MY NAME IS MARYAN

my name is Maryan.

ALISON M. GINGERAS

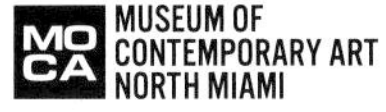

MUSEUM OF CONTEMPORARY ART NORTH MIAMI

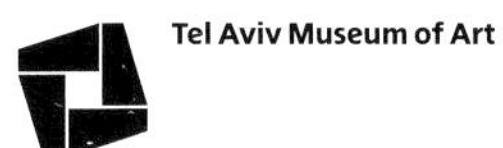

Tel Aviv Museum of Art

VERLAG DER BUCHHANDLUNG WALTHER UND FRANZ KÖNIG, KÖLN

CONTENTS

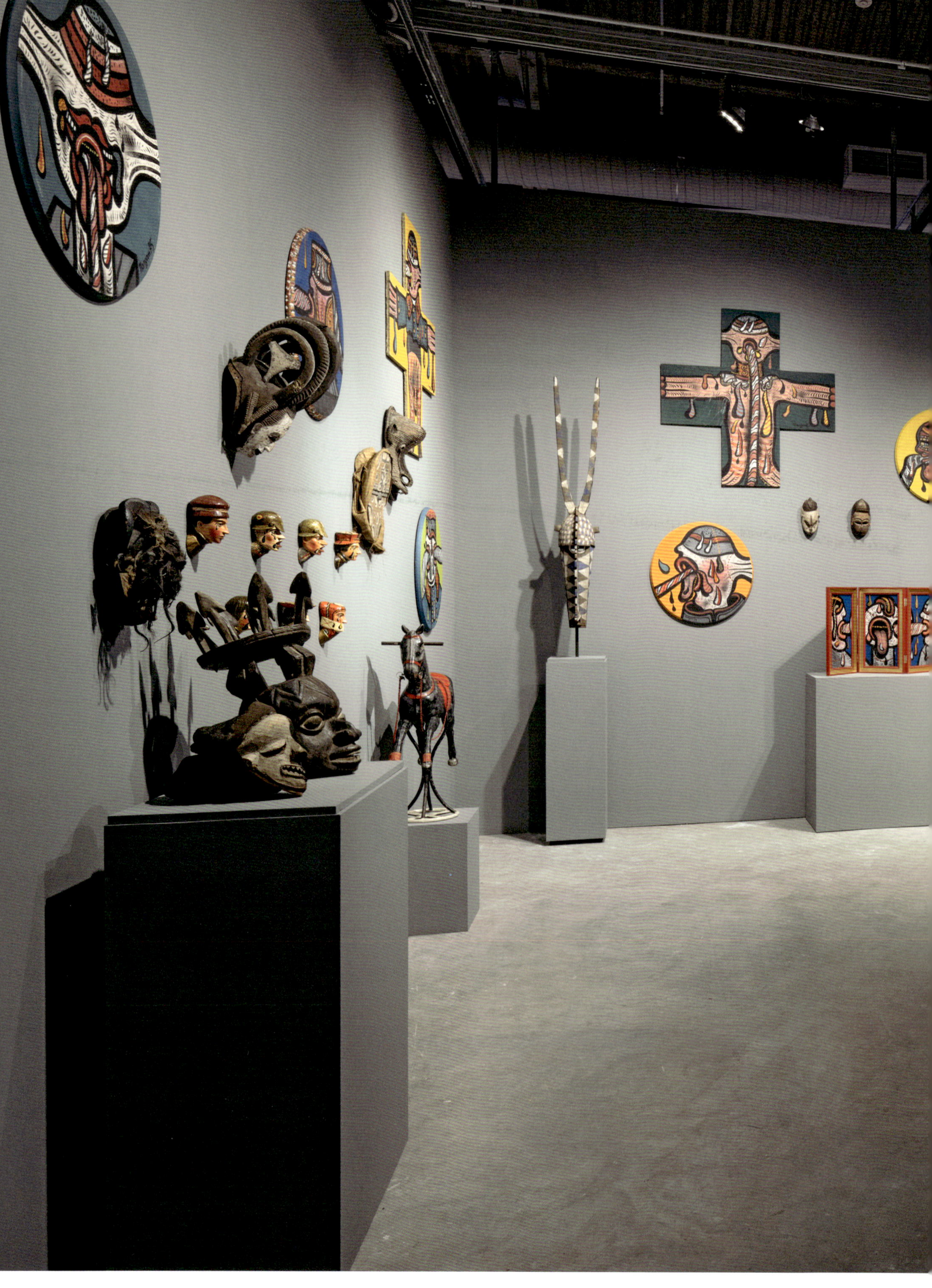

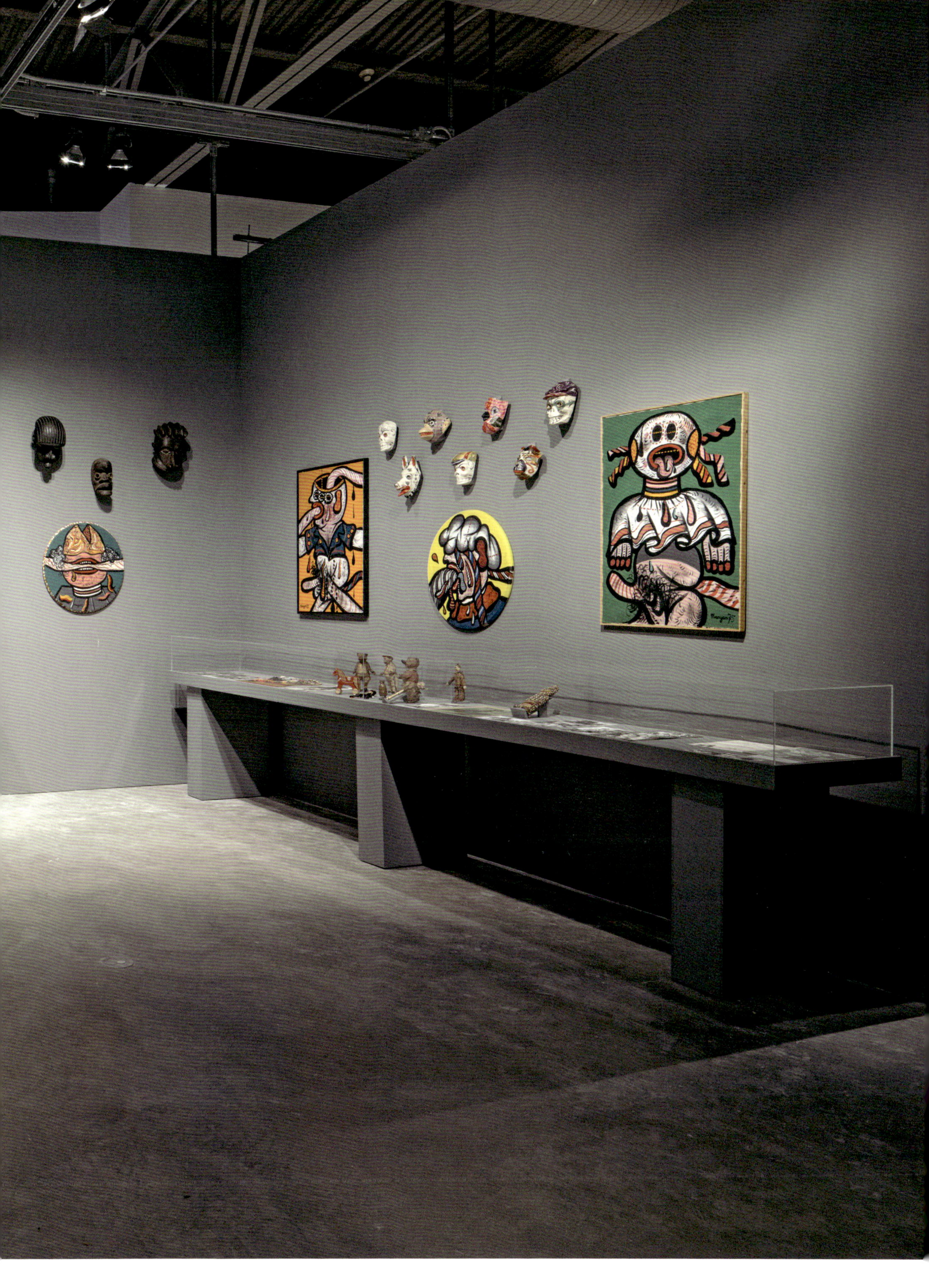

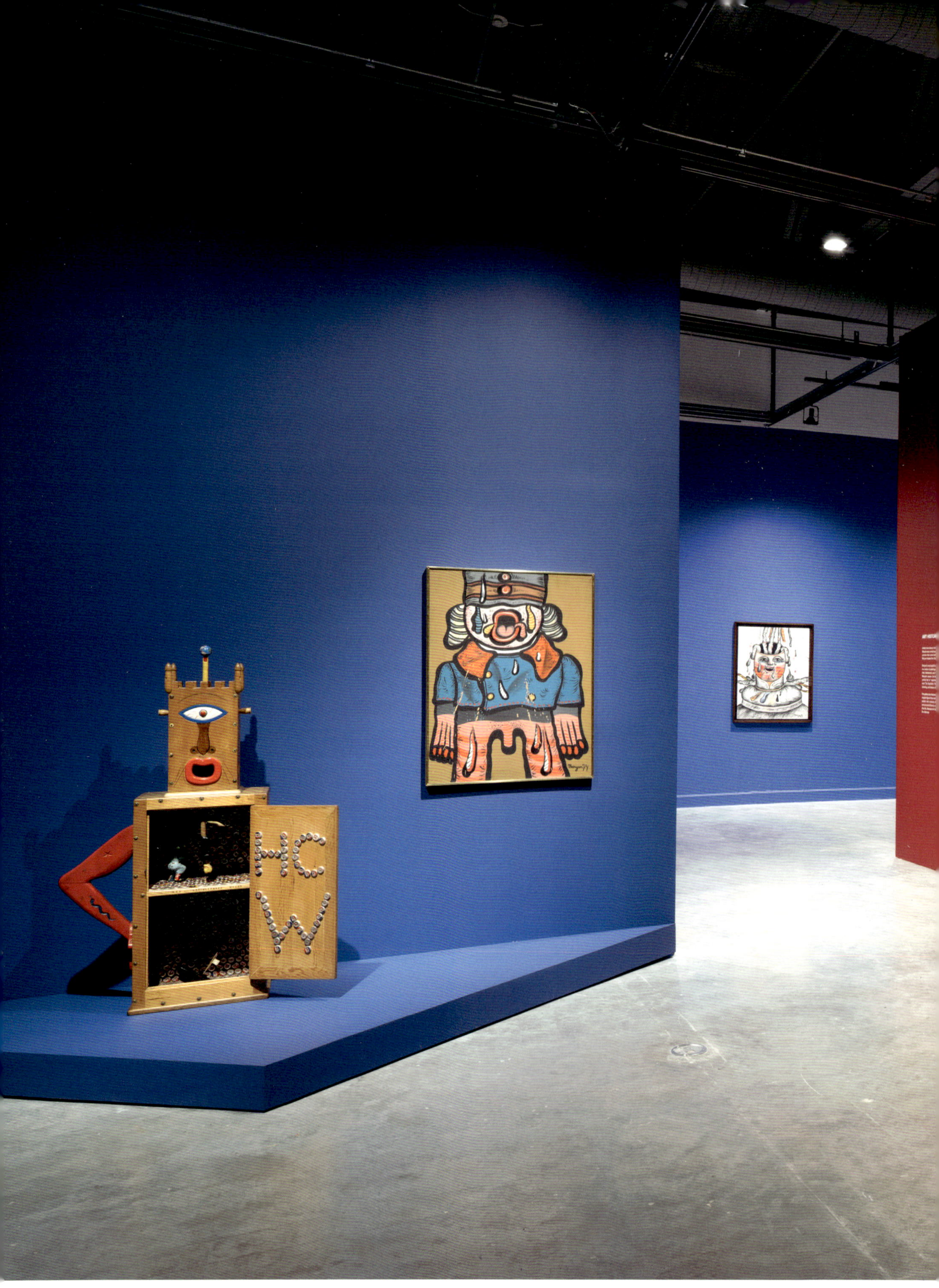

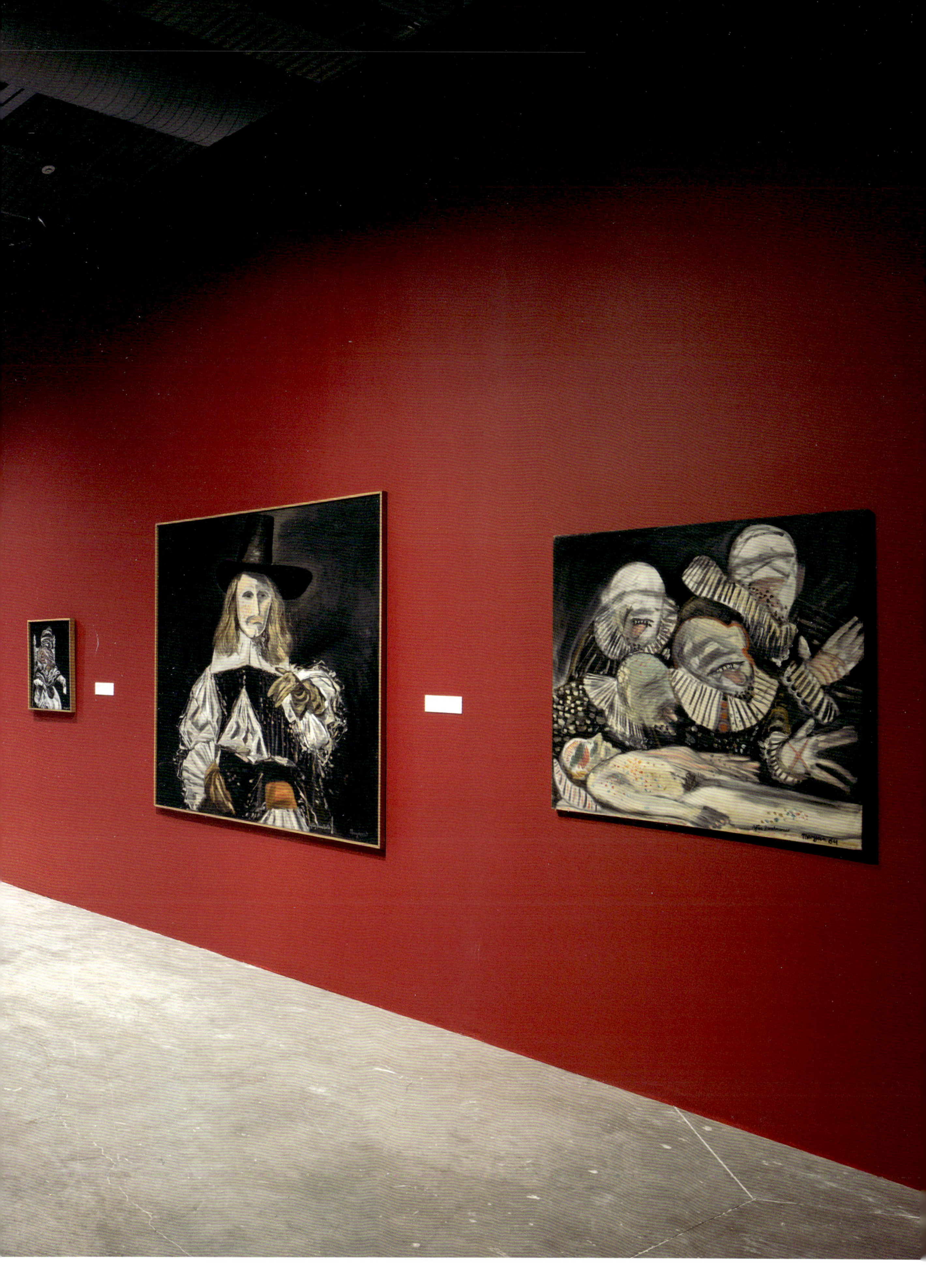

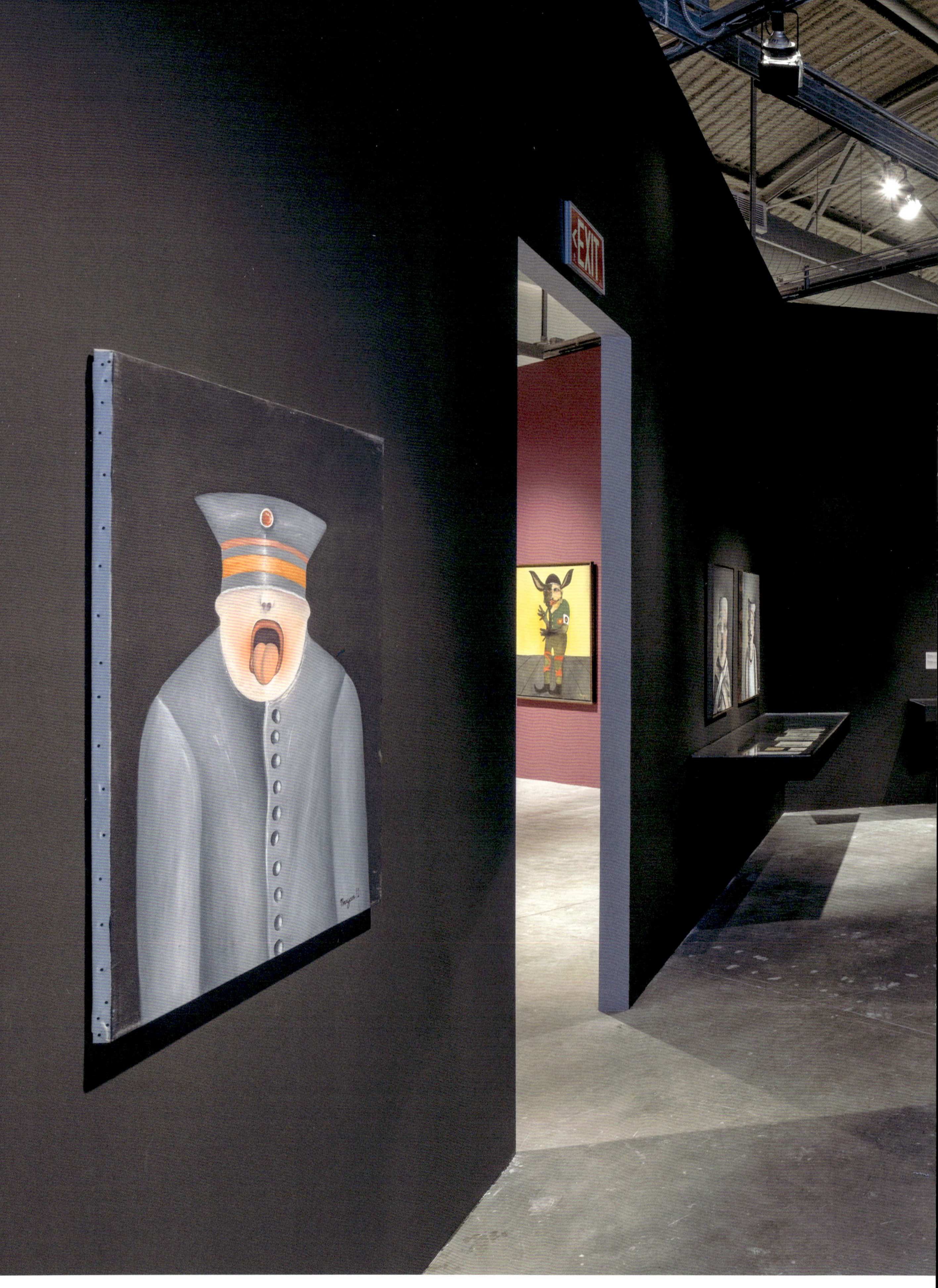

EXIT

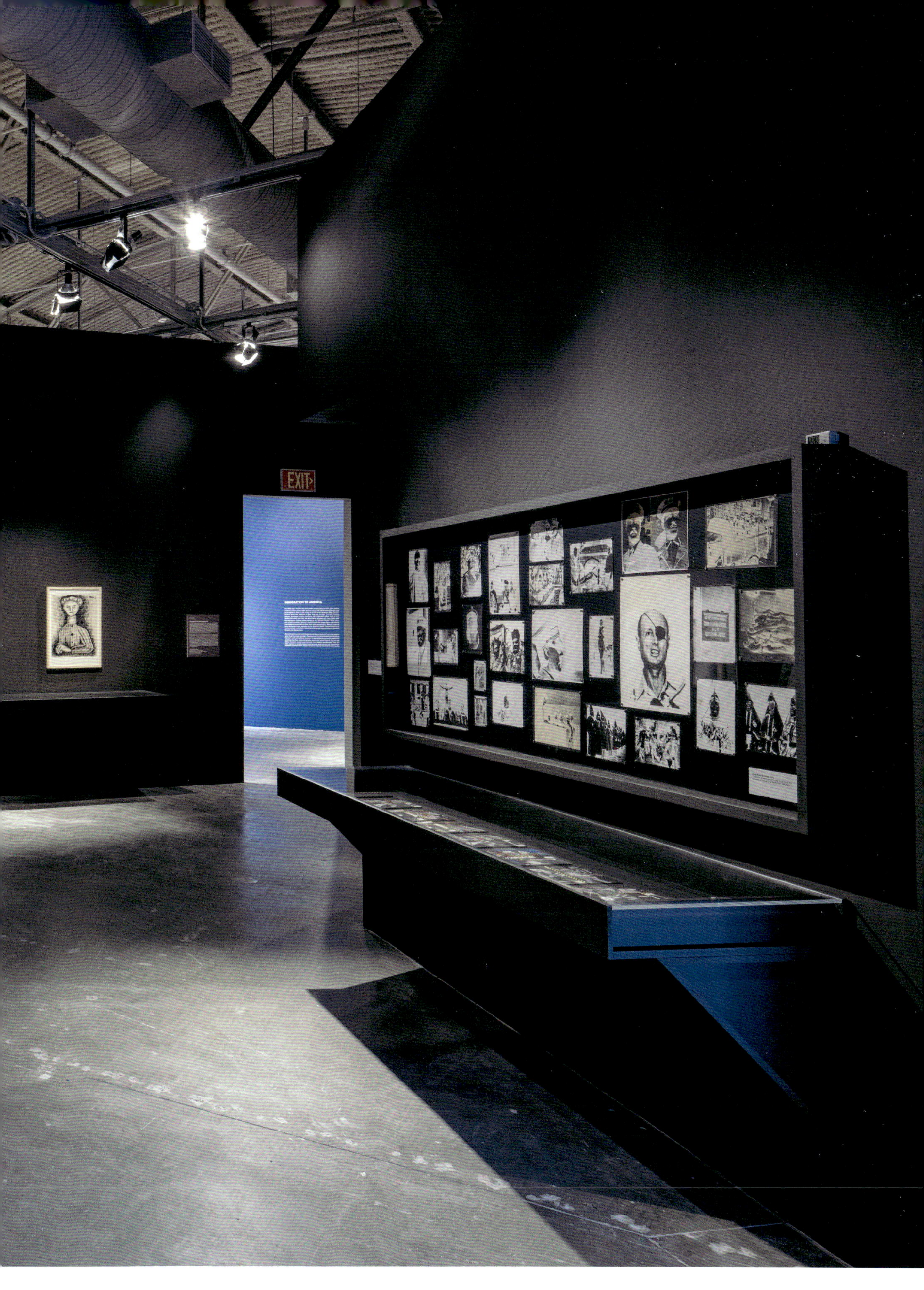

EXIT

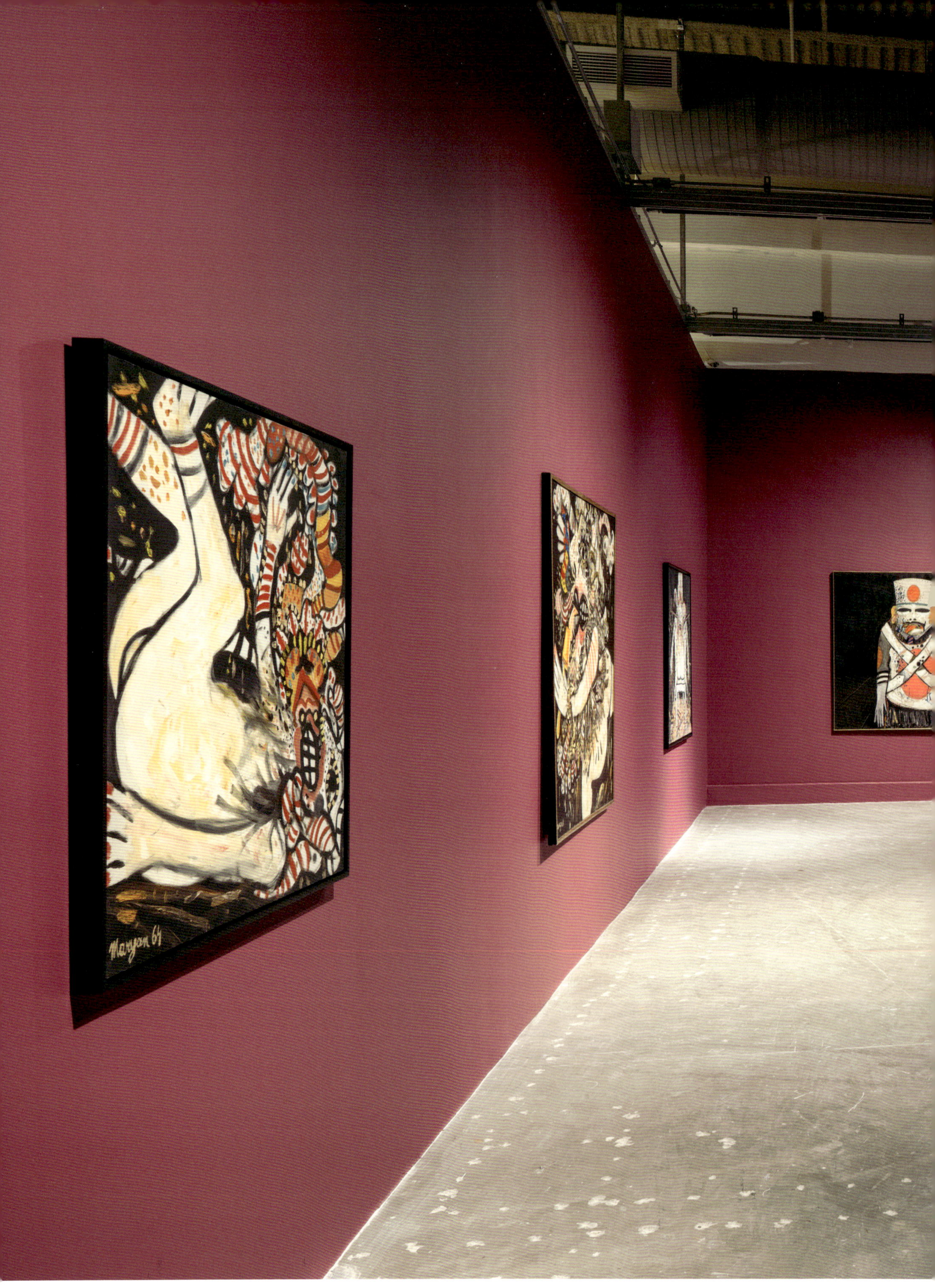

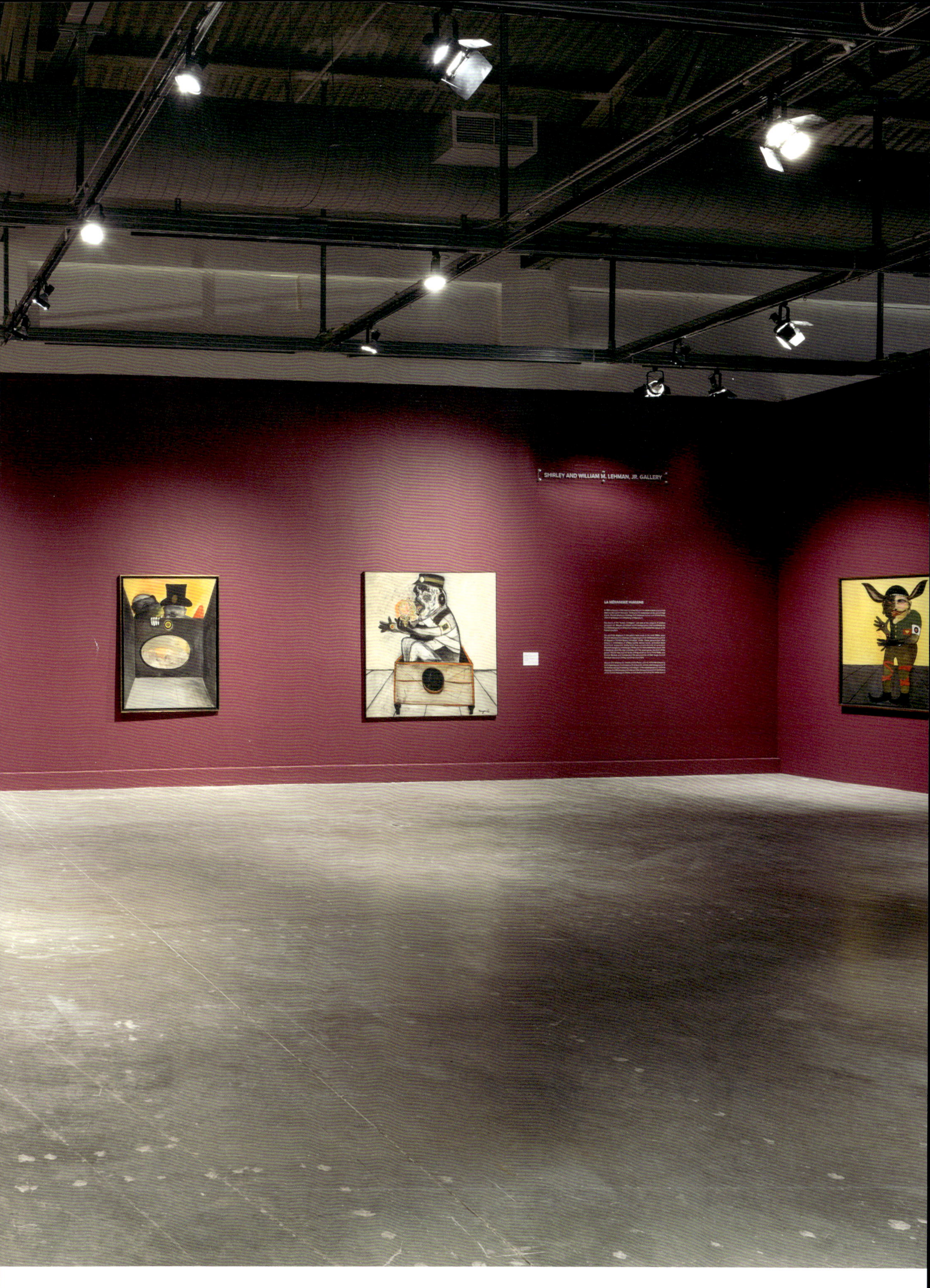

SHIRLEY AND WILLIAM M. LEHMAN, JR. GALLERY
LA MÉNAGERIE HUMAINE

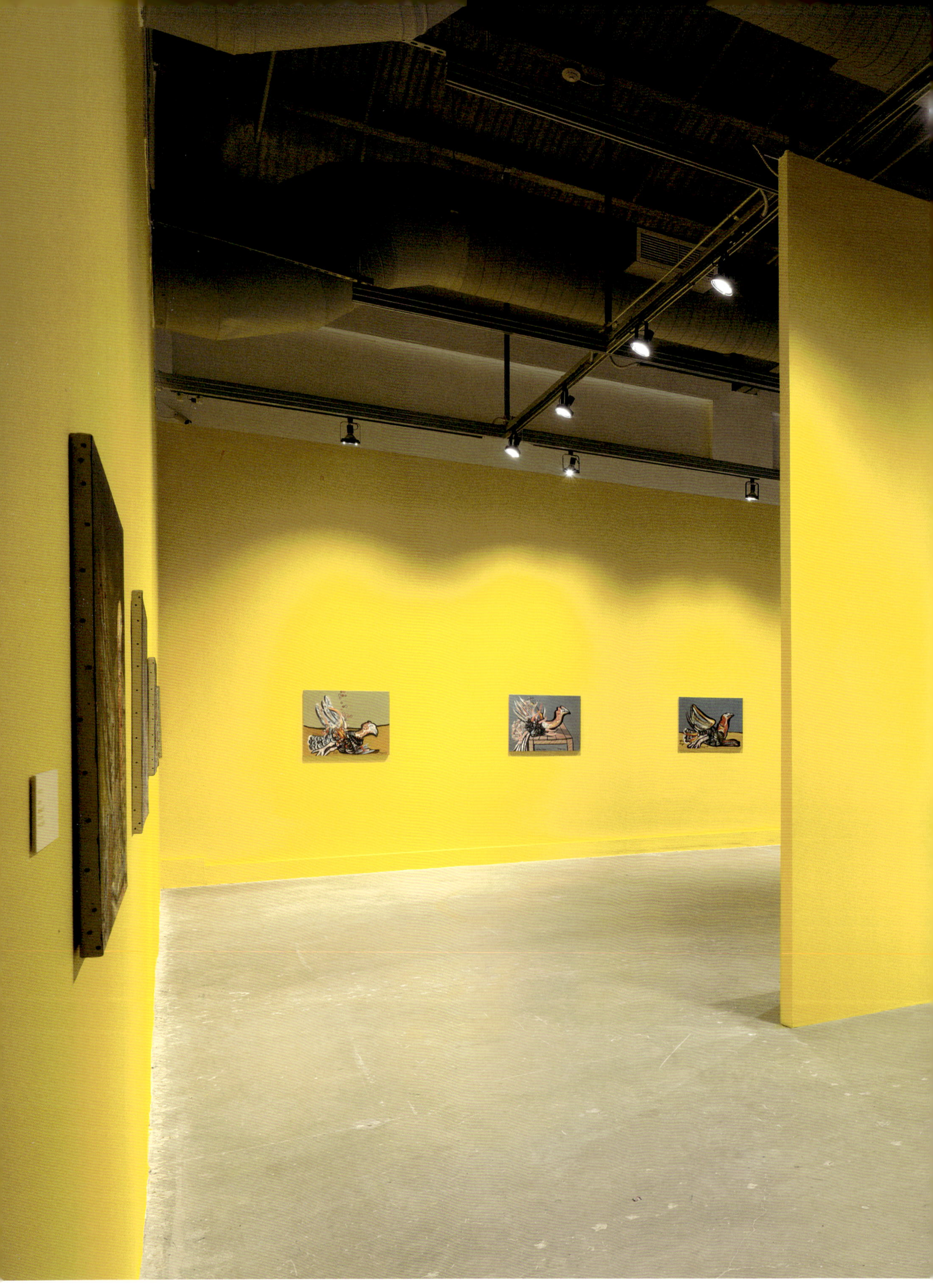

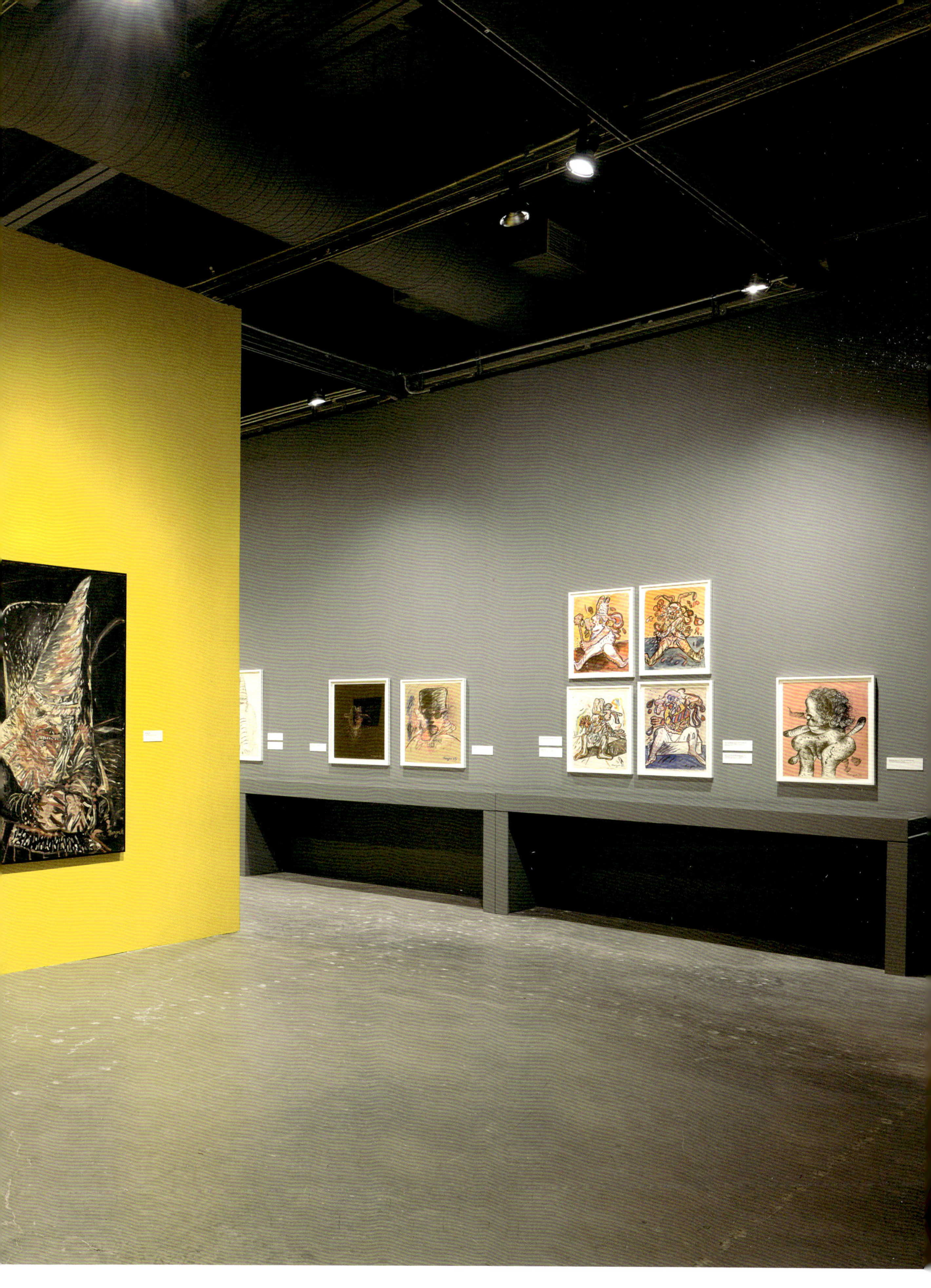

PREFACE

Chana Budgazad Sheldon
*Executive Director, Museum of
Contemporary Art, North Miami*

My Name Is Maryan, organized by the Museum of Contemporary Art, North Miami (MOCA), represents the most comprehensive assembly to date of work by Polish-born artist Maryan. This monographic exhibition presents four decades of paintings, sculptures, drawings, and film by the iconoclastic artist, who has largely gone under-recognized until now. Through the exceptional work of guest curator Alison M. Gingeras, the exhibition thoughtfully deconstructs the many layers of Maryan's practice, highlighting his unique form of figuration and exploring how, through his work, the artist connected his lived experience to a broader human experience. Moreover, the exhibition contextualizes Maryan's practice among those of his peers and reinserts his body of work into its rightful place in the art historical canon.

Born to Abraham Schindel and Gitla Bursztyn in Nowy Sącz, Poland, in 1927, young Pinkas, the artist who came to be known as Maryan, grew up in a traditional, working-class Jewish family. In 1939, Pinkas and his family were captured by the Nazis. He was imprisoned at various forced labor camps and finally Auschwitz and Birkenau concentration camps under his mother's maiden name, Bursztyn. He survived several near-death experiences and was the sole survivor from his family.

After the war, Bursztyn immigrated to then-Palestine to begin his artistic training, first in Jerusalem and then, beginning in 1950, at the École des Beaux-Arts in Paris. There is no denying that his artistic practice was informed by his experiences, but he also undertook a pointed study of art history. The young artist soon shed the name under which the Nazis persecuted him, and adopted the name Maryan S. Maryan. In the early 1960s he moved to New York City where his artistic practice thrived until his premature death, age fifty, in 1977.

My Name Is Maryan spans the entirety of this prolific artist's oeuvre, revealing its full complexity and including pieces that have never previously been exhibited or even reproduced. The exhibition takes us on the journey of an immigrant, from concentration camps to Palestine and Paris and then the States, where he finally found community. Through his work, Maryan speaks with a caustic, emotive lyricism to the human experiences of struggle and loss, and to the dogged perseverance of the human spirit.

MOCA celebrates over twenty-five years of creating a space for diverse voices and reflection through groundbreaking exhibitions such as this one. The museum's mission is to present contemporary art and its historical influences through exhibitions, educational programs, and collections. Inspired by its surrounding communities, MOCA connects audiences and cultures by providing a welcoming place to encounter new ideas and voices, and nurturing a lifelong love of the arts. MOCA strives to facilitate engagement and foster connections among artists and the local community, and to contribute to the global dialogue about critical issues of the day.

I would be remiss if I didn't share that this exhibition is personal. I am the granddaughter of two Holocaust survivors and was introduced to Maryan's work at an early age. My grandmother, Sabine Fox, was a hidden child in France with a number of other Jewish children and families—including Maryan's wife, Annette. My grandmother's bond with Annette lasted far beyond the years of the war. They both immigrated to New York mid-century and stayed in touch through letters, phone calls, and reunions. The bookshelf of my childhood home contained a collection of small publications of artwork by Annette's late husband.

In 2001, when I started working in the arts, Annette invited my mother and I into her Upper East Side apartment, to which I understood few were given access. To my amazement, the apartment was filled with paintings, flat files holding works on paper, and even paintbrushes on the drafting table, as though they had not been moved since the last time Maryan painted in that room. It was a time capsule; Annette acted as the guardian of these treasures and the keeper of Maryan's legacy. On subsequent visits, Annette read to me from Maryan's journals and shared stories about individual works and ephemera in her home.

In 2018, as the newly appointed Executive Director of MOCA North Miami, I unexpectedly encountered a handful of Maryan's paintings. The work had a powerful impact on me, and, as I thought about the museum's audiences and mission, I realized Maryan's story would resonate with our region's immigrant communities. The work felt urgent and timely. Through pieces such as *Ecce Homo*, Maryan attempted to create a parallel between the Holocaust and the sociopolitical struggles of the contemporary moment.

My sincerest appreciation to guest curator Alison M. Gingeras for her research and scholarship around this exhibition. Her expertise in French, Polish, and American postwar art and her compelling approach to curating have brought so much to this project. This three-year journey has been nothing less than thrilling. The resulting exhibition is a tremendous gift to Maryan's legacy, and a great source of pride for the museum.

I also want to extend my gratitude to the entire staff at MOCA who worked tirelessly to bring this project to life and oversee its travel to Tel Aviv. Thank you Adeze Wilford, Sophie Bonet, Arasay Vazquez, T.J. Black, Amanda Covach and MOCA educators and gallery interpreters, as well as Kevin Arrow, Alex Garcia, Danielle Damas, Stella Ford, and Dudley Alexis, each of whom greatly contributed to making this exhibition a success.

I am deeply appreciative of the contributions by Noa Rosenberg, Curator of Modern Art and 16th–19th Century European Art at Tel Aviv Museum of Art, and art historian Piotr Stodkowski, as well as Marlene L. Daut, Erica Moiah James, June Leaf, and Mackenzie Moon Ryan, who enriched this book with their thoughtful reflections and insights. For their support in the creation of this publication, my thanks to Todd Bradway, Joseph Logan, Miles Champion, and Franz König.

The exhibition was made possible through generous loans from private collections, galleries, and museums. I am grateful for the extraordinary collaboration and support of Adam Lindeman and the Venus Over Manhattan team, including Anna Furney and Zach Fischman, whose efforts made this colossal undertaking possible. I want to extend my heartfelt thanks to the Estate of Maryan for the generous loan of the exceptional artwork in its care and the many oral histories shared over the course of the exhibition's development. My sincerest gratitude to our colleagues at the Tel Aviv Museum of Art, with special thanks to the museum's director, Tania Coen-Uzzielli, for her commitment to this collaboration, and Noa Rosenberg for the extraordinary research that enabled the exhibition's expanded presentation in Israel.

Exhibitions like this one take the efforts and support of a community. I would like to acknowledge the contributions of Kenneth Roth, Human Rights Watch, and Oren Baruch Stier for their written contributions and the opportunities their texts provide for us to reflect upon and connect to ideas and histories. Thank you to Carl-Philippe Juste for organizing the photography section in the entrance gallery of the museum, and creating a space for contemplation, with works by Maria Daniel Balcazar, Maggie Steber, Vanessa Charlot, Woosler Delisfort, and Colin Finlay. My thanks also go to the local institutional lenders, whose contributions added to the richness of the exhibition, including the NSU Art Museum, Fort Lauderdale, and Patricia and Phillip Frost Museum of Art at FIU, among others, for their generous loans.

An exhibition of this scale requires the partnership of a number of key funders, who have our eternal gratitude. I am thankful to the Terra Foundation for American Art and Shirley and William M. Lehman, Jr. for believing in this project from the earliest stages of its development. Thanks to the Miami-Dade County Tourist Development Council, the Polish Cultural Institute New York, the Wege Foundation, and the Simkins Family for acknowledging the importance of this project and supporting the museum in realizing it. We appreciate the support of the Funding Arts Network, the Galbut Family, and Adele and Joel Sandberg, and the generosity of BNY Mellon Wealth Management, Florida Humanities, the William Louis-Dreyfus Foundation, Ariela and Benito Esquenazi, Arlene Kahn, and Richard Yulman. I would like to acknowledge Kamel Mennour and Mindy Solomon for supporting the publication; special thanks to Helen Chaset, David and Sydney Schaecter, and Jared Margolis for being champions of this project.

My deepest thanks and appreciation to MOCA's dedicated board of trustees. Led by Chairman William M. Lehman, Jr., their support has been and continues to be critical to the success of our institution. I sincerely thank the City of North Miami Mayor and Council and the North Miami City Manager, Theresa Therilus Esq., for their partnership and support. MOCA is generously funded by the Miami-Dade County Department of Cultural Affairs and the Cultural Affairs Council, the Miami-Dade County Mayor and Board of County Commissioners, the State of Florida, Department of State, Division of Arts and Culture, and the Florida Council on Arts and Culture. Founding support for the MOCA Sustainability Fund was provided by the Green Family Foundation Trust. I also thank our MOCA Members for their meaningful support.

Finally, I would like to acknowledge the six million Jewish victims of the Holocaust and the millions of other victims of Nazism. With the passing of the last survivors, the Holocaust is moving from memory to history. Maryan's work bears witness to that history, and carries relevance to the present day. I am wholeheartedly grateful to Annette Maryan, who died in 2011, for sharing his legacy and for fiercely protecting her beloved husband's artwork.

Annette and Maryan, studio on rue des Suisses, Paris, 1955

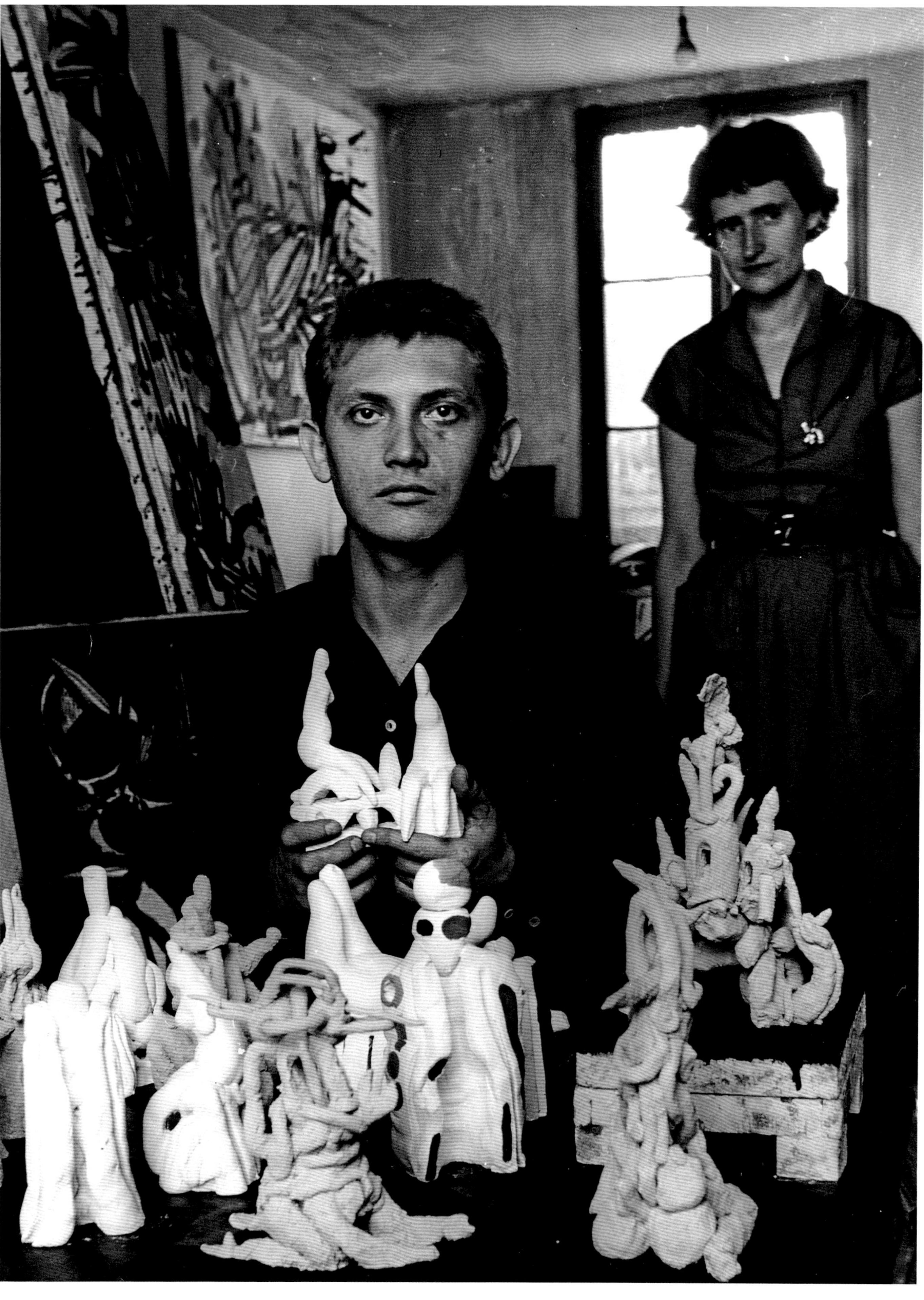

FOREWORD

Tania Coen-Uzzielli
Director, Tel Aviv Museum of Art

Pinkas Bursztyn arrived in in Mandatory Palestine in 1947 and left in 1950, when it was the State of Israel. His own story in Jerusalem in those years is, in many respects, the story of Israel as a young state, and the story of the art figures and institutions active there at the time. The reencounter with Pinkas Bursztyn, aka Maryan, teaches us about our local history just as much as it teaches us about him.

This is Maryan's second retrospective at the Tel Aviv Museum of Art. The first was in 1979, two years after his death. There is no better time than the ninetieth anniversary of the Tel Aviv Museum of Art, celebrated this year, to return to the artists who were active here—if only for a brief while—and to ensure that their place in the local history of art remains.

I wish first and foremost to thank Adam Lindemann (Representative of the Maryan Estate in New York) and Amalia Dayan, President of Tel Aviv Museum of Art American Friends (TAMAF), for the wonderful "matchmaking" between the Museum of Contemporary Art, North Miami (MOCA) and Tel Aviv Museum of Art, and for their ongoing professional and personal support and guidance. This collaboration would not have materialized without their encouragement.

Thanks also to Chana Budgazad Sheldon, Director of MOCA, for her professional engagement and collaborative work in the two years leading up to the exhibition. I am sure this is the beginning of a wonderful friendship between the two institutions.

Thanks to Kamel Mennour (Representative of the Maryan Estate in Paris) for their help and for lending many of the works that make up the Tel Aviv Museum exhibition.

Heartfelt gratitude to everyone, in Israel and abroad, who gladly loaned works for this exhibition.

Thanks to the Terra Foundation for American Art for its support of the exhibition and this illuminating catalogue.

Thanks to Mira Lapidot, Chief Curator of the Tel Aviv Museum of Art, for her incisive and generous assistance; Ronili Lustig Steinmetz, Head of Exhibitions and Collection Management, for getting all the pieces together; and Nathalie Andrijasevic, assistant to the exhibition's curator at Tel Aviv Museum of Art, for her dedicated work.

Lastly, thanks to Alison M. Gingeras, the exhibition guest curator at MOCA and joint curator of the Tel Aviv exhibition, and to Noa Rosenberg, Curator of Modern Art at Tel Aviv Museum of Art, for their comprehensive research, the results of which are published in this catalogue. I am sure the exhibition will be a milestone in our local culture, just as it was in Miami.

MY NAME IS MARYAN: INTRODUCTION

Alison M. Gingeras

The exhibition *My Name Is Maryan* examines the story of an iconoclastic Polish-born artist who reinvented himself after surviving World War II. Spanning four decades of paintings, sculptures, drawings, and film, this publication documents Maryan's unique approach to figurative art through the lens of struggle. Drawing upon new scholarship and a trove of never-before-exhibited works from the artist's estate, *My Name Is Maryan* is the first museum retrospective to holistically examine all periods of Maryan's life and work.

Born to Abraham Schindel and Gitla Bursztyn in Nowy Sącz, Poland, in 1927, young Pinkas, the artist who came to be known as Maryan, grew up in a traditional, working-class Jewish family amid a vibrant Polish Jewish community. In 1939 twelve-year-old Pinkas along with his entire family were captured by the Nazis. He was imprisoned under his mother's maiden name, Bursztyn, at various forced labor camps and finally at the Auschwitz and Birkenau concentration camps. Pinkas Bursztyn, who survived several near-death experiences, was the sole survivor from his immediate family.[1]

After the war, Bursztyn recovered from physical injuries that necessitated having his leg amputated when he was still in Poland. After staying in various displaced persons refugee camps in Germany, he immigrated to then-Palestine in 1947. Despite being promised that he could pursue his artistic training in Jerusalem, Bursztyn was deemed "handicapped" by the Israeli state and his options were limited. In response to this stigma, Bursztyn decided to leave for Paris in 1950 in order to complete his studies at the École des Beaux-Arts in Paris. Early in his Parisian period, the artist shed the birth name under which the Nazis persecuted him. In tandem with finding his artistic voice, he adopted the name "Maryan"—asserting his new identity as a radical act of self-identification. From that point onward, he exclusively used this mononym in his work as in his everyday life.

Living in Paris for over a decade, Maryan forged a distinct style that was independent from yet adjacent to the École de Paris and the CoBrA group. Exhibiting in prominent galleries such as the Galerie de France and Galerie Claude Bernard, Maryan garnered a loyal following in Paris and began to receive invitations to show in the United States. In 1962, Maryan moved to New York City where he further pushed his

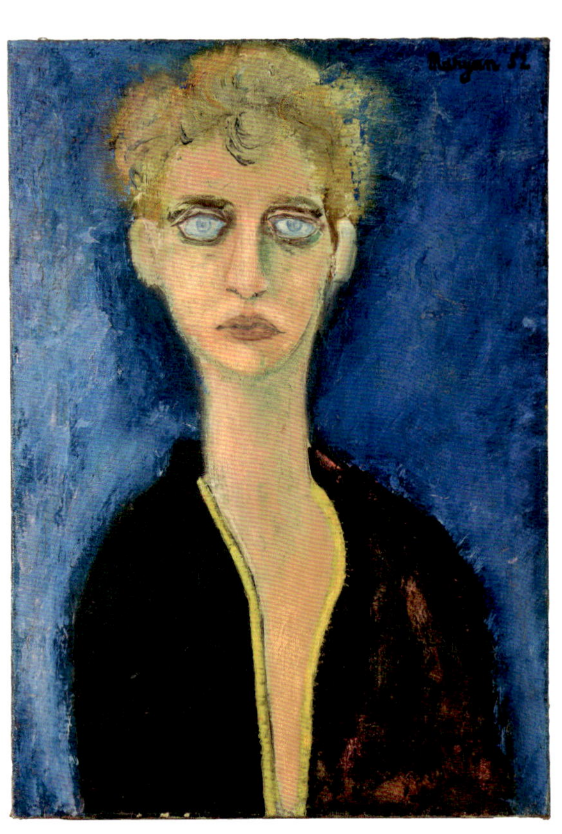

Maryan, *Self-Portrait*, 1952. Oil on canvas, 29½ × 21 inches (75 × 53.4 cm). Private Collection

notion of the *personnage*—the French term for "character"—to title the fictitious figures that dominated his mature oeuvre. His *personnages* became powerful vehicles for complex narratives and served as a conduit for the formal evolution of his distinctive painterly language.

Throughout the remainder of the '60s, Maryan showed extensively with Allan Frumkin Gallery in New York and Chicago, forging kindred artist friendships among a small circle of American figurative artists such as H. C. Westermann, June Leaf, and others. Maryan's American period was particularly prolific, and he was included in important group exhibitions at the Whitney and Guggenheim museums.

The trauma of Maryan's wartime experiences in the early 1970s caused profound upheavals in his personal life and in his work. After separating from his wife, Annette, Maryan moved to the famed Chelsea Hotel during the 1970s, where his *personnage* motifs became explicitly more tormented and darker in their subject matter. His '70s works explored psychosexual tropes as well as historical and fictional figures from Jesus Christ to Napoleon to Ubu roi.

While his last decade was extremely prolific, the emotional and physical turbulence were overwhelming. He had always refused being pigeonholed as a "Holocaust artist"; nevertheless, the psychological fallout of Maryan's experiences overwhelmed him in the early '70s. Under the care of a psychiatric doctor, Maryan filled notebooks with drawings and text that provide insights into the recurrent motifs of his art. In his only film, *Ecce Homo* (1975), Maryan paired a first-person testimonial of his experiences in Nazi prison camps with images of contemporary social-protest movements. All of these works made at the Chelsea Hotel—arguably his most important and most radical—are the cathartic result of his lifelong quest to question the very nature of humanity after his traumatic survival. Maryan died prematurely of a heart attack at the age of fifty in 1977.

My Name Is Maryan places the artist's act of renaming himself at the center of his complex artistic pursuit. Maryan paints what Primo Levi describes as his own quest after surviving the Shoah: ""The question of how to define a human being is not an idle one."[2] Empowered by his new, self-forged identity, Maryan imagined a defiant yet questioning form of humanism that he dubbed "truth-painting" (*peinture-verité*).

Through the lens of postwar humanism, these exhibitions have engendered new understandings of Maryan's complex oeuvre and have argued for the reinsertion of Maryan into a larger narrative of postwar European and American art history.

The essays, testimonials, documents, and images that compose this book chronicle Maryan's extraordinary biography while simultaneously exploring his prolific oeuvre. At the heart of this publication, the transcript of Maryan's monologue-testimonial in the *Ecce Homo* film is published for the first time, accompanied by a never-before-seen archive of photographs the artist used to make the film's montage. As the fulcrum of Maryan's American period, this groundbreaking film and its first-person narrative serves as a Rosetta stone that can help decode the entirety of his practice. Three intensely researched essays bookend the *Ecce Homo* transcript, offering new insight and information. Each essay explores a relatively little-known chapter of Maryan's life: Piotr Słodowski's excavation of Maryan's Polish childhood and his relationship to other Polish Jewish artists in the postwar period; Noa Rosenberg's deep dive into Maryan's crucial period as a burgeoning artist in Jerusalem amid other refugees and the emergence of the Israeli state; and the book's opening essay, which traces Maryan's life in New York, ending with his most radical period in the 1970s when he lived and worked at the Chelsea Hotel. The remainder of the book features reproductions of Maryan's works, organized in thematic sections that unfold in chronological order, documenting the various paintings, drawings, and other ephemera featured in both the Miami and Tel Aviv exhibitions. As the first ever publication to address the totality of Maryan's life and work, *My Name Is Maryan* insists that the understanding of his work cannot be reduced to his Holocaust experiences, but also that these experiences are a key part of a holistic oeuvre that reflects on the perseverance of the human spirit and the transformation of Maryan's traumatic memories and survival into the lifeblood of his art.

1. There are many different variants of Pinkas Bursztyn's name in the existing literature, in French, English, and Hebrew. For this publication, the editor/author has restored the original Polish spelling of his name.
2. Primo Levi, "A Bottle of Sunshine," in *The Complete Works of Primo Levi*, vol. 3, ed. Anne Goldstein, trans. Antony Shugaar (New York: Liveright Publishing, 2015), 2343.

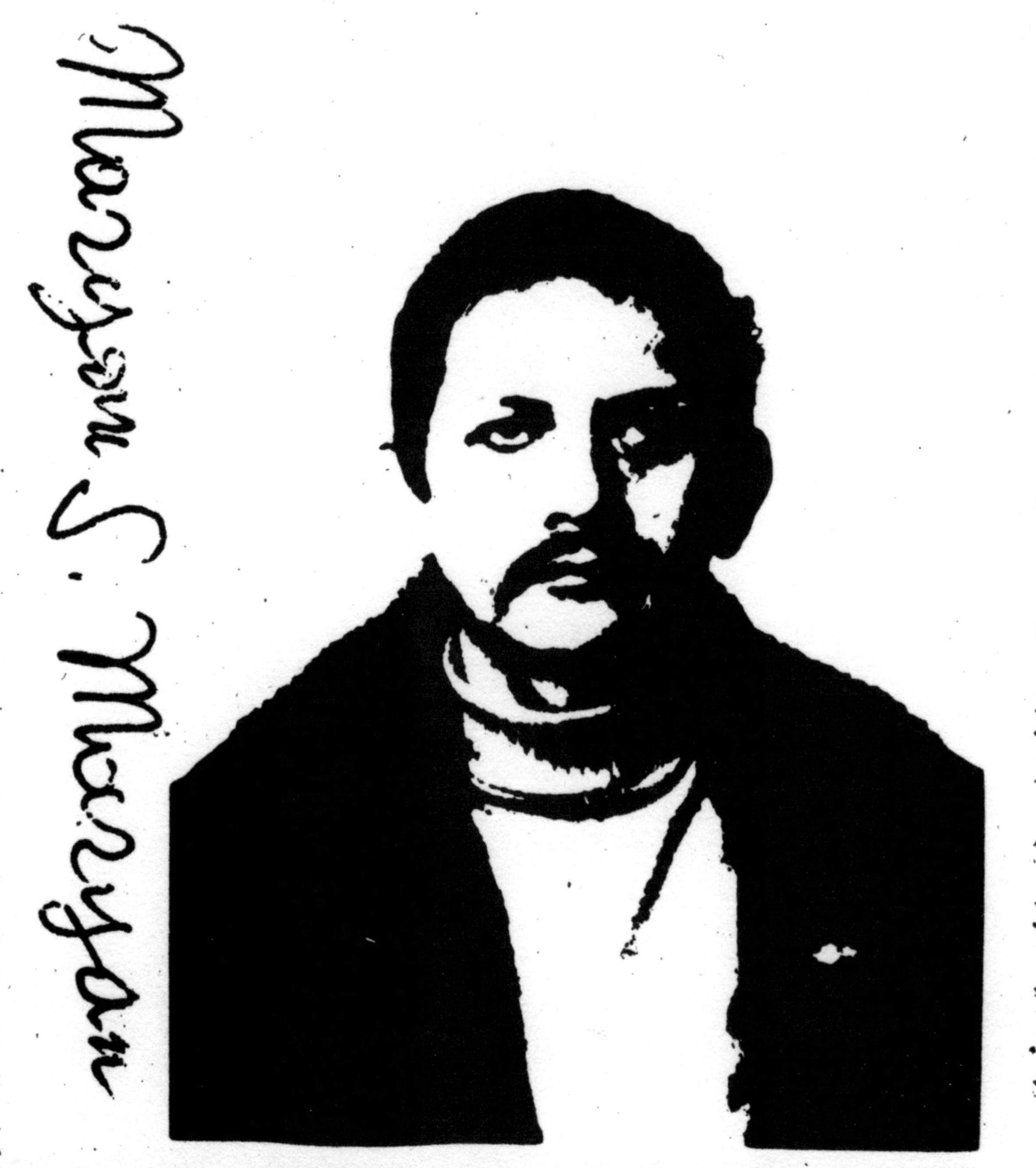
Marion S. Morgan

ID UNTIL SIGNED BY THE BEARER. PERSONS
T USE THIS PASSPORT FOR TRAVEL UNLESS
RER.

U. S. IMMIGRATION
NEW YORK, N. Y. 990

JUN 23 1976

ADMITTED________________________
(CLASS)
UNTIL
U. S. IMMIGRATION
NEW YORK, N. Y. 953
YORK, N. Y. 929

SEP JUN 18 1975 1976

ADMITTED ADMITTED________________________
(CLASS)
UNTIL UNTIL
(CLASS)

My name is Maryan S. Maryan. I was born in No
was truly the most beautiful part of the country
but not in other subjects. When I was seven or ei
"You know, my son is the best artist in town." N
mother was very nice to me, but I could not sta
time and in front of us kids, this surely marked
my father. They had been to a bris. He was smok
world, and at that moment, my mother gave hin
remember having received a spanking myself tha
camp with many kids who came from all over P
summer we all said see you next year same place
instead of the summer camp, I found myself at A
there, I will let you guess. Sometimes I regret th
have been sent to the camps and I would still hav
guys from the Gestapo came. There was one in
named Gavron. They chose 22 out of 44 of us an
Poniatowski Square and lined us up. I was the la
went on first period since the two Germans wer
cervical center, and they would miss and every
with extra bullets. • My turn arrived, I already fe
missed. Obviously, I am still alive. Having surviv
with me feelings of guilt. • It reminds me of the st
who specialized in kosher butchering; he missed
hook and run around the courtyard with its hea
my father went to fetch the chicken in my place.
put labels on it. For example, "denunciative pai
"it doesn't surprise me given his experience in
written about me is crap and they say that I am a
painting, I officially declare that I would rather
was also a rocking horse that nobody used at t
there through the yard. And I wanted it and the
horse, brand new, made by the same craftsmen
immediately. Obviously, I am too big to climb on it,

ącz, Subcarpathian Poland (January 1, 1927). It
school, I was very good in art, like all painters,
ears old my mother would tell all the neighbors,
ays it seems to me that she was too modest. • My
e slaps and blows she threw at my father. All the
affected me. • One holiday, she came home with
a cigar with a vodka and feeling at ease with the
h a knock that it made the house shake. I do not
med to show such feeling. I was sent to a summer
d at a place just near my town. At the end of the
e kids left and I stayed in my town. The next year
witz. • If you don't already know what happened
was born a Jew simply because then I would not
parents. • In 1943 it was very cold outside. Some
iform named Esther and one in civilian clothes
was among the 22. They led us to a place called
line to be shot, so I had to watch everything that
unk as donkeys, they would aim at the neck, the
was screaming and stirring, and they were shot
othing; they aimed at my neck and naturally they
any such farces, it is not surprising that I carry
about a chicken for which I was sent to the rabbi
of the time, as well the chicken would get off the
nging by a thread. And me I ran home. After that
o not expect anyone to like my painting but don't
g," "unrestrained aggression," or they will say,
oncentration camps." • Most of what they have
an person. But that is true. • But, in regard to my
l it "peinture-verité" or truth-painting. • There
eighbor's house, just next door, and I could get
used to give it to me. Last year, I found the same
y native town, in a big toy store, and I bought it
elieve me, it isn't because I wouldn't like to. • 1977.

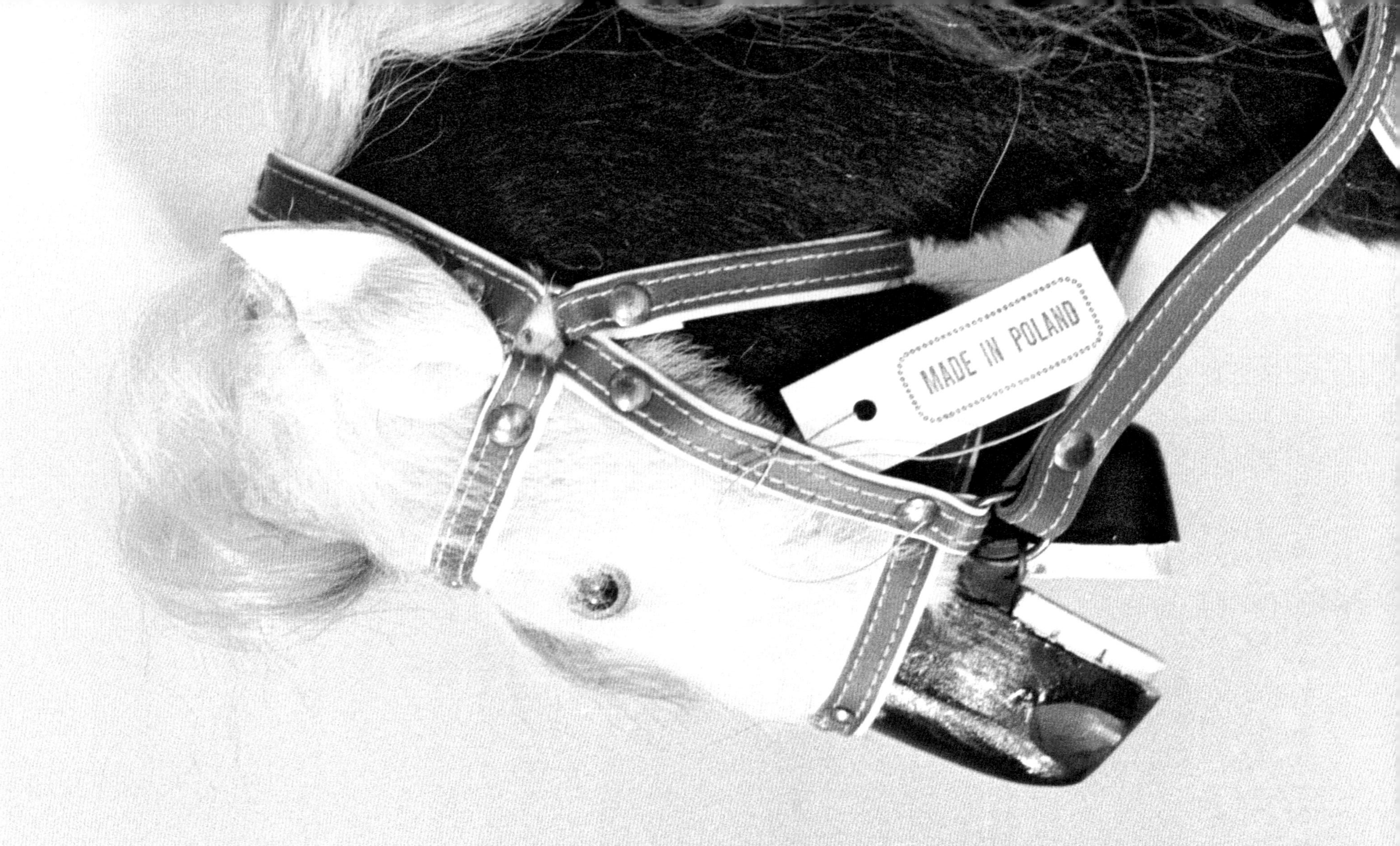

MADE IN POLAND

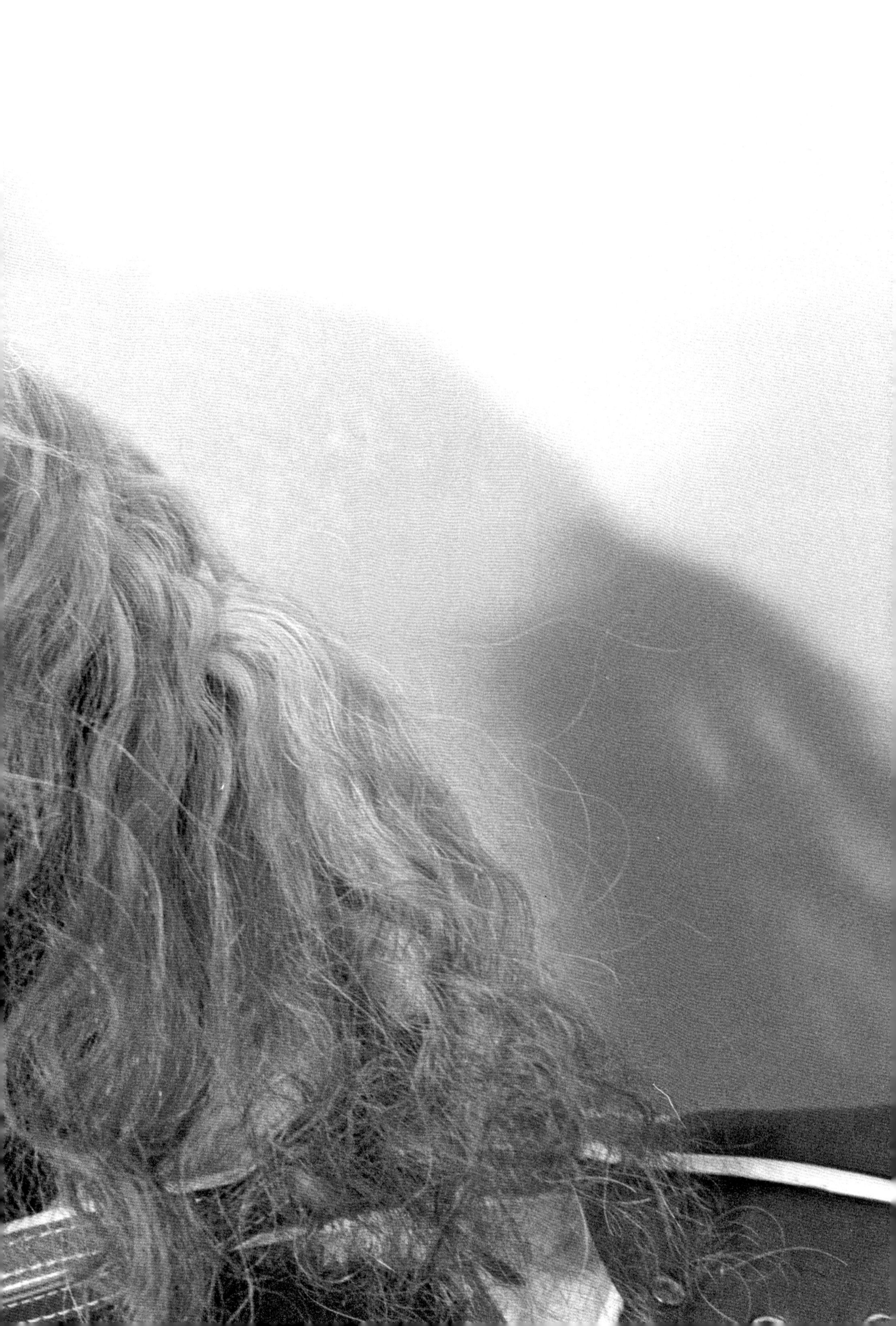

ROCK AND ROLL AFTER AUSCHWITZ: MARYAN AT THE CHELSEA HOTEL

Alison M. Gingeras

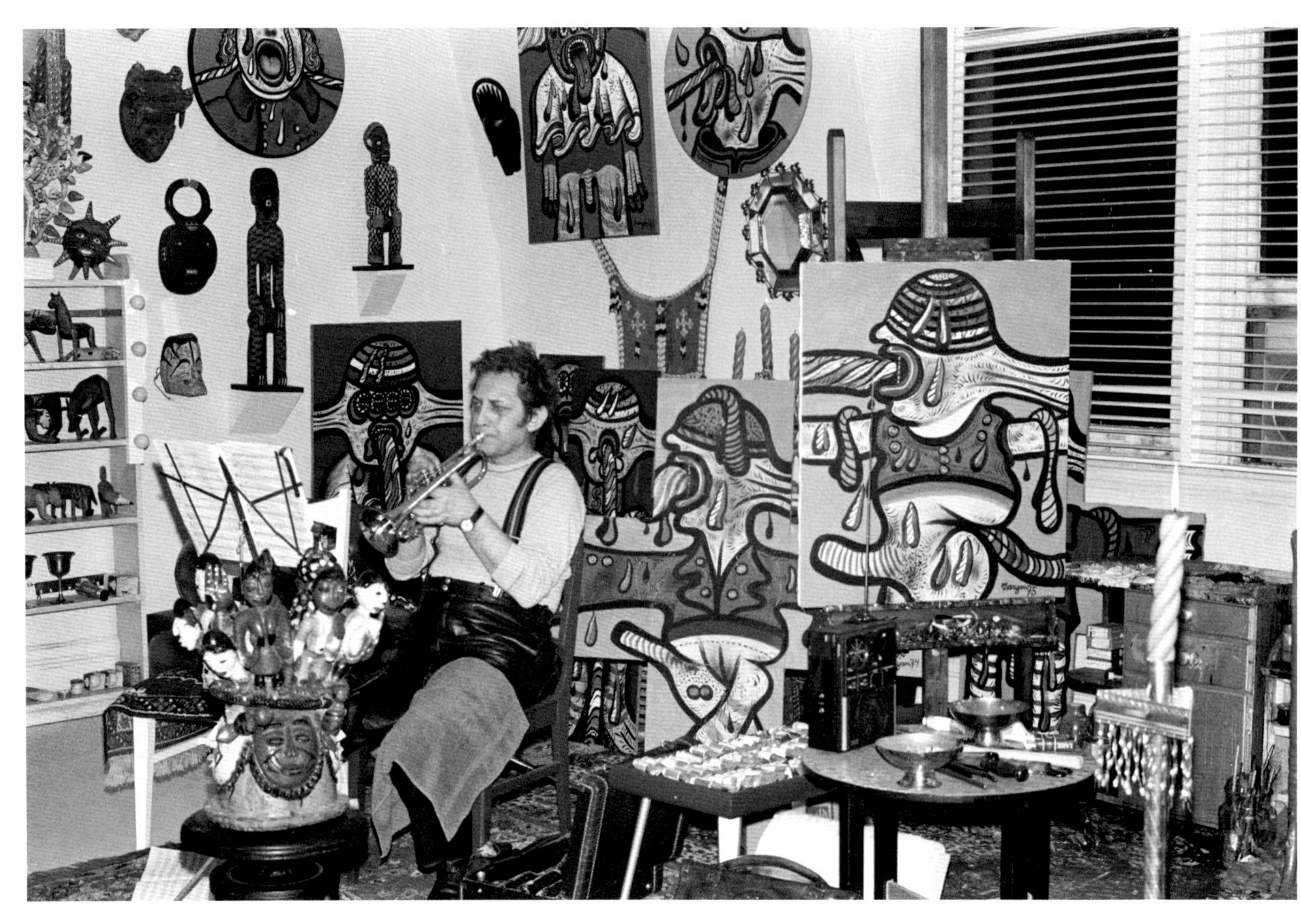

Horror Vacui

It was a case of horror vacui at the Chelsea Hotel.
Visitors to Maryan's studio-cum-apartment would
have been overwhelmed by the optical onslaught
of the artist's extended visual universe. No
surface was bare, no space left unadorned. The
Polish-born artist—who miraculously survived
imprisonment at Auschwitz, immigrating to Israel
and France before ultimately settling in New
York in the early '60s—had enacted this "fear of
empty space" when he filled up his new residence
at the Chelsea around 1972.[1] A trove of never-before-published photographs documents Maryan's
last haven where he made some of his most radical works.[2] The triple-height ceilings could barely
contain the figures and faces that hung salon
style—the visual maelstrom at times blurring the
distinction between what was made by Maryan's
own hand and works by other artists that he had
collected and arranged to create this immersive
environment. Maryan's distinctive *personnage*
paintings—depicted in his signature bright palette
with heavy black outlines and a cartoonish figurative style—dominated the main room. Whether
rendered on circular, rectangular, or crucifix-shaped canvases, Maryan's fictional characters
embodied states of torment and struggle, their
mouths frequently agape. A thread of Technicolor
streams—bodily fluids? vomit? a mysterious
life force?—seemed to connect one *personnage*
painting to another, a snaking line virtually
linking canvas to canvas. It is unclear if these
colorful streams were emanating from or going
into their mouths. A secondary, electric (if esoteric) dialogue also emerges between Maryan's
paintings and the other objects he assembled.
The African tribal masks that Maryan collected
occupy any wall space left empty of paintings.[3] A
formal and emotional synergy between Maryan's
personnages and these sculptural, highly stylized faces rendered in varied materials vibrates
throughout his hotel rooms. To crib the title of the
seminal MoMA exhibition of postwar humanist
art, Maryan's eclectic ensemble confronts us with
New Images of Man.[4]

An equally profound part of this menagerie
were the many non-art objects, charged with
personal meaning, that dotted the room: a wooden
rocking horse that was identical to the toy he cov-
eted as a child in Poland,[5] other small toys, folk
objects from Mexico and Poland, and pinup posters of blonde beauties Jean Harlow and Marilyn

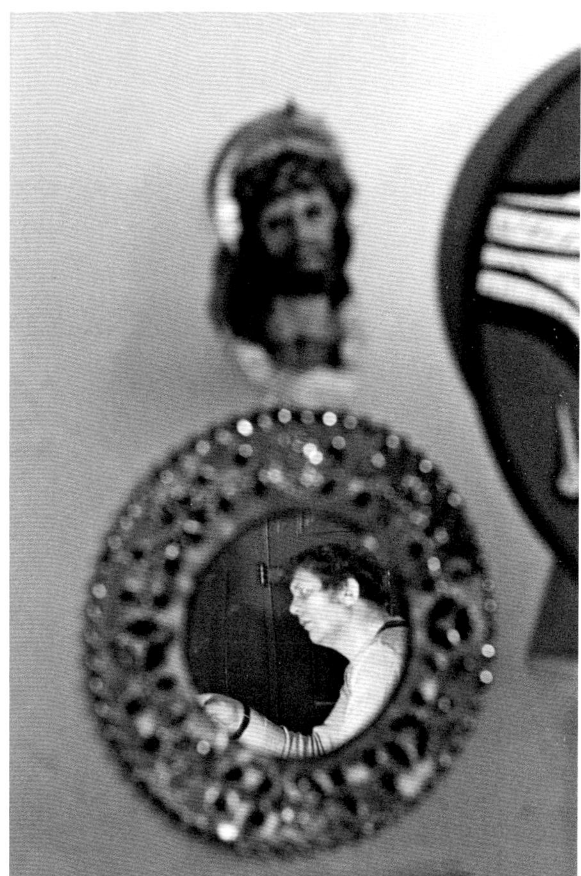

Monroe (Maryan was known to his friends as a
ladies' man). Judeo-Christian religious symbols
punctuated the space: ceramic effigies of the
Virgin and Child and Jesus Christ from a cheap
religious goods store hung on the wall. One
poignant portrait of Maryan taken in the Chelsea
apartment shows his pensive face reflected in
a round mirror with a figurine of Christ as the
Man of Sorrows hanging directly above. This
Christic overidentification, constructed against
the backdrop of a dense communion of human
likenesses, encapsulates the central themes he
explored during his Chelsea period. "The difference between the Jews that were murdered in the
concentration camps and Jesus is that Jesus was
forewarned that his end would be bad and bitter,
and he went to the cross in full consciousness,"
Maryan explains in a late interview. "I did many
sketches of Jesus for my doctor [psychiatrist].
Jesus was poor, a kind of idiot on the cross."[6]

The culmination of Maryan's preoccupation
with humanity, survival, and suffering took the
form of an autobiographical film entitled *Ecce
Homo* (1975) that he staged in his apartment with
the help of fellow artist and filmmaker Kenny
Schneider. *Ecce Homo* prefigures the genre of
the filmed Holocaust testimonial, predating
Claude Lanzmann's epic documentary *Shoah* by

a decade.[7] *Ecce Homo* is not a straight documentary. It opens with an experimental montage of the sociopolitical struggles of the day, such as the civil rights and anti–Vietnam War movements of the '60s and '70s, before Maryan begins delivering his first-person testimonial. His opening salvo presents his intersectional understanding of fascism and genocide. "It's one section of the My Lai massacre, which looks the same too. Absolutely the same," Maryan cries in response to his own opening montage. Facing the camera, Maryan speaks in a style that seems more like a therapeutic stream of consciousness than a dispassionate account of the historical record. At different moments in the film, Maryan dramatizes his recollections with symbolic costumes, alternating between two straightjackets, one with the Star of David and the second with a swastika painted on it. Fake blood oozes from his mouth and a toy machine gun peppers the soundtrack at key moments. Marshaling the Latin phrase for "behold the man"—a reference to the Catholic veneration of Christ's suffering and martyrdom—the film's title also characterizes the mash-up of paintings, masks, and other humanoid images that kept him company in his studio, where he toiled day after day, reflecting upon the human condition, until his untimely death of a heart attack at age fifty in 1977. It was at the center of this visual overload that Maryan found refuge. Amid this

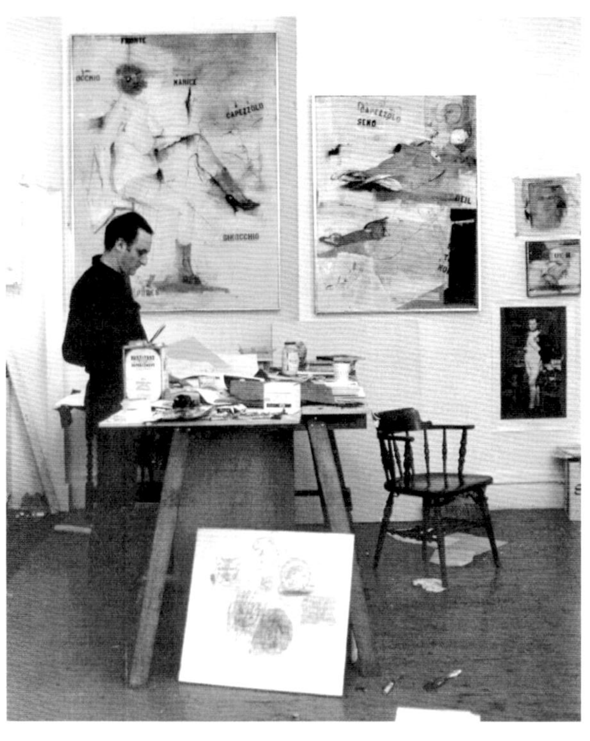

Larry Rivers at work in his Chelsea Hotel studio, New York, 1964. Photo by Basil Langton

horror vacui, testifies his friend and fellow resident Ruth Shomron, "it was only at the Chelsea that Maryan finally felt at home."[8]

For most people, the Chelsea Hotel was no "safe space." It might seem an unexpected trajectory for an artist who, until then, as if in reaction to surviving the Shoah, spent most of his postwar life married and living in rather comfortable, stable settings. Over the course of the 1960s and '70s, this infamous bohemian enclave on West 23rd Street "had become a veritable Ellis Island of the avant-garde, with more than twenty artists from Europe and the United States in residence."[9] By the beginning of the 1970s, when Maryan arrived, the Chelsea was at a turning point. "It was the period in which the Chelsea Hotel began to take on a tabloid character," noted one resident. "It moved from the realm of a bohemian hotel to a kind of hot spot. Rock-and-roll people began to stay there."[10] Patti Smith observed in her memoir *Just Kids*, "The Chelsea was like a doll's house in the Twilight Zone, with a hundred rooms, each a small universe."[11] Smith was another soon-to-be-famous denizen of the hotel's tenth floor, where she lived with the then unknown Robert Mapplethorpe. Her quip perfectly describes Maryan's own psychically charged room, and perhaps it is no coincidence that Smith's residency briefly overlapped with Maryan's time at the Chelsea, as did the tenures of many other illustrious figures from the creative classes, including poet Allen Ginsberg, artist Larry Rivers and Warhol Factory alumni Brigid Berlin, Viva,

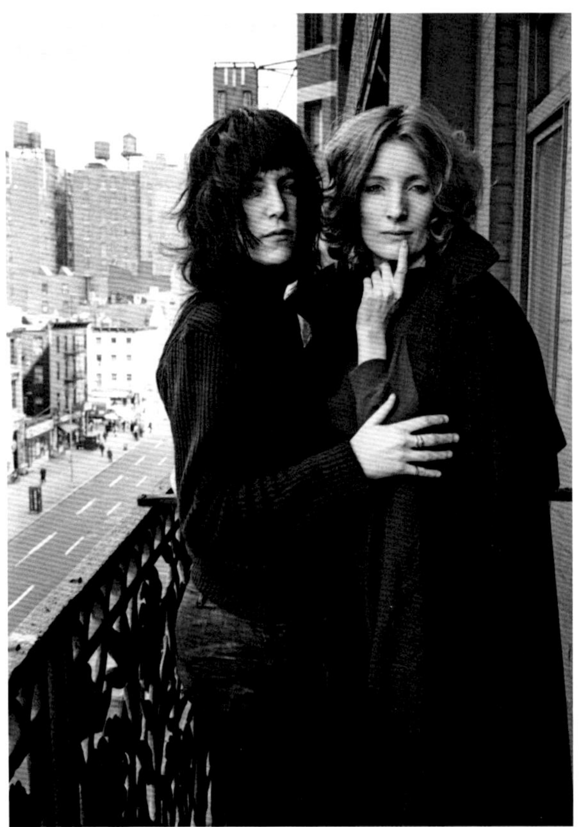

Patti Smith and Viva at the Chelsea Hotel, New York, 1971. Photo by David Gahr

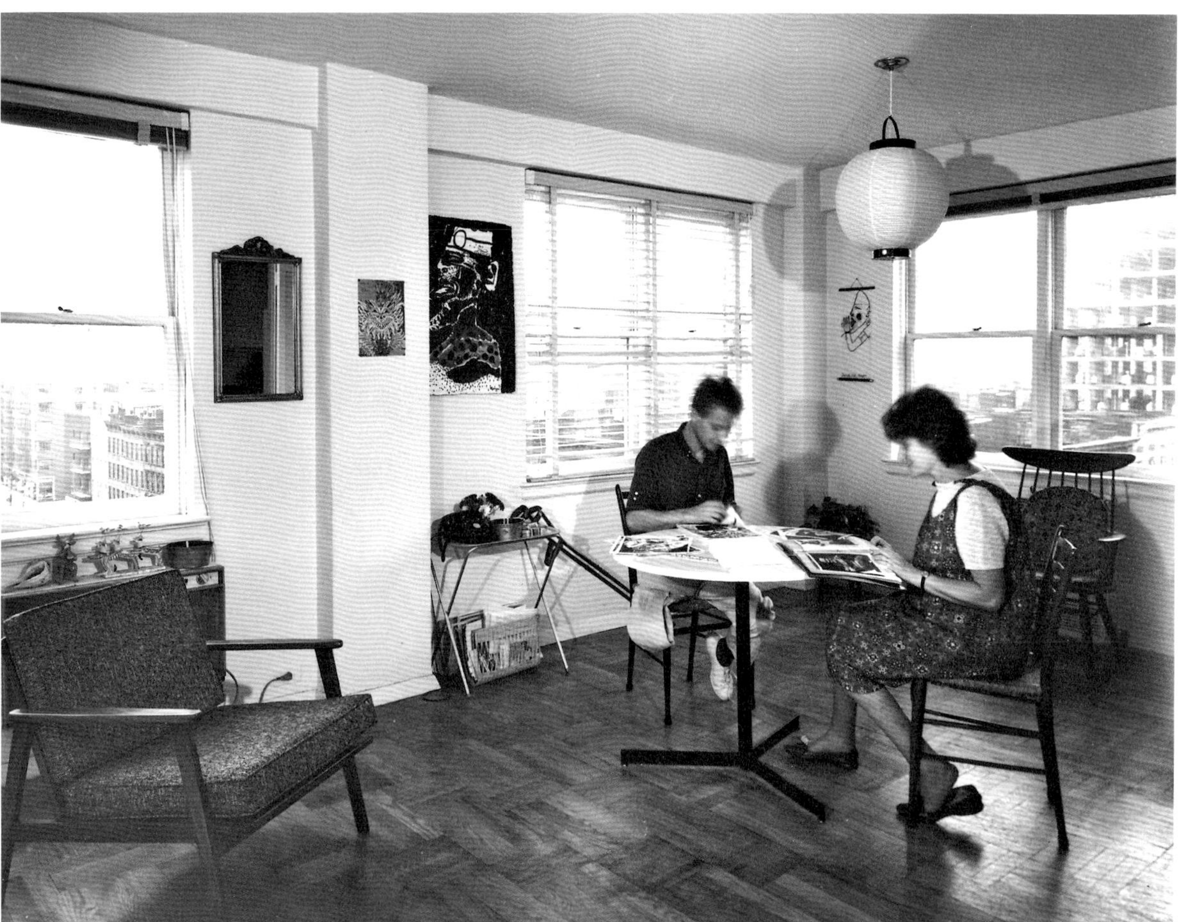

and Viva's then husband, artist Michel Auder. Recalling occasionally meeting Maryan in the lobby and elevator, Auder recounted the artistic and social hierarchy of the Chelsea Hotel floor by floor, explaining, "prostitutes and dealers came and went on the first and second floors, groupies were on the third floor, and rockers like the New York Dolls lived on the fourth and fifth floors . . . the higher you'd go up, the more established the artists, writers, and composers were."[12] Living at the top of this transgressive hive of experimental culture, Maryan's own "doll house in the Twilight Zone" was a far cry from the apartment in which he had spent the previous decade.

In a Rather Bourgeois Apartment

Maryan spent the majority of the 1960s in what his American dealer Allan Frumkin described as a "rather bourgeois apartment on the Upper East Side."[13] Along with his wife, Annette, Maryan immigrated to New York in 1962 after a decade in Paris where he made a name for himself in Europe as a promising, iconoclastic painter. In sharp contrast with the Chelsea photos, snapshots of Maryan's uptown existence show the proper,

middle-class interiors where Maryan painted in a tidy spare bedroom. Like clockwork, Maryan reliably produced enough paintings, watercolors, drawings, and lithographs to stage more than ten solo exhibitions at Allan Frumkin Gallery from 1963 to 1969. At a pace of two shows a year at both Frumkin's New York and Chicago outposts, Maryan steadily built his American career as part of Frumkin's stable, maintaining his maverick independence while connecting to a small circle of similarly unclassifiable artists such as H. C. Westermann, Irving Petlin, and June Leaf, who also showed with Frumkin. Postcards and letters exchanged by Westermann and Maryan testify to their artistic solidarity and tender personal friendship, as do the personal writings of June Leaf on Maryan.[14] United by their commitment to expressive figuration, Leaf and Westermann were often grouped together with other postwar artists from Chicago such as Leon Golub, Dominick di Meo, and Seymour Rosofsky under the nebulous appellation "The Monster Roster." Legendary art critic and curator Dennis Adrian summed up the commonalities of these artists: "Chicago artists recognized an intensity of feeling lodged in the human reference that centered largely on an extreme, often painful, transforming awareness of the world and of the sacred . . . [they] sought to rival such emotional intensities, recognizing their relevance to the dystopic and fragmented modern world of the 1950s and '60s."[15] Adrian's identification of a through line of existential angst and emotional intensity was also applied to the burgeoning reception of Maryan's own figurative work of the 1960s. His most iconic canvases made during this period were composed around single *personnages*, depicted in turbulent states, exuding frenetic energy. Explicit references to his Holocaust experiences remain sublimated in this period—only to explode into the fore in his Chelsea period—bottled up much like the bourgeois confines of his Upper East Side home. His figures are rife with coded symbols, polymorphous fixations, and visceral bodily emissions. The subtext of the humanist struggle in the paintings was legible to reviewers such as Nancy Marmer, writing in the pages of *Artforum* in 1964:

> The paintings, each containing a single figure of a man-animal, function together as a cast for some gigantic tragi-comedy that might be called, "Man: this thing of darkness." They sneer, sit, strut, stick their tongues out, smile enigmatically; others bellow, sprinkle confetti, exhibit themselves, sit in Beckett baskets, or change into hybrids . . . Certain symbolic details recur: the military armbands, confetti, stigmata. These are Chicago School monsters gone to play at German Concentration camps. Unlike Chicago "new images," these paintings have the redeeming virtue of comedy, and, especially in the black and white figures, a raw expressionistic power.[16]

As this snippet from the period confirms, despite never being an official member of the Monster Roster, Maryan was frequently compared to his Chicago compatriots. He was critically discussed in anthologies such as *The New Humanism* alongside Golub[17] and included in group shows with them, such as the Whitney Museum's 1969 show *Human Concern/Personal Torment*—an attempt to trace the existentialist, humanist zeitgeist that was roiling through American contemporary art.

Beyond his growing recognition on the art scene, 1969 was certainly a turning point for Maryan's life. It was in that year that he became

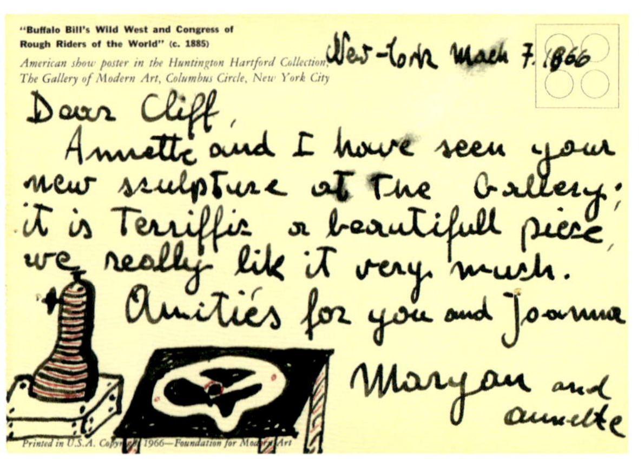

Maryan, Annette Maryan and H. C. (Horace Clifford Westermann, *Think the new sculpture at the gallery is terrific. Illustration of two of HCW's sculpture including Antimobile. Postcard: Buffalo Bill's Wild West, 1885*, March 7, 1966. Handwritten and illustrated postcard, 5⅝ × 4 inches (14.3 × 10.2 cm). Collection of The David and Alfred Smart Museum of Art, The University of Chicago, The H. C. Westermann Study Collection, Gift of Joanna Beall

an American citizen—marking the end of his postwar statelessness. More importantly, it was when he officially assumed his mononym. His new American passport read Maryan S. Maryan.[18] His naturalization cemented his decades-long process of reinvention that had begun when he decided to shed his birthname, Pinkas Bursztyn, and its painful associations with his Nazi imprisonment and his Paris years in the early 1950s. While he may have signed his canvases with his new name when he was a young artist studying at the École des Beaux-Arts, he only received permission from the French state to sign his name as Pinkas Bursztyn "dit Maryan" (known as Maryan) in 1956. He was also denied his request to become a French citizen, a partial catalyst for his decision to leave for New York in 1962.

Names were a fraught subject for many who survived the Shoah. Several Polish Jewish artists who survived hiding under Christian names were faced with the choice of whether or not to revert to their explicitly Jewish names. For example, the avant-garde painter born Henryk Streng opted to continue his postwar career under his assumed name Marek Włodarski, even going so far as to erase his former name from his prewar canvases and replace it with his new name.[19] Conversely, Polish artist Erna Rosenstein, who survived the Shoah under a series of fake identities, was adamant about reassuming her Jewish identity. Over the course of her seven-decade career in Communist Poland, Rosenstein prominently inscribed each of her canvases with her full name, flourishing "Rosenstein" with her distinctive cursive script.

With such stories in mind, "Maryan" emerges as a curious choice. According to his widow, the name was chosen because "it was a popular Polish masculine first name."[20] While impossible to verify, it is provocative to conjecture a psychoanalytical significance to his renaming.

Maryan is an overtly Christian name, a masculinized tribute to the Virgin Mary—keeping perhaps with Maryan's nascent overidentification with the suffering and martyrdom of Christ. Completely removing both matronymic (Bursztyn) and patronymic (Schindel) traces, Maryan is proclaiming his own virgin birth—no father or mother needed. Enacting a kind of parthenogenesis, Maryan was self-hatched. This act of self-generation is reenforced by the doubling of his name. Maryan S. Maryan: as if he is screaming to the world, "I told you once and I told you twice: don't you forget about me. Maryan Maryan."[21]

Even more unsettling, it is impossible not to see the word *Aryan* that is imbedded in the heart of his chosen moniker. Could this be a jarring manifestation of the artist's unconscious? For a survivor of genocide who sought to exorcise the trauma directly linked to his Jewishness, the presence of *Aryan* in his chosen name certainly conjures a host of conflicted and inchoate desires for his new life after Auschwitz. Tragically Maryan died too soon, and in the throes of his post-traumatic torment, for any definite conclusions about the motivations behind his self-nomination.

Despite this new identity and nationality, there was no stability in the cards for Maryan. Whatever attempt he and his wife made at living a "normal" life fell part around 1969.[22] Mirroring the societal turmoil of the late '60s in New York—the escalation of the anti-war movement, civil rights protests, the Stonewall riots, the rise of feminism—Maryan embarked on his own period of extreme turbulence. Before moving to the Chelsea Hotel, and ultimately leaving his wife to take up with a girlfriend, Maryan suffered a series of psychological crises in 1969–71. Under the treatment of a psychologist, Maryan was encouraged to make drawings to work through his traumatic memories. Drawing, rather than talking, was his analyst's solution to help him overcome his primary symptom, the inability to verbally communicate, which struck him around 1970. The resulting 478 drawings made in nine spiral-bound notebooks depict significant autobiographical vignettes from Maryan's prewar childhood, his imprisonment, and even references to difficulties in his marriage. Rendered in a cartoonish style in black ink, almost every drawing is captioned in Maryan's handwriting.

Preceding his film *Ecce Homo* by four years, these drawings can be understood as Maryan's first attempt at a testimonial, a visual-historical record of his own experiences that simultaneously decodes many of the repeated tropes, symbols, and characters that have populated his paintings in previous decades. Lost facts about his family emerge from the study of these drawings, and, in this way, the nine notebooks function posthumously like a Yizkor book—the grassroots practice of making publications that narrate and commemorate destroyed Jewish communities of Eastern Europe, written by surviving members of the diaspora. Maryan's account of Jewish life in prewar Poland does not progress in a chronological sequence; rather, it unfolds in a free-associative fashion. The notebooks reveal that Maryan's father, Abraham, was a baker; the baker's distinctive hat, along with bagels and pretzels, makes multiple appearances in the *personnage* paintings. His mother, Gitla, is portrayed selling bagels, saying Shabbos prayers over the table, and, on numerous occasions, fighting with her husband. In happier times, Maryan and his brother are playing "circus" in the backyard—references to theatrical costumes and carnivalesque tropes abound in his paintings. "I want the Horse!" The infamous toy appears multiple times with a crying boy Maryan, drawn in the same style as his *Screaming Ones* series. Maryan also recalls his "Kosher distress" and the "insane ritual" of the kapparah—the sacrificial killing of a chicken as an act of atonement—that left an indelible memory during his prewar childhood. The sacrificial bird is another trope in his works, from the

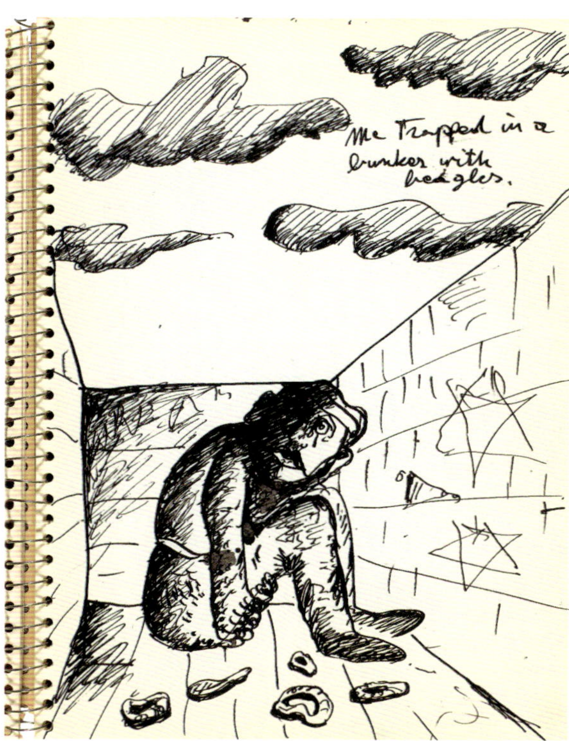

Maryan, page from *Carnet de dessins no. 1 - 9* (Notebook drawings, nos. 1–9), 1971. Chinese ink on paper, in 9 spiral-bound notebooks, dimensions variable. Musée National d'Art Moderne, Centre Pompidou, Paris. Gift of Annette Maryan

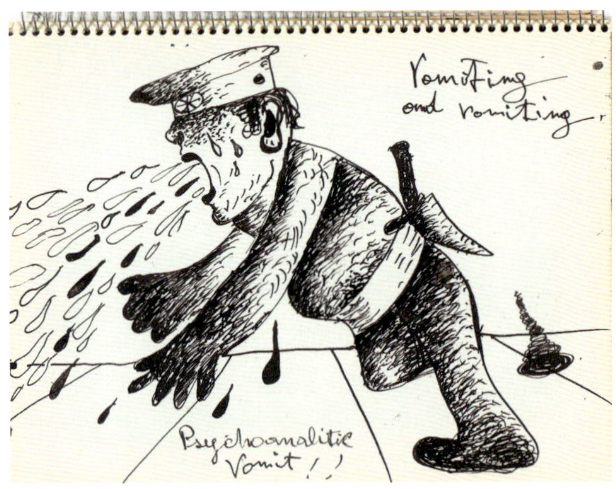

Maryan, page from *Carnet de dessins no. 1 - 9* (Notebook drawings, nos. 1–9), 1971. Chinese ink on paper, in 9 spiral-bound notebooks, dimensions variable. Musée National d'Art Moderne, Centre Pompidou, Paris. Gift of Annette Maryan

early '50s to his last series, *After Goya*, in which he repeatedly revisited the old master's still life *Dead Turkey*.

Yet it is the scenes of his camp experiences that dominate these notebook drawings. "The Box," drawn like a stylized stage, is the charged site of his traumatic recollections that are often presented in a theatricalized, rather than realist, manner. Characters that we know from his paintings are explained in the drawing captions: scary Gestapo figures, "Polak Policia," Nazi SS soldiers, Jewish Police (Żydowska Służba Porządkowa—the ghetto police that collaborated with the Nazis), the rabbi in the camp, his dying father. Visceral manifestations of his bodily disgust in response to the death and horror he witnessed are perhaps the most significant theme across these nine notebooks: wounded bodies, mouths, anuses, various orifices streaming fluids, spit, shit, vomit. Vomiting is the primary mode for Maryan to express his disgust in these drawings. Vomiting occurs in the camps as well as in scenes of his present-day life, even as part of his therapy. "Vomiting and vomiting. Psychoanalytic vomit." "The nausea is driving me crazy." "Nobody understood my vomiting. Everyone is laughing at me." In one of the only texts on these notebooks, the psychoanalyst Gérard Wajcman explains:

Rather than in the ear of an analyst, the artist confides his intimacy to his eye, to the paper, where, instead of the couch, he lays his life down on the pages of a notebook; it is where he stages Maryan's symptom, even if it means reinforcing it. He makes visible, and as it were palpable, that a deep disjunction runs through all his work, which haunts him, between what is said and what is visible.[23]

Wajcman surmises through his analysis of the notebooks that Maryan's linguistic silence is a result of the very impossibility to articulate in words what Maryan has survived. The mouth is the vehicle for spoken language. For Maryan, the mouth is the compositional center of action in so many of these notebook drawings as well as in his mature paintings. Based on a literal reading of these drawings, the oral emissions of so many of his painted subjects might be understood as purely autobiographical: stylized versions of his propensity to vomit, going back to his time in the camps. When asked about his recollections of Maryan, the artist Pierre Alechinsky (the only living member of the CoBrA group) offered a revelatory anecdote:

Myself, Pol Bury, John Lefebre and Maryan, were on a road trip from New York to Pittsburg.
Maryan: "The doctor told me I should stop from time to time so I can eat a little something, every half an hour."
Lefebre: "I hope you ate something before leaving."
Maryan: "No, but I already threw up."[24]

Beyond autobiography, this trope of vomit can also be understood on a more profound level as a visual manifestation of the inadequacy of language for the survivor. Little matter that it is reviling, vomit is Maryan's life force—the capacity to be disgusted, as scholar William Ian Miller wrote, "is human and humanizing."[25] In Maryan's case, the vomit-as-life-force is what separates him from all the inhumanity, death, and abjection that he witnessed. As Julia Kristeva wrote in her famous treatise *Powers of Horror: An Essay on Abjection*, "The spasms and vomiting that protect

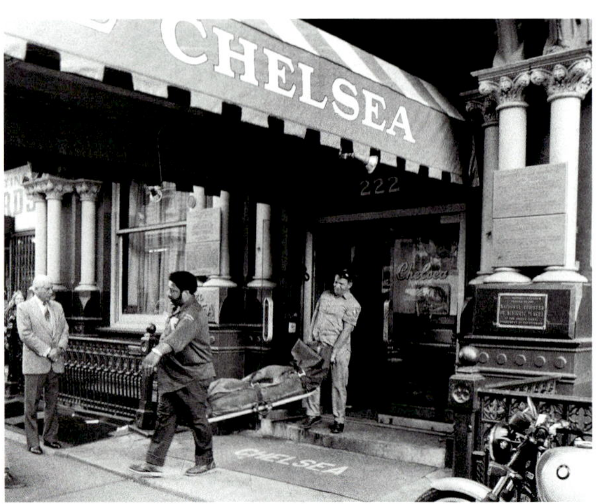

Attendants carrying Nancy Spungen's body from the Chelsea Hotel, New York, after Spungen had been stabbed to death by Sid Vicious, October 12, 1978. Photo by Hal Goldenberg

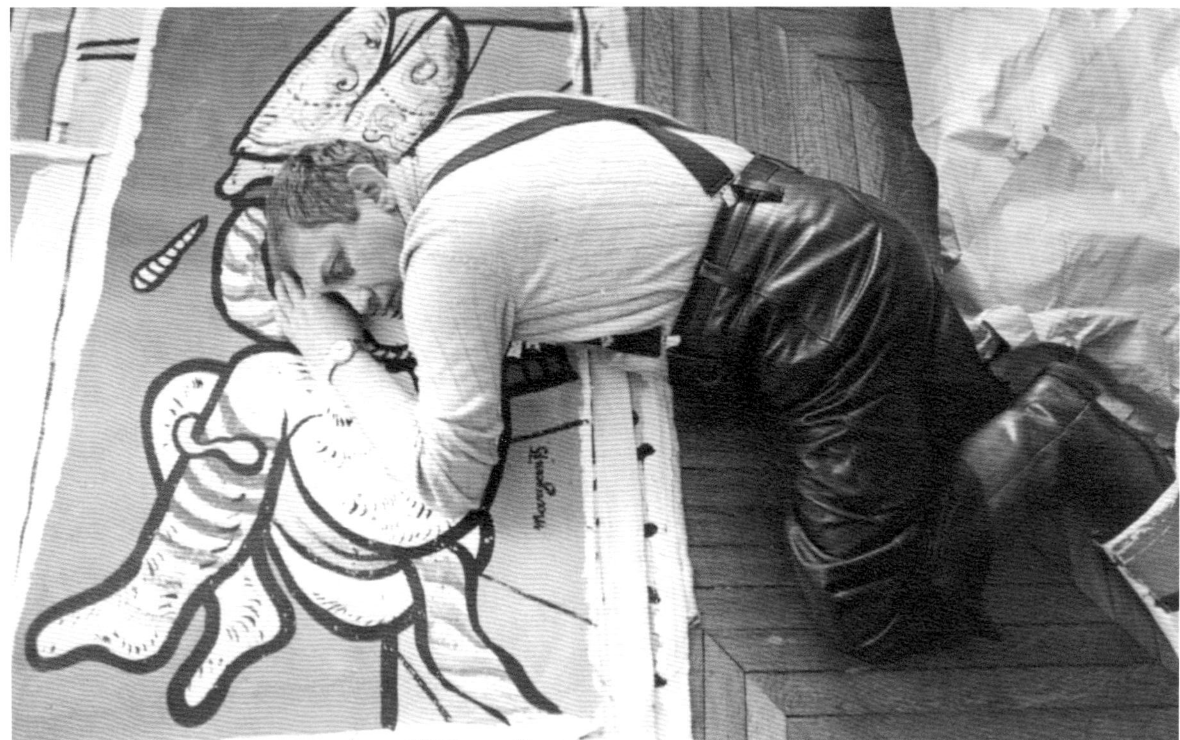

Maryan, ca. 1976. *Ecce Homo* Archives, 1975. Collection of ephemera from the *Ecce Homo* film. Courtesy of Venus Over Manhattan, New York

me. The repugnance, the retching that thrusts me to the side and turns me away from defilement, sewage, and muck."[26] Vomit—both on the canvas and in life—replaces words. It temporarily protects him, separating him from the traumatic pain of survival.

Rock and Roll after Auschwitz

Theodor Adorno articulated one of the most famous proclamations about art after the Holocaust, "To write poetry after Auschwitz is barbaric."[27] What would he make of Maryan's rock and roll after Auschwitz? If the bourgeois conventions of poetry were barbaric, how would he characterize the punk rock of the 1970s? Maryan's radical move to the Chelsea Hotel— living at the epicenter of this nihilistic, anarchistic zeitgeist—catalyzed his (albeit temporary) liberation. This was not the clean-cut pop rock of the 1960s Beatles; it was more seedy, edgy, à la New York Dolls and Sex Pistols. By 1975 the Chelsea Hotel epitomized rock's darker incarnation—Maryan had long traded his tweed suits and skinny ties for leather pants and suspenders. Kenny Schneider recalls the pervasiveness of the drug culture of the Chelsea Hotel and remembers Maryan himself struggling with addiction to pain pills. Not long after undergoing his psychological treatment that resulted in the notebooks, Maryan was unable to resume the status quo of his Upper East Side life. His neighbor and confidante Ruth

Shomron recalls that from the very first moment he arrived at the Chelsea, Maryan spoke about his insatiable drive to make his testimonial movie. Filming *Ecce Homo* literally broke his silence. This was a massive reversal: as a man, Maryan spent much of his life grappling with his survivor's guilt, while as an artist, he fought throughout his career to thwart the reductive label of "Holocaust artist." Goaded by this punk rock atmosphere, Maryan finally confronted these demons, unleashing all that he worked so hard to repress in previous decades, making his Chelsea years his least understood but most significant period.

Dramatic shifts in attitudes toward survivors also contributed to this watershed moment for Maryan. As Shoshana Felman explains, "It is a well-known fact that prior to the Eichmann trial, the Holocaust was not discussed in Israel but was rather struck by shame, silence, and widespread denial. Holocaust survivors did not talk about their past and when they did, they were not listened to. Their memories were sealed in muteness and in silence. Their stories often were kept secret even from their families."[28] With this context in mind, it becomes understandable why Maryan would have thought that his oeuvre could not simultaneously be considered "high art"—recognized and admired as advanced, modern painting on a par with the very best of his mid-century peers: Philip Guston, Francis Bacon, Leon Golub—while simultaneously embodying

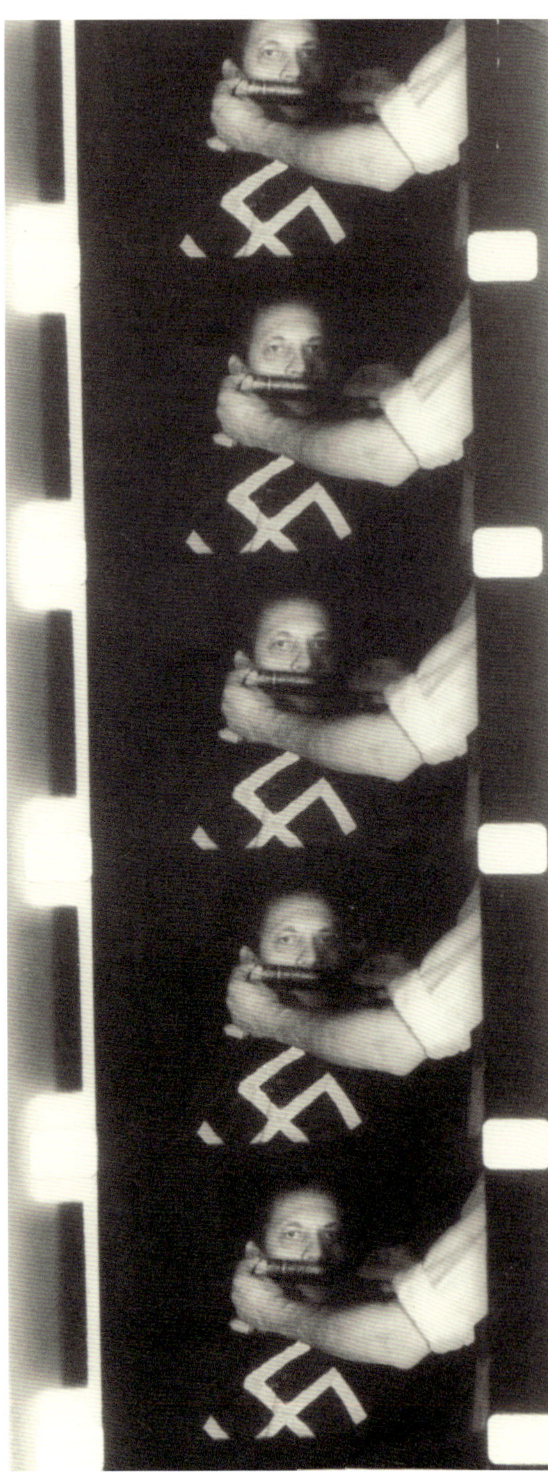

Maryan, film strip print from the *Ecce Homo* Archives, 1975

crippling disability was now being reclaimed as an empowering and proudly shared political and moral identity."[29]

On a private level, Maryan similarly experienced a personal transformation in his Chelsea Hotel studio. The taboo dividing himself as an artist and as a survivor began to erode, paving the way for his work to fully function on both levels concurrently. At the height of his painterly power, his canvases made at the Chelsea vibrate with chromatic and graphic intensities. The *personnage* heads painted on tondos and crucifix-shaped canvases in saturated shades of yellow, green, blue, and brown are triumphant examples of his "American period" style. These canvases, hung edge to edge, crowded around Maryan to bear witness to the extraordinary personal narrative he delivers in his opus, *Ecce Homo*—itself a groundbreaking work of experimental film *and* a groundbreaking document of the Holocaust. His late *personnage* paintings are visual totems of his artistic autonomy and a pictorial Greek chorus that reinforces the tormented story Maryan struggles to immortalize on film. "I can't anymore. I am not getting crazy, I think. It hurts too much, you know. I am not getting crazy," Maryan proclaims in the middle of the film. His *personnages* scream silently, their mouths full of vomit-words, echoing the pain caused by his broken silence. Two years after completing the film, Maryan died of a heart attack alone in his tenth-floor room—abetted by the psychic trauma and turbulence of his last years. Alone, except for the crowd of his *personnages*, his tragic, premature passing finally liberated him from his earthly torment.

Adorno ultimately recanted his prohibition: "Perennial suffering has as much right to expression as a tortured man has to scream; hence it may have been wrong to say that after Auschwitz you could no longer write poems."[30] Maryan's transformation at the Chelsea Hotel—what this essay has tried to chart as his "rock and roll after Auschwitz" becoming—further refutes Adorno's dictates about the impossibility of artistic representation in the wake of the Shoah. This exhibition, and its accompanying catalogue, very deliberately tells Maryan's story starting from its last years, rather than starting at the beginning. As such, his last radical chapter provides the primary lens through which we attempt to chart a holistic understanding of his complex life and artistic trajectory. *Ecce Homo*: we must behold a man *and* an artist. Maryan pioneered an independent vision

invaluable sociopolitical and historical significance as a firsthand visual testimonial of the Shoah. The burden of history canceled aesthetic merit. Yet, as Felman points out, after the public testimony of over one hundred survivors was broadcast around the world on television during the 1961 trial, the status of the survivor-witness had undergone revolutionary transformation. "For the first time victims were legitimized and validated and their newborn discourse was empowered by their new roles, not as victims but as prosecution witnesses within the trial . . . . A Jewish past that formally had meant only a of postwar figuration while concurrently wrestling with what it meant to be human after suffering such inhumanity. Looking backward from the perspective of his mid-1970s Chelsea Hotel room, this duality is the through line that connects his oeuvre, from his first paintings made in Israel in the late 1940s to his very last series, *After Goya*, executed before his death in 1977. "My painting is autobiographical. Everything I do must be auto-biographical. I will be myself in any color that I put on the canvas."[31]

NOTES

1. The exact chronology of Maryan's residency at the Chelsea Hotel is difficult to establish (there are no known archives of the hotel from that period). In an unpublished interview with the author, Maryan's close friend Ruth Shomron, who still resides at the Chelsea Hotel, recalls that Maryan was moved to the Chelsea around the same time she moved there in 1972. Ruth and her husband, Daniel Shomron, immigrated to New York from Israel that same year and remained very close to Maryan until his death in 1977. Daniel Shomron found Maryan the day he died in his Chelsea apartment.

2. The art dealer John Lefebre—whose eponymous Lefebre Gallery in New York showcased numerous postwar artists from the CoBrA movement and the École de Paris—took these photographs in the 1970s. The author is grateful to his daughter Marion Lefebre, who shared these never-before-published images from his archive.

3. Scholar Erica Moiah James identified masks by the Gelede, Bamileke, Ejagham, Igbo, Chokwe, Kifwebe/Luba, Dan (Yakuba), Guere, and Pende peoples in the photographs of Maryan's Chelsea apartment. See "Maryan and African Art in the Chelsea Hotel: Two Perspectives," in this volume, 176.

4. Peter Selz, the legendary curator at the Museum of Modern Art who emigrated from Germany in 1936 after fleeing Nazi perse-cution, organized *New Images of Man* in 1959. In the exhibition catalogue, he writes, "The revelations and complexities of mid-twen-tieth-century life have called forth a profound feeling of solitude and anxiety. The imagery of man which has evolved from this, reveals sometimes a new dignity, sometimes despair, but always the unique-ness of man as he confronts his fate . . . these imagists take the human situation, indeed the human predicament rather than formal structure, as their starting point. Existence rather than essence is of the greatest concern to them." See Peter Selz, ed., *New Images of Man* (New York: Museum of Modern Art, 1959), 11. While Maryan was not included in this exhibition, Selz's entire conceit uncannily fits Maryan's approach to figuration like a glove.

5. In a 1976 text that begins "My Name is Maryan," he writes, "There was also a rocking horse that nobody used at the neighbor's house, just next door, and I could get there through the yard. And I wanted it and they refused to give it to me. Last year, I found the same horse, brand-new, made by the same craftsmen of my native town, in a big toy store, and I bought it immediately. Obviously, I am too big to climb on it, but believe me, it isn't because I wouldn't like to." This autobiographical statement was first published in the catalogue *Ariel 42* for Maryan's exhibition at Galerie Ariel, Paris, in February 1977. It was reprinted in *Maryan's Personnages: Works in Chicago Collections*, 1958–75, ed. Michele Vishny (Chicago: Sper-tus Museum of Judaica, 1983), 23 (in the editor's translation).

6. Joseph Mundy, "Conversation: Maryan at La Coupole," in Vishny, *Maryan's Personnages*, 54.

7. It is difficult to pinpoint the existence of filmed testimonials that predate Maryan's film. In July 1946, David Boder, a Latvian American psychologist, recorded audio interviews with Holocaust survivors who were living in displaced persons (DP) camps—these are among the earliest known testimonials. In 1979, the Holocaust Survivors Film Project started to videotape testimonials of survivors and witnesses. This has become part of Yale University's Fortunoff Archive. The author is grateful to professors Oren Baruch and Noah Shenker for sharing their research on this subject.

8. Ruth Shomron, interview by the author, October 6, 2021.

9. Sherill Tippins, *Inside the Dream Palace: The Life and Times of New York's Legendary Chelsea Hotel* (New York: Mariner Books, 2014), 164.

10. Nathaniel Rich, "Where the Walls Still Talk," *Vanity Fair*, October 8, 2013, https://www.vanityfair.com/culture/2013/10/chelsea-hotel-oral-history.

11. Patti Smith, *Just Kids* (New York: Ecco, 2010), 139.

12. Michel Auder, interview by the author, October 12, 2021.

13. Unpublished 1978 interview with Allan Frumkin, Juliette Elkon Hamelecourt papers, 1911–2000, bulk 1940s–2000. Archives of American Art, Smithsonian Institution.

14. See June Leaf, "About Maryan," in this volume, 142.

15. Dennis Adrian, *Monster Roster: Existentialist Art in Postwar Chicago* (Chicago: Smart Museum of Art, 2016), 12.

16. Nancy Marmer, "Maryan," *Artforum*, December 1964, 16.

17. "Leon Golub has created one of the most ambitious represen-tational arts in our time . . . Maryan S. Maryan has also created one of the most ambitious representational arts of our time . . . His art became an exorcism of authority, a psychological journey into and beyond the crisis of contemporary life." Barry Schwartz, *The New Humanism: Art in a Time of Change* (New York: Praeger, 1974), 154–56.

18. The "S." stood for "Simson" or "Samson," according to inter-views with his widow, Annette Maryan. His Polish birth certificate indicates his birth name as Pinkas Simson Bursztyn.

19. See the recent scholarship by curator Piotr Słodkowski around his exhibition *Henryk Streng/Marek Włodarski and Jewish-Polish Modernism*, Museum on the Vistula, Warsaw, February 5–May 16, 2021, https://artmuseum.pl/en/wystawy/henryk-streng-marek-wlo-darski-i-modernizm-zydowsko-polski.

20. See Vishny, *Maryan's Personnages*, 10n4.

21. This last passage on Maryan's virgin birth, parthenogenesis, and doubling has been developed in conversation with my colleague, scholar and analyst Tracy Morgan, who helped expand my thinking through of the possible psychoanalytic understandings of Maryan's act of naming himself. The quote comes from Morgan.

22. Jeanne Marie Wasilik, *Maryan: Behold a Man and His Work* (Chicago: Spertus Institute of Jewish Studies, 1996), 248.

23. Gérard Wajcman, "Help!," in *Maryan: La ménagerie humaine* (Paris: Musée d'art et d'histoire du Judaïsme, 2014), 90.

24. Pierre Alechinsky to Alison M. Gingeras, October 17, 2021. In the same letter, Alechinsky writes, "During the sixties at the Galerie de France, I showed with three 'unijambistes' (one-leggers), Maryan, Hans Hartung, and Roger Edgar Gillet . . ." The dark humor of Alechinsky's neologism also testifies to the pervasiveness of profound wounds that were visible after the war.

25. William Ian Miller, *The Anatomy of Disgust* (Cambridge, MA: Harvard University Press, 1997), 11.

26. Julia Kristeva, *Powers of Horror: An Essay on Abjection*, trans. Leon S. Roudiez (New York: Columbia University Press, 1982), 2.

27. Theodor W. Adorno, *Prisms*, trans. Samuel and Shierry Weber (Cambridge, MA: MIT Press, 1983), 39.

28. Shoshana Felman, "Theaters of Justice: Arendt in Jerusalem, the Eichmann Trial, and the Redefinition of Legal Meaning in the Wake of the Holocaust," *Critical Inquiry* 27, no. 2 (Winter 2001): 231–32.

29. Ibid., 232.

30. Theodor W. Adorno, *Negative Dialectics*, trans. E. B. Ashton (New York: Continuum, 2007), 362–63.

31. Mundy, "Conversation: Maryan at La Coupole," 52.

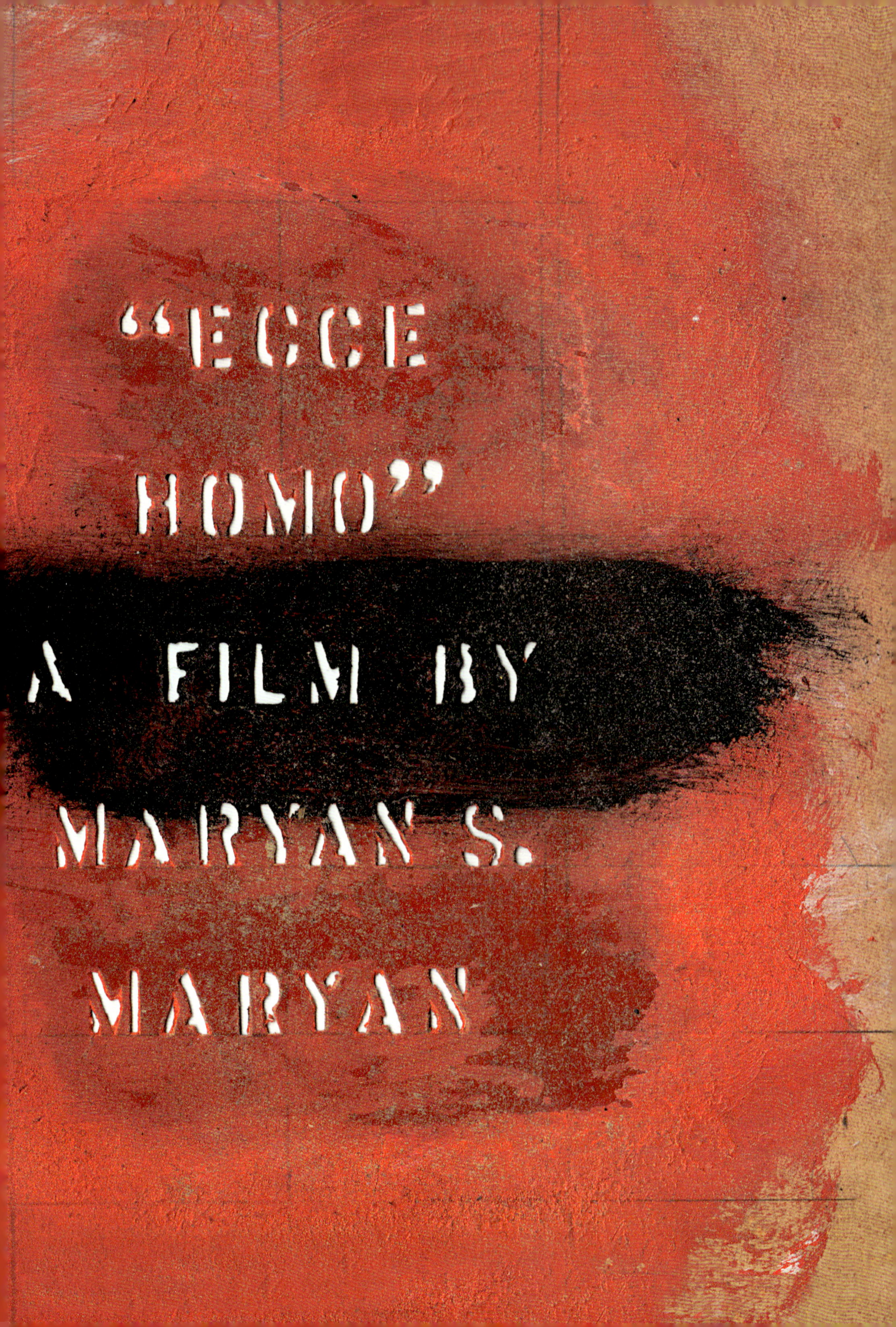

"ECCE
HOMO"
A FILM BY
MARYAN S.
MARYAN

ON *ECCE HOMO*

In 1975, Maryan created an experimental film titled *Ecce Homo*. Shot in his studio in the Chelsea Hotel by fellow artist Kenny Schneider, this groundbreaking work combines Maryan's first-person testimony of his experience in the Nazi camps, spoken directly to the camera, with still imagery of contemporary historical events and images of the contentious political subjects of the day.

The Latin phrase *ecce homo* translates as "behold the man." Frequently used in Christian art that depicts the suffering of Christ, the phrase was attributed to Pontius Pilate, the Roman governor of Judea (26–36 CE) who mockingly addressed the Jews demanding the crucifixion of Jesus (John 19:5).

Maryan knowingly appropriated this loaded art historical reference and made it a recurrent trope in his late paintings. In an interview conducted just before his death in 1977, Maryan spoke about the reference. "The difference between the Jews who were murdered in the concentration camps and Jesus is that Jesus was forewarned that his end would be bad and bitter, and he went to the cross in full consciousness," he said. "The Jews who were slaughtered did not know until the last moment that they were to be murdered. I did many sketches of Jesus [at the urging of] . . . my doctor. Jesus was poor, a kind of idiot on the cross."[1]

In the last decade of Maryan's life, he grappled with the unresolved psychological turmoil of his childhood, his experience in the camps, and its impact on his life after surviving. The film *Ecce Homo* is the culmination of his processing of his experiences, as well as an attempt to create an equivalence between the Holocaust and the sociopolitical struggles of the day, such as the civil rights and anti–Vietnam War movements in America. As a filmed Holocaust testimonial, *Ecce Homo* predates Claude Lanzmann's epic film *Shoah* (1985) by a decade.

A never-before-exhibited archive of still images that Maryan used to make *Ecce Homo* was uncovered during the research for this publication. The photographic images of current events were captured by the Black Star Photo Agency, which was known for photojournalism made by some of the most prominent documentarians of the twentieth century. *Ecce Homo* includes Black Star images of Adolf Hitler, Yasser Arafat, Mustafa Kemal Atatürk, Mao Zedong, Moshe Dayan, Benito Mussolini with Pope Pius XII, Black American protestors being attacked by police dogs, members of the KKK, and victims of the Mỹ Lai massacre in Vietnam. *Ecce Homo*'s typewritten prologue proclaims it is "a painting on film that speaks and moves: a startling anti-genocide work of art."[2] By making these associations between his own memories and some of the most tumultuous sociopolitical events and figures of the twentieth century, Maryan's *Ecce Homo* precociously articulates an intersectional relationship between his Holocaust survival story and other anti-Fascist, anti-racist struggles around the world.

—Alison M. Gingeras

1. Joseph Mundy, "Conversation: Maryan at La Coupole," in Maryan's *Personnages: Works in Chicago Collections, 1958–75*, ed. Michele Vishny (Chicago: Spertus Museum of Judaica, 1983),

2. See facsimile of unpublished prologue by Allan Rich, 1976, in this volume, 62-63.

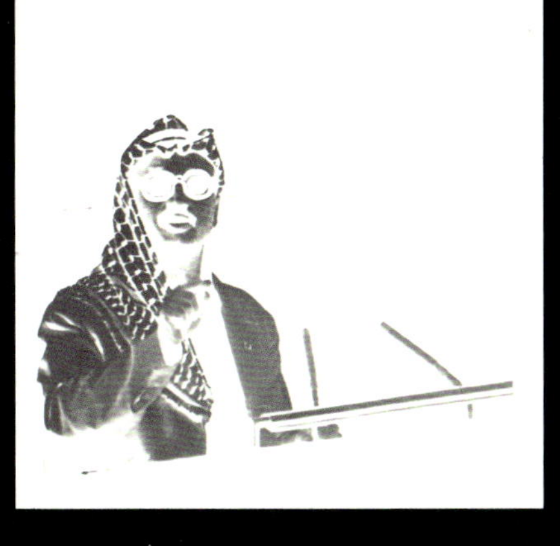
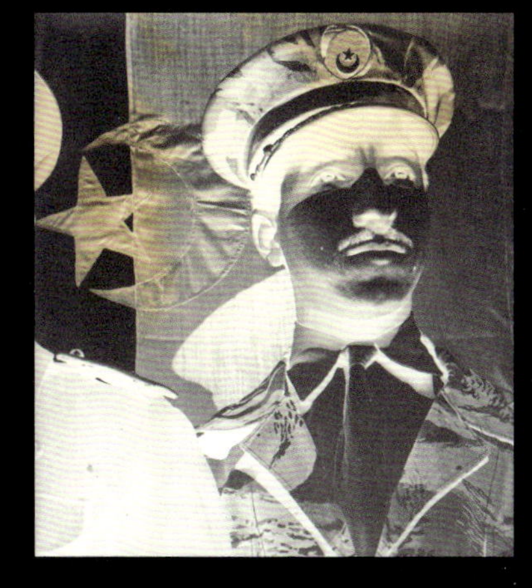
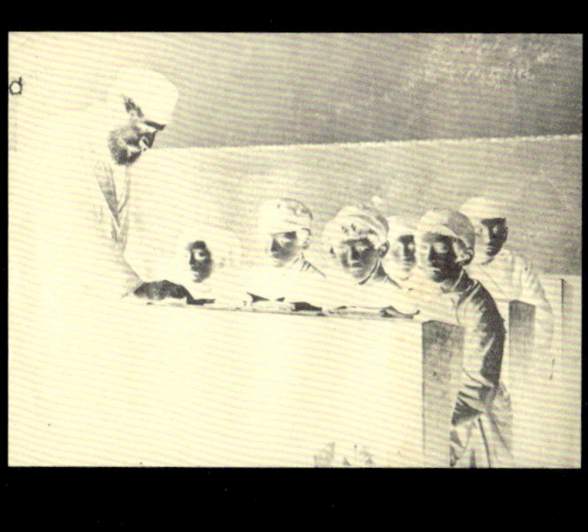
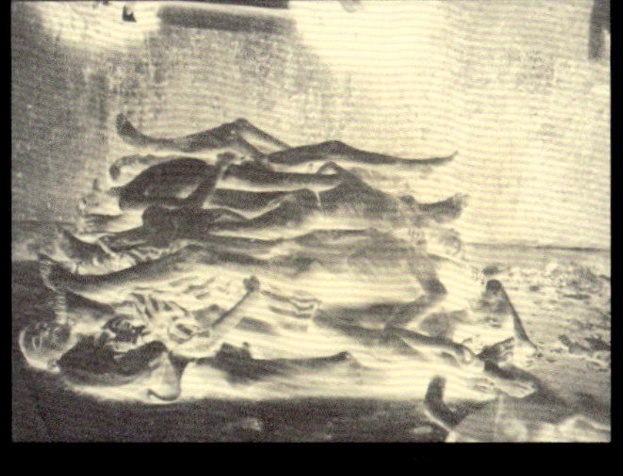
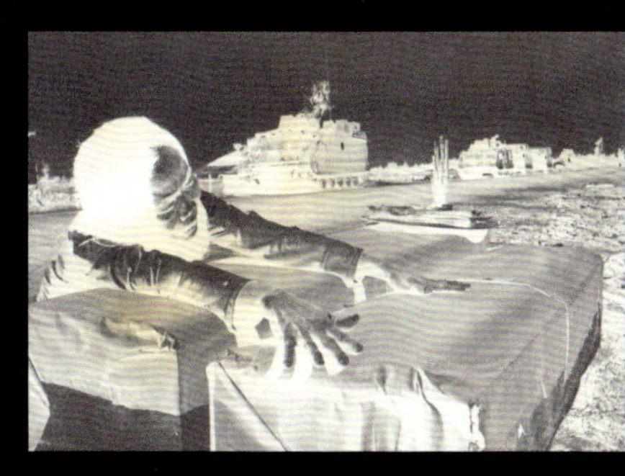
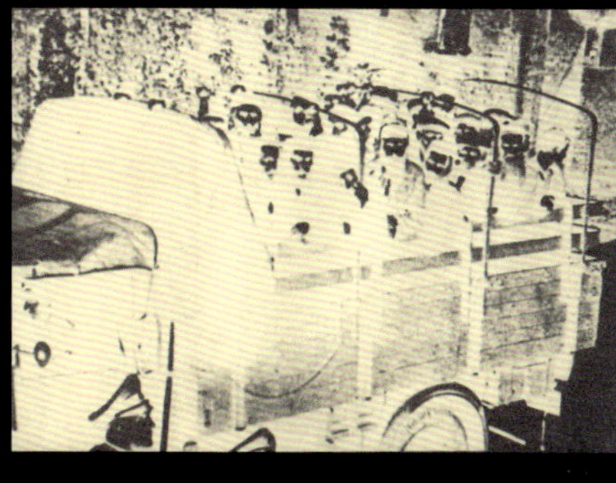
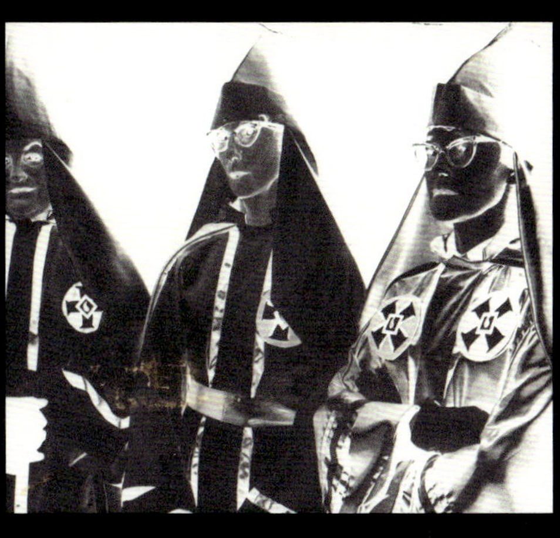
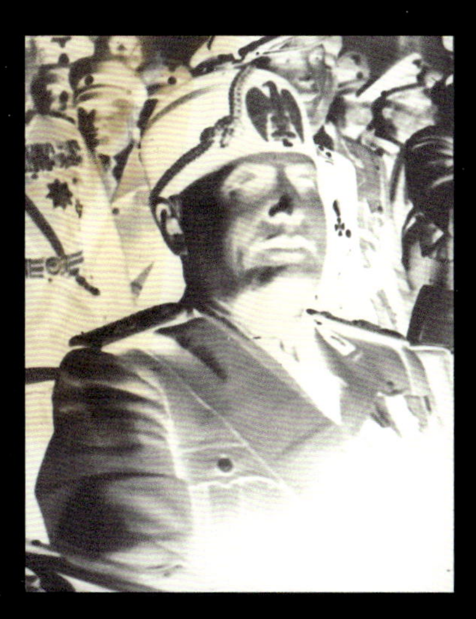
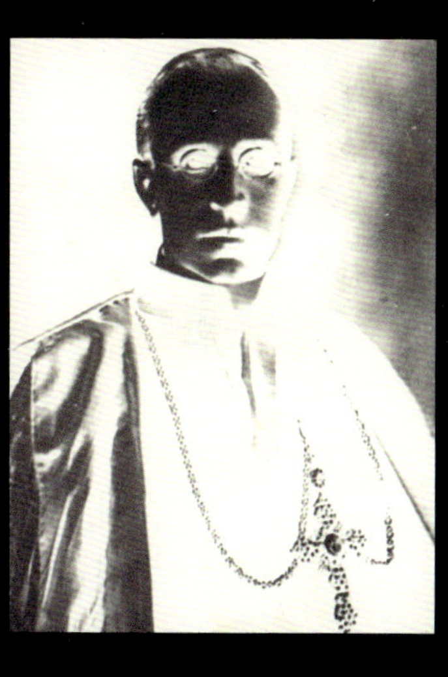
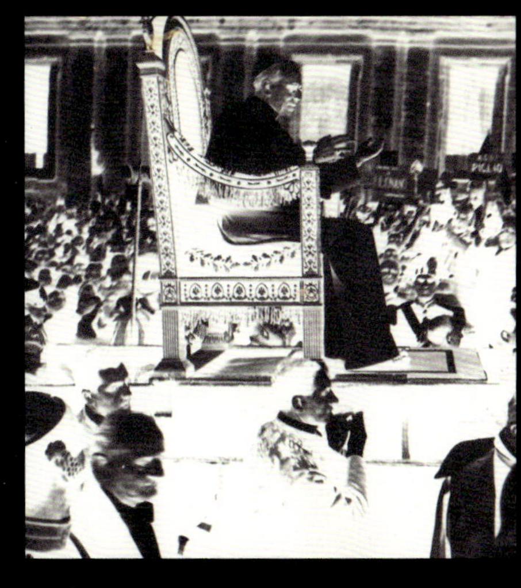
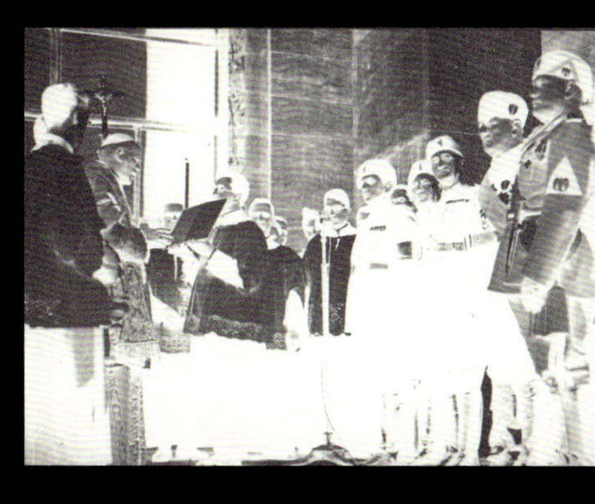
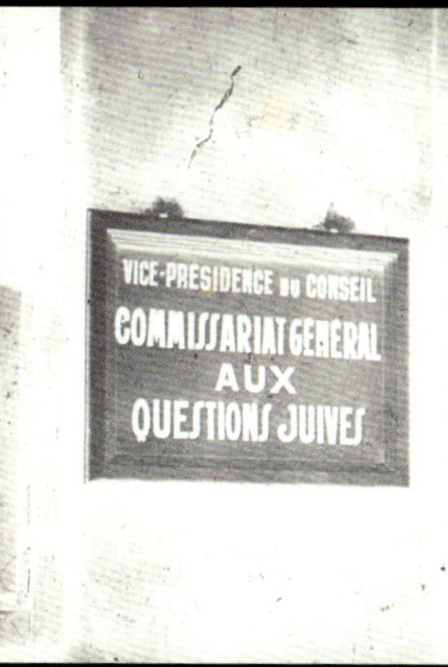
VICE-PRESIDENCE DU CONSEIL
COMMISSARIAT GÉNÉRAL
AUX
QUESTIONS JUIVES

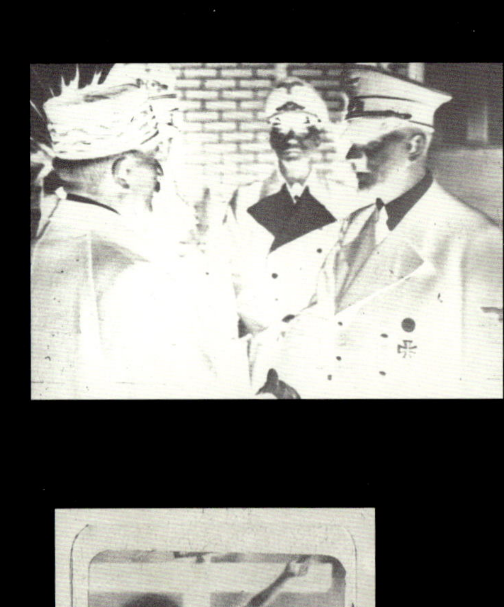
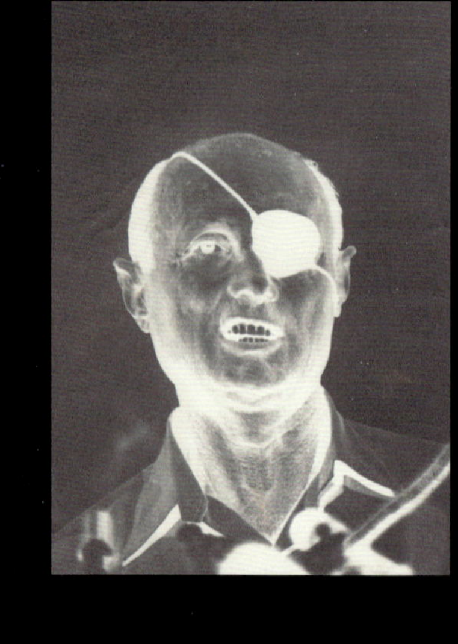
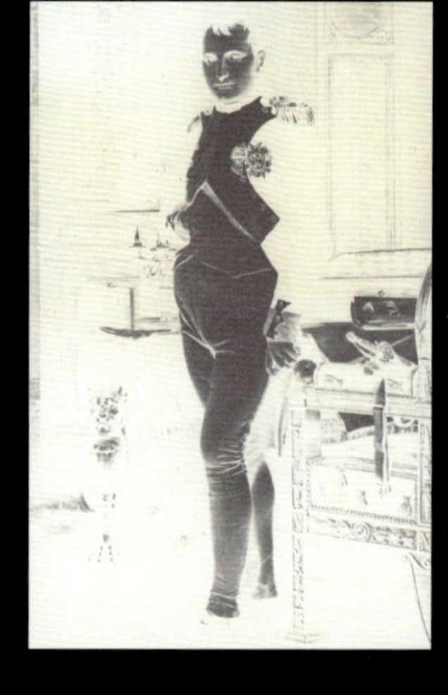
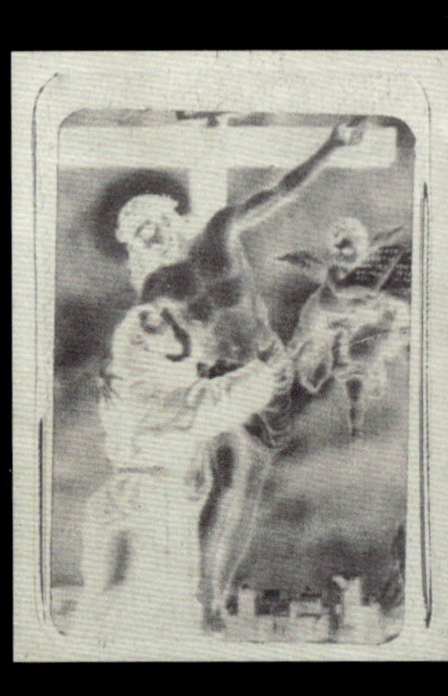
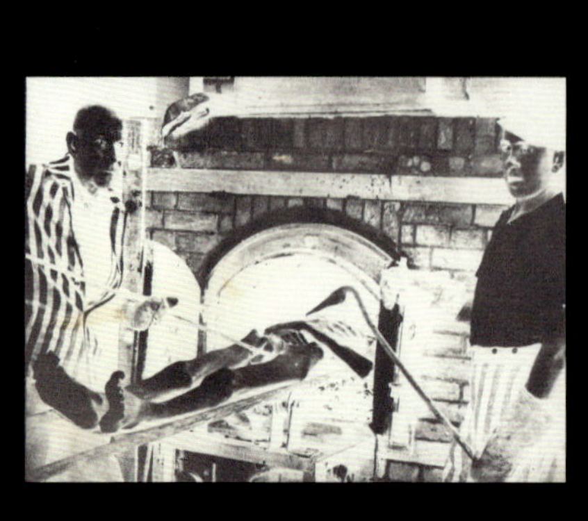
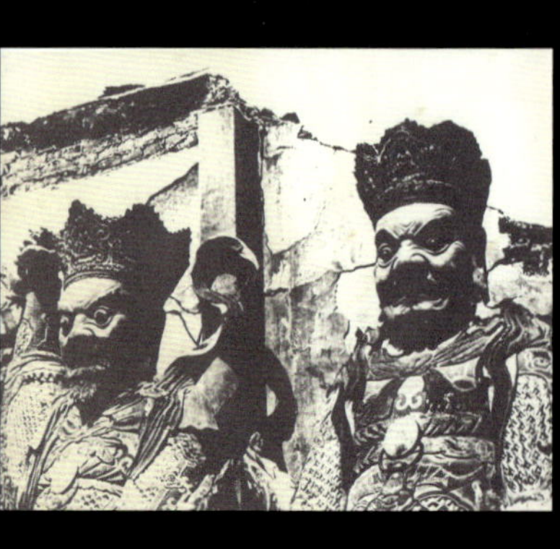
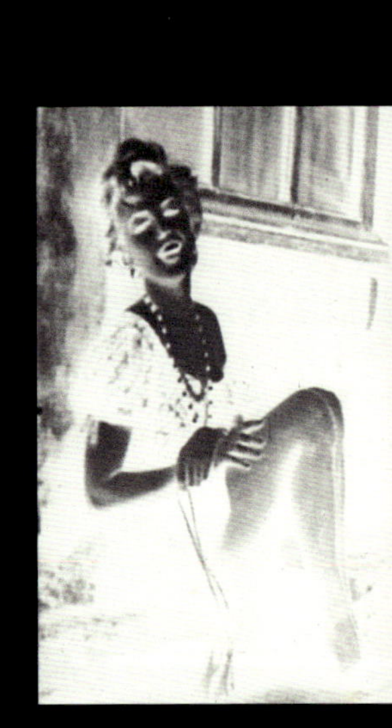
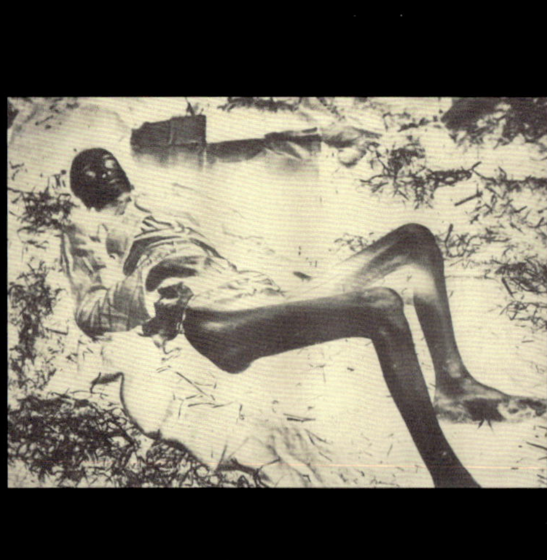
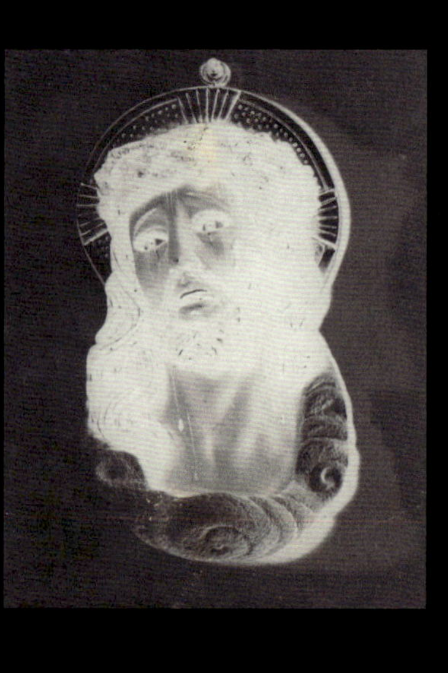
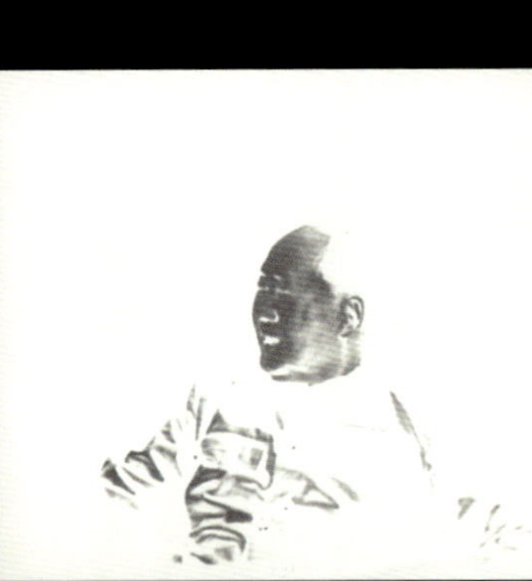
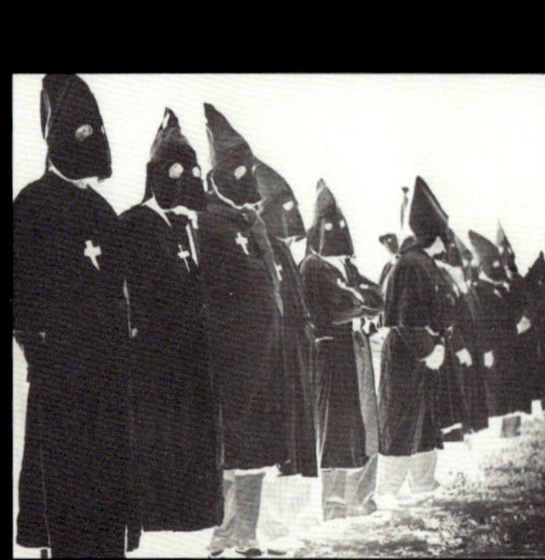
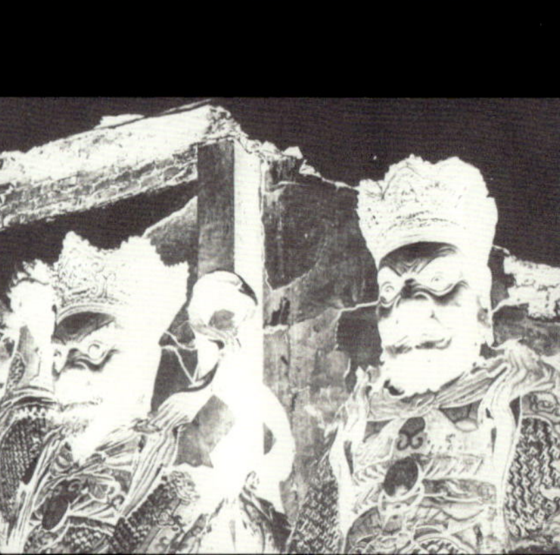

Transcript of Ecce Homo Monologue (1975)[1]

Maryan S. Maryan

The film opens with a musical recording of "Rozo d'Shabbos" (The Secret of Shabbos, lyrics in Aramaic)[2] sung by Pierre Pinchik (1893–1971), the famous Cantor of Leningrad. A montage of still images, mostly taken from the collection of the Black Star wire service, unfolds in tandem with the music.

Maryan: That's how we were . . . that's how we were transported to the concentration camp. Ah . . . ugh . . . I saw these wagons full of dead, you know, like, about hundreds of them. Oh, no! I cannot even say anything about this.

[Still image of Mỹ Lai massacre]

It's one section of the Mỹ Lai massacre, which looks the same too. Absolutely the same. That's another pile-up . . .

[baby crying]

Mỹ Lai.

[baby crying; baby stops crying abruptly]

I can't anymore. I am not getting crazy, I think. It hurts too much, you know. I am not getting crazy.

Two guards, you know. I even remember their names. One was in civilian clothes, and one was in their German Nazi clothes. One was named . . . one named Esther Hildergarden. They took us. We were twenty-four . . . twenty-two people. Also, I think, children. They shut us into . . . till . . . till we came to the place where they wanted to shoot us.[3]

They shoot a few . . .

No, I . . . No! [moans] Er . . . *Ja* and . . .

We were standing in a road waiting for the bullets. They shot . . . they used this German Mauser, you know. They even got their machine gun there to shoot . . . [moans]

Then they had to shoot everybody separately. And I was watching.

I don't know why I was there. They were drunk. These bastards were drunk. The Nazis . . . they didn't kill anybody. They just . . . they had to shoot them several times later. To get them dead. Then my . . . my two came. Frankly, I don't know. It's kind of . . . I wanted to . . . I wanted to be dead before.

And he . . . he gave me one shot in the neck, and the bullet came out in the front, on the eye. First lying there not realizing that I am not . . . dead.

Instinctively, I decided not to move and not to breathe. I don't know how the hell I knew that they would check again and over. Check whether it is not . . . dead. Then place another bullet.

The guy near me . . . like mine, his head was touching my head and he was moving, half-dead, screaming, yelling. He got a dozen bullets, and he didn't touch my head.

And they went and they came back with dogs. The dogs started to smell who would breathe. They shot again. I didn't breathe. I didn't breathe.

1. All dialogue spoken by Maryan unless otherwise indicated. The transcript has been lightly edited to correct some of Maryan's English grammar.

2. The final lyrics as sung by Pinchik translate as "And so all the forces of evil, and all enemies, will disappear."

3. Pinkas Bursztyn was transferred in the winter of 1942 to Rzeszów, where he was to be executed. Despite being shot in the face and neck, he survived.

I cheated. Maybe I cheated. That is my guilt.

Do you think I am guilty?

[Kenny Schneider, from behind the camera:] No.

And I went into a house and knocked on the door and nobody wanted to open it for me.

They were scared. I didn't understand, but now I understand they were scared. I was dead for them. Nobody would hide me.

Finally, the . . . the Jewish policemen, all of them, came with the Dachau forces in a black wagon to take them, and they wanted to take me too.

I say, "No, you won't."

He said, "Yes, you will be missing. An hour they will shoot everybody."

I said, "I don't care."

He won't take me somehow. I don't know what happened.

They put me in the local prison. And the same people came, all the Gestapo, all the police, the Polish . . . and even the Polish policemen of the town, the doctor came to see how I survived. I was sure they were going to place another bullet. Oh! Hmph. They let me live. They even say things I didn't understand. I was wondering why they . . . I was astonished why they let me live. Just for the kick out of it they let me live. For kicks! Just as they last night shot everybody for kicks.

Now I can smell the gun, the powder of the gun. It is getting so demagogic, you know. Yeah, I smell . . . actually, I smell the powder of the gun. I've tried to get rid of that guilt for a few years. Everybody says I am not guilty. I didn't do anything wrong. I was going to tell myself that I didn't do anything wrong! But it doesn't help me.

Oh no!

[Maryan sobs]

Let's stop! Let's stop for a while.

How to survive.

I got this power knowing how to . . . not to get the . . . not to get shot immediately. To gain time, you know. Like in one camp. That was before that shooting, which I told you.

I still was with my father in the camp.[4] They were all sick. I had been sick of . . . typhus. But I . . . I made it. I got over it. So, I went for some water and by the time I saw everybody from the camp, they took everybody from the camp on a platform. Also, with horses. I ran there with rubber tires. It didn't occur to me that they took my father too. Then I ran with the water around there to the barracks to see. There was this big guy. This Gestapo guy. His name was Knoth. How can I remember names? It was a long time ago.

He said, "Where are you going?" He was pointing the pistol at me.

I say, "I'm . . . I'm cleaning this shithouse."

Actually, it wasn't true. I say, "I'm going to clean this shithouse."

It so happens that it was nearby. It looked like it because I had water. My pail.

4. From 1940 to 1942, Bursztyn and his father were forced to work in the Biesiadka, Dębica, and Huta Komorowska Nazi labor camps. Bursztyn's father was killed at Huta Komorowska. Bursztyn survived, despite suffering from typhus.

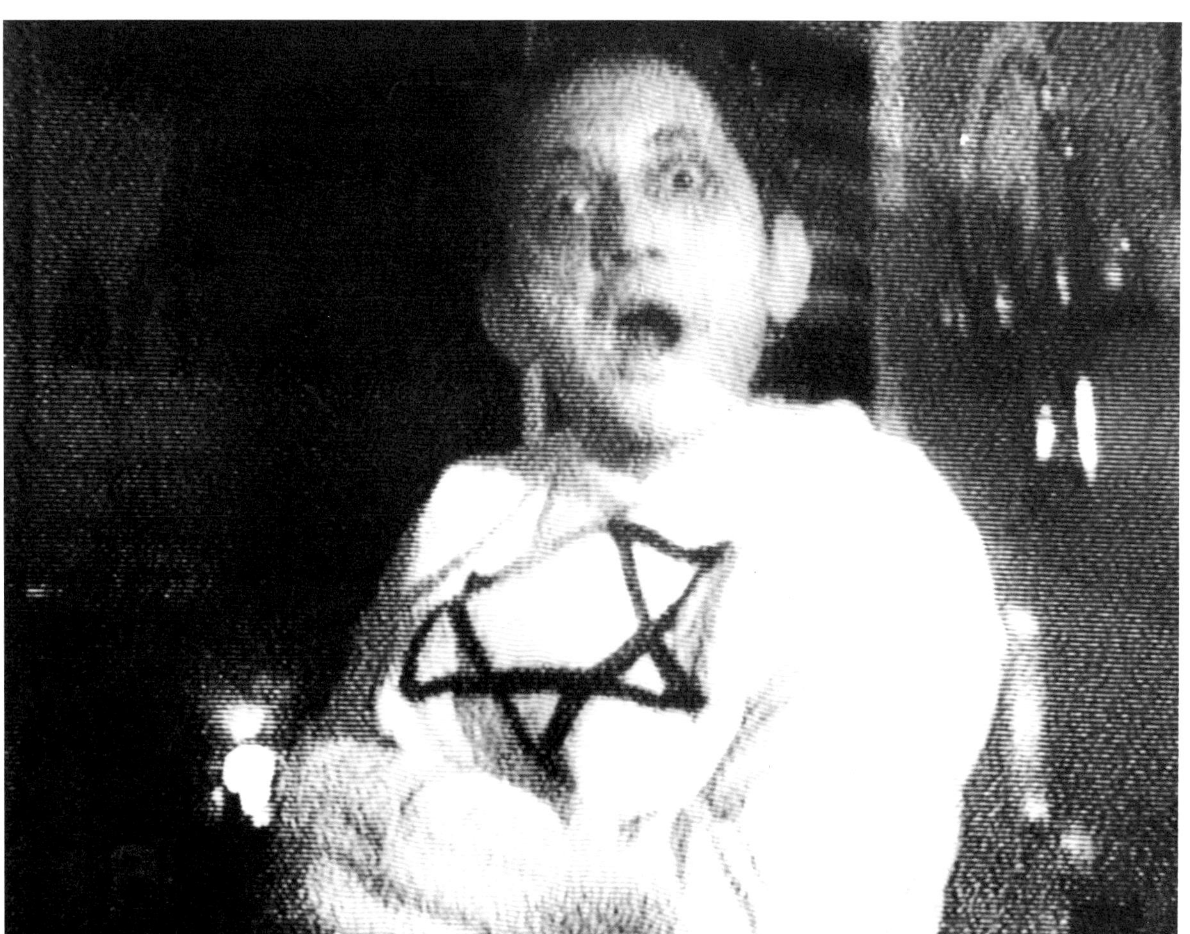

And he says, "Why should you survive at all when everybody is gone? You have to go too."

Tell me, how come? How come? That it is more difficult for me today to negotiate with other people, to communicate, and I was fifteen years old, and I could negotiate with him, with the Gestapo, who was shooting everybody. And I could convince him. Am I so strong? To convince a Gestapo, don't shoot me?

He said, "Okay." He went away.

Automatically, I went to the shithouse. And I was working with the shit to my knees! That is how it was. That is how it was dirty. I actually couldn't clean it. I poured out the whole water on it, and . . . ran to the barracks and went in and I saw they took my father. I started to cry. I didn't believe it until a few days later when I was at work, you know.

There's this German, watchman, with a big machine gun, and he tells me, "Hey, you! Why didn't you go with your father? You would be better off to go with your father. That's not good what you have done," he said.

I was only sixteen years old. Maybe fifteen. Oh fifteen, surely. Not sixteen.

Since he told me this, I took that differently, you know. I took it differently, he say, "If you would've gone with your father, you could have saved him."

That's what is in my mind, which is still now. Why did he tell me this?

He knew my father very well. I remember that they were at work. My father used to speak German, properly. He kind of liked that, and they discussed literature, and he knew, from time to time, he gave him a piece of bread, which we shared.

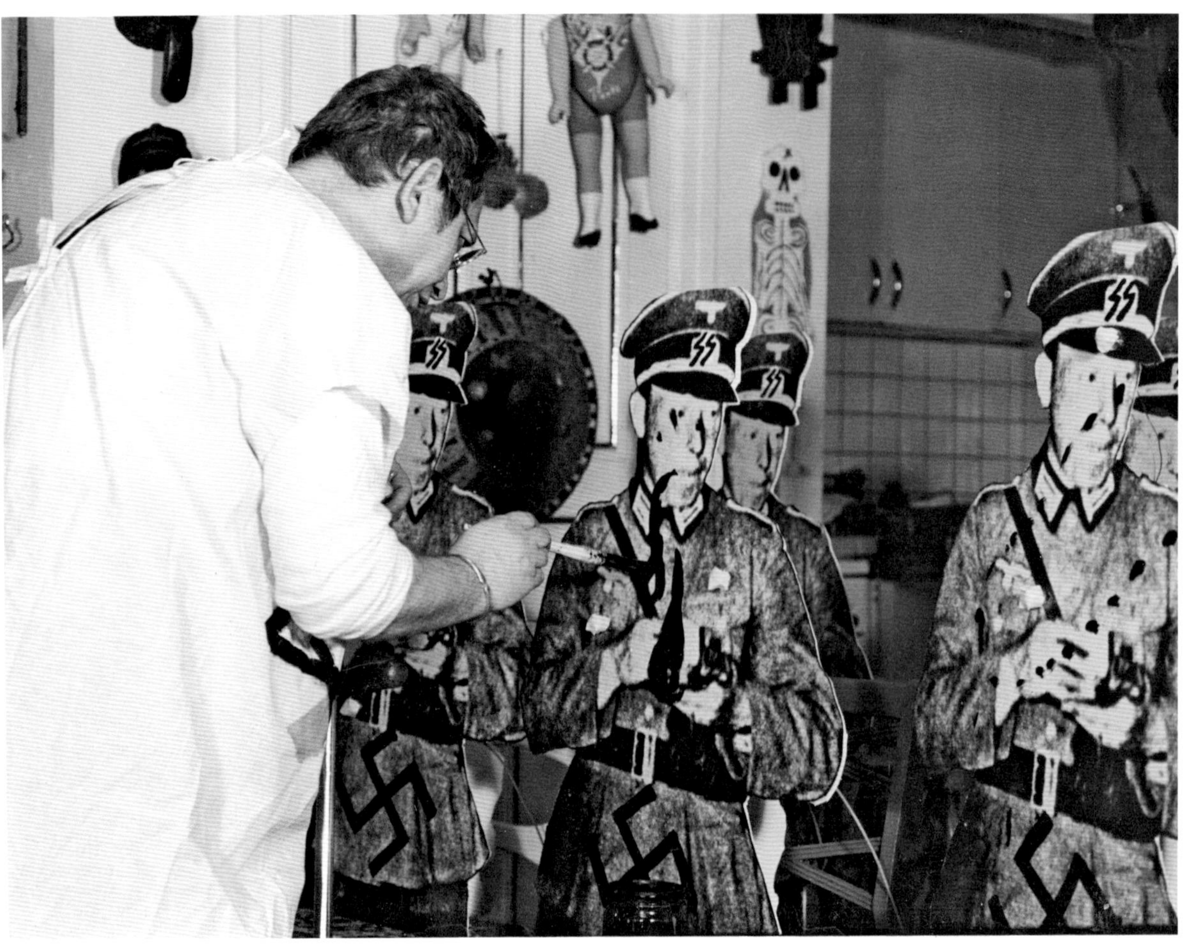

Production still from
Ecce Homo, 1975

That's why he asked me later on, why didn't I go with my father?

I understood that I could have helped him, but he meant something else. I see what he means! He knew that everybody was going to be exterminated. He was a fanatic.

I forgot his name. Nickel. Nickel was his name.

I saw him shooting people like nothing. He never touched me.

He said, "I am shooting you," to everybody, "because . . . so you won't suffer. You suffer too much in a concentration camp."

That's how he talked to us. Maybe he was right. Actually, he was right that we were suffering the whole time. And at the end, we would be killed anyway. He knew that.

But is there a reason that he owns the right to shoot people?

A few days later . . . he came to the work . . . place and the woods needed chopping. It froze.

It was about six o'clock in the morning. We just came, and what did we see?

There were two little boys, twins. One of them lying shot and Nickel, the guy, the German . . . he goes, "I did it. Because he was suffering."[5]

Actually, the guy was, you know, hiding and napping behind a tree. And his mouth, of the guy, of the boy, was open. His brother was lying, and he'd been crying. He went down to work later, and by twelve o'clock, they brought the soup for everybody.

And . . . I go and have my portion of soup, and the guy who actually brought the soup, came from

5. "After the outbreak of the German Soviet war, Jews were sent to work in Biesiadka, Dęba and Huta Komorowska . . . Polish policemen were the guards and frequently beat the Jews. . . . They receive passes to visit their families from Saturday afternoon until the roll call on Monday morning, but they chose to return Sunday afternoon to make sure they were not late. A German by the name of Nickel got drunk and announced that he must kill two Jews to prove himself to his friends he shot and killed two brothers." *The United States Holocaust Memorial Museum Encyclopedia of Camps and Ghettos, 1933–1945*, vol. 1, *Early Camps, Youth Camps, and Concentration Camps and Subcamps under the SS-Business Administration Main Office (WVHA)*, ed. Geoffrey P. Megargee (Bloomington: Indiana University Press, 2009), 482.

the . . . from this camp where they killed my father. He didn't want to tell me they killed my father. The reason that he looked me up there on that spot while they were distributing the soup, it's because a few days before, or one or three days before, I gave him a package, which contained a pair of shoes. I remember, with wooden soles, to give it to my father. Because they told me where they take them. And I knew he was working there. He took it. He was supposed to give it to him. But this time, he gave me back the package.

I say, "What happened?" I say, "What happened?"

He says, "Your father is dead!"

I say, "That is not true! That is not true!"

He said, "Yes."

And then, everybody was . . . working. I was lying. I was lying in and crying. Crying, and yelling, and crying, and what must have been for the first time of my concentration camp staying, was that I didn't eat my soup. I was there, lying and screaming, crying, and . . . didn't touch the soup. And . . . for five hours, five or six hours till then, I ran by . . . I know somebody from the same town.

I told him, "Weinach, they killed my father, Jurgen."

He said nothing.

I said, "They killed my father! They killed my father!"

Nobody answered. Nobody heard it. Came to the camp, went into the barracks. Suddenly I was hungry. I was screaming to everybody, "They killed my father!" And I was hungry.

He has got a wooden box under a lock keeping there pieces of bread sometimes and lock it. I go check if there is not a piece of bread, I knew there was supposed to be one. Tried to open the box. I saw it was . . . forced. Somebody checked the doorway, and actually, the guy who stole the piece of bread was sitting on his bed across and watching me.

I said, "Why did you have to do it? You know I am hungry."

He said not one word. Can you imagine?

For hours I asked him, "Why did you have to take the piece from that case, from that box?"

And he sits and watches me, he doesn't say anything.

I think I converted, transferred the fact that my father was dead to hunger, and I was crying often over that piece of bread, until I got tired, and I don't remember what happened later.

What was it? Nothing. I never checked again. At least for a few months, I didn't check the box, whatever was left there. Pair of shoes, the separate shoes of my father, which was returned.

One day I saw a guy . . . was making business in the camp. He gave . . . he traded bread against . . . against golden pieces, valuables, like men's watches. I haven't got anything to give him. I was thinking, suddenly, suddenly I got the idea, ran quickly to my barrack, and went to the box. They were wrapped in a piece of brown paper. My father's teeths, false teeths were actually . . . There was a lot of blood inside. I mean, I'm not . . . I thought it was enough that maybe it could be traded, but I didn't hope for anything. I thought he wouldn't like it. Then anyway, I took a chance, I took it away from him to the other barrack and said, "Look, I need bread, and I have something."

"What do you have? What do you have?"

I say, "I have this."

"Okay." He said, "Okay. It's . . . yes, it's gold, it is fine."

Actually, he was nice to me. Because he gave me a loaf of bread. Big. Very big. Huge. I got it for a long time. Almost a week. He didn't cheat me. The fact that I read the memory of the bread doesn't bother me about the teeth. And yet, still I didn't think I didn't do anything wrong.

For years, I couldn't look at my own food. Could never see somebody having false teeth because it's, actually, it is sometimes visible.

I didn't get anything anymore to trade. Nobody got it. People were dying near me . . . and *I* didn't say anything either, anymore. It's like I don't see them. It's like I haven't seen them.

I think I cannot talk more about this now. It's too much! It's too much! I can't . . . I can't . . . talk . . .

Machine gun.

Shoot all the Nazis.

But I can't.

Take the place . . .

Ugh . . .

Give me the machine gun.

I'll shoot . . .

[toy machine gun]

[arms the gun]

But I am shooting down dummies, anyway.

Oh, no! Shot dummies!

[coughs and unties himself noisily]

[picks up the toy machine gun and arms it]

Dummy machine gun shoot dummy Nazis.

I remember that it was one morning, and they came with a list of people. And that was where we lived in that place, and my mother taught me you know what, go hide yourself in the shithouse in this and this backyard. So, I went in and stayed there for one hour, maybe, and I didn't know, really, what the difference was between going or not to go, anyway.[6]

But I heard someone calling my name. The Germans were calling my name off the list . . . for half an hour. And my mother couldn't do otherwise. They'd come . . . and open the shithouse inside and I'd have to go. I'd gladly go. I went.

Then they put us on these trucks, these . . . these . . . heavy-duty trucks.[7] Mercedes-Benz. I didn't know. I didn't realize then, that I was taken to a concentration camp, riding in a Mercedes-Benz. Without saying goodbye to our families.

Down below reaching their hands. Everybody was reaching their hands. Either there was some package

6. On September 1, 1939, the Nazi army invaded Poland. Bursztyn (then aged twelve), together with his older sister and younger brother, fled to Baranów Sandomierski.

7. In 1940, Bursztyn and his family were captured by the Nazis. The family was separated and Bursztyn never saw his mother and siblings again.

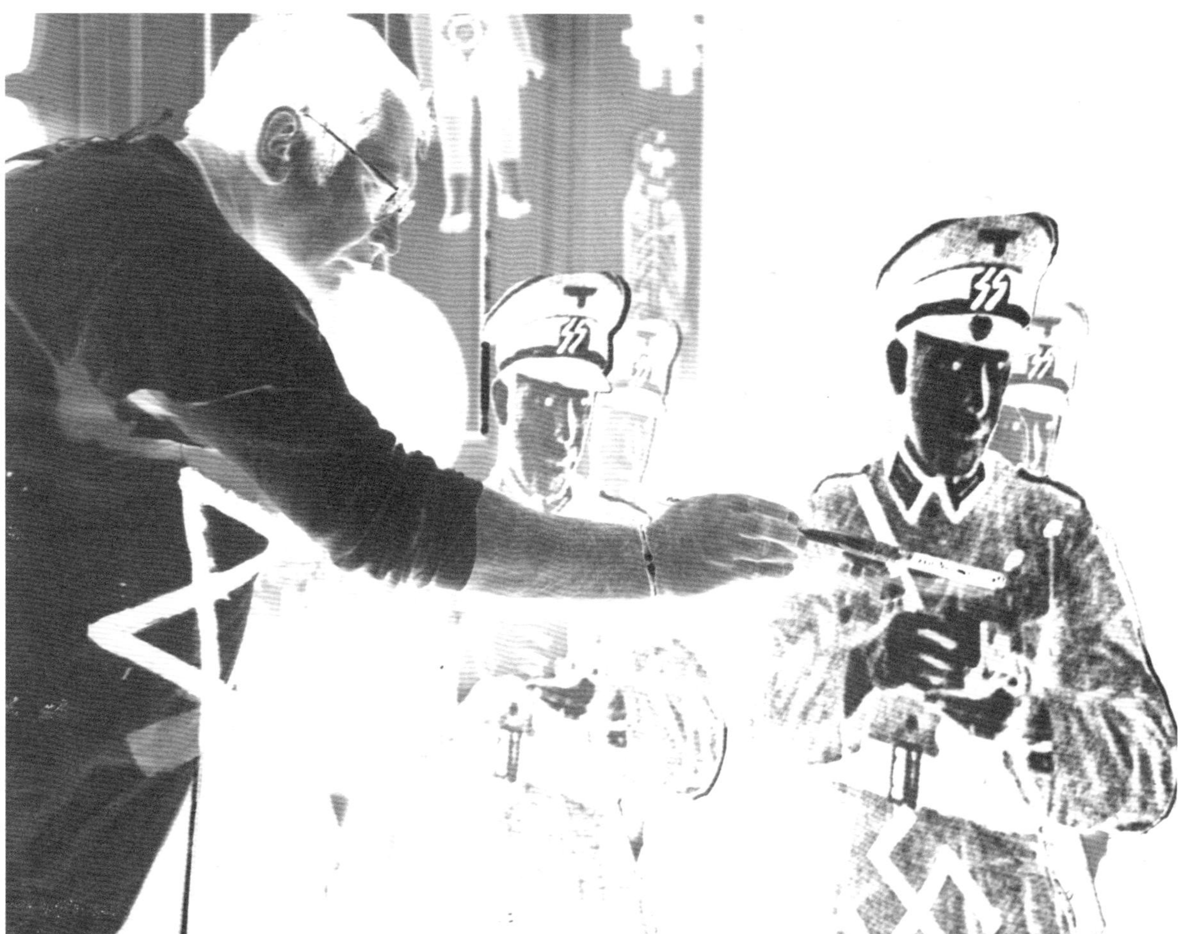

Production still from
Ecce Homo, 1975

or something. I remember my mother. That was the last time I saw my mother. And she gave me a loaf of bread. And that was the last time I saw her.

Then I came to the camp. My father was there. I think that I didn't want to realize what was happening. It is not because I was very young, and I didn't know what was happening. I didn't want to know. My father knew. He knew because he wasn't talking. As if he had shut it down completely. I think maybe he went crazy. He never talked since then.

And I never questioned, "Why don't you answer me?"

I ask him "what's" questions and he barely answers by "yes" or "not" or "no."

8. "In the spring of 1942, a number of forced laborers were transferred to a labor camp in Biesiadka where they cut down trees . . ." Megargee, ed., *Early Camps*, 567.

9. "In Biesiadka, Jews and Poles, separated from each other, were conscripted to cut beech trees for the German Fisher company and assist the Muller company to transport them to Melic by truck. Jewish laborers were treated as prisoners." Ibid., 516.

Every day we are working . . . we are sawing the feet of the trees in the woods in pieces, you know.[8] And these guys, this Polish employee, and the Germans to watch us, with guns, and very big sticks, clubs, they decided, for kicks, of course, to beat up everybody, although you were working. If you didn't make any mistakes.[9] That was not his order. And everybody got . . . a few bangs on the back with a big stick, big heavy piece of wood.

I remember my father was saying, "*Ai, yi, yi!*" It must have hurt him.

I didn't say anything. Few minutes it was over.

That was not Auschwitz, if you only know Auschwitz. Mauthausen, Buchenwald. But these are small death camps. Nobody knows what happened there, and everybody died, anyway. There's no trace at all.

So, they took us. Whoever left, whoever had been alive . . . and they took us from one camp to another, to one camp to another.

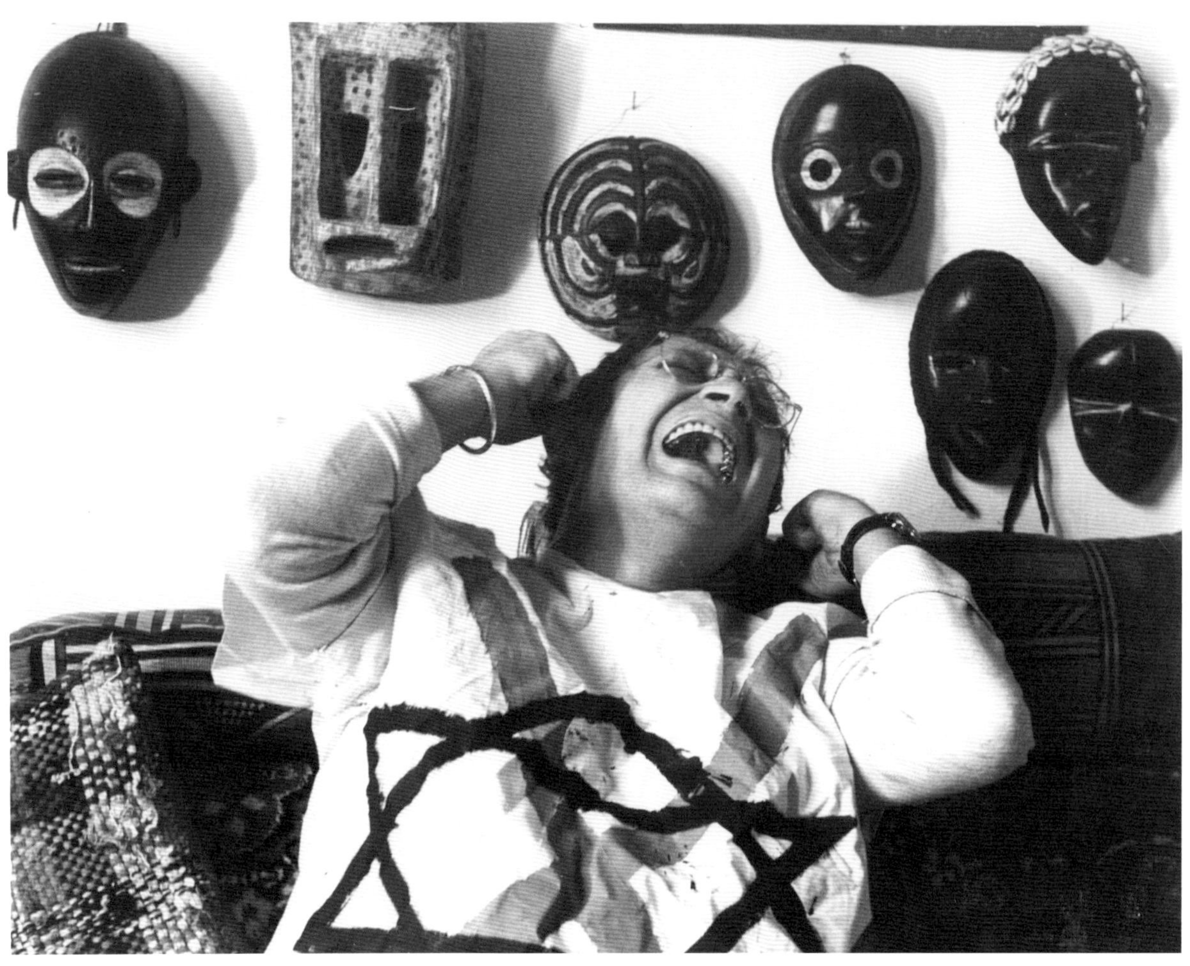

Production still from
Ecce Homo, 1975

I remember one day; it was very cold. It was very cold. Everything was freezing. Got no clothing. I decided not to go to work. But then, this guy, a Jewish kapo, a bad guy . . . there were some good ones too. But this one was bad. He beat me so badly up. And I had to go anyway, without shoes, I said, "No, I don't understand, I don't believe it."

After a few minutes, being there I decided to escape, I ran into the woods. I throw . . . my tools, the axe, and another piece of tool on one side, the other on the left side, so, they cannot trace me. But actually, I forgot they can trace me after my footprints.

And I ran . . . I ran very deep in the woods, maybe three miles, four miles. And suddenly, what do you think, who is behind me, pointing, in my back, a gun. One of these Polish watchmen.

And he says, "You son of a bitch! You miserable Jew!"

Slapped me back, took me back and there was this Nazi and, I remember he got a big gun like this and, knocked me out. I thought he was going to shoot me, but he just knocked me out. He beat me up on the head.

I got up, I didn't know what was happening, and I started to work. How can that be?

When the night came, they had to put . . . There were these trucks waiting for us to take us back to the camp, you know.

When we came to the camp I heard somebody's cries . . . screaming out and along, my name. They want me. I didn't expect they were going to punish me again. They put me in a bunker. It's a cellar, without windows. A whole while and then I was up, another guy there already, I didn't know why, and I didn't ask. How could one survive in that kind of a . . . cold . . . frost? Everything was freezing.

I was bleeding from my head. My blood on the sheets was frozen. Pieces of ice I took up . . . took them up, a little packet. It's like pieces of little candy, like candy sticks. I saw all red blood, but frozen blood I have in a vessel.

Said to him, "Look, frozen blood."

He said, "C'mon, shut up!"

And in the morning. They open the door and they let us go, and nothing else happens anymore. I felt actually victorious by not being punished more than that.

From that camp, actually, they took us in another Mercedes-Benz fancy truck, they called me in the list, and the list . . . they've got a list . . . everybody went into the truck.[10] The guy, the German, the Nazi who run the camp. He was always going around with his pistol, and shooting. Shooting like nothing, people. He was standing there. We were walking up on the . . . on the . . . we were walking up on the truck, inside it was piling up. I remember there was one couple, they held each other, you know. I was sitting on the side, and before they were closing the truck, this . . . guy, Schmidt . . . gave one shot, just like this, wherever it goes, and he went away. Well, we didn't know who got hurt.[11] Maybe nobody.

Suddenly, I see a woman is crying, she is holding her husband's head, they hug. He was actually touched by that shot. So, after he was shot, we went to the ghetto, to one ghetto in Rzeszów in Poland. He came to the gate. There were other Gestapo people, the Jewish police. Star of David, here, and here, and here. They were counting us. How many we are.

But then there's this guy, I used to know him since a few years before the camp. His legs, his feets were frozen, you know. He couldn't walk. I have to carry him.

One of the Gestapo guys says, "You have to carry him. Carry him down. Put him here in this . . . place. This corner. There on that corner."

And he goes and he shoots him. And I am standing here watching. And that was the place where a few days later they took us to this execution place. Oh!

After that, they literally shot, I survived. And they took me for one night to the same place from where they took us, there were other people. There we were supposed to be shot the next day. They were scared stiff. Seeing me, losing your voice, full of blood on the . . . face.

Couldn't talk. Something in the vocal cords happened, probably. I was lying. I was lying. What do you think? I asked for food. I asked. I didn't know what to ask. And they gave me food. They brought me some tea there and bread, I remember. I don't remember eating it. I remember lying, and bleeding very heavily.

And this guy, who was distributing the food, said to the other, "He is going to die. He is dying. In a few minutes he is going to die."

I heard that. I say, "Oh, no! I am not going to die."

Actually, the more they saw me, that I was denying the thing, and I wasn't dead. They send a doctor to the ghetto. All they could do. He says, "It's nothing, he will be okay." He put a Band-Aid on, on the front and on the back, that was all. Actually, I wasn't suffering.

I suffered later when I got infections. Stools were running. And I was around in this ghetto later, survived this.

So, they also got an epidemic. Sickness, illness, the same one, typhus, I already got. So, I could watch whether anybody was dying, I didn't know what to do. I didn't get anything.

10. This part of Maryan's monologue refers to the summer of 1942 in Rzeszów.

11. "In their recollections, survivors from Zolynia, Rzeszow and Kolbuszowa have specifically recalled a German commandant named Schmidt at both Huta Komorowska and Pustków in 1942 and 1943. From descriptions, it is apparently the same man; he may also be the same Schmidt who supervised the forced roundup of Jews in Rzeszów for labor at Biesiadka and Huta Komorowski earlier in the occupation. They identify Schmidt as a sadist, personally shooting or hanging numerous inmates at random to prove his control." "Seven Concentration Camps: Group of Zolynia Jews, August 1942 to January 1945," Zolynia Memorial, accessed March 1, 2022, https://www.zolynia.org/other-camps.html.

To survive, I carried corpses. For every dead person carried to the morgue, there were two guys in a team. They get a piece of bread.

I remember myself, having these pockets here, full with pieces of bread coming out, and carrying this guy, who died. He just died from typhus. He had just got one eye eaten out, from a rat, you see, a rat! One eye was missing completely. It was a big hole. I didn't pay much attention. It didn't do me anything, I don't know. Probably it did. That is why I am talking now about it, then in the morgue.

And then, I was working, you know, in a factory, in a . . . in a workshop, with shoes, and the . . . the manager of this . . . section said, "How about we make you a nice pair of shoes?"[12]

On the stand there's leather, everything is going tomorrow.

And they make me, you know, a pair of shoes, overnight, I have never got in my life! They were so nicely made by a specialist, you know. A pair of shoes. Wonderful! And I got them on, in the morning and then, we *then*, we went on these trains, inside, it was dark. And all with no air. Probably some people were dead, from the lack of oxygen, and water. And everybody took off his shoes and, nobody thought anymore about this life, things, you know, and it took me four days, suddenly come in the tracks.

We built anything in Auschwitz, you know, until the crematorium.[13] Just drive inside, you know. And somebody opened the door, and you didn't see any soldiers, nobody, which was a sign that you are inside, not outside. But, other fellows, prisoners, Jews, work there, who are doing the job.

They opened and they said, "Out!" "Out!" Everybody got out, some . . . some were dead.

I got out. It was dark outside and inside, but I didn't want to know the reality was going to happen, I saw the whole reality. And, as I said before, I never wanted to see. I have some strong defences.

And, so I think, "Where are my shoes? My good shoes, my best shoes? Never, never got such shoes!"

The guy says to me, "Listen guy, you won't need any shoes here."

I say, "What do you mean?"

"You won't need anything here. You will see that in a few minutes. It will only take a few minutes. You won't need anything."

And I still heat up the more he says, I . . . I insisted on the shoes. I say, "As I have to find my shoes . . ."

So, finally, and of course, he got angry and pushed me away. Dragged me to the road. A bunch of people, we were together, and we were going . . . We were walking like half a mile, you know. In the dark. It was maybe four o'clock in the morning.

And, er . . . I saw all kinds of barracks, you know, and, people going out, and, in their shirts, you know, like from their sleep, and they go and, it is cold, the men surrounded by what was a kind of a container, everybody came, I saw five, ten, ten, eleven, maybe more of them. Because you can't sit around, you know. While I was walking, I saw that. And . . . I got the whole picture in, anyway.

And then they took us to a very big place. A hall . . . very huge hall, actually, with a cupola, around a . . .

[Kenny Schneider interjects:] Dome.

Dome.

And there was nothing inside but water. We start to drink water. After a few minutes, we were waiting and suddenly, Germans came with the, no, elegantly, nicely dressed, with monocles. Some of them

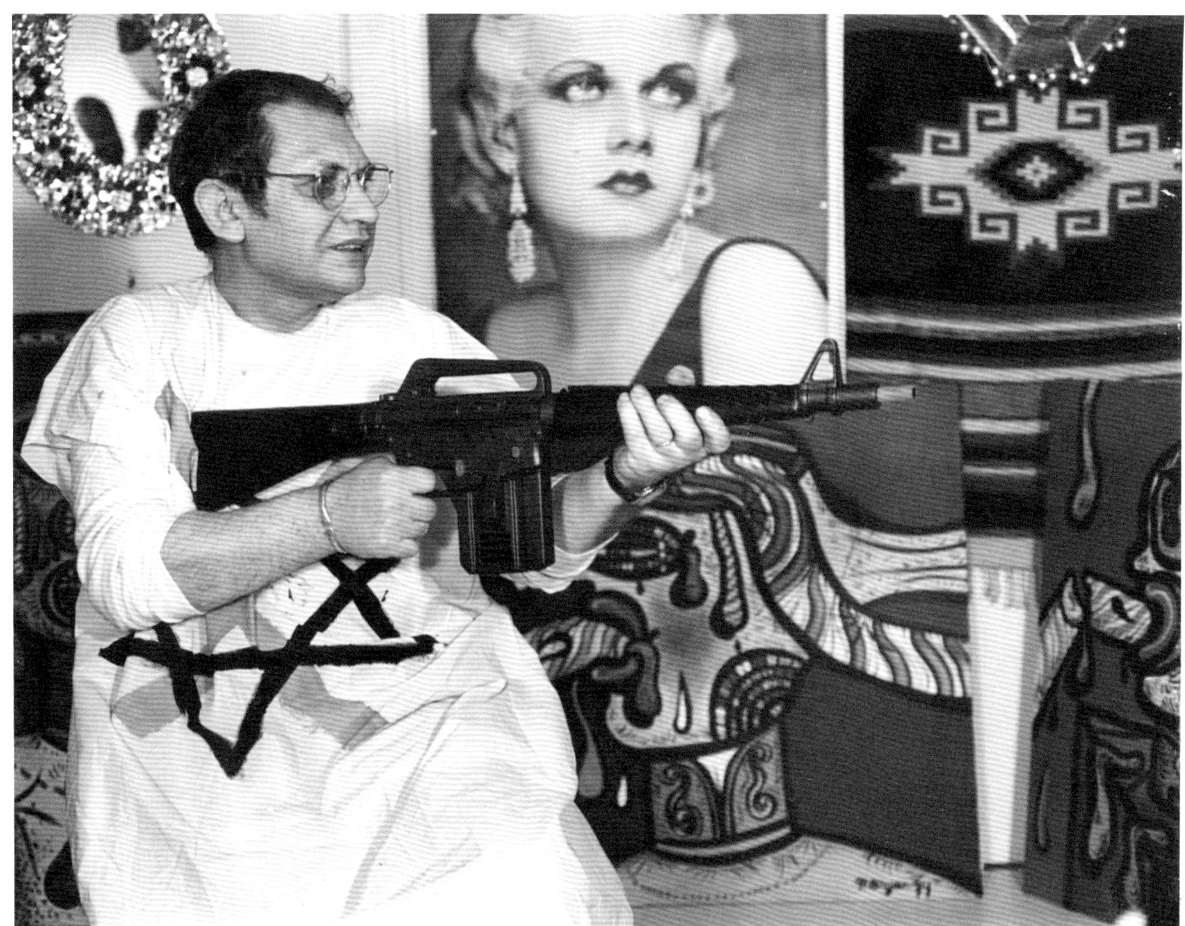

Production still from
Ecce Homo, 1975

have got white gloves, can you imagine? And holding the German Shepherds, the dogs. And telling us . . . to undress because we are going to have a shower. And so be it, we undress.

Everybody was naked, waiting. Actually, I knew that before, some people were talking . . . What they really do. What they really do, and . . . And you are waiting and waiting and waiting.

It took a very long time, and since it took a long time, you know, an hour, two, three hours. I imagine, maybe, you know, longer, and the longer it takes, the longer you have the chance to survive. If we are older, maybe old, you know, and actually, it was half true because they didn't decide to put us directly in the gas chamber.

And we did not get a shower, nothing. However, they gave us some . . . clothing. I remember . . . a tall guy got a pair of pants from a very little guy, and vice versa. Wooden shoes, one shirt, and no underwear. You know, punishment, no underwear for the . . . trousers for, you know. It was very rough to wear a pair of pants without it, you know that.

And that was . . . and then it was already daytime, in the morning, and they took us where they called it Zigeunerlager, Birkenau.[14] That's the worst part of the . . . that is where they make the decision if they keep you, if they need you, they don't keep you, they don't need you.

And . . . came there . . . There was a guy, also a kapo. He was one prisoner. A German, I think, and he started to beat up people. He started to beat us up. I thought . . . I did . . . We were lying . . . We were lying, you know. And I'm bad, like . . . aged people. And there was no space for anybody, so legs . . . legs or hands were hanging in the air, down, you know, from the bed. Super post beds, three or four. So, everybody who got his hand out, hanging, got a bang from the big stick from the guy. I already survived that night, and next night we . . . They gave him a stick, and we were sitting and waiting, but we knew.

14. "Zigeunerlager in Birkenau existed until August 2, 1944. That evening, the approximately 4,200 to 4,300 men, women, and children left in the camp were loaded onto trucks and driven to the gas chambers. The prisoners attempted to resist, but the SS crushed their opposition brutally." "Sinti and Roma (Gypsies) in Auschwitz," Auschwitz-Birkenau State Museum, accessed March 1, 2022, http://www.auschwitz.org/en/history/categories-of-prisoners/sinti-and-roma-gypsies-in-auschwitz/.

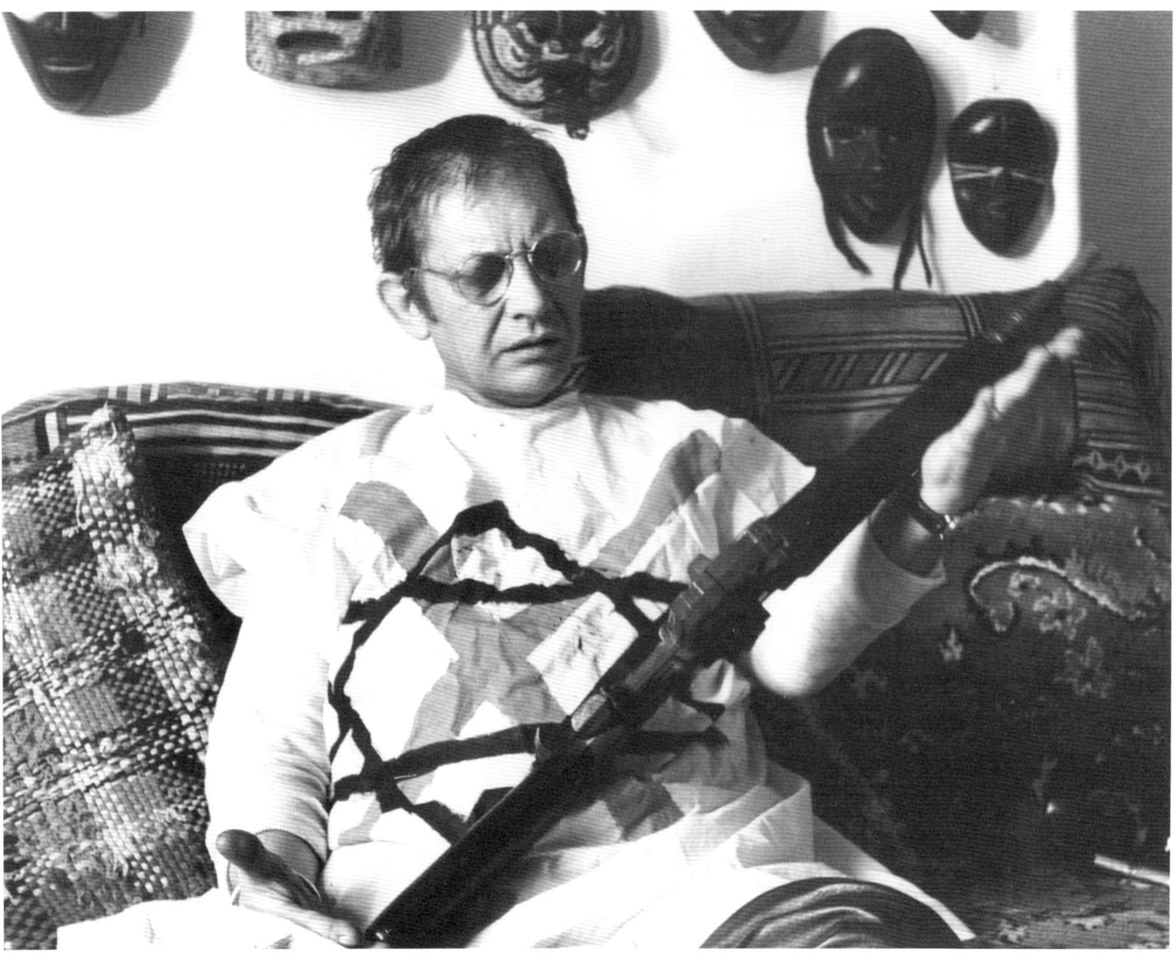

Production still from
Ecce Homo, 1975

We were there sitting and waiting. Suddenly, I see a guy, you know, a young boy, he belonged to our group. He went quite near to the . . . wires, to the electrified wires, and the guy at the watch post from the upstairs, he shot him. It was a child, I think. I am sure it was a child. I am sure he was . . . about eight, nine years old, maybe less. It was far worse and the whole world was sitting and watching it and didn't say anything.

The whole world was looking, and you know, we were . . . being cremated.

People every day by thousands went to the washrooms and there were plenty of Jews, greet Jews, they even didn't know why they are there because they didn't know even they are Jews.

All they would say is, "Hmm, hmm, *shalom*." Which means that he will say that he is Jew too.

I say, "*Ai*, another one!" I know what I want to do with him too.

Suddenly . . . some . . . creatures of the Gestapo came and they . . .

Take that photo still. To light . . . [Kenny Schneider hands Maryan a photograph]

I mean . . . to dress, er . . . to undress. Probably there were some physicians, doctors, they wanted to check how, you know, everybody looked, say, physically. They took out a few. I remember they took one guy. He wasn't going very well. They took him. They took another one. And a few minutes later, I hear a few shots.

Millions of us! And nobody says anything.

The whole world . . . They are working! On our baths! Kind of working things like . . . on bombs! You know, on bombs, like in a . . . They got all over Hiroshima.

You know . . .

The smell of the gas chamber. You got very near to it. And there were bones all over.

They were taking us to the place where the crematorium is. We were working in front, until they opened the door. That was the who, who was part . . . who was part of this . . . Why do they open the door?

And one says, "They got finished."

The other said, "No, what do you say?"

Suddenly, they opened the door, and they let us in.

They let us in and say, "Undress! And go wash yourself."

I say, "Eila! They are going to kill you!"

We washed ourselves, and then there's this guy who . . . who . . . cuts the hair. I say to myself, if they cut our hair and put it all over, you know, they cut every hair, of the whole body, all over, and then they put . . . ah . . . some kind of liquid, it was burning, like Lysol. We were dancing like a bear. It was burning. Disinfecting. But on the other hand, I knew that they weren't going to kill us, because they are . . . I mean . . . they need us. And then they gave us uniforms, striped. Striped uniforms. But the terror of the uniforms, which actually, I am not scared of uniforms.

I am painting uniforms, actually. I thought so.

People said, "You are painting uniforms because you are scared of uniforms."

And I am never scared now, since quite a while. From a kapo, or something. Maybe supposed to, but I wanted to care for a uniform myself. Go through to the same . . . power. We can have power without the uniform, but the uniform . . . but the uniform was . . . gives you . . . a power. Even if you are not powerful.

It wasn't so easy because we got out of the crematorium on one side and on the other side I . . . I remember now they took people. I remember there were women and children, and old people. They were putting them through each other . . . they were . . . Leading them through another door, you know.

So, I say to myself, oh, a few are alive.

And I cannot forgive myself by just thinking this. How could I think like this? Maybe I wasn't thinking this. We are alive, that is the main thing. I wouldn't say that today, no. I couldn't stand up . . . I . . . I couldn't . . .

You know . . . What is impossible is when you build up your own fantasy, I feel guilt, you know. Even though I didn't do anything. I didn't do anything wrong, you know. I was just . . . thinking that we had a life, so good. That going through it will really be shot or gassed, killed.

And I didn't know about this. I just remember right now.

There was something else. No, they were taking them. There were a bunch of us. About five hundred thousand people. Throughout the door and sight.

And they gave us . . . they made us a tattoo number on the left hand of everybody which was also a sign of, of a kind of a provisory permanency. Later on, came a few trucks and a few guys from the army, German army, some, one Gestapo guy.

And he said, he asked, "Who . . . who is a welder, welding. Who knows how to weld in metal?"

So, there was one who said, "I!"

"Who else? Second."

And I say, "Me too!"

Ha . . . ha. Can you imagine, can you imagine, I was . . . I was fifteen years old and I . . . and I bullshitted him, that I am . . . that I know how to weld. I don't know. He probably didn't believe me, but . . . he got just a moment of a . . . of a . . . He didn't care, you know.

And he was in a hurry. He said, "Okay."

So, everybody finally came and turned out to be welders. Everybody knows how to weld, so we went on the trucks, and they led us to a camp. That was quite a few months before the end of the war.[15]

And that camp wasn't so bad. It wasn't so terrifying. Nobody was shot. There was no gas chamber. There was no . . . there was no . . . I mean there was no gas chamber, there was no . . . torture chamber. I haven't seen any piles of dead like there, you see. And . . . I wish that it could have a happy ending, but it didn't.[16]

Because actually, they took us away from there. They took us away. We had to walk on the snow. We walked, and walked, and walked. And incidentally, it so happens that our camp, the Nazis who kept our camp, the watchmen, Nazis who kept our camp, they were very old men, and it so happens that they didn't shoot, while we were marching slowly, like they did with other camps also. Evacuate them. Whoever couldn't walk, whoever couldn't walk, they shot them. Whoever couldn't keep up with every . . . with the others, path . . . path . . . Sometimes they wind up to come to this big camp . . . the Germans . . . with two or three people only. The rest was shot. Like, you know, the whole . . . I remember seeing . . . So, actually, it was winter, snow. Snow was red! Can you imagine? Completely red![17]

Then we came into the camp. We didn't know why that is, what a place, nothing. It was a fair total disorder. And the next day . . . the next day. I saw people running. They were running from the place where, where food is, in a place into the kitchen. There was some, suddenly, access. It wasn't controlled. So, they went to take whatever it was to take. So, I . . . run . . . also. I come to the place, and I see potatoes. I filled up a hod full of potatoes. Went back to the barracks, inside. No one was inside. And while I was peeling the potatoes, to make them ready to cook . . . and everybody was outside running, running, by thousands, and then the machine guns, startled, knocked like, man, everybody outside. But I was sitting inside. And there has been like shit . . . You see . . . the thing is . . . the thing is . . . Would I be outside, running for the food, going there or back? Today I would say always, I would say if I wouldn't go out, I wouldn't have been shot in my leg. But I cannot say this, because I was inside, which is good. Which is good, I cannot blame . . . one thing I am positive about is not to blame myself.

And they shot maybe a few thousand. Maybe ten, fifteen thousand of them. They stopped later and I looked out and I couldn't look. But I saw the next day when they were carrying me to this kind of a hospital, which was not a hospital, I think that, Kenny.

I saw . . . the guys who carried me, they couldn't walk, they had to walk on the dead. I remember they were crying.

They must, too, felt guilty, I thought.

Maybe I wasn't going to go there, they wouldn't shoot, but I wasn't alone, I was one among thousands. And the . . . the day when they shot, I mean the day before I was lying and had a big birth of consciousness and was listening to people.

15. In 1944, Bursztyn worked in an ammunition factory as a welder in the Gliwice Camp. "A sub-camp founded in March 1944 at the rolling stock repair yard in Gliwice (German: Gleiwitz). The first several score prisoners transferred from Auschwitz were sent to work assembling seven wooden residential barracks and a kitchen, hospital, storage area, and workshops. On the sides facing the road and the rail tracks, the sub-camp was screened by a wall of concrete slabs topped with barbed wire, and on the other sides there was barbed wire strung on concrete posts. . . . The prisoners worked repairing damaged sides of cars, in the machine shop and smithy, and building roads and a nearby airstrip. From the late summer of 1944, they were taken out to work on two 12-hour shifts. . . . Almost a hundred Gleiwitz I prisoners died as a result of mistreatment, hunger, and backbreaking labor. At least five were shot while trying to escape, and two Russians hanged for the same offence. The number sent to Birkenau after selection cannot be established. The sub-camp population just before evacuation in January 1945 was 1,336 prisoners, mostly Jews, Poles, and Russians. They marched on foot to Gross-Rosen." "Gleiwitz I," Auschwitz-Birkenau State Museum, accessed March 1, 2022, http://www.auschwitz.org/en/history/auschwitz-sub-camps/gleiwitz-i/.

16. In September 1945, when it became clear that the German army was trapped between the Soviet troops to the east and the advancing Allied troops from the west, the evacuation from Blechhammer (Polish Blachownia Śląska) began. The SS forced the inmates of the concentration camp to march westward in the so-called "death march." During the march Bursztyn was shot several times in the leg. Liberated by the Soviet army, he was transported to a hospital in Częstochowa. Bursztyn, who survived several near-death experiences, was the sole survivor from his family.

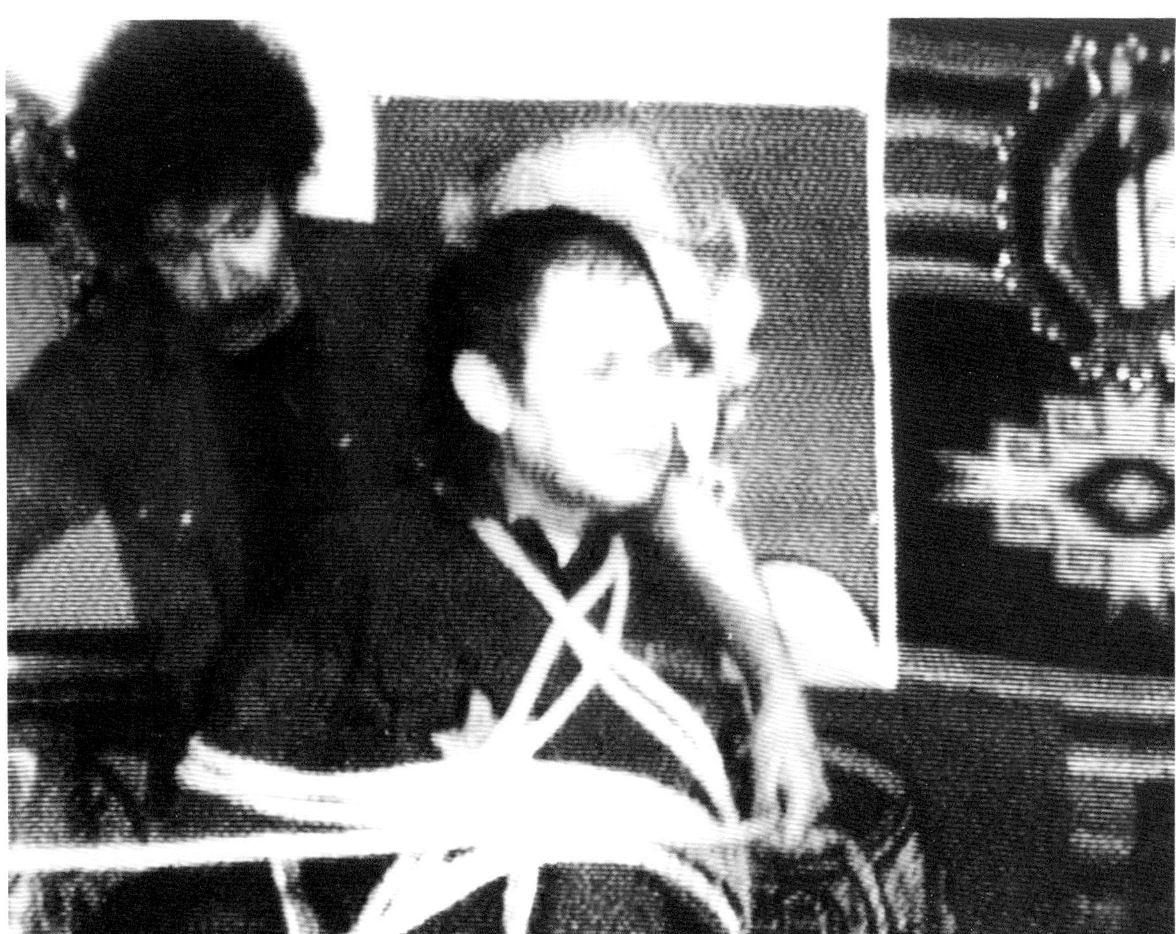

17. "The almost nine thousand prisoners left behind in the Main Camp (Stammlager), Birkenau, and the sub-camps as unfit to join the evacuation march found themselves in an uncertain situation. The majority of them were sick or suffering from exhaustion. The SS intended to eliminate these prisoners, and only fortunate coincidences prevented them from doing so. The SS did manage to murder about 700 Jewish prisoners in Birkenau and the sub-camps in Wesoła (Fürstengrube), Gliwice (Glewitz IV), Czechowice (Tschechowitz-Vacuum) and Blachownia Śląska (Blechhammer) between the departure of the final evacuation column and the arrival of the Red Army. The majority of the SS men on duty in the guard towers left Auschwitz on January 20 or 21. However, larger or smaller SS units continued to patrol the camp. Wehrmacht units also passed through, and joined the SS in plundering the camp warehouses. Some prisoners took advantage of the confusion and risked escape." "The Escape of the SS and the Final Victims," Auschwitz-Birkenau State Museum, accessed March 1, 2022, http://www.auschwitz.org/en/history/liberation/the-escape-of-the-ss-and-the-final-victims/.

They were talking. And they say, "You know, I just was outside, and you know what happened?"

"What?"

"They shoot . . . one guy, one Gestapo guy."

Just took a few people, like a bunch of thirty people, and killed him. One by one. And he was enumerating people, "Don't shoot me. Don't shoot me. I will bury them. I will help to bury them. But don't shoot me."

But they shot him, anyway.

His name was Warshawsky.

One day before I was shot. A German said, "Go to hell, everybody goes. Go home, don't go home. Go wherever you want."

They were panicking. We did not panic. We didn't really know what to do. If we go, they might shoot us outside. If we stay, they might shoot us inside. And what do I see . . . trucks.

Ah, again! The nice fancy trucks, Mercedes-Benz loaded with . . . loaded with . . . hundreds, and hundreds and hundreds on one truck, a big pile like this, you know. But the blood was running, running down, it was running. You know. On the . . . on the tires, and it is like a leak of gas or oil, but it was red. The Russian army was not far.

One thing I was thinking about: Why are they not coming now? Now before they shoot us.

 And then I was all night, and I was lying in this hospital, without help, without nothing. There was

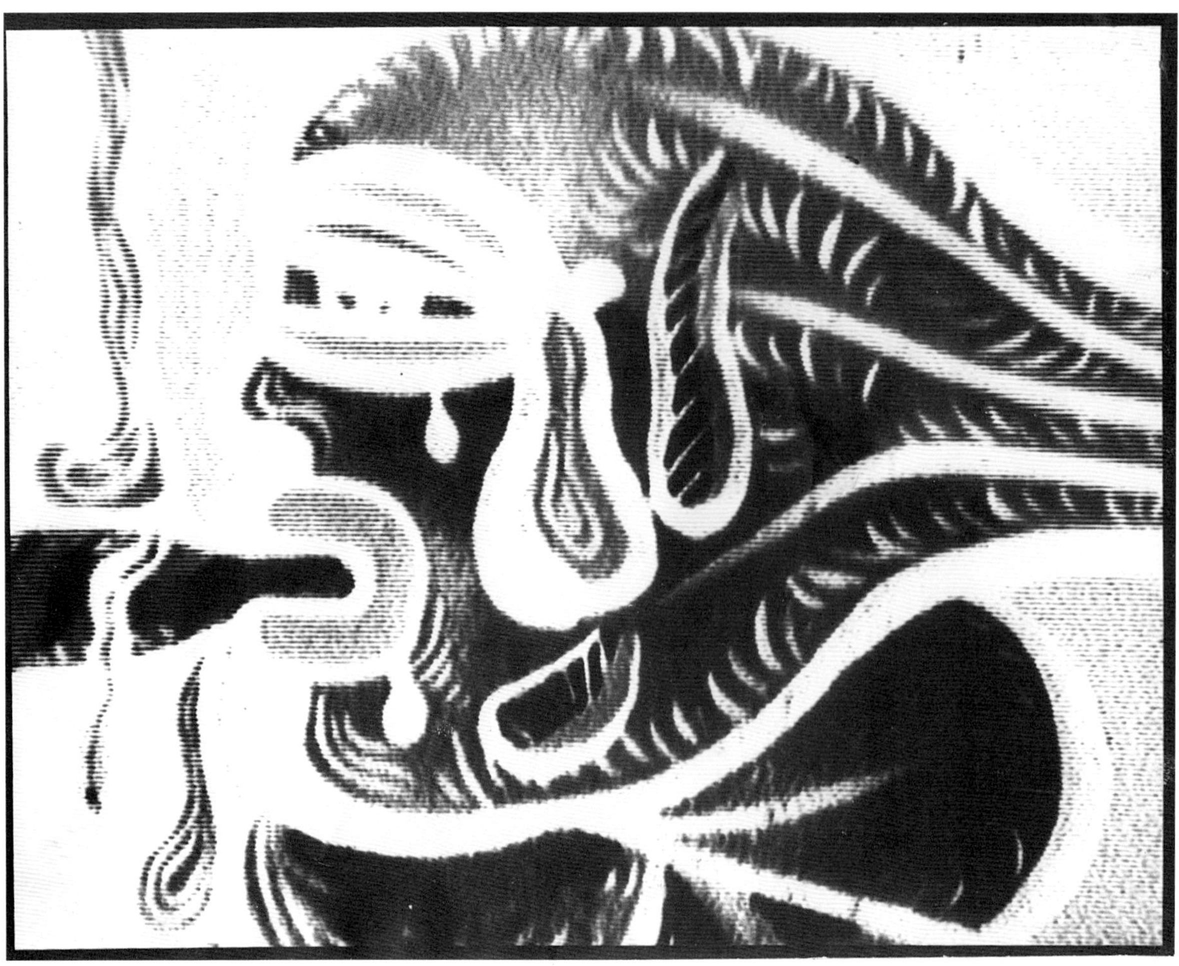

nothing. They were shelling the camp. The Russians, they didn't know. They were shelling the Nazis. They flew. The Nazis flew away. Then they stopped shelling, they came. The next day they came.

They liberated us.

Now I have to . . . Huh, I had to learn how I had to live with that.[18]

So, people used to say to me, right after the camp, "Don't think about the past. Because it is terrible. It's happened."

So, I didn't. But secretly, secretly, every minute, everywhere I was there might have been something, which reminded me. A smell, a noise, somebody say a word. And I am living with this. I decided to get rid of . . . Although, one of my shrinks used to say all this, ugh!

"It's not only this, it must be the child prophecies."

Maybe . . . maybe . . .

I said to him, "Look, doctor . . . What I told you, do you hear that every day?"[19]

I want to be alone. I knew I . . . I knew it was not true. I couldn't be alone.

He said, "Of course. I got patients of the Korean war telling me stories."

I get angry. He was minimizing my real story. It didn't help me.

It didn't help me at all. Since then, I have tried to help myself. And find all kinds of means, you know. How to get rid of, at least, a part of it. A small part of it. That's why I decided to make this show [film].

18. After the liberation of Auschwitz, Bursztyn had his leg amputated and he stayed in a recovery house until July 1946. He is listed in the Register of ill persons, Committee in Warszawa-Praga, District 5, Committee in Czestochowa; see the Holocaust Survivors and Victims Database, United States Holocaust Memorial Museum, accessed March 1, 2022, https://www.ushmm.org/online/hsv/person_view.php?PersonId=3083513. Then he went to an UNRRA (United Nations Relief and Rehabilitation Administration) displaced persons camp in Germany.

19. Maryan was under the care of a psychiatrist from the early 1970s. He was hospitalized at the Payne Whitney Clinic in 1974 for approximately one month as the result of an emotional breakdown, and again in 1977.

To run this show. It doesn't help.

I would never have . . . you know. I would never . . . I couldn't do what I did. I don't know how again, I don't exist. Being homicidal, but to come to such a genocide, and people didn't say nothing.

Many countries. All countries! All countries! Big countries and powerful countries. They didn't want to say anything, or they were, or they were impotent.

Sometimes I know. I think, you haven't? How come?

I couldn't kill anybody. I wouldn't be able to kill anybody.

A Nazi, I say to myself, all right. He is a human being. Nazis are human beings.

So, if you were to kill a human being, you can kill any human being.

No.

Yes, a Nazi, yes.

I don't know why I had this in mind. Why a Nazi?

Why this kind of human being, yes, and not anybody else?

I feel thankful. I know many people in my case. They were also in concentration camps, and they say, "You damn, you get a gun and do it. You let them shoot. Nazis . . . they do it."

I am the same. The same feeling. I said it last time.

[toy machine gun sound effects]

Told you. They are dummies. [Maryan shoots cardboard Nazi cutouts]

See, that is what I can do.

Shooting the dummies.

[toy machine gun sounds; Maryan hums along with Pierre Pinchik]

That's the end of the show.

Or this -- An old black tells his life's tale in truth, full,
full with descriptions. From the time he was ripped from his mother's
arms in a slave market, and sold into bondage. He speaks of how he
survived, what he is left with -- his thoughts -- his feelings --

But there are no films -- it's all heresay. All second, third,
fourth hand -- opinions, opposing opinions, points of view -- just
various human points of view, and all just a bit abstract.

Grist for fiction --

"Ecce Homo" by the painter Maryan S. Maryan is a unique, stark,
unrelenting truth. A painting on film that speaks and moves!
A startling anti-genocide work of art.

To sum up -- a man in Paris was asked what he thought of the
film that you are about to see. He said, "All the time I wanted to
walk out, but I knew if I did -- I would be walking out on my own
life."

"ECCE HOMO"

A Film

by

MARYAN S. MARYAN

You are about to witness a human document! It is a document
for all time -- for all men --

"It's something new" "A first" "A real original"

Picture this! It's 1 B.C. A follower of Jesus is mysteriously
given a 16 mm. sound camera. He follows Jesus through everything,
ending with the crucifixion. And it's all there, on film --
in sight as well as sound.

A flick for all men -- for all time! No acting; a real man,
telling a real story -- his own story.

Or this -- It's the winter of 1812 -- the Napoleonic siege
of Moscow. Plague, typhus, death, filth, and a constant shelling
by French guns. Frozen corpses cover the grey rubble strewn streets,

MARYAN'S EARLIEST TESTIMONIES OF THE HOLOCAUST IN GEOHISTORICAL MOTION: NOWY SĄCZ, AUSCHWITZ, JERUSALEM, PARIS

Piotr Słodkowski

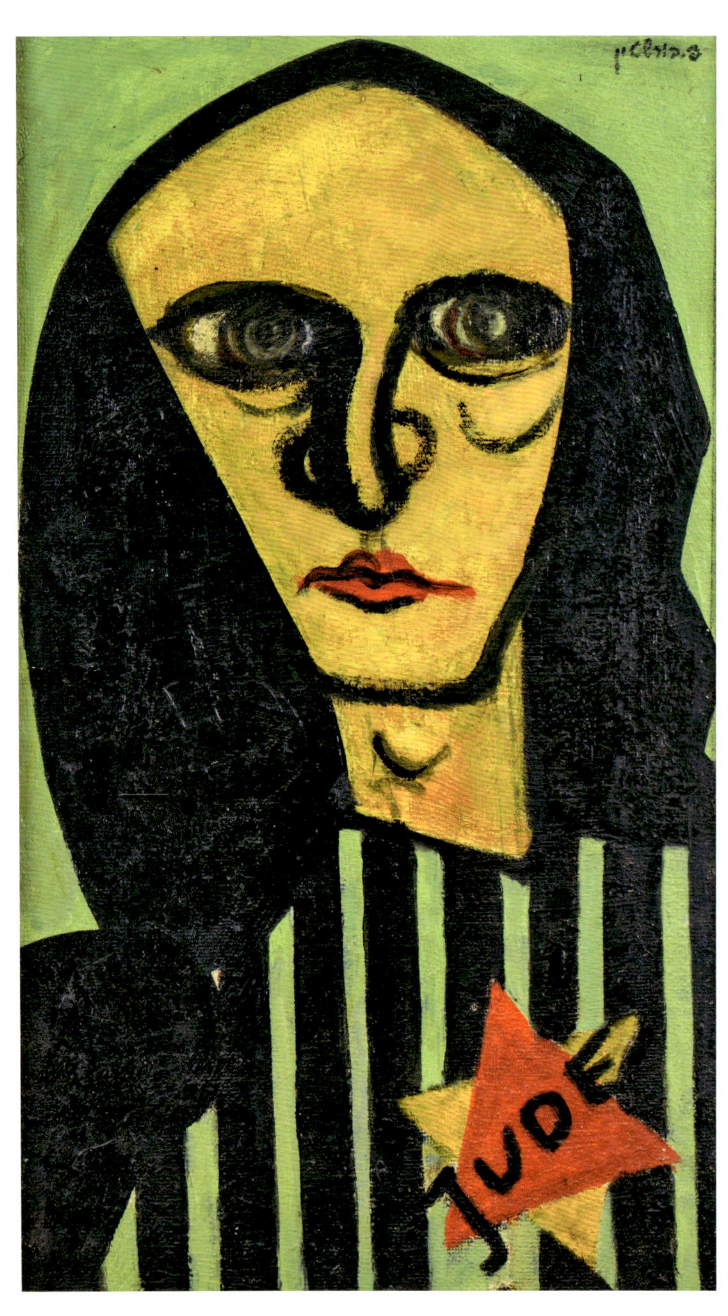

Maryan's works challenge ideas of the history of contemporary art that are rooted in conservative clichés of national artistic canons, notions of centers and peripheries, and in assessment criteria imposed by high modernism. This Polish Jewish painter, born Pinkas Bursztyn, who emigrated from Poland after World War II, gained recognition in France and the United States. Yet he remains relatively unknown in Poland, even though his art offers an impressive take on a key question for Central Europe, namely, the extermination of European Jews. This essay will examine the geohistorical diversity of Maryan's biographical experiences, using this as a lens through which to view his earliest testimonies to wartime limit events. By attempting to reconstruct his cultural background in the small town of Nowy Sącz in southern Poland, this essay will also explore how memory of the Shoah and being part of the community of survivors weighed upon the artistic education Maryan received in Jerusalem and Paris. This perspective clearly reveals how a modernist aesthetic aided him in creating visual testimonies to the Holocaust that enter into interesting dialogue with works by other Polish Jewish artists. In seeking to trace these relations, I also consider the social visibility of testimonies from this period, thus providing a spotlight on how Maryan's activities were connected with other efforts to maintain memory of the Shoah that were being produced in the country of his birth. It is only through such a comparative approach that Maryan's significance as an artist can be revealed. As a result, he does not appear as an isolated figure but, on the contrary, as an important member of the international, transregional, and global—yet also therefore dispersed—community of Jewish witnesses to the war.

The cultural landscape of Pinkas Bursztyn

In 1952, by which time Maryan was already in Paris, the Israeli writer and journalist Mordechai Tsanin published in Tel Aviv the book *Iber sztejn un sztok: A rajze iber hundert chorewgeworene kehiles in Pojln*, a poignant report describing his journey around Polish towns in 1946–47. From the perspective of those living after the Holocaust, Tsanin's testimony, as a pioneering report on encounters with a world that had been destroyed, had a tremendous impact on the development of textual genres. It offers a mosaiclike description of a confrontation with

the once vibrant and very rich culture of Polish Jews, of which there remained only ruins and cinders immediately after the war. Tsanin's reportage presents a testimony reflective of an entire generation while at the same time being immersed in detail, thus making readers aware of the geohistorical diversity of former Jewish communities: the diversity of levels of education, the diversity of attitudes toward the Jewish faith and politics, and the diversity of social and professional positions.

Many artists of Jewish origin who have entered the canon of Polish modern art belonged to Polonized families from interwar Poland's large cities; the avant-gardists Henryk Berlewi and Henryk Streng (later known as Marek Włodarski) were, respectively, from Warsaw, the capital, and Lwów (today's Lviv in Ukraine), the main center of Galicia. It is of crucial significance that, in contrast to them, Maryan—then known as Pinkas Bursztyn—was raised "in a practicing Jewish family"[1] in Nowy Sącz (or Nay Sanz, or Sanz), a small town in Eastern Galicia on the Dunajec River. The town was famous among religious Jews because of the achievements of Chaim Halbertam (who died in 1876), an outstanding rabbi and tsadik who founded the Hasidic Sanz dynasty that promoted Orthodox teaching of the Torah and demonstrated notable conservative traits that were embodied both in education and everyday practices.[2] It is hardly surprising, then, that in his description of the town in the period following World War I, Samuel D. Kassow valued the long-standing nature of this tradition, with Sanz remaining "a heavily Hasidic town."[3] This must have had an impact on Bursztyn's formative cultural encounters as he grew up in the Jewish neighborhood of Zakamienica that later came to be known as Piekło (Hell). This was the most impoverished part of the town center, as evidenced by the very poor sanitary conditions. Photographs and postcards from the time documenting Lwowska Street, the district's main thoroughfare and where Maryan lived before the war, show simple brick houses and modest two-story tenements on both sides of the street.

In 1910, Galicia was home to "the most numerous Jewish diaspora in the world," with some 871,000 members.[4] In the interwar period, the Jewish minority continued to form a significant portion of the population of Nowy Sącz. Regional studies show that in the 1931 census— taken when Pinkas was four years old—nearly a

Pinkas Bursztyn, *The Yellow Star*, 1947–49. Oil on cardboard, 21¾ × 33 inches (55 × 84 cm). Private Collection

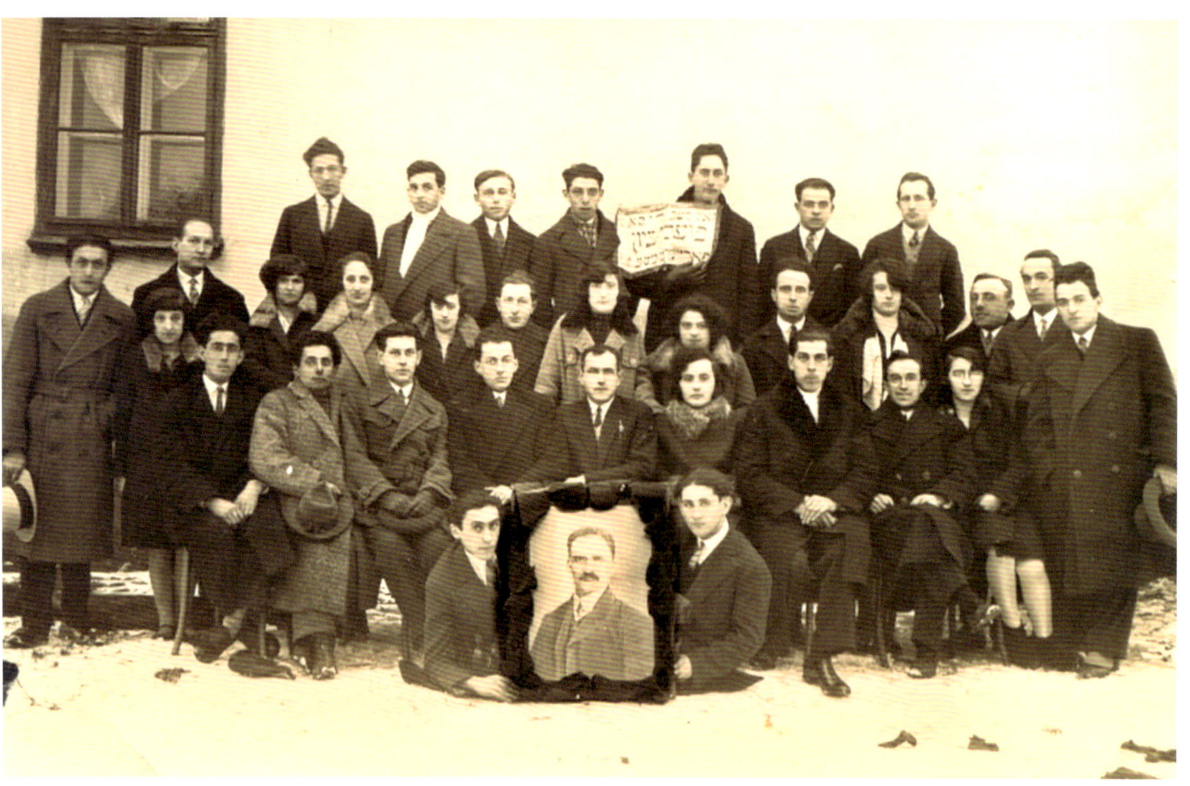

quarter of the town's 50,000 inhabitants (12,000) were Jews who professed Judaism.[5] According to the historian Łukasz Połomski, this group managed to maintain its religious and political autonomy while at the same time proving highly mobile, as it mediated between other ethnic and national groups.[6] Its members largely worked in trades and as merchants, primarily in the textile and food businesses—as was the case with Bursztyn's father, the baker Abraham Schindel. As in other parts of Galicia, the Jewish population of Nowy Sącz was highly diverse in terms of political outlook, economic standing, and cultural background. Orthodox organizations (Agudas Israel) existed alongside Zionists (Hitachdut, Haszomer Hacair, and Mizrachi, among others), socialist-Zionist factions (including the left-wing workers' movement Poale Zion), and a cell of the Communist Party of Poland.[7] Besides the owners of exclusive shops and hotels, there were also market stallholders. Just as there were large numbers of people who lacked education and could not speak Polish, there was also a Jewish intelligentsia, including lawyers who, in 1930, owned over half the town's law offices. This reveals a great deal about the social stratification of the local community, although it should be noted that Pinkas himself did speak Polish.[8]

How did this diversity of life in Nowy Sącz translate into Pinkas Bursztyn's cultural background? Given his family's social position, it is more likely that he encountered amateur and folk art more often than high culture. This kind of folk culture was often centered around the Purim holiday, which involved dancing and joyful revelry. Purim was a grateful subject for art, including for the Jung Idysz group operating in Łódź in central Poland, which looked to reflect the Jewish tradition through a modern artistic form. Purim also strongly influenced theatrical aesthetics in Galicia and had a lasting impact on the motifs Maryan used in his later work.

Evidence suggests that in childhood he showed interest not only in the fine arts but also theater, a beloved art form of the population of Nowy Sącz generally that was more than capable of competing with cinema. Many professions (workers, clergy, and soldiers) formed their own theater groups. It is quite possible, then, that Bursztyn watched theater productions and musical shows staged by amateur theater enthusiasts involved with the Szymon Arski Jewish Drama Society (Żydowskie Towarzystwo Dramatyczne im. Szymona Arskiego), which was founded in 1929 and performed plays in Hebrew that attracted significant audiences. Led by the tailor Jemieliah Kornmehl in the 1930s, the society also established a revue company involving workers and craftspeople, with its light entertainment pieces largely attracting poorer members of the community.

In 1936, Bursztyn's family left Nowy Sącz for Dębica, around 100 kilometers away.[9] The man who became the artist Maryan would never return to his hometown, where Hasidic culture had been prevalent, even as the subsequent years of his life saw him move home regularly. In the precise chronology of Maryan's life, we can read that "September 1939 marked the beginning of the family tragedy. When the German army invaded Poland on September 1st, twelve-year-old Pinchas, together with his parents, older sister, and younger brother, fled to Baranów Sandomierski. In May 1940 the family was separated. Pinchas never saw his mother or his siblings again."[10] During the war, he was a forced laborer in Biesiadka and Huta Komorowska (both north of Dębica) in 1940/41, before being placed in the Rzeszów ghetto in 1942, a forced labor camp in Pustków the following year, and the Auschwitz Concentration Camp (Roma camp) in 1944, before finally landing in a camp in Gleiwitz (Gliwice) in 1944–45, from where he was sent on a "death march" to Blechhammer (now Blachownia in Opole Silesia, Poland). His migration experiences did not end with the war. He ended up in hospital in Częstochowa in 1945–46, followed by a displaced persons' camp in Germany, before going to Haifa in May 1947. He was then in Jerusalem from 1948 to 1950, before moving to Paris, where he remained until 1961.

Maryan never returned to the country of his birth, an experience quite typical for Polish Jews. Indeed, the history of communist Poland was marked by several waves of emigration. The first, in 1945–46, was primarily a result of popular and economic anti-Semitism, including the associated pogroms and other forms of organized or spontaneous violence against Jews. The two subsequent periods of intensified migration, in 1956–57 and 1968, were caused by political, state-sanctioned anti-Semitism that was exploited effectively by the communist regime.

Both during the Stalinist period (in Poland, from around 1949 to 1954) and in the 1950s and 1960s, the politicization of war memory and cultural and historical policies were not conducive to the affirmation of Jewish identity and the unique experience of the Holocaust. Despite these unfavorable circumstances, it is possible to speak of memory and identity being maintained. The Jewish Historical Institute in Warsaw played a major role in this process, headed by the eminent art historian Józef Sandel, who did much to preserve the memory of Jewish artists active before World War II.[11] Moreover, not all of them decided to leave the country. A large group of prominent Polish Jewish modern artists were active in the Polish art world after 1945, including: Artur Nacht (after the war: Nacht-Samborski), Erna Rosenstein, Jonasz Stern, Henryk Streng (after the war: Marek Włodarski), and Alina Szapocznikow, who received her artistic education in Prague (1945–46) and Paris (1948–50) before returning to Poland in 1951. The experience of WWII and the Holocaust manifested itself in their works with different dynamics: in some cases as early as the 1940s; in others, only intensifying much later. Regardless of personal artistic differences, these artists formed a symbolic community of artist-witnesses, so that their visual testimony can be related to the work of those who produced testimonies of the Holocaust far beyond the borders of their native country.

Modernism in the shadow of the Shoah

The entanglement of local forms of Jewish tradition and wartime limit events that shaped Maryan's biographical experiences in the 1930s and 1940s had an impact on the development of his mature artistic practices. One of his letters sent from Paris includes a list of the most renowned figures of high modernism in France: "Matisse, Picasso, Rouault, Modigliani, F. Léger . . ." Alongside this list, Maryan notes: "I don't know how to paint and what to paint."[12] His simple declaration is crucial to understanding more fully his earliest visual testimonies to the Holocaust.

Maryan's artistic education together with his works from the turn of the 1950s are immediately striking primarily because they both diverge from the master narrative of the history of modern art, which is grounded in the expansion of Euro-American modernism. It is worth noting

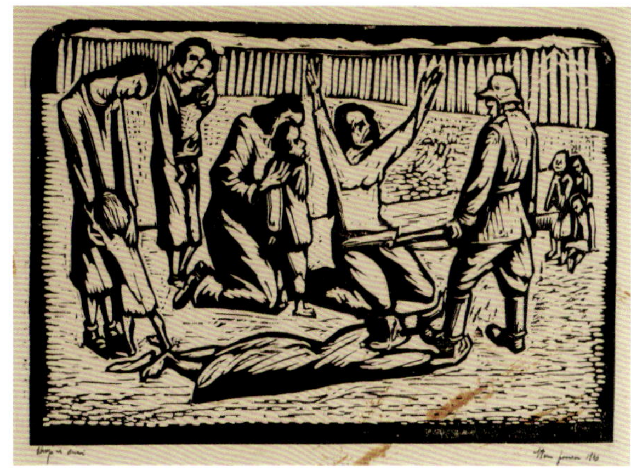

that from this perspective, the initial postwar period was primarily a time of struggle for global hegemony fought between the old and new art capitals, as Serge Guilbaut has masterfully demonstrated in his seminal work, *How New York Stole the Idea of Modern Art*. This dominant conception of modernism thus effaced all differences in identity, as the outstanding historian of Central and East European art, Piotr Piotrowski, later noted: "Modernism avoided individual identification—one could even say any identification: ethnic, local, gender, sexual and so on—in the name of a universalizing utopia of unity. The adjective 'international' means 'among' nations, or 'beyond' and 'outside' national characteristics and identities . . ."[13]

The case of Maryan completely contradicts these assumptions. He began his artistic education on the margins of the global tension spanning Paris and New York, namely in Jerusalem. There—in contrast to Euro-American universalism—art and identity were naturally linked, specifically the distinct Jewish identity that had been devastated by the war. In 1947, Bezalel Academy of Arts and Design enjoyed a boom in popularity, as, for the first time, it admitted students who were Holocaust survivors. Maryan was a member of this pioneering cohort. The fact that, within a year, he had established close contacts with a group of Central European Jews who had lived in small towns in Poland, Czechoslovakia, and Romania before the war shows that the community of people who shared experiences of the Shoah was at least as important to him as the community of artistic ideas. Among his many acquaintances, he was friends with the painter Yehuda Bacon (born in Ostrava, Czechoslovakia), who, like Maryan, was raised in a religious Orthodox family and spent time at Auschwitz-Birkenau (1943–45). Another person who was important to him was Mordecai Ardon, an artist born in Tuchów (some fifty kilometers from Nowy Sącz) and one generation older than Maryan. In the 1920s, Ardon studied at the Bauhaus and the Academy of Fine Arts in Munich, drawing inspiration both from the poetics of Paul Klee and from the artworks of the old masters Rembrandt and El Greco. Ardon left for Palestine after Hitler took power, gaining recognition as an outstanding Israeli painter. At the turn of the 1950s, when he and Maryan were in touch, Ardon employed a synthetic artistic language, with his simple figures outlined by precise drawings that were filled with a rich mosaic of colors forming an expressive, impasto texture.

It is noteworthy that Maryan felt frustration at being labeled handicapped by the Israeli state and therefore he left Jerusalem in 1950, moving to Paris, becoming a student at the École nationale supérieure des beaux-arts. He studied primarily under Fernand Léger, at that time a master approaching the end of his life and primarily engaged in monumental art: designs for murals, mosaics, and stained glass windows. Still, in his paintings, Léger continued to employ his typical quasi-mechanical mode of figuration and striking black contours.

Images from the earliest period of Maryan's works are indicative of the formative role played by the cultural community that his representations reconstruct. Two ink drawings from 1950, *An Inmate in the Auschwitz Camp and Nude Female Figure, Upper Torso*, portray human figures in an identical pose/frame: a stiffly straight Auschwitz prisoner wearing a hat and striped uniform, and a woman bearing her breast, struggling to conceal her body with her shoulders. The striped uniform below her suggests that she, too, is a prisoner of the camp who, given her pose, has been forced to strip naked. These modest works on paper contain a significant degree of tension that emerges from the juxtaposition of the media used and the aims of the images. Essentially, the artist turned to some of the most traditional subjects of art that are evident in the works of the old masters as well as in contemporary art: a half-figure portrait and a nude. Portraits usually serve to ennoble the subject, yet in this take the form has the opposite impact: the intention is to commemorate a person, who has been stripped of subjecthood, and their face, which has been replaced by a number. In this sense, Maryan's drawing establishes a connection with many portrait-based testimonies produced in ghettoes and camps that also attempted to maintain the human dignity of fellow prisoners, with the works of Halina Ołomucka (imprisoned in Majdanek and Auschwitz) and Maja Berezowska (who was sent to Ravensbrück) being just two examples of this. The works of the latter, in particular, offer an interesting point of reference given her contrasting take on the same subject matter. Berezowska attempted to emphasize the beauty of the women who sat for portraits with her, treating their eroticism as the

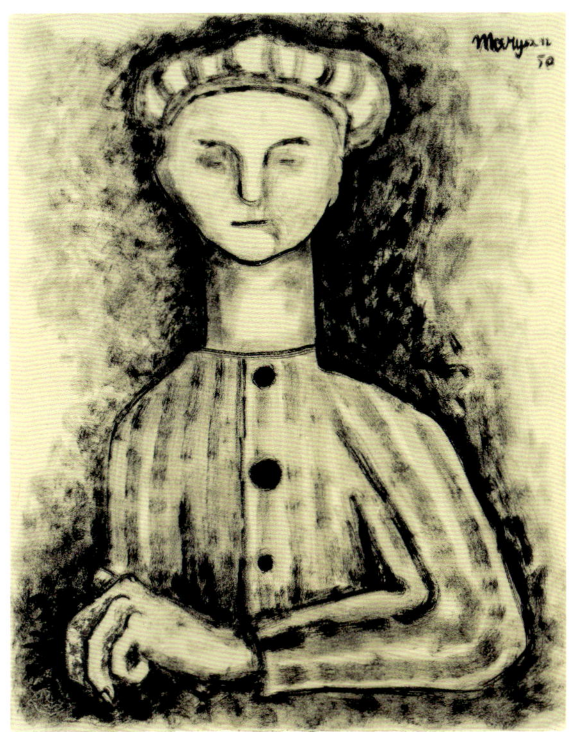

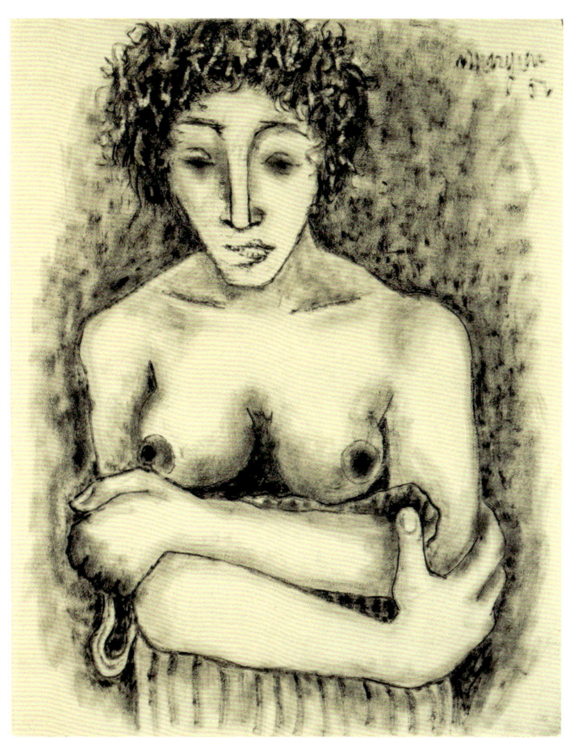

source of their strength. Maryan's nudes, how-ever, produce completely different connotations: marked by force and sexual violence, his images suggest the powerlessness of women.

In Jerusalem, he created the painting *The Yellow Star* (1947–49), which combines the themes of portraiture, identity, and stigma. The expressive and highly synthetic image is con-structed using thick, black contours and pale, flat colors. From this severe figuration there emerges the thin face of a woman with large eyes and dark black hair falling onto her striped uniform, onto which is sewn a red-and-yellow star bearing the inscription "JUDE." The simple—indeed, mini-malist—composition focuses exclusively on the meaning-making relations between the face and the badge. In this way, it enters into dialogue with Nathan Grunsweigh's undated *Self-Portrait*. The Krakow-born painter Grunsweigh left for France in 1908 and spent the Nazi occupation there. In his self-portrait, Grunsweigh depicts himself brush-in-hand as an artist at work, while display-ing "two attributes of the Jewish community: the traditional yarmulke and the imposed yellow star of David."[14] In both paintings, neither figure averts their gaze. Indeed, in Grunsweigh's work the figure looks discreetly at the viewer from the corner of his eyes, while the woman in Maryan's portrait looks directly at the viewer with great intensity. Despite the hopeless situation of the female prisoner, her expression means that her face emanates an internal force that does not seem

to cohere with the figure of a weakened victim, an identification that is certainly reductive and super-ficial precisely because it is determined by factors external to her.

Where *The Yellow Star* emphasizes the face, *Crematorium in Auschwitz* (1949) employs sim-ilarly expressive figuration in order to depict a group deprived of individuality. The twisted lines produce a tangle of amalgamated pale bodies that fill the frame of the composition to the edges, leaving just a small space at the margins for the flames. As Ziva Amishai-Maisels points out, Maryan was one of the first artists to see with his own eyes and depict on canvas the mass genocide carried out at the concentration camps through a combination of gassing and burning in the crematoria. Importantly, according to the Israeli American art historian, Maryan does not portray Jews one-dimensionally as innocent victims. Trapped in the crematorium, they in fact climb over each other in a tragic attempt to survive at all costs, which this dimension of the artist's testi-mony makes even more poignant.

Wiktor Simiński depicted similarly expres-sive bodies located at another limit space of the camp in an almost identical fashion. His drawing *In the Gas Chamber* (1944) features a complex mesh of pencil lines forming overlapping limbs and torsos. Aside from the time of their creation, the main difference between these works lies in the fact that Simiński limits his artistic meth-ods to a minimum, creating the impression of a

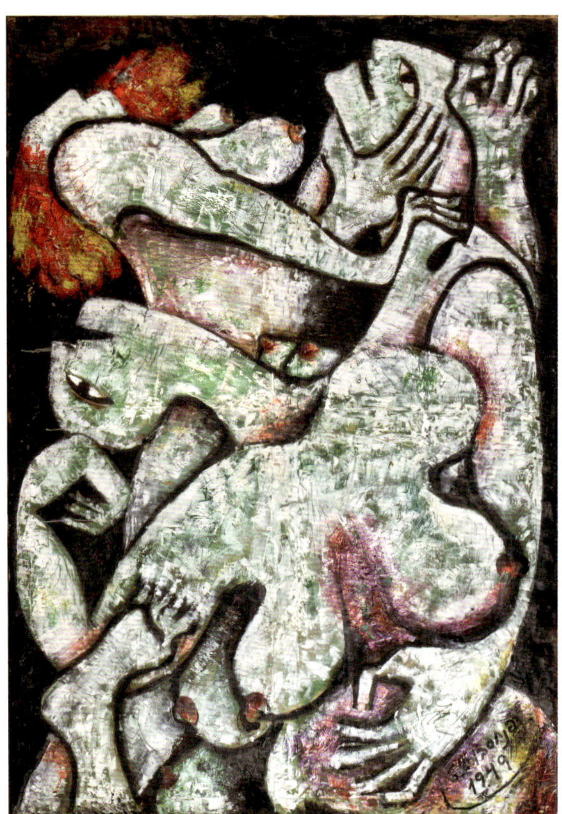

touching document, while Maryan makes use of synthesis, with his flat forms giving emphasis only to what is essential. The aesthetics adopted by the painter enters into a dialogue with another painting, *Extermination Train* (1947–48) by Erna Rosenstein, who, in the 1940s, belonged to one of the most important circles of modern art in Kraków. Although Rosenstein does not depict a gas chamber, but rather the claustrophobic interior of a train car, she engages in a similar visual language based on the poignant contrast between the cramped space and the group of crowded human silhouettes. Both Maryan and Rosenstein give us the best examples of how, just after the war, artists tested the limits of 1940s modernism in order to establish that it was indeed the most appropriate language in which they could express the horror of concentration camps.

How to paint just after the war: The visibility of Holocaust testimonies

How to paint and what to paint? This apparently banal question that Maryan posed at the very outset of his career can be understood in two ways if we remain aware that his entry into the art world was marked by the close relationship between modernism and both immigrant and post-Shoah identities. It is clear that this geohistorical framework ensured that he posed questions not only about particular artistic idioms, but also about the importance of subject matter in art and the ability to actually bear witness to the Holocaust. This issue must be examined through a broader comparative lens.

Essentially identical questions regarding the condition of art after 1945 were posed in both Central Europe and in Western Europe and North America. Citing Barnett Newman's well-known statement, Éric de Chassey sensed a burning desire in Euro-American art for a new beginning: "What it meant for me was that I had to start from scratch as if painting didn't exist, which is a special way of saying that painting was dead."[15] Paris, the city to which Maryan immigrated, was not only the capital of the avant-garde but also a location of debates about art after the war. As postwar art historian Sarah Wilson's analyses have shown, art indeed developed in highly diverse directions.[16] The 1948 *HWPSMTB* (Hartung, Wols, Picabia, Stahly, Mathieu, Tapié, Bryen) exhibition confirmed the significance of Tachism, which sought to challenge high culture as such. At the same time, the wave of criticism of modernism also led to calls to adopt Socialist Realism and conservative art. As early as 1936, there was a debate on *Quelle du réalisme*, while the Catholic group Jeunes peintres de tradition française was active throughout the 1940s. After the war, calls to return to academicism and national art forms under the auspices of David grew stronger, thus creating something of a contrast with the vision of Paris as a center of artistic innovation. In Poland, an interesting point of reference given Maryan's biography, the situation was equally complex, but for different reasons. There, as was the case everywhere else behind the Iron Curtain, the end of the war saw the implementation of a new communist form of statehood. Art referring to the war and works specifically seeking to bear witness to the Holocaust necessarily emerged within the prevailing context

Pinkas Bursztyn, *Crematorium in Auschwitz*, 1949. Oil on canvas, 63 × 41⅜ inches (160 × 105 cm). Collection of Marsha and Assaph Caspi, Israel

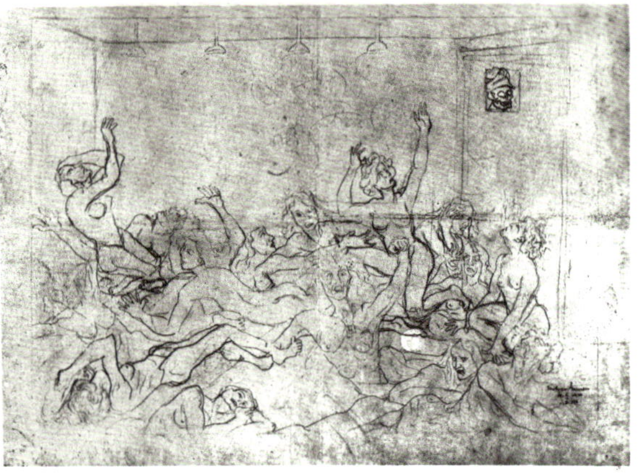

Wiktor Simiński, *In the Gas Chamber*, 1944. Pencil on paper, 14 × 24 inches (35.5 × 60.9 cm). Janina Jaworska Collection, Warsaw

of socialist and Socialist Realist art—something that is perfectly illustrated by the works of Andrzej Wróblewski.[17] Whereas Wróblewski was a keen advocate of communism and its official aesthetics, at the end of the 1940s he also tried to create a visual language of engaged figuration called "direct realism" that was expected to be more vivid than conventional schematic Socialist Realism. His cycle of paintings entitled *Shooting* (or *Execution*, 1949) remains a sharp example of this artistic attitude.

Since it was the case that, in the various parts of the world linked to Maryan's life (Poland, France, and the United States), questions were being asked regarding the ways in which the war had powerfully transformed perceptions of art, it is therefore worth exploring, in relation to his early works, just what degree of visibility the testimonies to limit experiences he produced could have achieved at the time. It is generally accepted that for Western societies, one of the first important catalysts for developing collective knowledge of the Holocaust came only with Adolf Eichmann's notorious trial held in 1961. However, such knowledge was transmitted completely differently within societies where communities of survivors had once lived. In order to establish the broader context and proper significance of Maryan's early works, I suggest positioning them in relation to the efforts to generate awareness and visibility of the Holocaust that were taking place in parallel in Poland. Political developments there meant

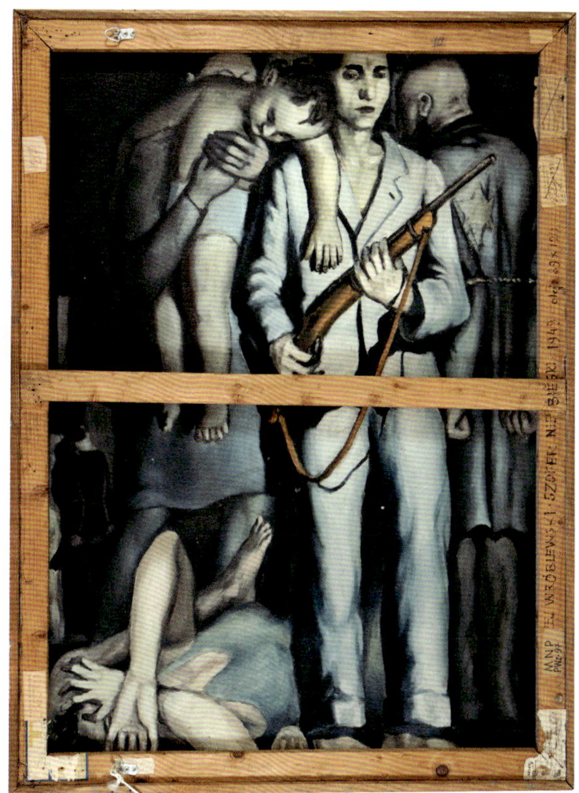

Andrzej Wróblewski, *Likwidacja getta* (Liquidation of the Ghetto), 1949. Oil on canvas, 45¼ × 35 inches (120 × 89 cm). Private Collection

that the dynamics of awareness and ignorance of this event differed from those in the West and in Israel.

It is notable that favorable conditions for forming and maintaining memory of the Shoah existed for only a very short period in communist Poland, namely up until 1949, at which point Stalinism became the official doctrine in the country, forcing the effacement of any claims regarding the exceptional nature of Jews' wartime experiences. Very soon after the war, exhibitions featuring art that documented the concentration camps were organized. Pioneering in this respect was the 1945 exhibition of works by Ukrainian Jewish artist Zinovy Tolkachev, *Majdanek w sztuce* (Majdanek in Art).[18] Over the next four years, the Central Jewish Historical Commission in Poland published reprints of documents, analyses, and photo albums, while also calling for the collection of source material and thus acquiring numerous witness testimonies itself. After 1949, the situation changed completely, as is illustrated clearly in the activities of the painter and curator Marek Oberländer, who, like Maryan, came from a small-town Jewish community. In 1953, Oberländer looked to organize an exhibition marking the tenth anniversary of the Warsaw Ghetto Uprising. He wanted to stage it in New York, but his material was ultimately rejected by American Jewish communities. He did succeed in organizing, in Poland in 1955, the *Ogólnopolska*

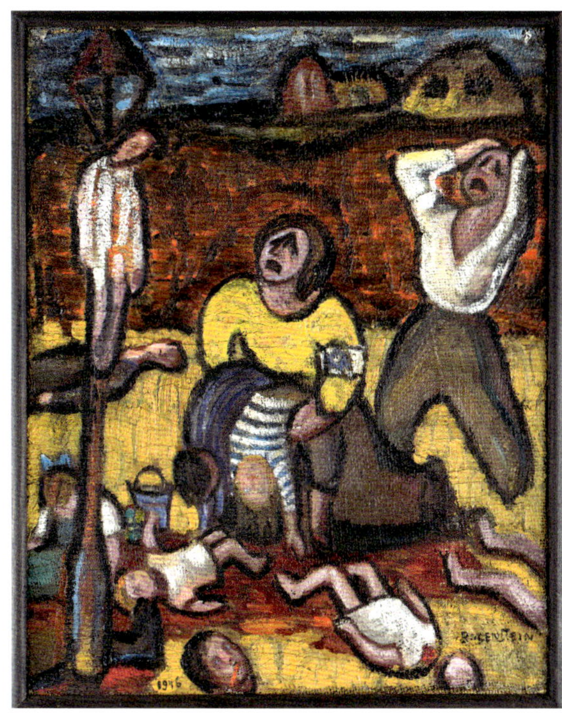

Erna Rosenstein, *Getto* (Ghetto), 1946. Oil on canvas, 19 ⅝ × 16 ⅛ inches (50 × 41 cm). National Museum, Poznań

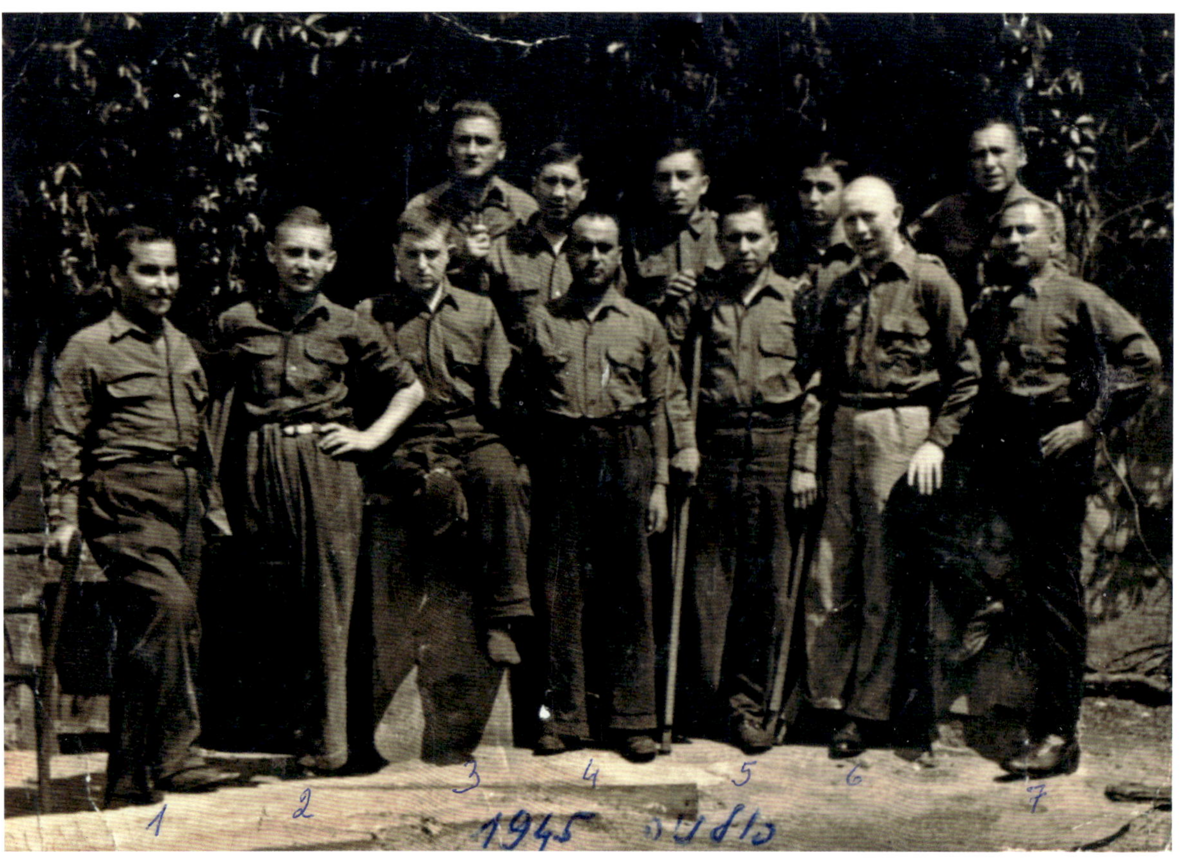

A group of Jewish Holocaust survivors (Maryan is second from the left) in Czestochowa, Poland, in 1945. They lived in a "House for the Cripped" at 11 Garibaldi Street after their discharge from various hospitals beginning in May 1945. Photographic print, 8 × 11 inches (23.3 × 28 cm). Courtesy of Ghetto Fighters House Archive, Israel

Wystawa Młodej Plastyki (National Exhibition of Young Artists), in which oil paintings based on photographic testimonies of ghettos and Nazi camps (thus referring directly to the Holocaust) were indeed exhibited, albeit within the framework of the propagandistic rhetoric of anti-fascist struggle. It was only in 1961 (vide the Eichmann trial) that he was able to develop an exhibition on the Warsaw Ghetto, which was then shown in Northern and Western Europe, namely in Aalborg, Amsterdam, Copenhagen, and Stockholm, so far behind the Iron Curtain.

The similarities between Maryan and Oberländer are striking. They not only shared a similar cultural background and dedicated much of their work to bearing witness to the Shoah, but they were also both pioneering in generating access to these tendencies, albeit within the limits of their particular political and geohistorical conditions. It is only when placed in the context of the activities of the Polish Jewish community of the 1940s, in particular Oberländer's efforts in the 1950s, that the significance of an exhibition held at the YMCA in Jerusalem in 1950 becomes clear. Maryan's first individual show, organized with the assistance of the art critic Miriam Tal, was recalled powerfully by Yehuda Haezrahi from the position of a witness to history: "It was more than fifteen years ago. One day, I met the art

critic Miriam Tal, who told me enthusiastically that a new, highly significant exhibition had just opened by a young painter. The painter's name: Pinkas Bursztyn. An unknown name that meant nothing."[19] Describing Maryan's earliest works featuring portraits of concentration camp prisoners, Haezrahi stated concisely: "I viewed those paintings and was touched to tears. I must admit, I was terrified of this emotion."[20]

At the outset of his career Maryan, like Oberländer, maintained the memory of a traumatic past. But he did so in Jerusalem in 1950, where Stalinists were not in power, and artists were not forced to adopt Socialist Realism. Nevertheless, were his fate to have taken a different turn—i.e., had he remained in Poland—I believe he would still have sought to produce a similar exhibition. This argument leads to an important conclusion. Piotr Piotrowski emphasized that when writing about Central European art, it is necessary to avoid comparisons to Western art and instead stress the differing social and political frameworks that prevailed: "Although observed forms may sometimes be similar, our 'framing' will give them distinct meanings. We should therefore focus more on the frame than the idiom."[21] While certainly an important lesson to take on board, the cases of Maryan and other Polish Jewish (or Israeli) artists demonstrate that the opposite could indeed be the case. Occasionally, such artists built a fragile community based on biographical experiences that were far more significant than artistic forms or the prevailing political situation. While keeping sight of geohistorical differences, it is worth drawing attention to the intuitive dialogue among artists that took place in—and between—Israel, France, and Poland. In this way, it is possible to avoid their marginalization within particular national canons, with Jewish cultural identity and post-Holocaust identity thus emerging as a source of agency and strength. All of these artists were constantly searching for the best source of expression of limit experiences, often oscillating between realism (or figuration) and generalized metaphor. Over time, Maryan himself began to incorporate an increasingly symbolic rather than realistic language into his best-known works. But in the final phase of his work—in *Ecce Homo* (1975)—he returned to more direct constructions of representation. This shows that the significance of his earliest testimony should not be underestimated.

NOTES

1.   Ewa Andrzejewska, Krzysztof Bojarczuk, and Anda Rottenberg, Pokój Maryana. Maryan (Pinchas Burstein) w Nowym Sączu i w Nowym Jorku / Maryan's Room: Maryan (Pinchas Burstein) in Nowy Sącz and in New York City (Nowy Sącz: Stowarzyszenie Maryan, 2016), 9.
2.   Yivo Encyclopedia of Jews in Eastern Europe, s.v. "Sandz Hasidic Dynasty," by David Assaf, accessed May 7, 2021, https://yivoencyclopedia.org/article.aspx/Sandz_Hasidic_Dynasty.
3.   Samuel D. Kassow, *Who Will Write Our History? Emanuel Ringelblum, the Warsaw Ghetto, and the Oyneg Shabes Archive* (Bloomington: Indiana University Press, 2018), 23.
4.   Łukasz Połomski, "Między zacofaniem a nowoczesnością. Społeczeństwo Nowego Sącza w latach 1867–1939" ("Between Modernity and Backwardness: Society of Nowy Sącz, 1867–1939") (PhD diss., Uniwersytet Pedagogiczny, Kraków, 2017), 60.
5.   Ibid., 58.
6.   Ibid., 60.
7.   Tadeusz Duda, "Eksterminacja ludności żydowskiej Nowego Sącza w okresie II wojny światowej" ("Extermination of the Jewish Population in Nowy Sącz during WWII"), *Rocznik Nowosądecki*, no. 19 (1988–1990): 209–49.
8.   In one of his testimonies referring to this period of time, Maryan stated: "I was sent to a summer camp with a lot of kids who came from all over Poland, and it was right near my town. We all used to say to each other, 'See you next year, same place.' The kids would leave and I would remain. Instead of summer camp the year after, I found myself in Auchwitz." Maryan S. Maryan, "A propos de l'exposition Maryan à la Galerie Ariel, Février 1977," *Ariel 42* (Paris: Galerie Ariel, 1977), 6–7.
9.   Andrzejewska, Bojarczuk, and Rottenberg, *Pokój Maryana / Maryan's Room*, 7.
10.   Ibid.
11.   See Jakub Bendkowski and Mikołaj Getka-Kenig, *Art History and the Fight for Memory: Józef Sandel (1894–1962), Founder of the Jewish Historical Institute Museum: An Exhibition at the E. Ringelblum Jewish Historical Institute in Warsaw, October 6, 2016–March 19, 2017* (Warsaw: Emanuel Ringelblum Jewish Historical Institute, 2016).
12.   See Maryan's letter sent from Paris on May 19, 1950.
13.   Piotr Piotrowski, *Art and Democracy in Post-Communist Europe*, trans. Anna Brzyski (London: Reaktion Books, 2009), 38.
14.   Maria Muszkowska, *The Masters of the École de Paris*, ed. Maria Muszkowska (Konstancin-Jeziorna: Villa la Fleur, 2020), 122.
15.   Newman's words were used as the title of the exhibition *Repartir à zéro: Comme si la peinture n'avait jamais existé* (1945–1949) at the Musée des Beaux-Arts, Lyon, October 24, 2008–February 2, 2009. See the accompanying catalogue, ed. Eric de Chassey and Sylvie Ramond (Paris: Hazan, 2008).
16.   See Sarah Wilson, *Paris: Capital of the Arts, 1900–1968* (London: Royal Academy of Arts, 2002).
17.   See *Andrzej Wróblewski: Avoiding Intermediary States*, ed. Magdalena Ziółkowska and Wojciech Grzybała (Warsaw: Andrzej Wróblewski Foundation and Adam Mickiewicz Institute; Ostfildern: Hatje Cantz, 2014).
18.   On the Tolkachev exhibition, see Agata Pietrasik, "Symbol, Testimony, Evidence: Representations of Majdanek in the 1944–1945 Works of Zinovy Tolkachev," *Miejsce*, no. 6 (2020): 112–35.
19.   Yehuda Haezrahi, "The Wandering Paintbrush," *Maariv*, no. 24 (June 1966): 23.
20.   Ibid.
21.   Piotr Piotrowski, *In the Shadow of Yalta: Art and the Avant-Garde in Eastern Europe 1945–1989*, trans. Anna Brzyski (London: Reaktion Books, 2009), 27. See also Piotrowski, "How to Write a History of Central-East European Art?," *Third Text* 23, no. 1 (January 2009): 5–14.

(1) REGISTRATION NO.

5799

Original ☐

M

F

BURSZTYN   Pincha

Family Name   Other Given Names   (

.1.1927.   Nowy Secz   Poland

Birthdate   Birthplace   Province   Cou

Number of Dependents:

Bursztyn   Abracha

(10) Full Name of Father

(12) DESIRED DESTINATION

Palestine

City or Village   Province   Country

ART. PAINTER

) Usual Trade, Occupation or Profession   (15) Performed in W

(18) Do You
to be a
oner of

lish   Jewish German   c

) Languages Spoken in Order of Fluency

) Signature of Registrant: *Bursztyn Pinches*   (21) Signature of Regist

) Destination or Reception Center:

Name or Number

)Code Issue	1	2	3	4	5	6	7	8	9	10	11	12	

(24)

ATION RECORD

uplicate ☐

For coding purposes

A.	B.	C.	D.	E.	F.	G.	H.	I.	

Single ☒ Married ☐
Widowed ☐ Divorced ☐

(4) Marital Status

Polish Jew

(5) Claimed Nationality

Jewish

(7) Religion (Optional)

(8) Number of Accompanying Family Members:

Bursztyn Gitla

(11) Full Maiden Name of Mother

) LAST PERMANENT RESIDENCE OR RESIDENCE JANUARY 1, 193

Nowa Targ

City or Village	Province	Country

ind of Establishment | (16) Other Trades or Occupations

none [handwritten]

Yes   No   (19) Amount and Kind of Currency in your Possessi

Date **2.V111.46**   Assembly Center No. **581**

City or Village					Province					Country		
15	16	17	18	19	20	21	22	23	24	25	26	27

RKS

DR-1
16—3978

THE HUMAN MENAGERIE: ON DEMONIC DOGS AND OTHER ANIMALS

Noa Rosenberg

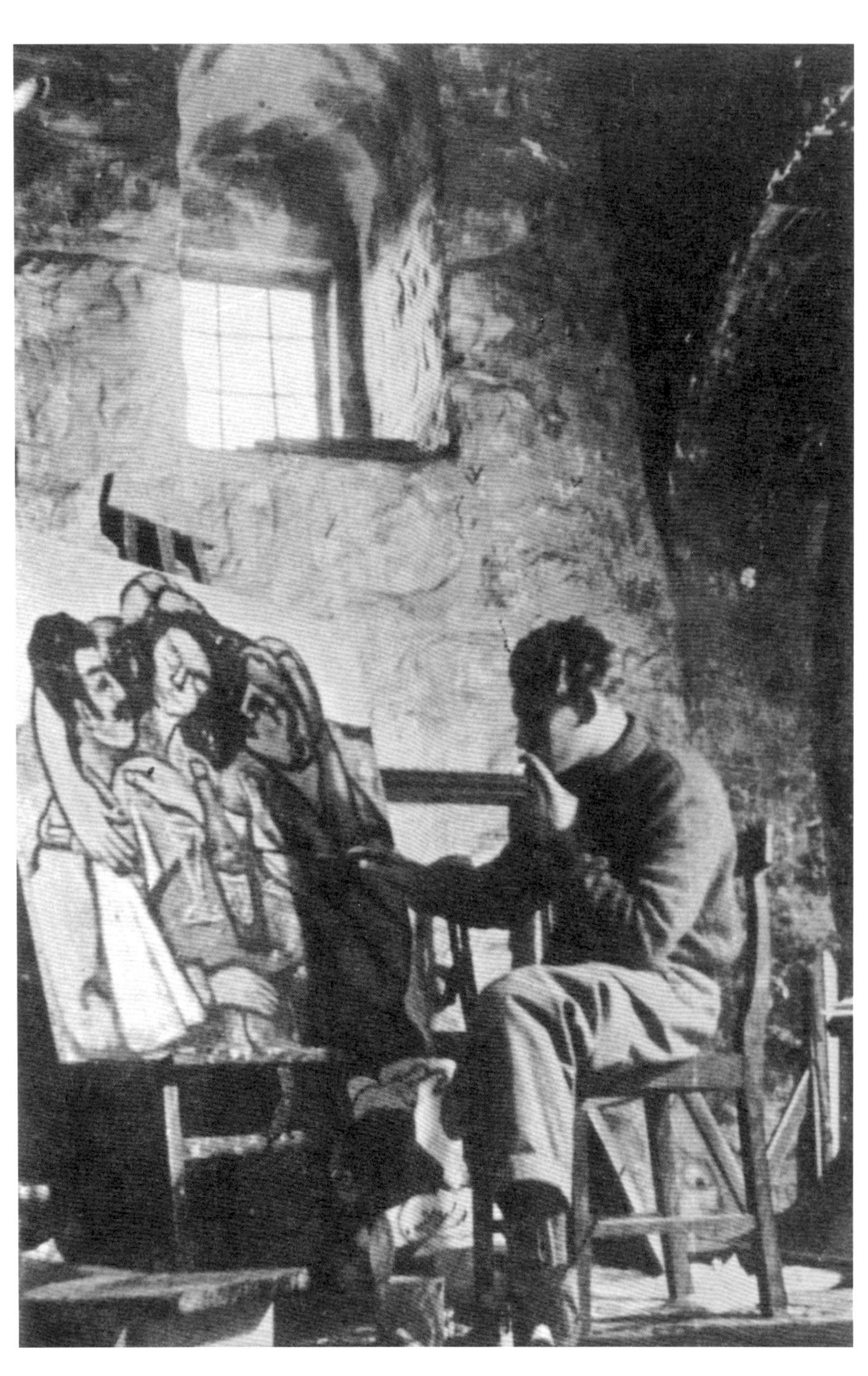

Pinkas Bursztyn in Palestine–Israel, 1947–1950

In the spring of 1947 a ship docked at the Port of Haifa. Pinkas Bursztyn disembarked alone. After a brief interview and physical examination he was handed an identity card. There, under the occupation clause, appeared the word "disabled." No one had come to meet him. He sat down on a stack of orange crates ready to be shipped and waited. Ironically, Bursztyn, a young Auschwitz survivor, sat exactly on Zionism's "vitamin C": the orange. But unlike the fantasies of Zionist advocates, the national fruit failed to fill him with a passion for life and the bright sunlight did nothing to restore his mind and body. Instead, he was overcome by a death anxiety.

> When the ship arrived in Haifa, I received an identity card with the word "disabled." Can you imagine . . . they stamped my paper with "disabled"! I came from the concentration camps! After getting the card, they left me alone on the dock. Nobody came to me. I found a stack of orange crates and I sat down on it . . . I waited. Yes, I waited for someone to come and get me . . . I waited for several hours and suddenly I felt a terrible dread. I began to see the truth. Nobody had waited for me . . . They left me on the dock. After some time I understood that it was worse than in the concentration camp because there I hadn't been alone, we were all going to die together. Yet on the dock of Haifa port I was about to die alone.[1]

Since the late nineteenth century, the new Jewish nation in Eretz Israel expressed itself primarily through the body, as is manifest in the term *muscular Judaism* (Muskeljudentum), coined by Max Nordau.[2] Hebrew literature endorsed discourse on the deficiency of the body of the diaspora Jew, which it presented as lacking Eros and creativity. The national Jewish diaspora body was often described as impotent, "an old, dying man, whose body is bruised and wounded, crushed under the weight of the decrepit books that contain his misfortunes."[3] The revival of the body took center stage in Zionist ideology where it reflected a desire for a new Jewish masculinity, a body at once whole, native, and omnipotent. In the 1930s and '40s, when the flow of immigrants from Europe to Eretz Israel grew, a gap opened between the diaspora Jew and the local Hebrew/Israeli, known as the Sabra.[4] This name marked the difference between those who grew up in the homeland, under the bright sun, and those who withered in the dark rooms of Europe.

Pinkas Bursztyn was sent directly from the orange crates to an "old people's colony" near Haifa.[5] The youth immigration official needed just one glance at Bursztyn's amputated body to know that in this case, national revival through the body was not a valid option. Therefore, Bursztyn had no place on a kibbutz or in a youth group and must sit among those unable to contribute to building a new society: the elderly. Bursztyn described this period, in which he felt "imprisoned" in the old people's colony without understanding why and for what, in terms of a trauma equal in its intensity to his imprisonment in the concentration camps.[6] An early series of paintings, from the beginning of the 1950s, shows void spaces punctuated by figures facing the nothingness. This survivalist-existential waiting continued, so he felt, from when he was twelve until the age of twenty-two: in the ghettos, the work camps, the death camps, the Port of Haifa, and the old people's colony. He later described his time there: "I stayed for a year and a half, without studying, without doing anything, and at that time I was eager to study, to read—I wanted to have back all that I had lost as a child. I was there, among the old people, for a year and a half . . ."[7]

It is not coincidental that the term "old people's colony" evokes Franz Kafka's story "In the Penal Colony," where we find similarities with the descriptions and feelings Bursztyn experienced at that time.[8] The events in Kafka's story unfold in a mysterious chronotope, occurring to people who are described as blank-faced and mute, and who have no idea why they are being punished. Their slow execution is performed by a torture machine that inscribes the sentence of each condemned prisoner on their skin.

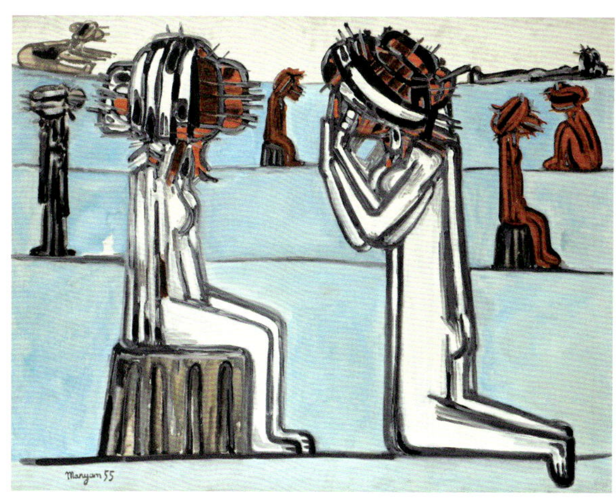

Maryan, *Untitled*, 1955. Oil on canvas, 35 × 45 ⅝ inches (89 × 116 cm). Private Collection, courtesy of Kamel Mennour

Pinkas Bursztyn painting in his Jerusalem studio, ca. 1947–50

Written on the Dog's Skin

The inscription of a mysterious sentence on the skin of the blameless recalls the dog Balak in S. Y. Agnon's novel *Only Yesterday*.[9] The novel's main protagonist, Yitzhak Kummer, who arrived in the country on the Second Aliyah, works as a painter, painting signs on the streets of Jerusalem.[10] In an inexplicable act, he paints the words "crazy dog" on the skin of a stray dog called Balak, before kicking him hard in the ribs, sending the wounded dog running off, bleeding. Balak then sets out to pursue "the man with the damp paintbrush" who inscribed his skin, wishing to understand the act of writing. In his wanderings, the "crazy dog" is banished by the residents of Jerusalem's Orthodox neighborhoods with shouts and kicks, thus worsening his injury, until finally he contracts rabies. Eventually Balak finds Yitzhak Kummer and sinks his teeth into his palm, into the fingers that held the paintbrush that had brought on all the trouble that befell him. Kummer then contracts rabies, his mouth froths as he howls like a dog, walks on all fours, and tries to bite anyone who comes near him, until he dies in great agony.

The aftertaste of Balak's encounter with his tormentor's flesh leads the dog to believe that Kummer acted absentmindedly. This realization shocks him to the core and brings about his most extreme "doggish" behavior. From hereon he lusts after the taste of human flesh:

> And after he dug himself a hole in the flesh of the painter and dripped the truth from it, the truth should have filled all his being, but in the end, there is no truth and no nothing . . . Balak became sad and angry. But his teeth that had tasted human flesh began longing and wanting more . . . And once again he was amazed, for man is made of special material, yet in the end, his flesh is no different from most animals.[11]

Bursztyn identified strongly with the dog Balak, to whom he referred in his works several times over the years, sometimes directly, by painting Balak and other dogs, and sometimes indirectly, for example when inscribing the canvas "skin" with the number tattooed on his own skin in a coded self-portrait.[12] Prisoners and the dog Balak appeared in Bursztyn's work after he left Israel. "I am not liberated from the Kafkaesque world," he said. "He suffered from the same nightmares that I suffer from. Fear of authority, fear of being unloved. Fear of not being accepted by society. I read a story by Agnon twenty years ago that also impressed me: 'Formerly' this dog Balak wandered around Jerusalem. I found myself in this story. He wrote it very beautifully."[13]

The literary critic Baruch Kurzweil, author of a seminal essay on the symbolic meanings of Balak, called him a "demonic dog."[14] According to to Kurzweil, Balak gradually becomes a symbol of an anxiety-ridden existence that cannot be defined as constant because, were it constant, it would also be solved. Balak is "the symbol of lust, of vice, of primal forces, of untamed desires, madness and craziness."[15] Balak is all the mental strength Kummer needs to repress his anxieties, yet they rise to attack him and bring him down.

In her book *Written on the Dog's Skin*,[16] Michal Arbel understands the writing on the skin as an expression of the abject[17] and the demonic, which explains the desire to distance the act from ourselves. Moreover, it is an act that strikes the roots of artistic creation. By writing the words "crazy dog" on Balak's skin with a paintbrush, Yitzhak Kummer becomes, momentarily, an artist. He creates a conceptual-representational reality which, like an artist, he then sends into the world as an object at once attached to and detached from his body. The moment Balak begins running through

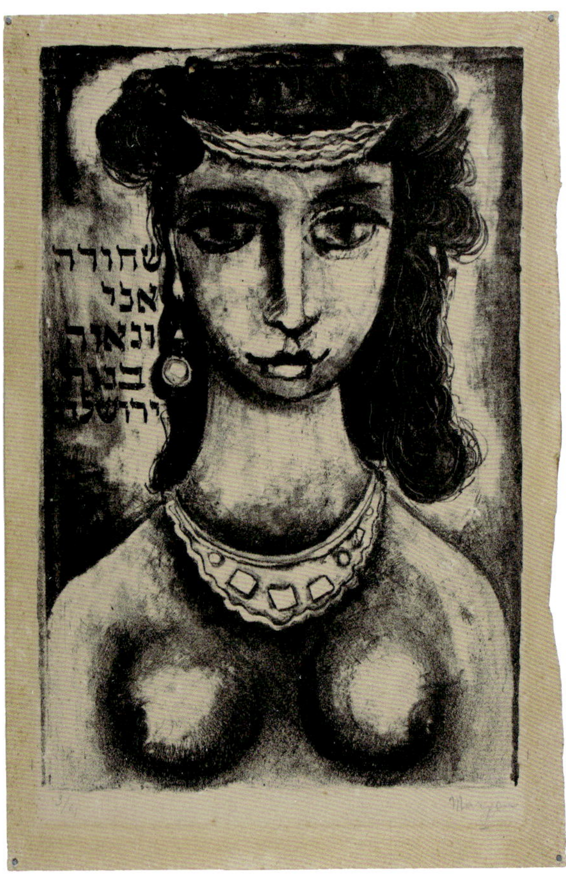

Maryan, *Shulamite (from Song of Songs)*, ca. 1950. Lithograph, 20 × 13 inches (53 × 34 cm). Collection of the Tel Aviv Museum of Art, purchase

the Jerusalem neighborhoods, he is Kummer's creation, now uncontrolled and free to gather independent insights.

Unlike Yitzhak Kummer, who became an artist for a moment, Pinkas Bursztyn arrived in the country with a laissez-passer that had "artist painter" written as his occupation. Bursztyn was considered a gifted painter already as a child in Poland. At the end of World War II he spent several months studying art in Poland, before moving to a displaced persons camp in Germany, where he worked as a set designer in the camp's Jewish theater.[18] The Haifa port official's act of "writing" on the "skin" of Bursztyn's identity card therefore creates a new reality—it made the term *disabled* both an identity and an occupation that threw Bursztyn off course.

Outcasts at the New Bezalel in Jerusalem

After three weeks in the old people's colony, Bursztyn submitted through the Jewish Agency an application to the New Bezalel Academy of Art in Jerusalem. His application was accepted and after a five-month wait, on October 7, 1947, the student Pinkas Bursztyn enrolled in the preparatory program for applied graphics at the New Bezalel.

When Bezalel reopened in 1935, the art academy endeavored to train weavers, metalsmiths, and the "Eretz Israelian graphic artist" to shape and convey the general national spirit as opposed to personal artistic expression. Three departments operated at Bezalel in the late 1940s: handweaving, metalwork, and applied graphics. All the academy students studied art history, drawing, theory of color and form, sculpture, and painting with the school's first director, the painter Mordecai Ardon.[19] Classes in the department of applied graphics focused on learning Hebrew script and designing posters for the upcoming national service. The school was close in spirit to the international Bauhaus school in Germany, of which Ardon was a graduate. In a 1942 memo from the Jerusalem City Archive, Ardon describes his vision for the department of applied graphics:

> The industry and commerce in the country
> need the work of the applied graphic artist
> in all areas. He must create a form for the
> commercial symbol, the dressing, the cover,
> the announcement, poster and stamp . . . Of
> course a graphic artist arriving from abroad
> cannot serve to fulfill these aims in the
> renewed spirit of the place and the people

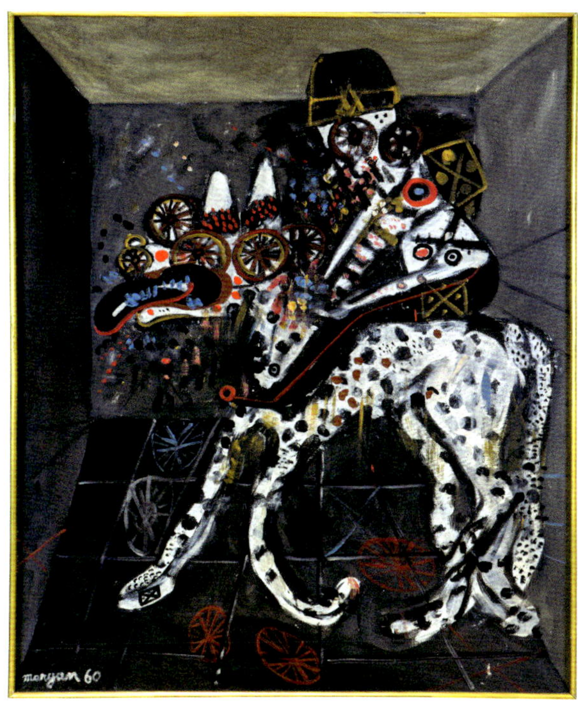

Maryan, *Balak, chien fou*, 1960. Oil on canvas, 51 × 37½ inches (129.5 × 95.2 cm). Private Collection

> . . . There is no alternative but to train and
> develop the Eretz Israel graphic artist. The
> school cannot see its mission as purely satis-
> fying the needs of the individual. The value
> of the institution rests primarily on its ability
> to serve the public.[20]

The Bezalel program was demanding, and Bursztyn studied every weekday from 8:00 a.m. to 7:00 p.m. and Fridays until 2:00 p.m. The attendance log reveals that some weeks Bursztyn was present in all the classes while other times completely absent.[21] His surviving works from the department of applied graphics illustrate Ardon's view of the department's national goals. The lithograph *Shulamite (from Song of Songs)* is likely an exercise in Biblical script, while the poster *Boy Reading Talmud* was probably created for a textbook or for one of the High Holidays.

Bezalel was also the place where Bursztyn found, for the first time since arriving in the country, a small group of friends his own age, all Holocaust survivors, including the painter Yehuda Bacon. Speaking in his Jerusalem home, Bacon recalls:

> We were the odd ones at Bezalel. Everyone
> knew that we were war refugees but at that
> time nobody talked about the Holocaust and
> the term "Holocaust survivor" didn't yet
> exist.[22] There were four of us friends, Maryan
> [Pinkas Bursztyn], Maryan Merinol [Meyer
> Leibner, 1932, Romania–1955, Israel],
> Avigdor Arikha[23] [1929, Romania–2010,

Paris], and me. We had one thing in common: all of us existed in various holes which we crawled out off. We were seventeen-, eighteen-year-olds and far from normal. Among ourselves we could talk about what we had seen but we knew that others would never be able to understand. Maryan and I were together at the broadcast of a newsreel that showed the liberation of the camps. Everyone was shocked and covered their eyes. We laughed out loud, because they showed something like ten bodies . . . nothing, compared to what we'd seen.

Our situation at Bezalel was difficult. The Youth Immigration paid part of our tuition but apart from that it was each man for himself. At the beginning Maryan slept in a Turkish building and later in a monastery.[24] Arikha was a bit better off because he'd already been in the country a few years and lived on kibbutz Ma'ale Hahamisha. While feeling an outsider at the kibbutz, he still had food and clothes. Maryan was in the worst state, especially because of his leg. I slept at the home of Dr. Be'echer, a German woman gynecologist. There I met all the greats of the day: Hugo Bergman, who wrote a letter of recommendation for me, Gershom Scholem, and Agnon. Maryan and I would go to hear their lectures.[25] On the one hand we felt fortunate to be included in this world of culture and to feel like human beings once more. Most of the lectures were in German, which we understood, and we worked on our painting and art. However, our situation was very bad. I lived through a Jerusalem winter in torn shoes. We went hungry for days. We later managed to organize our food. Each of us brought something and we all shared. Just like in the camps when we were used to looking out for one another. I felt that Mordecai Ardon, the director of the school, understood our situation and knew where we had come from, but we never discussed it with him. He treated us warmly and specially, offered us lunch, so we knew that at least once every few days we would have a decent meal. He also recognized our talent and gave us private lessons in color in the evenings and made sure we learned to speak Hebrew and to be less like suckers in our dealings with the Sabras and their snobbish attitude.

Bacon recalls a real incident between the Holocaust survivors and the Sabra students:

There was an opportunity to receive a small living grant. Maryan [Merinol] and I spoke to the other students and asked that it be granted to Pinkas seeing as his situation was worse than others and he was suffering terribly because of his leg. But they refused, saying that Pinkas could never be a painter because of his leg and that he is unable to contribute to the new society, to fight or to be an artist and therefore giving him the money would be like throwing it away. Maryan was very sensitive about his leg and his appearance in general, and felt inferior both physically and mentally, something that the Sabras kept rubbing in his face. He was aware of the things said behind his back and that was perhaps the reason he decided to leave. Ardon and the other teachers considered him gifted; the problem was mostly in relation to the Sabra students. Later Ardon introduced us to Miriam Tal.[26] She recognized Bursztyn's talent and took him under her wing.

Bursztyn maintained two things from his time in Jerusalem: a close friendship with Miriam Tal and his contempt for Bezalel. Two letters to Tal from 1950, his first year in Paris, speak volumes:

I met Mr. "Yehuda Razgor." He didn't even want to speak to me. He probably thinks I need something from him, but he's wrong. I don't need anything from any friend and anyway I don't want to talk to any person from Eretz Israel (I shit on them). There are people here who are much nicer.[27]

How is the "art" in the country? Are there exhibitions? Is there a scene? Whatever. Let those provincial painters have them. Steinhardt, Miron Sima, Bloom, Brunstein, Levanon, Pines and the young sculptors and poets, the Palmachnikim with their autobiographies . . . sorry . . . in other words: the "Fine" New Bezalel art school in Jerusalem.[28]

The three years Bursztyn spent in Jerusalem (1947–50) were eventful: the siege on Jerusalem, which led to severe hunger in the city; ceaseless firing from the Jordanians; the War of Independence,[29] in which many fighters were Holocaust survivors;

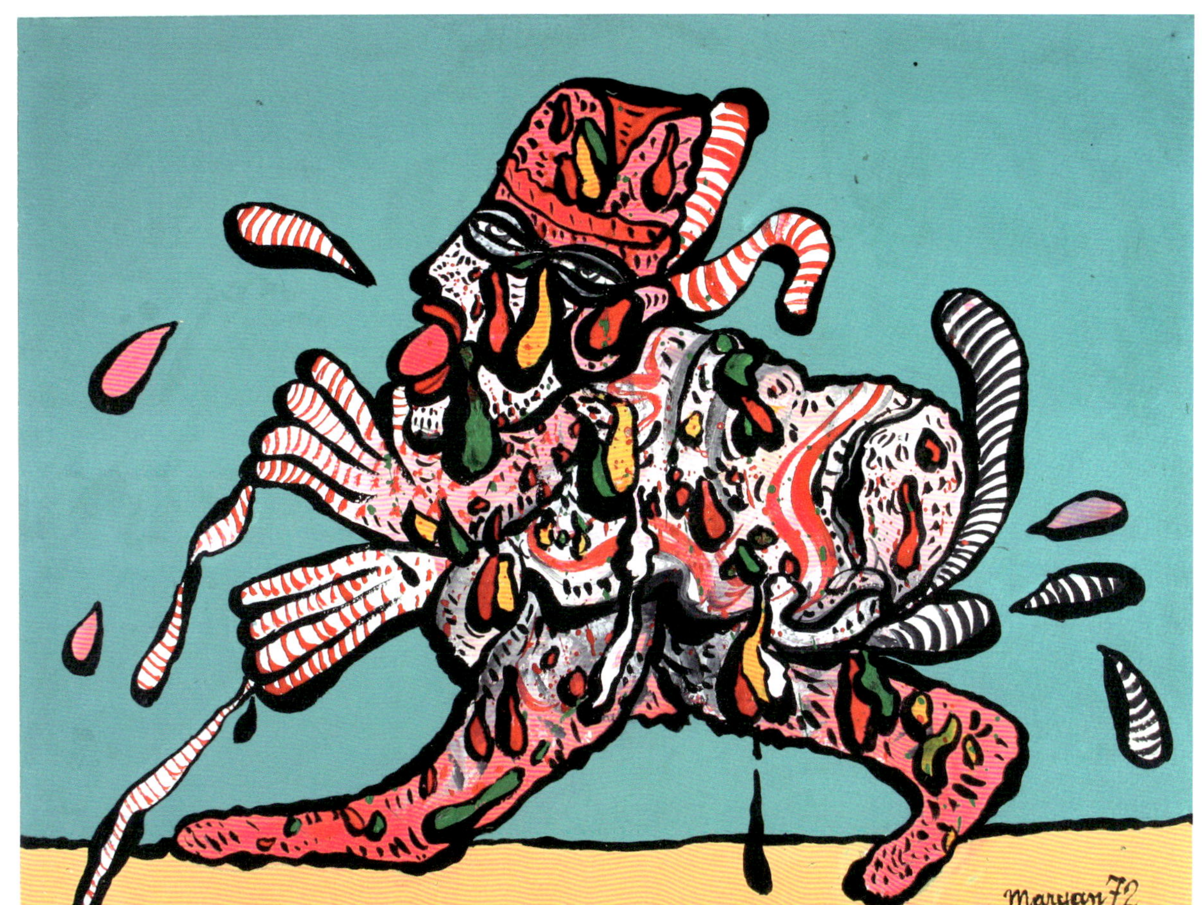

Maryan, *Personnage*, 1972. Acrylic and gouache on paper, 12 × 16 inches (30.5 × 40.5 cm). Collection of the Tel Aviv Museum of Art. Gift of Allan Rich, Los Angeles, through the American Friends of the Tel Aviv Museum of Art, 1983

and finally the transition from Mandatory Palestine to the establishment of the State of Israel, a country whose population was mostly new immigrants and refugees from Europe. The period was one of many different social narratives. The artistic discourse centered on questions of artistic concept: What is the nature of the local national art? Should artists aspire to a local or a universal art? In Tel Aviv several artists formed the influential group New Horizons, which claimed the precedence of abstraction and universality over "localness"; in the kibbutzim artists were active in socially engaged art; and in Jerusalem, a periphery in relation to the art field in Tel Aviv, the New Bezalel Academy worked to shape national symbols. Two values had sweeping consensus in Israeli art at that time: the glorification of the image of the fighters of the War of Independence and the reduction of the Holocaust into a symbolic event whose consequences must be studied. The second ethos strengthened the first.

A rare photograph from that period shows Bursztyn in an abandoned Ottoman prison, which was his home and studio, painting three injured Palmach fighters leaning on each other. This is most likely the only one of Bursztyn's paintings to toe the line of the ruling attitude in Israeli art at the time. At his feet, behind a chair, leaning with its

back to the viewer, is a work of art that seems to be the painting *Crematorium in Auschwitz* (1949). If indeed so, the photograph is charged with symbolism as it depicts both that which was considered "appropriate"—facing us on the easel—and that which must be repressed—facing the wall.

Yehuda Bacon's answer to my question—Were Bezalel students free to work on images of the Holocaust?—was a decisive "No":

All of us [Bacon, Arikha, Merinol, and Bursztyn] painted the Holocaust and spoke to each other about these paintings. But we worked on them mostly outside Bezalel, not as oil painting on canvas and so expressive! Pinkas was the only one who didn't care, and he did what he wanted. He was a tragic figure and could be very aggressive toward anyone who hadn't been in the camps or was dismissive of what we had gone through. He painted some of these works in Bezalel lessons as well. For example, if we had to paint a self-portrait, he would sometimes paint himself in a prisoner's uniform. The students would recoil from him, and the teachers would get angry. Miriam Tal would save him each time.

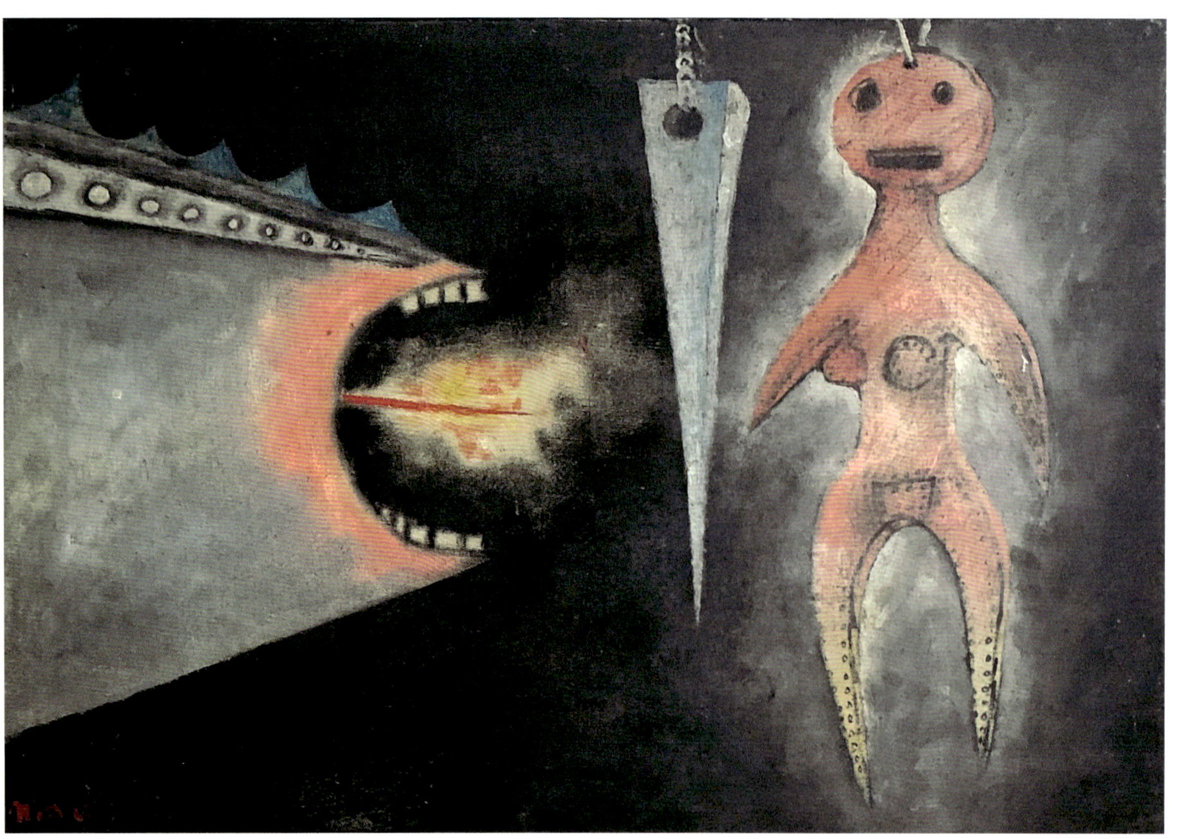

The description of Bursztyn's anger toward the Sabras over his provocative insistence on depicting images from the concentration camps in his art at Bezalel reminds us once again of Balak, the dog who returns and bites the legs of those who insisted on his despicability and shooed him away violently. The poet Nathan Zach,[30] who was friendly with Bursztyn, would go with him and Maryan Merinol to exhibitions at the Jerusalem Artists' House. He recalled Bursztyn bringing with him a razor blade and cutting the paintings he didn't like while saying, "Damn decorations! Everything decorations! Destroy!"[31]

However, not only repression and silencing were directed at the Holocaust survivors; there was also "victim blaming," whose verbal expression was a phrase from the world of animals: "Like sheep to the slaughter." In its modern context, this expression laid the blame on the victims themselves, showing them as passive "diaspora Jews" submitting to their extermination. Thus, for example, Agnon in his story "The Sign" decries the fate of his townspeople: "For the Land of Israel has given us the strength to stand up for our lives, while outside the land we went to meet the enemy like sheep to the slaughter."[32]

First published in 1944, "The Sign" was later included in the collection *The Fire and the Trees*, a title that recalls the biblical Sacrifice of Isaac. No other biblical story has been treated as obsessively by Israeli culture. In the context of the Holocaust, the Sacrifice joined the motif "like sheep to the slaughter," with Isaac perceived as the ultimate passive victim of a penal mechanism that is completely incomprehensible to its subject. The painting *The Sacrifice of Isaac* (1951), created by Maryan a year after he left Israel, has a "metal cutout" of Isaac hanging like a marionette facing a metal animal, part fish, part tank, part fire-spewing crematorium. Isaac is presented here as an androgynous figure, as are the figures in *Crematorium in Auschwitz*, who are also characterized by their gender fluidity. In this respect, Maryan's attitude is groundbreaking for his time and evokes a discourse that did not exist in Israel in the late 1940s.[33]

Metaphors from the world of animals were not only associated with the victims but also with the perpetrators, for example, the phrase "Nazi beast." The association of the Nazis to the animal world offers an explanation that comes with a certain relief: these were not human beings that perpetrated the Holocaust but savage animals. Following the Eichmann trial in 1961, these two central theses were undermined. Hearing the witness accounts of Holocaust survivors made clear that many of them were far from passive subjects walking "like sheep to the slaughter," acting at times against other prisoners in their attempts to survive. In parallel, the image of the "Nazi beast" was also eroded. It was Hannah Arendt who coined the phrase "the banality of evil"[34] in the context of Eichmann and the Nazis, seeking to understand the Holocaust not as an animalistic phenomenon but as the result of human bureaucratic behavior.

In this respect, it can be said that Maryan was different from his fellow artists in relation to the Holocaust. His work does not present a binary division between victims and perpetrators and there is no attempt to formulate a uniform symbolism or to present an "authentic depiction" of the camps and the extermination. He does not sit comfortably within the category later known in Israel as the "artist-witness." Maryan's figures recall Kurzweil's question to Agnon in a letter about Balak: "I have read the book three times or so . . . but I have doubts about Balak, there is no constant symbolism here."[35] In Maryan's works generally there is great complexity, even more when it comes to revealing himself and his biography: it contains both the mimesis of the artistic act, and its complete rejection as an "act of Balak." Often, when Maryan recounts his past, he turns to animals as symbols of sorts, which hold both his time during the Holocaust and the time that preceded it:

> They put us in a line, and I was the last one to be executed . . . they always aimed at the neck, which they missed, and everybody screamed and continued to move and were shot again somewhere else. My turn came and I felt nothing anymore. They shot at my neck and of course missed. As you know, I am still alive. Of course, after having been through such a "circus," it isn't surprising I carry such terrible guilt.

> It reminds me of my cock story. When I was obliged to go to the slaughter, he also half missed killing the cock. Because the cock was strong, it freed itself from the nail and

ran in the courtyard with its head hanging on a thread and I fled, running home . . . My father went to fetch it.[36]

Adam, Son of a Dog

Yoram Kaniuk (1930–2013) studied with Bursztyn for several months at the department for applied graphics in Bezalel. As far as we know, they had no personal connection. And yet it seems that, of all the artists active in Israel when Bursztyn lived there, Kaniuk is the closest to him artistically, even if he is the furthest from him in terms of biography. Born in Tel Aviv, Yoram was the son of Moshe Kaniuk, the first administrative director of the Tel Aviv Museum of Art. He joined the Palmach at seventeen and fought in the battles over Jerusalem in the War of Independence. He can be seen as the figure of the Sabra, in direct opposition to Bursztyn—the Holocaust survivor. And yet Kaniuk is fascinated by the figures of diaspora Jews, and writes about them:

> The attitude of Eretz-Israel Jews to the Holocaust survivors was shameful. And later when I returned from the War in 1948, I worked on the immigrant ship *Pan York*, and we brought 3,000 people on every trip. And the first time I returned from a trip of that sort, I wrote an article entitled "I Hate the Jewish people" and sent it to Shlonsky to publish in the daily *Al Hamishmar*. That is because a young kibbutz boy had said: "we warned them and warned them, and they didn't want to come—so they deserve what happened to them!" That is how it was, something that passed through our ranks. But on my second trip I looked at these Jews and I was fascinated by them. Afterwards I wrote books and stories and articles about these Jews, because they were the biggest survivors in history. They were strong, interesting and very miserable; I fell in love with them on the ship.[37]

In *Adam Resurrected* (1968), Kaniuk's first novel, Adam Stein, a circus ringleader and the most wonderful Jewish clown in Weimar Berlin, is sent to a concentration camp with his wife and daughter.[38] The camp commander, who used to watch him as a child in Berlin, turns Stein into his dog, making him walk on all fours and bark on command. At the peak of the novel Adam Stein entertains his daughter and wife on their journey

Maryan, *Untitled*, ca. 1950. Ink on paper, 8¼ × 10⅝ inches (21 × 27 cm). Private Collection

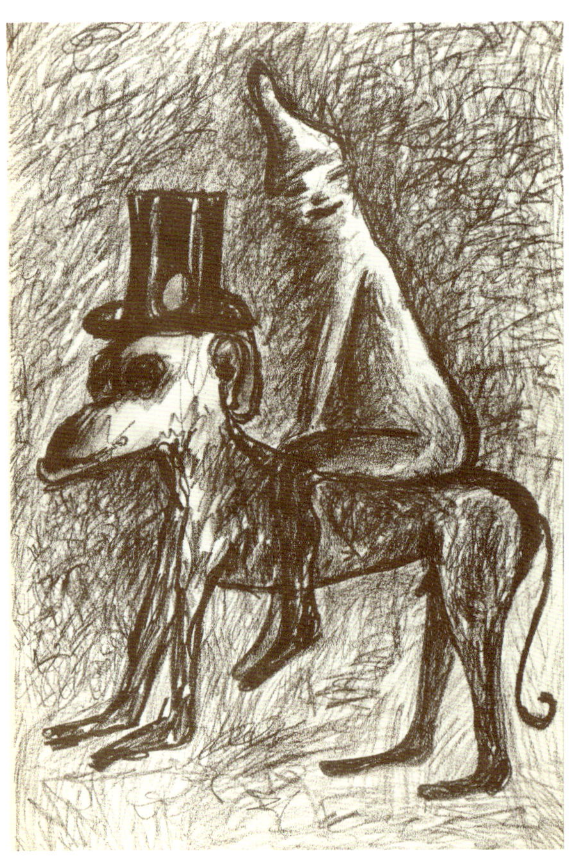 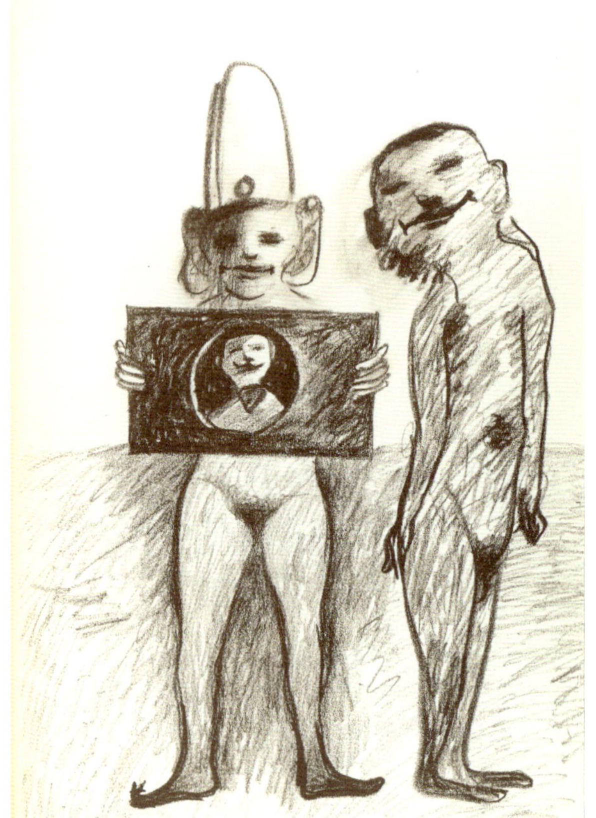

Maryan, *Untitled*, from the lithograph album "The Human Menagerie," 1961. Lithographs, 17¼ × 12¼ inches (43.9 × 31 cm). Collection of the Yad Vashem Art Museum, Jerusalem. Acquisition, courtesy of Barbara and Lewis Shrensky, Washington, DC

to the crematorium. The story unfolds in three heterotopic spaces: the circus, the concentration camp, and the psychiatric asylum, whose parallel dynamics merge in Adam Stein's mind. The story is told from Stein's time in Israel of the 1960s where he is sent to an asylum for Holocaust survivors in the desert. Stein is a victim consumed by guilt, but also a violent abuser of Gina, the asylum's head nurse, who he confuses in his mind with both his wife and a circus performer.

The artistic mechanism at work in *Adam Resurrected* is almost identical to that of the lithograph series *The Human Menagerie*, which Maryan created in 1961. The series presents marginalized human figures who act in a circus-like dynamic. They are weak and vulnerable just as much as they are barbaric and violent; humans who are demonic dogs, "sheep to the slaughter" who are also savage animals; figures active in sadomasochistic acts combining sex, death, pain, and pleasure. Maryan's pantheon of human–animal figures, like the multilayered figure of Kaniuk's Adam Stein, undermine the period's hegemonic-official Holocaust discourse because they do away with the binary division. Maryan's treatment of the Holocaust is part of his preoccupation with a chaotic human space and with dynamic power relations. The human and the animal interweave; viewers are attracted to

Maryan's work for its sense of danger and want to make sense of it, to glean some truth. Yet the closer we move our attempt to understand, the bigger the danger we get bitten by Balak.

Back to the Port of Haifa: Farewell Pinkas Bursztyn

We return to our opening image: a young Holocaust survivor disembarks from a ship at the Port of Haifa. The agency official on the dock gives one look at his body and declares him an invalid. If only he had been greeted by Odysseus's old wet nurse, she would surely have recognized him by feeling his stump and greeted him on his return home. The amputated leg and the number tattooed on his arm are Pinkas Bursztyn's "Odysseus's scar." In his book *Mimesis* (1946), which centers on the question of the representation of the world by means of art, Erich Auerbach understands Odysseus's scar as the meeting point of reality and fiction. The tragic hero's old wound becomes his attribute and, as in the artistic act, a representation of a past catastrophe.[39]

In the last six months of his stay in Israel, Bursztyn left Bezalel and prepared to travel to Paris. During this time he was busy trying to organize a solo exhibition in Jerusalem, which would summarize his three years in the country.

At Bezalel there was no one to help him, and he couldn't find a gallery that would agree to display his works. Finally, with the help of Miriam Tal and the sculptor David Palombo, Bursztyn opened his solo exhibition on January 8, 1950, in the YMCA building in Jerusalem. Forty-seven works were exhibited, and the binding of the exhibition pamphlet showed a cat with a curved spine. When the exhibition ended Bursztyn left most of the works in the country. Maryan S. Maryan departed the Port of Haifa for Paris, leaving Pinkas Bursztyn behind on the dock.

NOTES

1. Joseph Mundy, "Conversation: Maryan at La Coupole," in *Maryan's Personnages: Works in Chicago Collections, 1958–75,* ed. Michele Vishny (Chicago: Spertus Museum of Judaica, 1983), 50-51.
2. Max Nordau coined the term *muscular Judaism* at the Second World Zionist Congress, in Basel, in August 1898. Nordau argued the need for a "new Jew," healthy in body and soul, who was needed for the realization of Zionist goals.
3. Avner Holzman, "Old Jews, New Hebrews," *Haaretz*, April 2, 2002, https://www.haaretz.com/life/books/2002-04-02/ty-article/old-jews-new-hebrews/0000017f-f4e9-d460-afff-ffef40670000.
4. "'Sabra,' scion of the generation spawned by the pioneers of the early aliyahs, the first generation of the 'Hebrew revolution' . . . this classification includes natives of the country born in the first three decades of the twentieth century . . . The origin of the term is unclear apart from being a native cactus in Israel. It is common to see the term as an expression of external roughness and sarcasm." Oz Almog, "The Figure of the Sabra," in *New Jewish Time: Jewish Culture in a Secular Era—An Encyclopedic Look*, vol. 4 (Jerusalem: Keter Publishing, 2007), 298 [Hebrew].
5. "Old people's colony" is how Bursztyn referred to the place; it was a retirement home for new immigrants in the Bat Galim neighborhood in Haifa.
6. Yehuda Bacon, conversation with author, Jerusalem, May 15, 2022 (all quotes from Bacon are from this conversation). Bacon (born 1929, Czechoslovakia) is a Holocaust survivor and a friend of Bursztyn's from Bezalel Academy. He studied at Bezalel from 1946 to 1952 and then taught there, and was a witness at the Eichmann trial in 1961.
7. Mundy, "Conversation: Maryan at La Coupole," 51. In fact, Maryan was only there for five months. He arrived in the country on May 15, 1947, and began studying at Bezalel on October 7, 1947.
8. Franz Kafka's "In the Penal Colony" (In der Strafkolonie) was published in 1919. Maryan did not refer directly to the story; his main preoccupation was with Kafka's novel *The Trial* (he published an album of drawings relating to this book in 1953).
9. The dog Balak first appears in short stories by Agnon, and later in the novel *Only Yesterday*, published in 1945.
10. The Second Aliyah is the wave of immigration from Eastern Europe to Palestine in 1904–14.
11. S. Y. Agnon, *Only Yesterday*, trans. Barbara Harshav (Princeton, NJ: Princeton University Press, 2018), 631.
12. In Bursztyn's solo exhibition in Israel in 1950 there was a painting titled *A17986*, his number in Auschwitz. The painting was lost and is undocumented.
13. Mundy, "Conversation: Maryan at La Coupole," 53.
14. Baruch Kurzweil, *Essays on the Stories of S. Y. Agnon* (Tel Aviv: Shocken, 1975), 104 [Hebrew].
15. Ibid., 110.
16. Michal Arbel, *"Written on the Dog's Skin," S. Y. Agnon: Concepts of Creativity and Art* (Jerusalem: Keter Publishing, 2006).
17. "The abject confronts us, on the one hand, with those fragile states where man strays on the territories of animal. Thus, by way of abjection, primitive societies have marked out a precise area of their culture to remove it from the threatening world of animals or animalism, which were imagined as representations of sex and murder." Julia Kristeva, *Powers of Horror: An Essay on Abjection*, trans. Leon S. Roudiez (New York: Columbia University Press, 1982), 21.
18. In Jerusalem Bursztyn worked as a set designer for the Rina Nikova Ballet.
19. Mordecai Ardon (1896, Poland–1992, Jerusalem) was an Israeli painter and the third director of the New Bezalel Art Academy, from 1940 to 1952.
20. Mordecai Ardon, "Note for the Supervising Committee," 1942, Jerusalem City Archive, box no. 218, original file no. 63.
21. Student attendance log, 1947–48, Jerusalem City Archive, box no. 225, original file no. 251.
22. Hanna Yablonka, "The Absorption of Holocaust Survivors in the State of Israel—New Perspectives," *Studies in Zionism, the Yishuv and the State of Israel,* vol. 7, Ben-Gurion Institute, Ben-Gurion University of the Negev, 1997, 290 [Hebrew].
23. Arikha, like Maryan, was also preoccupied by the figure of Balak in the early 1950s and even mentioned the mental closeness he felt to this figure. Agnon's novel *A Stray Dog* was published by Tarshish Books (Jerusalem) in 1952, with drawings by Arikha.
24. The monastery is most likely Talitha Kumi near Bezalel. The building served as student lodgings at the end of the 1940s and in the early 1950s. Yoram Kaniuk's book *Soap*, published posthumously in 2018, recounts the story of four students who live at Talitha Kumi in the late 1940s.
25. Following the siege on Jerusalem and the Jordanian fire, the Hebrew University at Mount Scopus was closed and some of its classes moved to Bezalel, which is likely when Bacon and Bursztyn attended them.
26. Miriam Tal (1910, the Russian Empire–1981, Israel) was an art critic, writer, poet, and Israeli delegate in Brussels in the 1950s. She took Bursztyn under her wing, helped him in the early stages of his artistic career in Israel and in Paris, and was a supportive friend all his life.
27. Maryan to Miriam Tal, Jerusalem, May 19, 1950, *My Name Is Maryan* exhibition file, December 2022–June 2023, Tel Aviv Museum of Art Archive [Hebrew].
28. Maryan to Tal, Jerusalem, October 24, 1950, *My Name Is Maryan* exhibition file, December 2022–June 2023, Tel Aviv Museum of Art Archive [Hebrew].
29. The War of Independence began on May 15, 1948, and officially ended on July 20, 1949.
30. Nathan Zach (1930, Berlin–2020, Israel) was a major Israeli poet.
31. Nathan Zach, "Fighter with No Message," in *Maryan: Retrospective 1927–1977* (Tel Aviv: Haifa University Gallery and Tel Aviv Museum of Art, 1977), 9 [Hebrew].
32. S. Y. Agnon, "The Sign," trans. Arthur Green, *Response* 7, no. 3 (Fall 1973): 6.
33. This subject, worthy of future scholarship, is beyond the scope of this article.
34. Arendt coined this phrase in a book based on her reports from the Eichmann trial in Israel for the *New Yorker* magazine. In Israel the book generated a contentious debate and was published in Hebrew only four decades after its publication elsewhere. See Hannah Arendt, *Eichmann in Jerusalem: A Report on the Banality of Evil* (New York: Viking Press, 1963).
35. Baruch Kurzweil to S. Y. Agnon, January 1946, in *Kurzweil–Agnon–Uri Zvi Greenberg: Correspondence (1942–1971),* ed. Lillian Dabby-Joury (Ramat Gan: Bar Ilan University Press, 1987), 19 [Hebrew].
36. Maryan, "Autobiography," in *Ariel 42*, February 1977, 7. Brochure for Maryan's exhibition at Galerie Ariel, Paris, 1977.
37. Yoram Kaniuk, "Learning to be a Jew," talk given at Beit Bialik, Tel Aviv, on November 5, 2009, ahead of the republication of his book *The Last Jew*.
38. Yoram Kaniuk, *Adam Resurrected*, trans. Seymour Simckes (New York: Grove Press, 1971). The Hebrew title of the book translates literally as "Adam Son of Dog."
39. Erich Auerbach, *Mimesis: The Representation of Reality in Western Literature*, trans. Willard R. Trask (Princeton, NJ: Princeton University Press, 1953), 3–24.

תש"י

תערוכת

פנחס

בורשטיין

1950

EXHIBITION

OF

PINHAS

BURSTEIN

EARLY WORK

Pinkas Bursztyn's dreams of becoming an artist were forestalled by the devastating effects of World War II. From 1939, at the age of twelve, to 1945, Burstzyn was interned at various forced labor camps and at the Auschwitz and Birkenau concentration camps in Poland. Burstzyn miraculously survived despite being left for dead with eight bullets lodged in his body; his leg was amputated as part of the operation to save his life. He spent a year in recovery in Częstochowa, Poland, where he learned to live without his leg. He was later transferred to a United Nations Relief and Rehabilitation Administration displaced persons camp in Germany.

In 1947 an official of the Jewish Agency convinced Burstzyn to travel to what was then British Mandate Palestine, where Burstzyn was told he could live in a kibbutz and study art. Once he arrived in Haifa, he was labeled "handicapped" and placed in a settlement for elderly refugees. Burstzyn submitted an application to the New Bezalel Academy of Art in Jerusalem via the Jewish Agency. His application was accepted and after a five-month wait, on October 7, 1947, he arrived at the preparatory program for applied graphics at the New Bezalel. At Bezalel he mostly practiced applied arts. Despite these limitations, in this period Burstzyn began to pursue art, developing his own unique style of figuration.

At Bezalel students were encouraged to depict subjects that were in keeping with the positive national image projected by the newly formed State of Israel. While, outside of his coursework, young Burstzyn explored imagery that directly related to his experience in the camps, his official output explored more prosaic and secular subjects, dabbling in various established genres.

Among his surviving juvenilia are a number of self-portraits Burstzyn made using lithography as well as black-and-white line drawings. A surviving landscape painting shows the sun rising over Jerusalem, and Burstzyn also tried his hand at the classical nude (*Nude Women,* 1950) as well as a number of animal portraits, including his menacing *The Black Cat* (1948) and *Doves Wounded* (1949). Although the canvas does not survive, an early photograph of Bursztyn in his Jerasalem studio (ca. 1948–49)—a converted space in a former Ottoman prison that became Talitha Kumi convent—shows a painting in progress that typified the propagandistic imagery of the new state of Israel. Two figures are shown gathered around a table, a mustachioed man and a woman, both embodying the idealized native-born "Sabra," the healthy, heroic men who were conscripted in the fight for Israeli independence and who were symbols of the rising nationalism that unified the embattled country. While this canvas has been lost, it is emblematic of the early ideological struggles and prohibitions that imprinted upon Bursztyn's early work in Israel as he was simultaneously searching for his artistic voice. —AMG

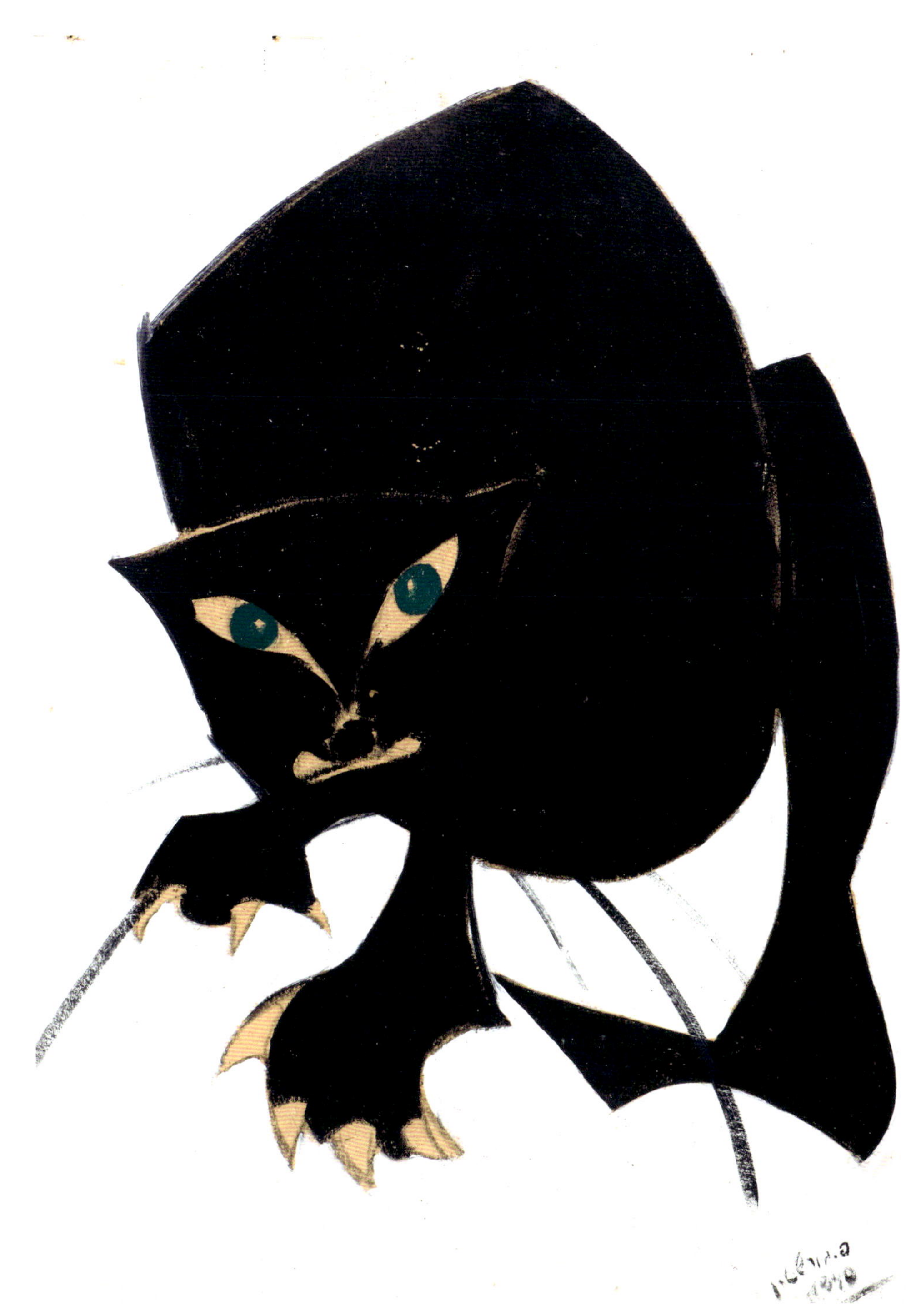

Pinkas Bursztyn, *The Black Cat*, 1949. Oil on cardboard, 33 × 22½ inches (84 × 57 cm). Levin Collection, Jerusalem

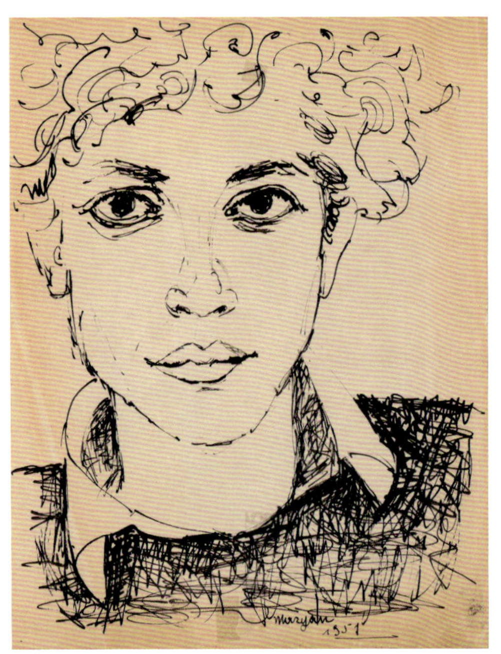

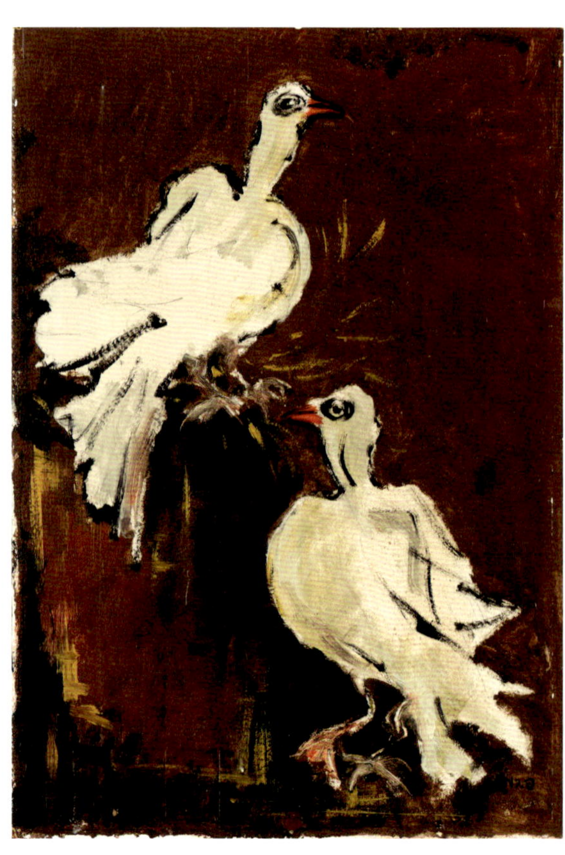

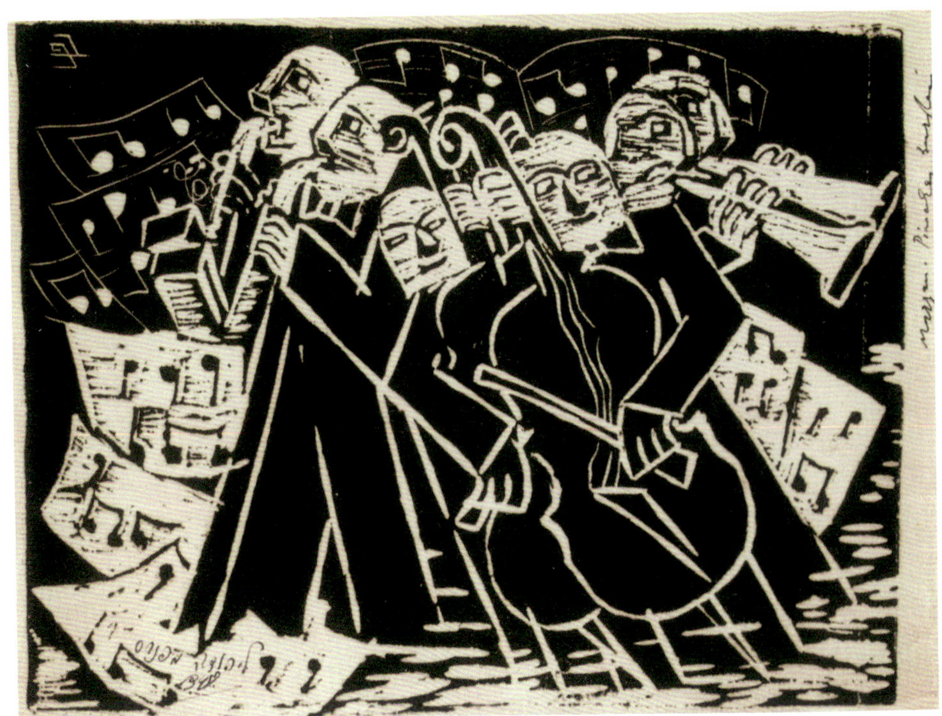

Clockwise from top left
Pinkas Bursztyn, *Self-Portrait*, 1951. India ink on paper, 10⅝ × 8¼ inches (27 × 21 cm)
Pinkas Bursztyn, *Doves (Wounded)*, 1949. Oil on wooden panel, 27½ × 19⅛ inches (70 × 48.5 cm). Collection of Neomi
and David Kolitz, Tel Aviv, Israel
Pinkas Bursztyn, *Musicians*, 1948. Linocut, 8⅝ × 13⅛ inches (22 × 33.5 cm). Estate of Yehuda Bacon, Jerusalem

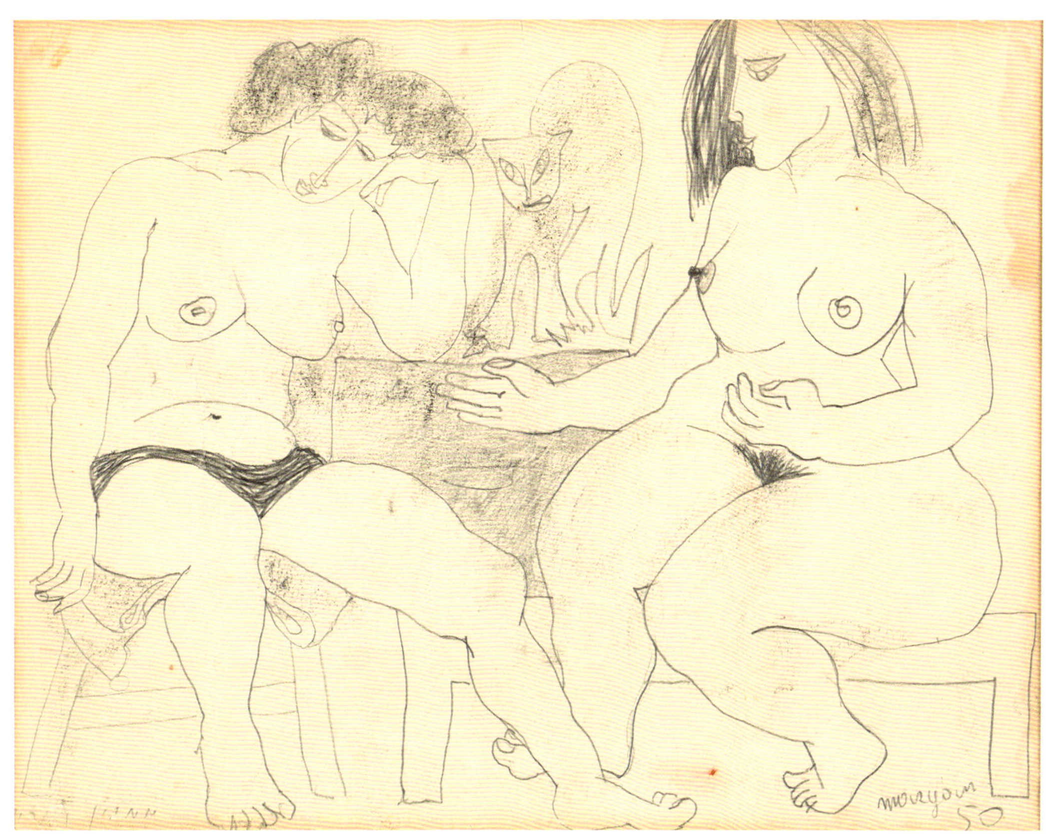

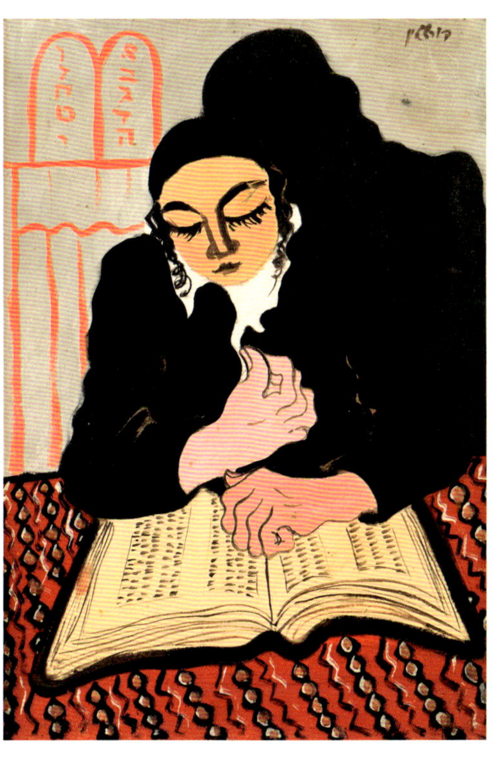

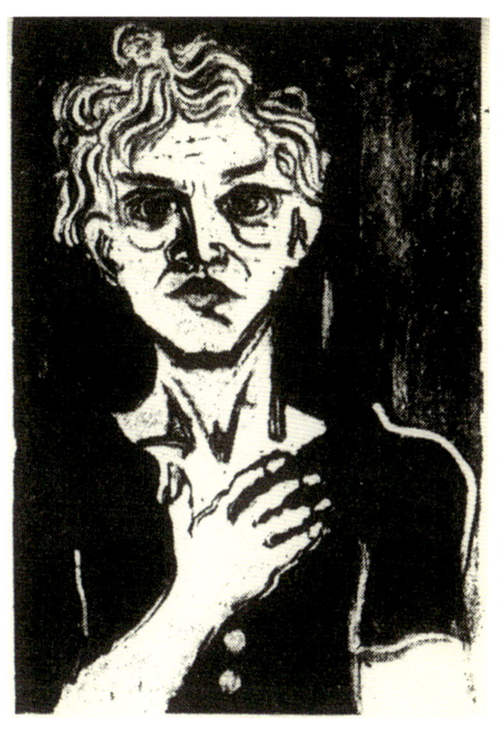

Clockwise from top left
Maryan, *Nude Women*, 1950. Pencil on paper, 9⅞ × 12¼ inches (25 × 31 cm). Private Collection, Ramat Gan, Israel
Pinkas Bursztyn, *Self-Portrait*, ca. 1948–49. Linocut, dimensions unknown
Pinkas Bursztyn, *Boy Reading Talmud*, ca. 1947–50. Oil on cardboard mounted on canvas, 27½ × 19⅛ inches (70 × 48.5 cm).
Collection of Tamar and Avner Keshet, Rishon LeZion, Israel

SHOAH AND JEWISH IDENTITY

Maryan's traumatic experience of the Holocaust is omnipresent in his work, although most of the references are veiled. In the late 1940s, however, when the trauma was recent, he was living in Israel, and had not yet changed his name, Maryan made direct representations of his experiences in Auschwitz and Birkenau. These include his haunting early painting *The Yellow Star* (1947–49) and the drawings now conserved at the Ghetto Fighters' House, a museum founded in 1949 by Holocaust survivors living at Kibbutz Lohamei Hagetaot in Israel. He returned to these explicit expressions of his trauma more than two decades later in New York.

The works produced in the late 1940s establish a visual language rooted in figuration yet gravitating toward an avant-garde aesthetic. Jewish identity is an important theme in Burstzyn's early works, in which he depicts archetypal subjects such as Talmud students, Yemeni Jews, and rabbis. He continued with some of these themes even after leaving Israel for Paris in 1950, when he used the name Maryan for the first time. Sacrificial lambs and rams are the subject of a series of drawings made early in his Paris tenure, in which he situated the biblical tale of the sacrifice of Isaac amid the barbed wire of the camps.

The Yellow Star, one of the artist's earliest known works, is a portrait of a Jewish concentration camp prisoner. Burstzyn made it while a refugee in Israel. The figure's emaciated face is depicted using the same yellow that is found on the Star of David, inscribed with the German word *Jude*, on the prisoner's striped uniform. Such graphic symbolism becomes a leitmotif in later Maryan works. The emotional intensity and autobiographical nature of *The Yellow Star* also prefigures the psychic intensity of later works.

In her groundbreaking 1993 book *Depiction and Interpretation*, Israeli American art historian Ziva Amishai-Maisels credits Maryan as being among the first artist-eyewitnesses of the Holocaust to directly depict on canvas the atrocities he experienced. *Crematorium in Auschwitz* (1949) portrays five stylized figures in the throes of death. Amishai-Maisels interprets this large canvas as combining gassing and burning in the crematorium. She conjectures that Maryan's anger is expressed in the figure's raised fist in the upper right of the composition. Amishai-Maisels notes the ambivalence of this painting, which is rooted in Maryan's personal knowledge of the camps. The figures are not portrayed only as innocent victims helplessly clinging together; they also scratch and climb over one another trying to escape. "In *Crematorium in Auschwitz*, he demonstrated the ambivalence of the state of being a victim or an oppressor—one can easily become the other."[1] This ambivalence, along with the malleability of human monstrosity and victimhood, are themes that become sublimated in Maryan's mature oeuvre. —AMG

1. Ziva Amishai-Maisels, Depiction and Interpretation: The Influence of the Holocaust on the Visual Arts (Oxford: Butterworth-Heinemann, 1983), 238.

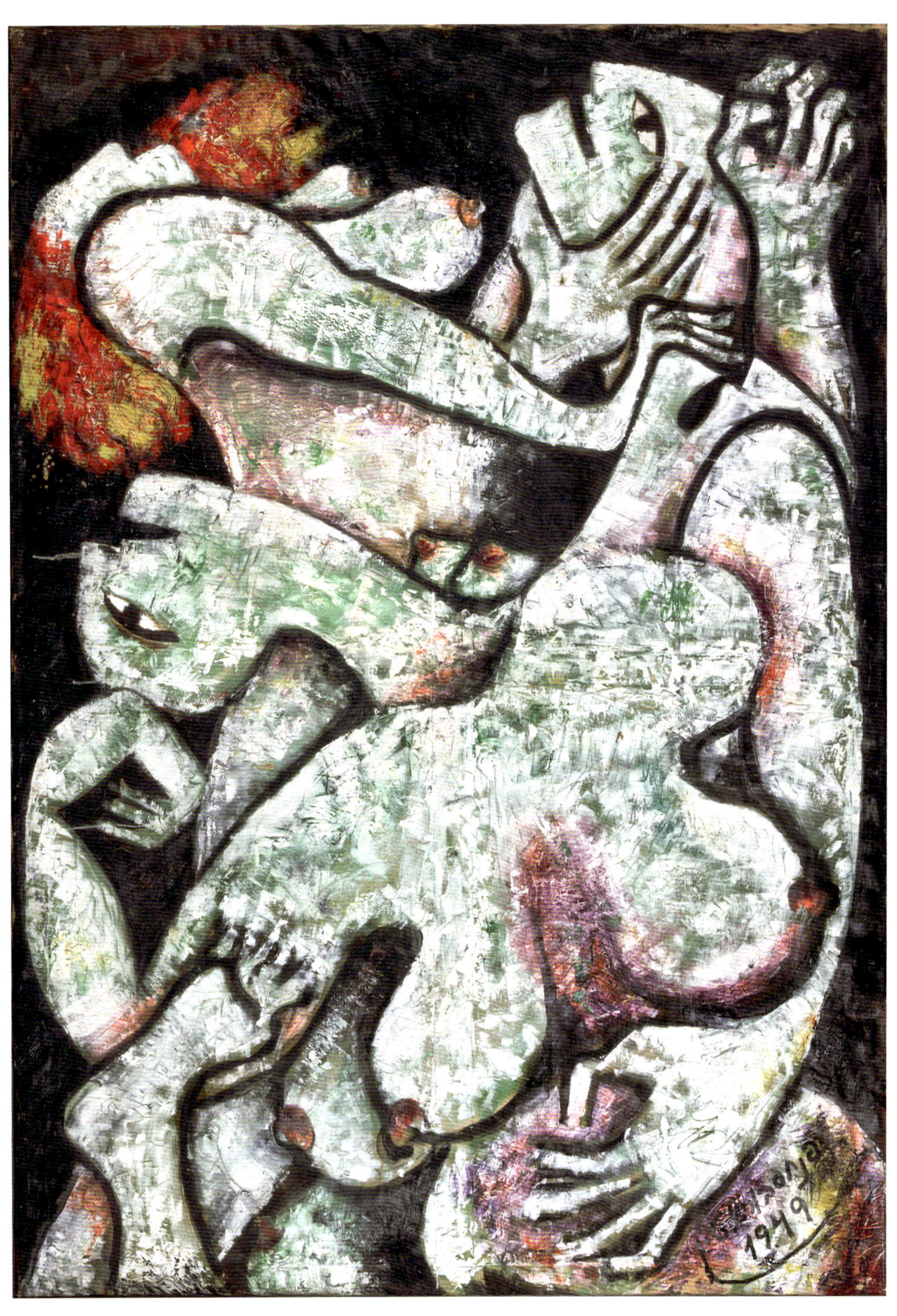

Crematorium in Auschwitz, 1949. Oil on canvas, 63 × 41 inches (160 × 105 cm).
Collection of Marsha and Assaph Caspi, Israel

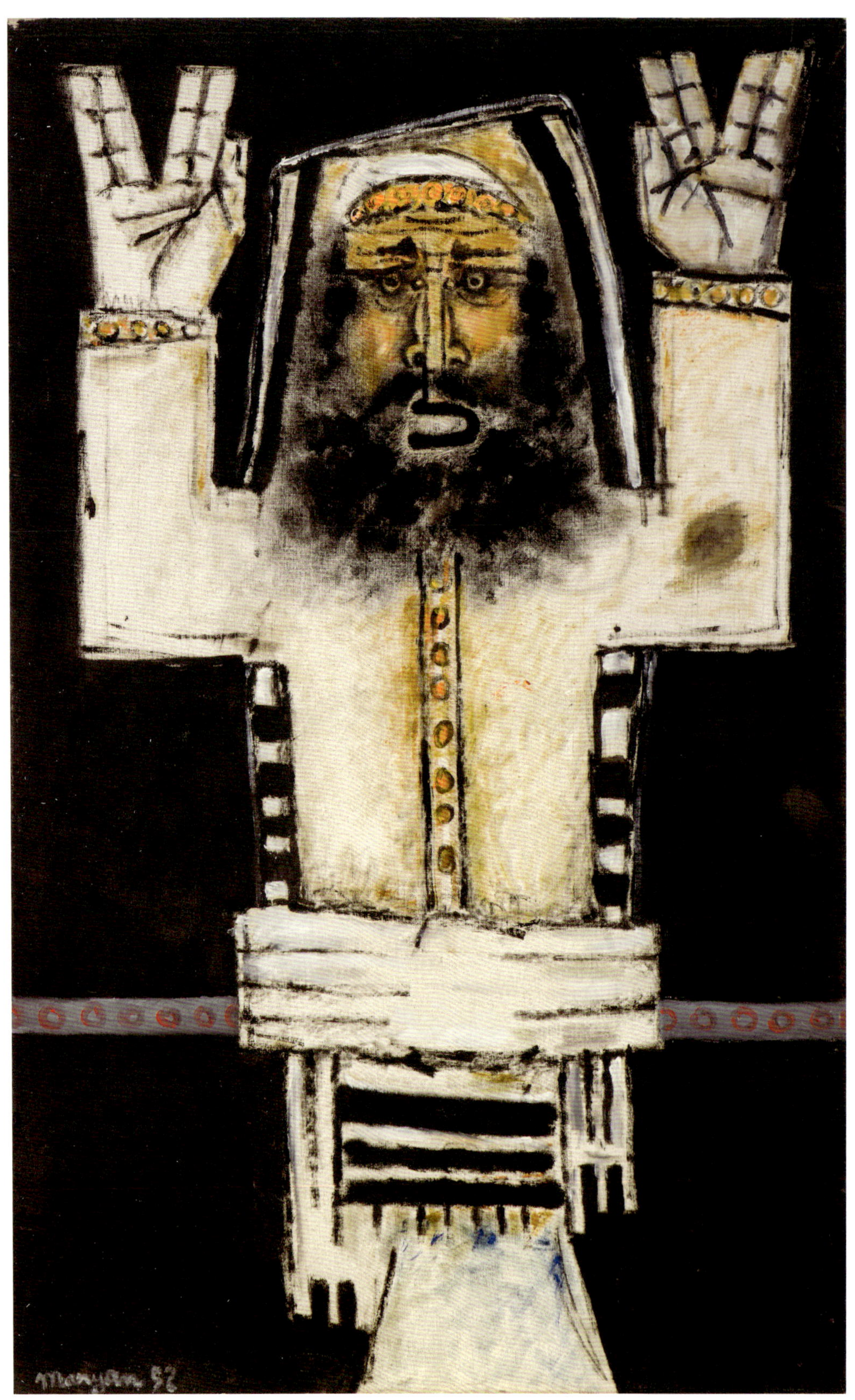

Untitled, 1952. Oil on canvas, 45 × 28¾ inches (116 × 73 cm). Private Collection

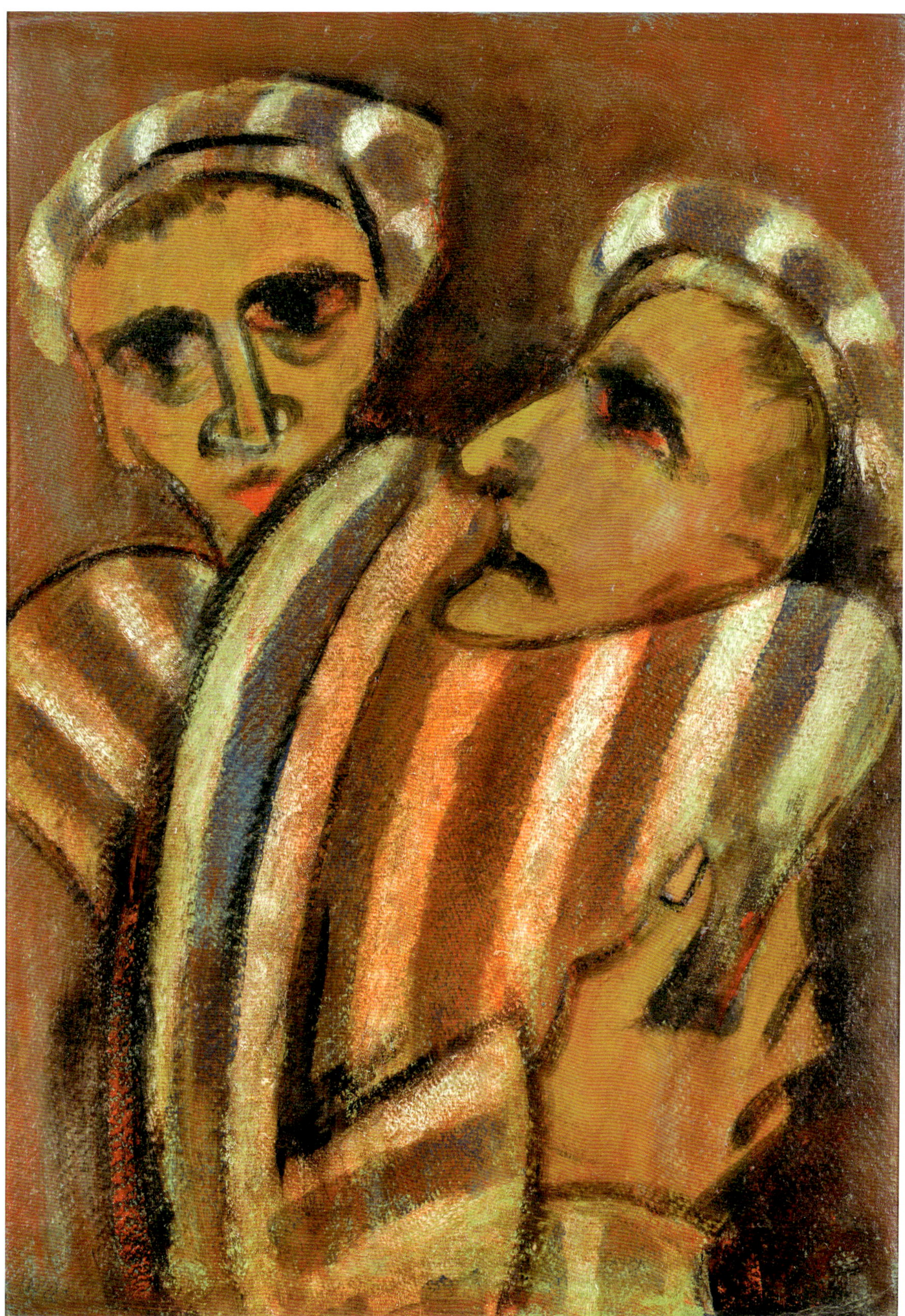

  Two Inmates, 1947–49. Oil on canvas, 27½ × 19 inches (70 × 50 cm). Courtesy of Ghetto Fighters House Archive, Israel

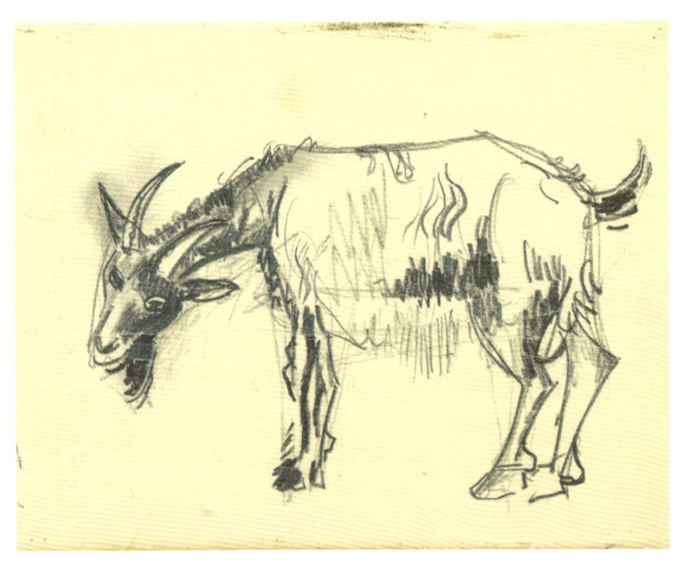
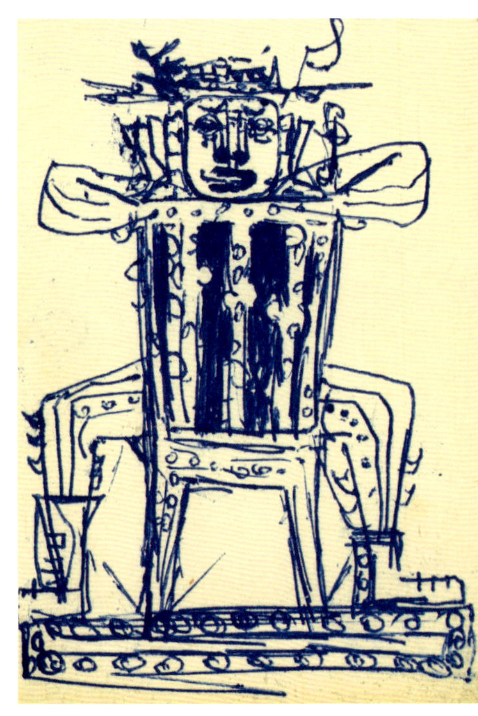
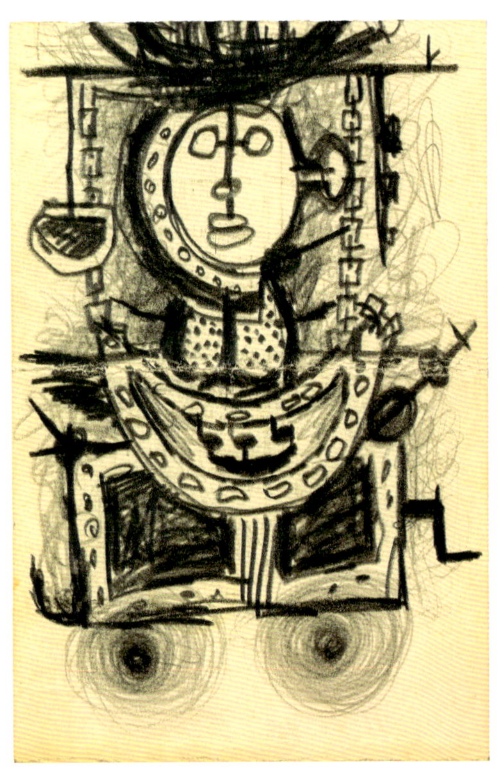
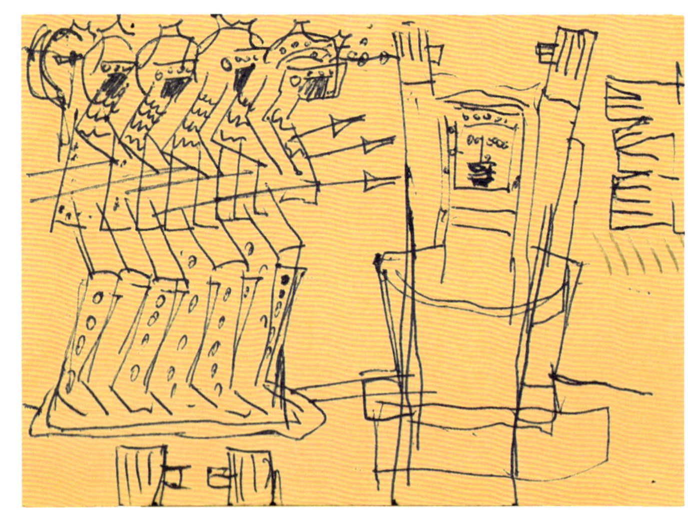

Clockwise from top left
Untitled, ca. 1950. Ink on paper, 8¼ × 10⅝ inches (21 × 27 cm). Private Collection
Untitled, ca. 1950. Ink on paper, 4¼ × 3 inches (10.7 × 7.4 cm). Private Collection
Untitled, ca. 1950. Ink on paper, 4⅛ × 5¾ inches (10.5 × 14.5 cm). Private Collection
Untitled, ca. 1950. Ink on paper, 5⅞ × 3⅞ inches (15 × 10 cm). Private Collection

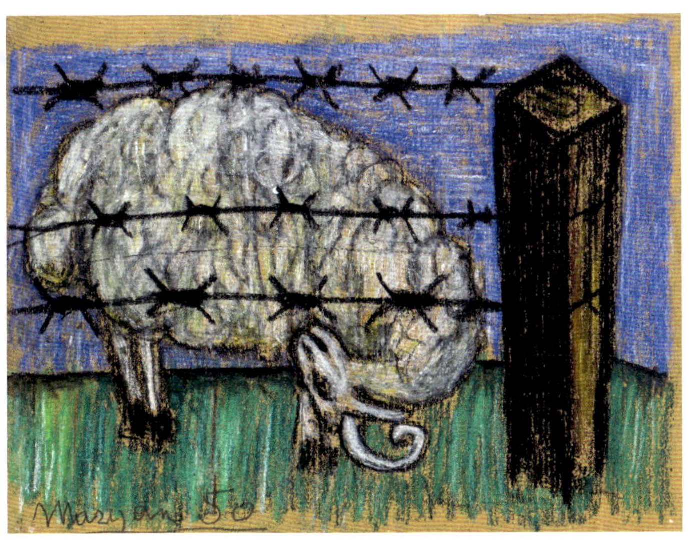

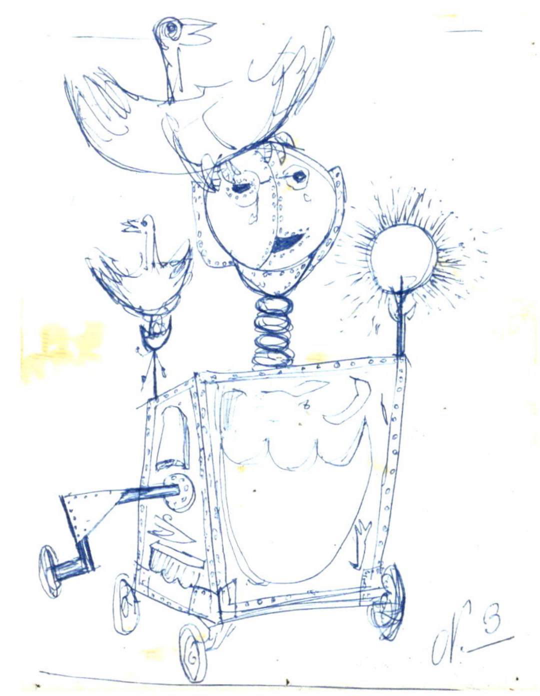

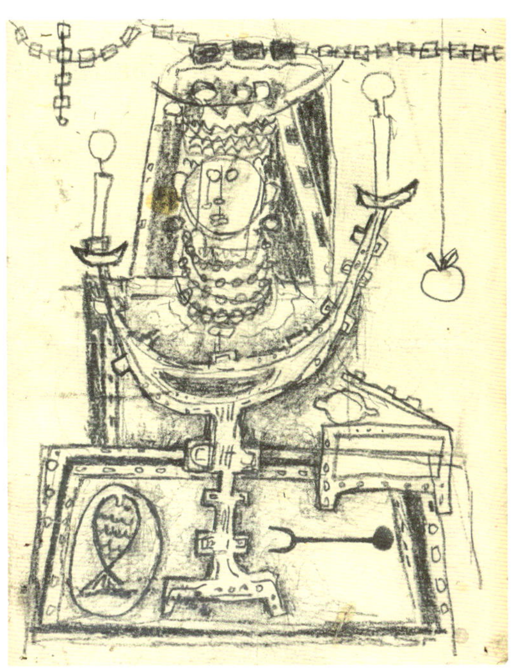

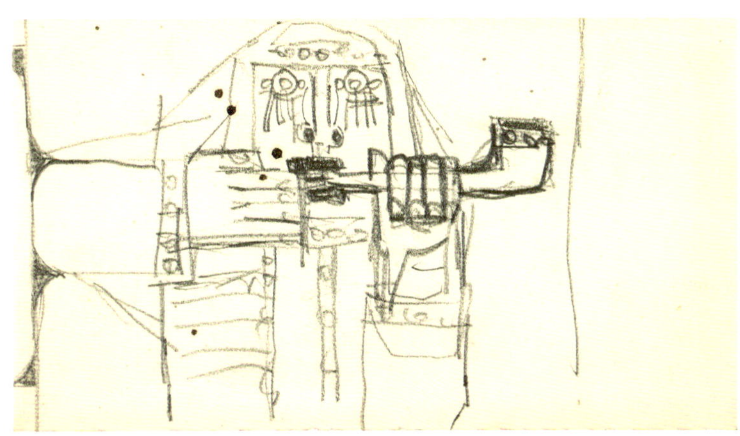

Clockwise from top left
Untitled, ca. 1950. Mixed media, 7½ × 10 inches (19.2 × 25.5 cm). Private Collection
Untitled, ca. 1950. Ink on paper, 10⅝ × 8¼ inches (27 × 21 cm). Private Collection
Untitled, ca. 1950. Ink on paper, 3¾ × 6⅝ inches (9.5 × 16.8 cm). Private Collection
Untitled, ca. 1950. Ink on paper, 8¼ × 10 inches (21 × 27 cm). Private Collection

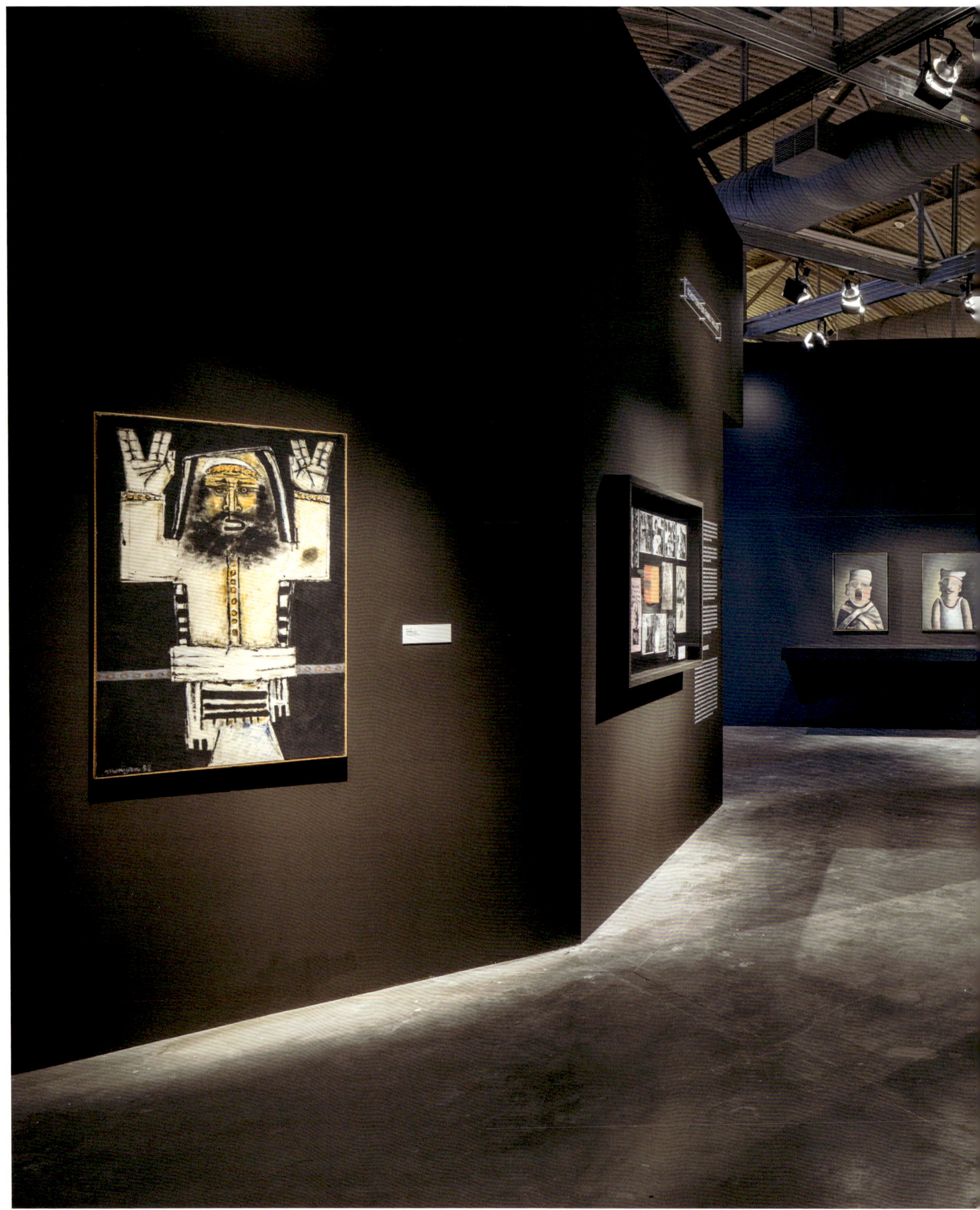

My Name Is Maryan, Museum of Contemporary Art, North Miami, 2022. Installation view

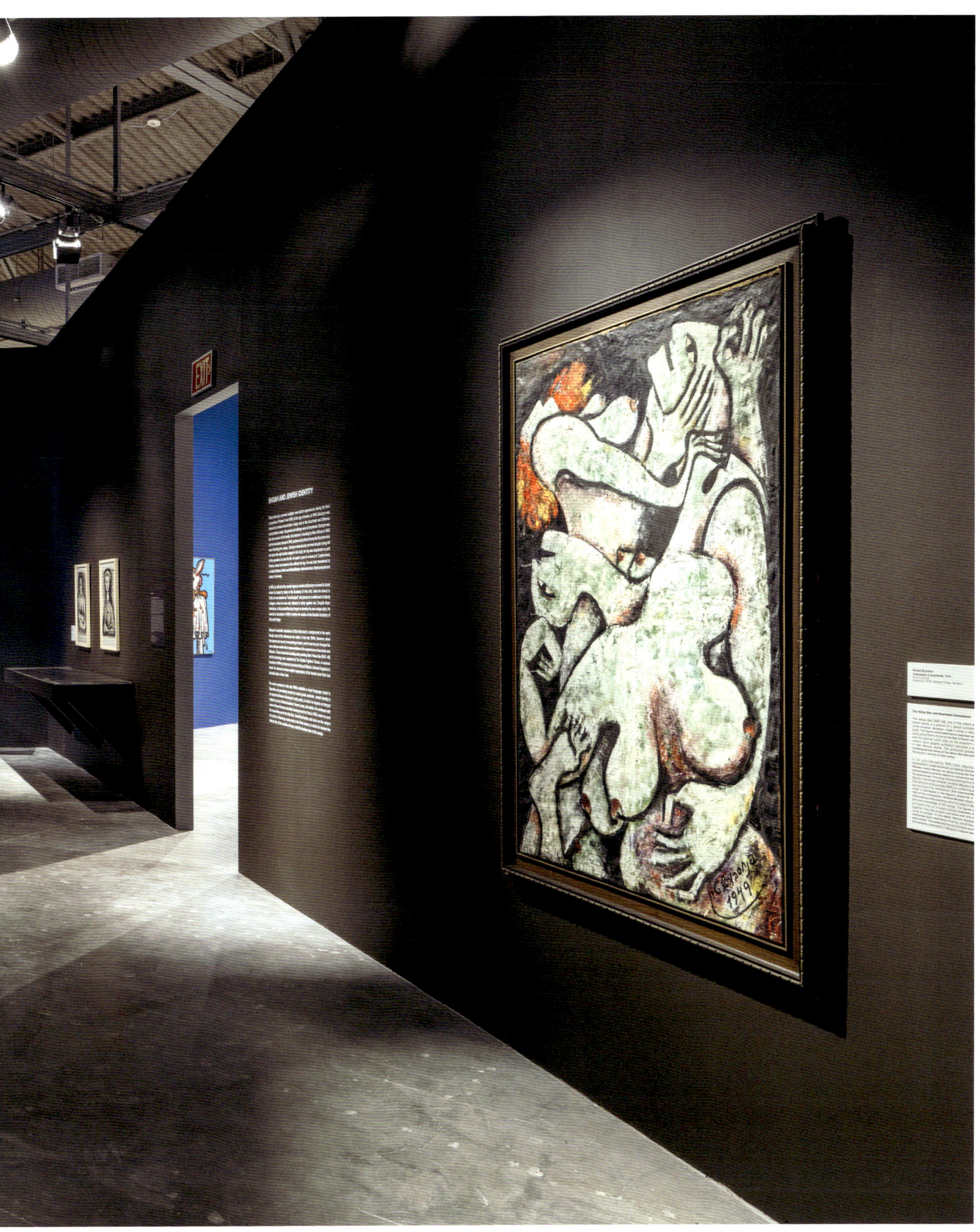

MARYAN IN THE 1950s

Moving to Paris to study at the École nationale supérieure des beaux-arts in 1950, Maryan found himself at the center of a diverse and vibrant artistic scene. Establishment figures from the prewar avant-garde, such as Pablo Picasso, Jean Dubuffet, Alberto Giacometti, and his teacher Fernand Léger exhibited alongside emerging postwar artists. While Maryan never formally aligned himself with any movement, his emerging art practice in the 1950s shared some formal and conceptual affinities with the CoBrA artists. Maryan became acquainted with CoBrA through Jean Atlan—a French Algerian Jewish artist and poet who was the main exponent of the movement in France.

CoBrA was an essential post–World War II movement named for its home cities of Copenhagen, Brussels, and Amsterdam. Abolishing divisions between figuration and abstraction, CoBrA began in the late 1940s as a loose, multinational artist collective. The eclectic CoBrA group was united by its political stance against Nazism and its desire to work through the traumas of the war. The artists' interest in experimental practices, non-Western art, the work of psychiatric patients and children, and ancient art formed their unique take on modernism.

At MOCA, key early works by Maryan from the 1950s were juxtaposed with an emblematic selection of works by CoBrA artists from the NSU Art Museum Fort Lauderdale's extensive holdings of the movement. This dialogue gives historical context to Maryan's seminal early works in which single figures, tormented animals, and complex landscapes emerge as among his signature themes. In parallel to the CoBrA group, Maryan was probing the grotesque and the menacing forces of the collective subconscious in the wake of World War II.

CoBrA artists attempted to theorize, in their eponymous journal and in their art, how the trauma of the war impacted society. An early manifesto stated, "A totally new creature comes into being, neither animal nor human, created by the artist's fantasy and in accord with human psychic needs."[1] While derived independently of each other, "human-animal" tropes in both Maryan and CoBrA works appear here in the menagerie of hybrid creatures, birds, snakes, and homunculi that populate the canvases in this ensemble. —AMG

1. Helhesten artists, "New Realism (Manifesto)," quoted in *Karen Kurczynski, The Art and Politics of Asger Jorn* (Farnham, Surrey: Ashgate, 2014), 47.

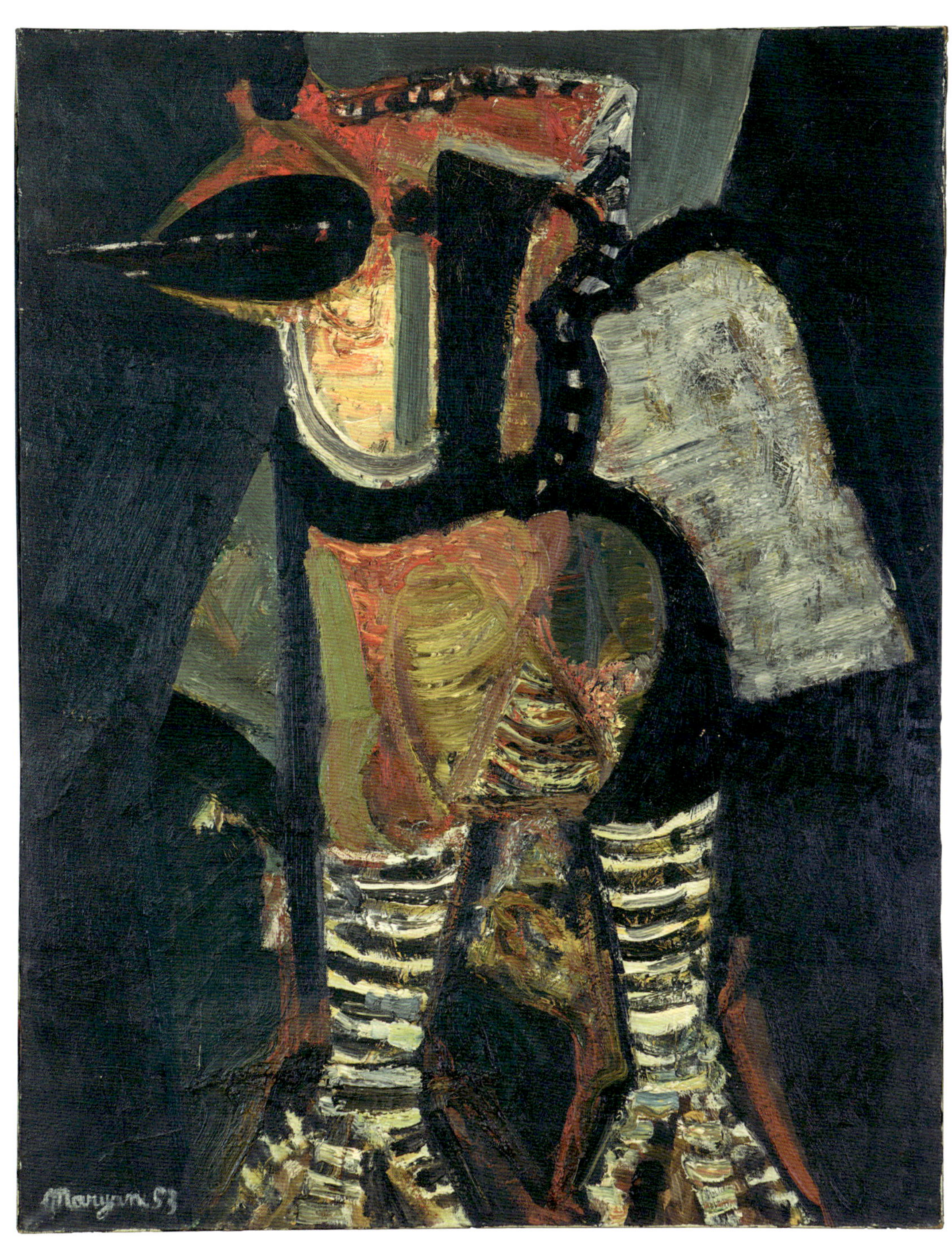

L'oiseau, 1953. Oil on canvas, 36 × 28¾ inches (91.4 × 73 cm).
Collection of Mr. David Rosenhaft, Stamford, CT, courtesy of Taylor Graham Gallery, New York, NY

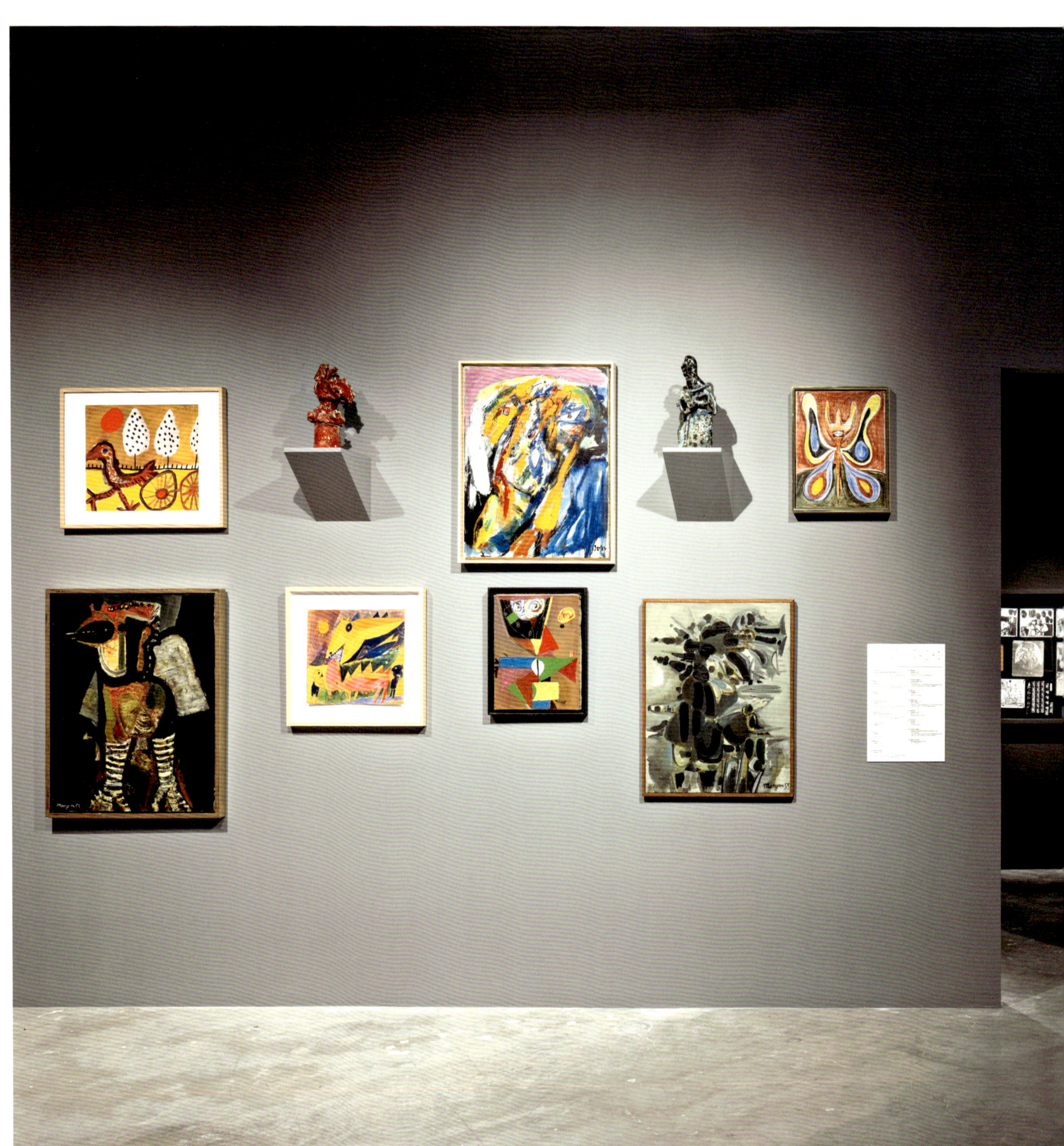

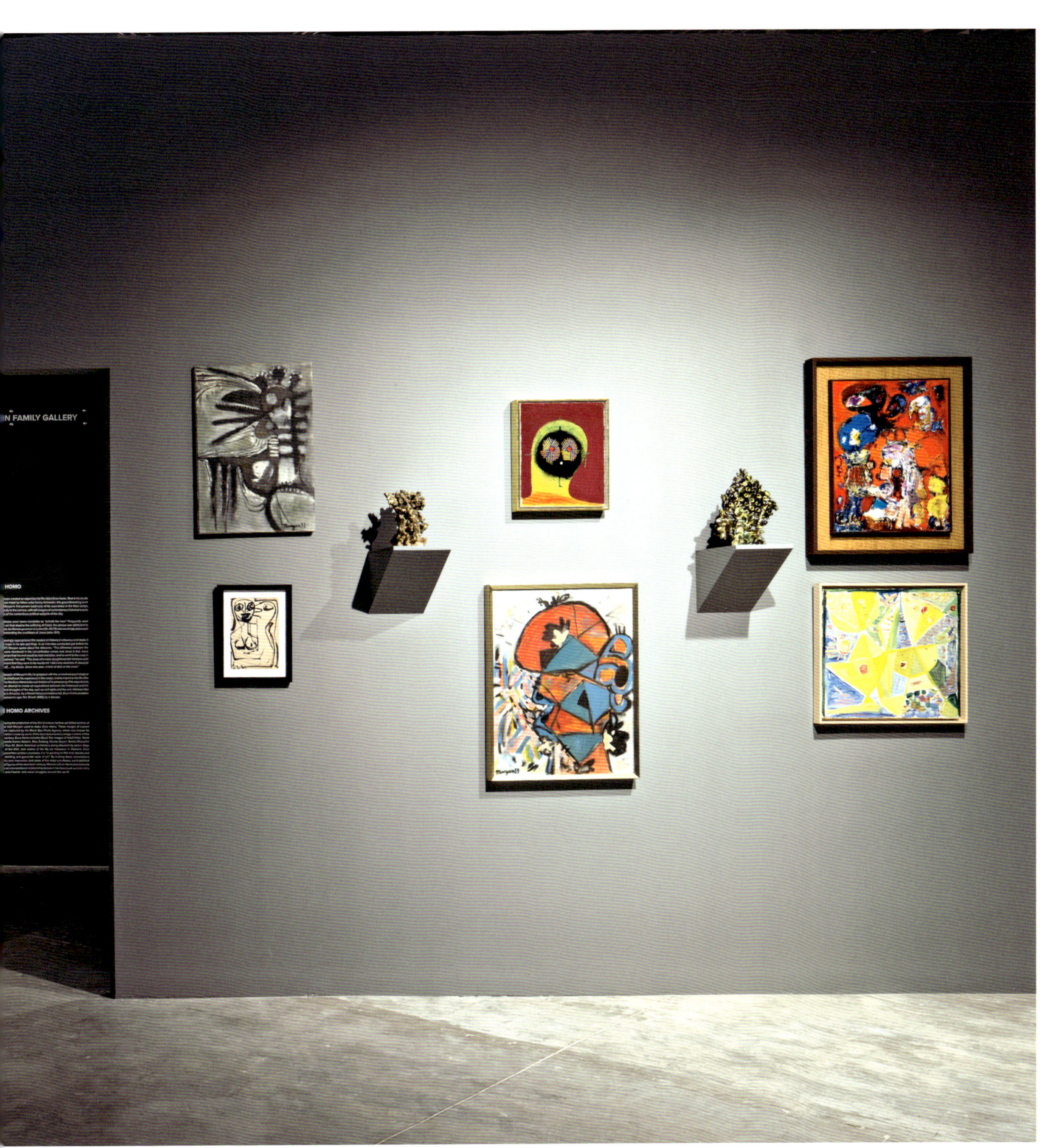

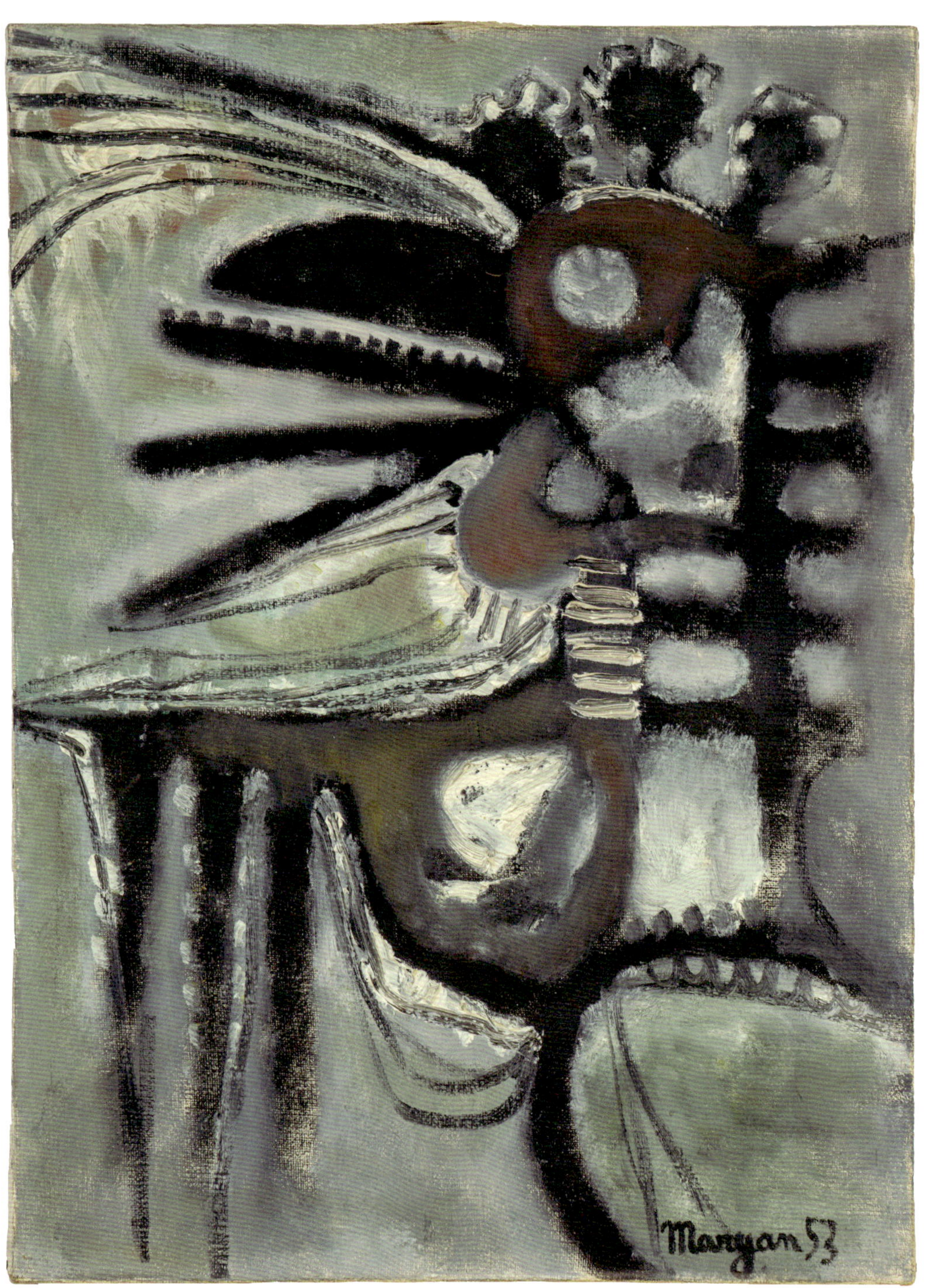

Untitled, 1953. Oil on canvas, 28¾ × 21¼ inches (73 × 54 cm). Courtesy of Galerie Claude Bernard

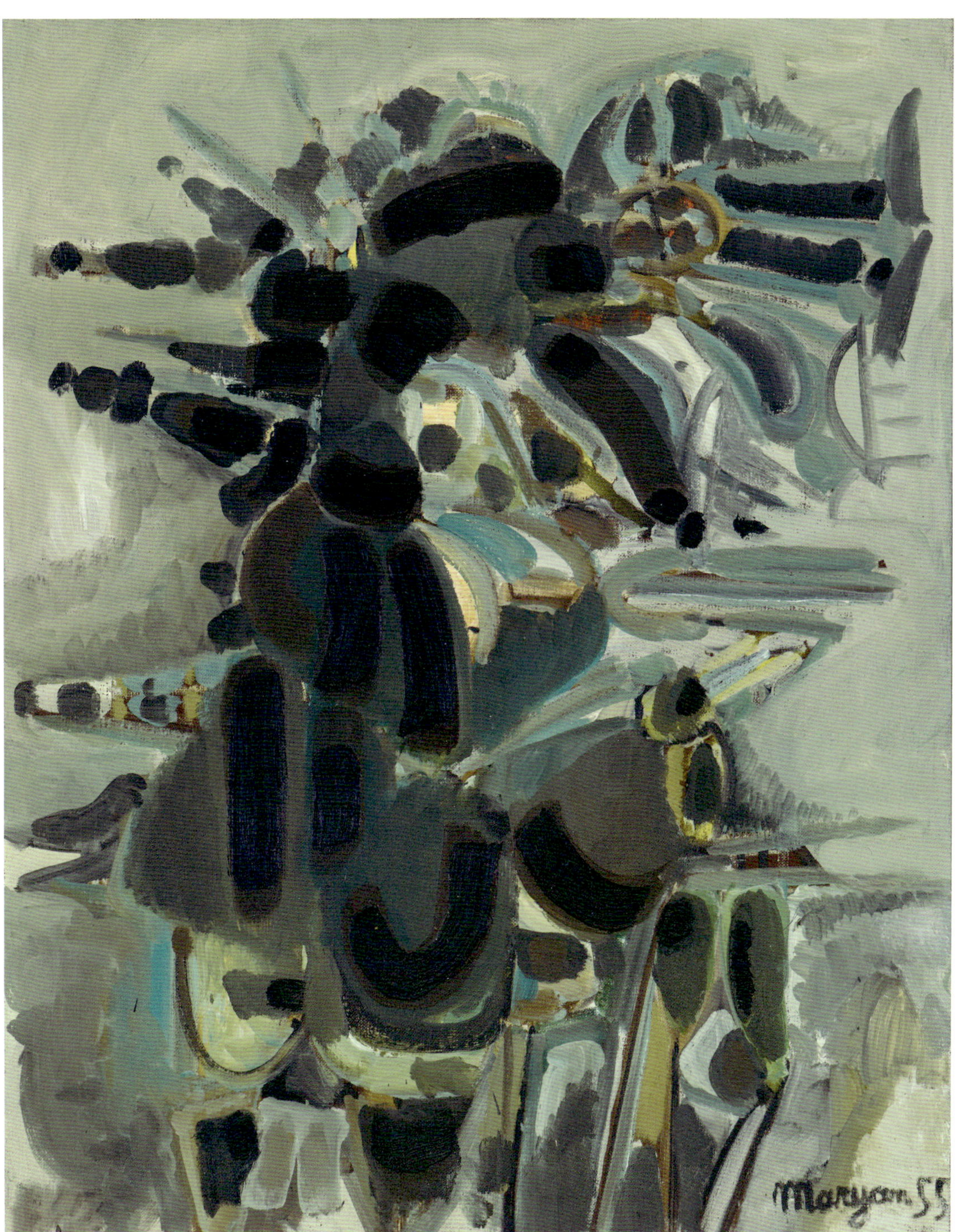

Untitled, 1955. Oil on canvas, 32 × 25 inches (81 × 65 cm). Courtesy of Galerie Claude Bernard

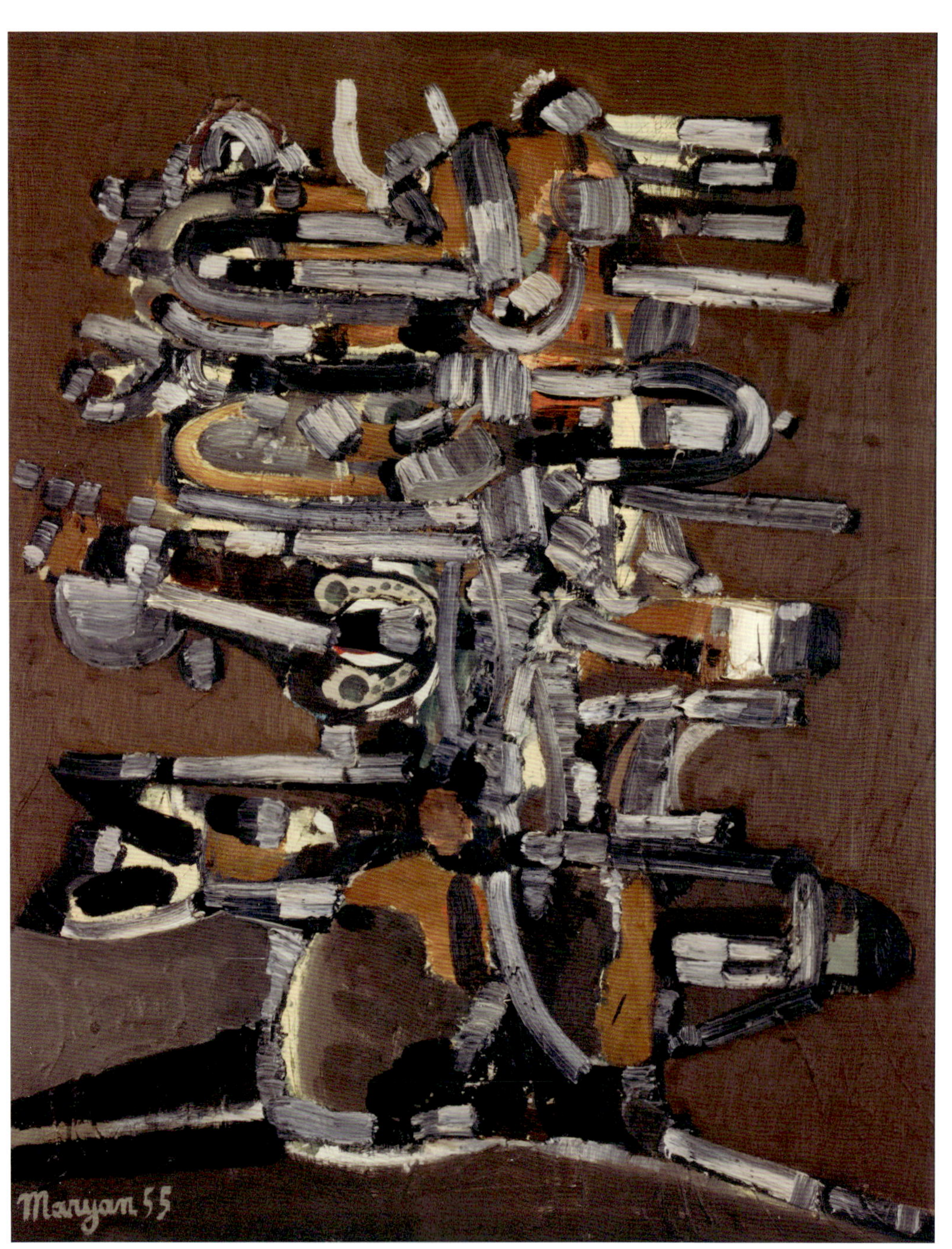

Untitled, 1955. Oil on canvas, 35¾ × 28⅜ inches (91 × 72 cm). Collection of the Tel Aviv Museum of Art, Gift of Claude Bernard, Paris

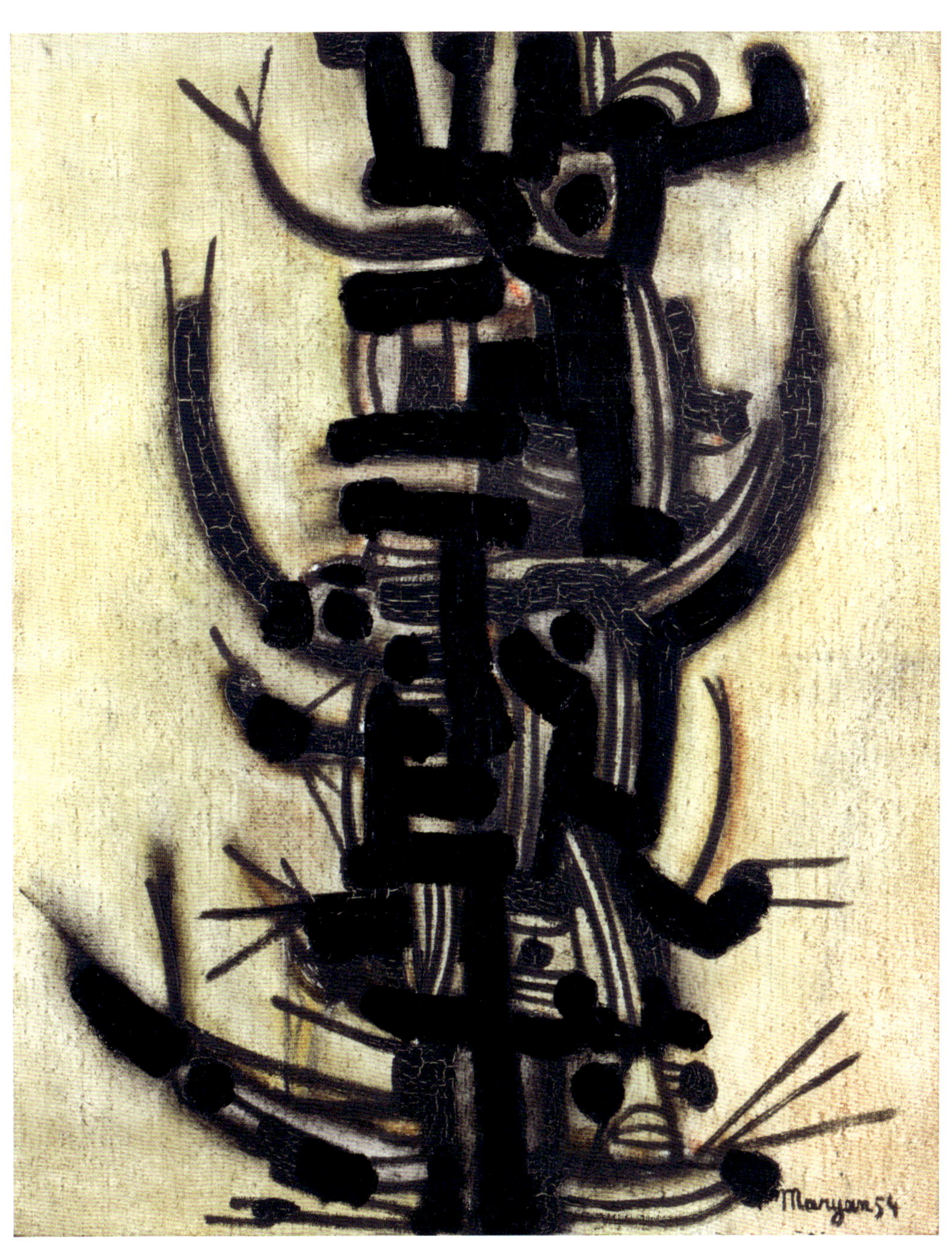

Composition, 1954. Oil on canvas, 31¾ × 25⅜ inches (81 × 64.5 cm). Collection of the Tel Aviv Museum of Art,
Gift of Claude Bernard, Paris

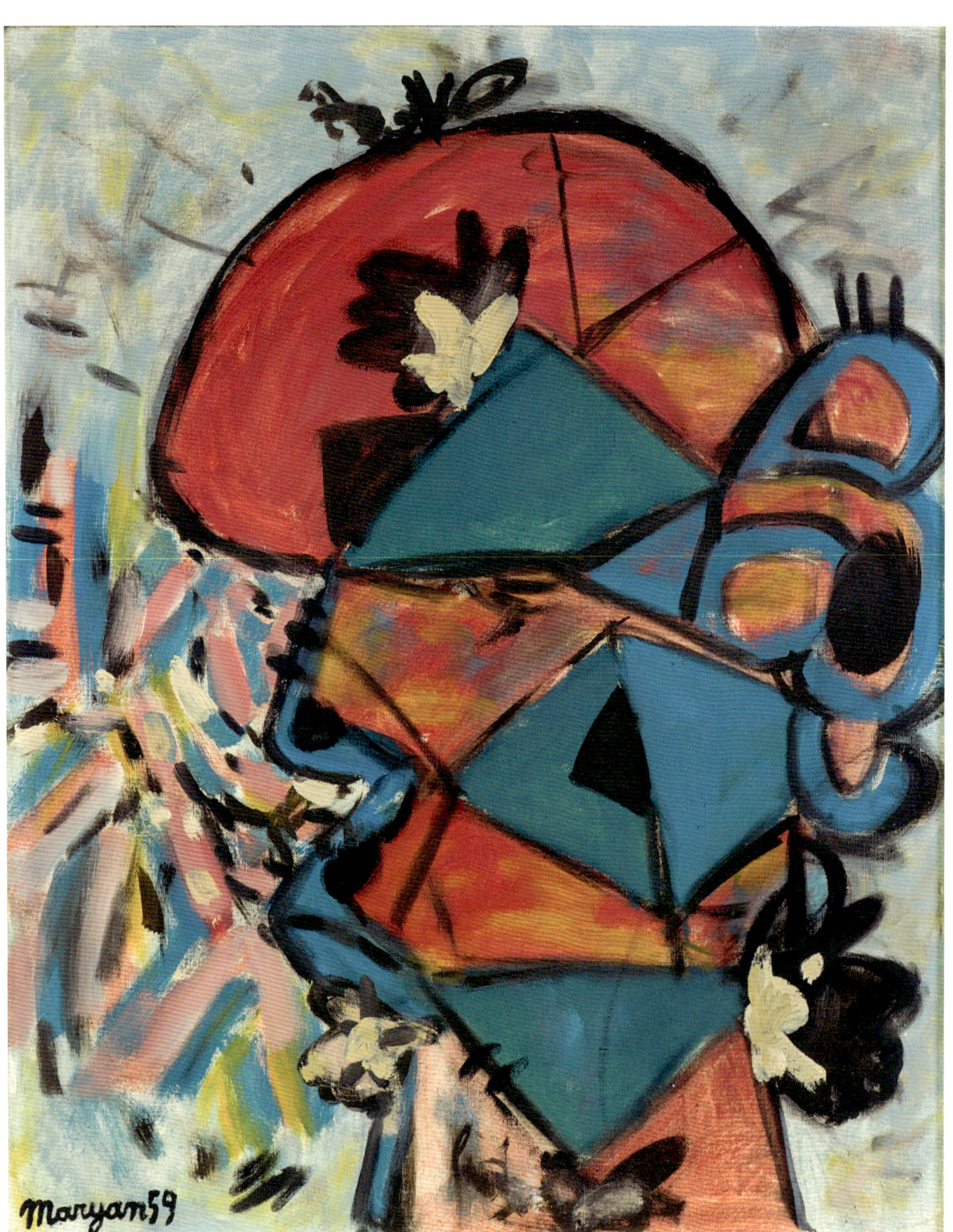

Untitled, 1959. Oil on canvas, 32 × 25½ inches (81.3 × 64.8 cm). Private Collection, Paris

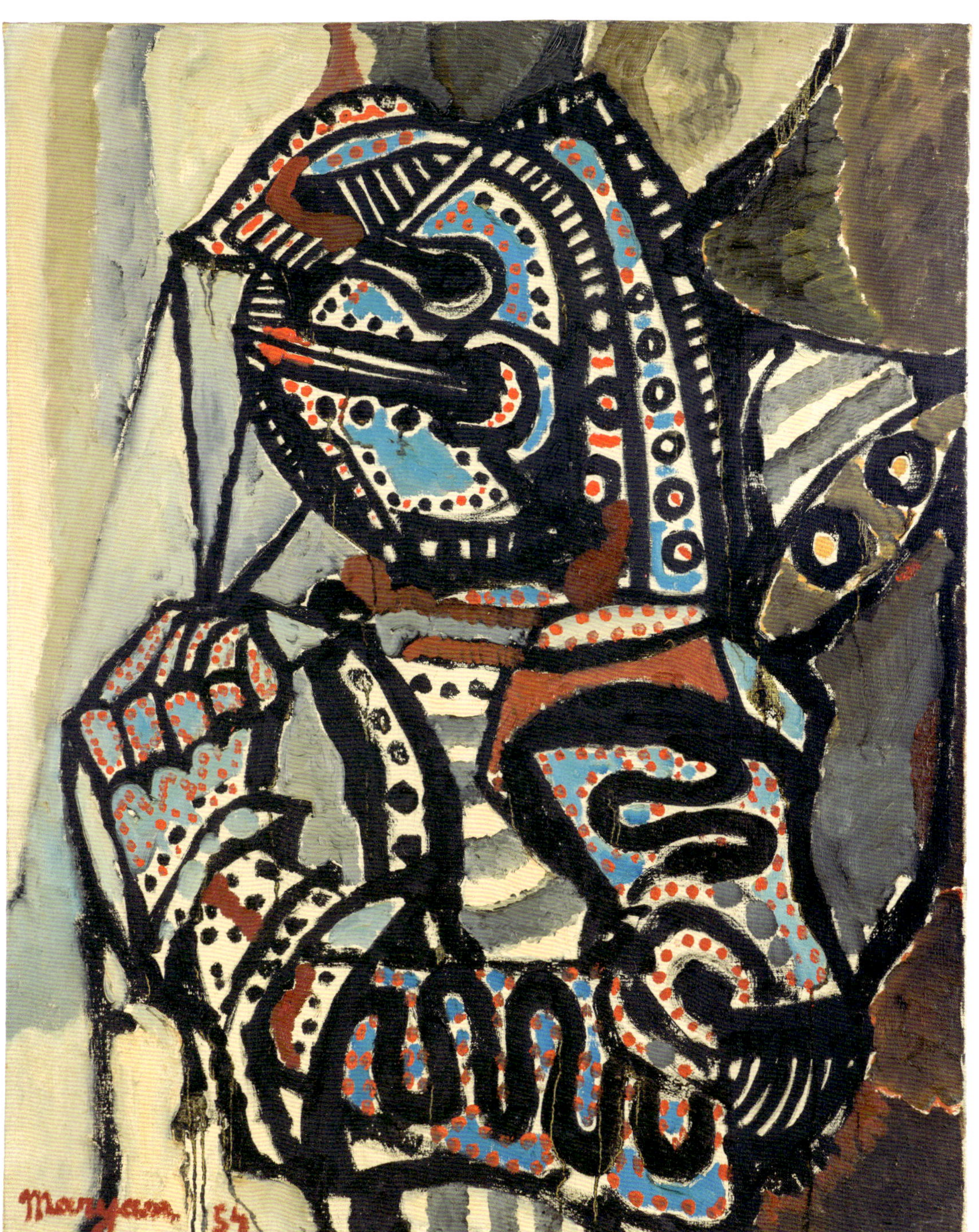

Chevalier, 1954. Oil on canvas, 39½ × 32 inches (100.3 × 81.3 cm). Private Collection

BIRTH OF THE PERSONNAGE

Between 1959 and 1960, Maryan began to focus on creating single-figure compositions. During this breakthrough period, he titled nearly all his works with the simple moniker *personnage*. Translated from the French as "character," these fictitious figures dominated Maryan's mature oeuvre and became a powerful vehicle for both complex narratives and the formal evolution of his distinctive painterly language.

The first group of *personnage* paintings were shown at the Galerie de France in fall 1960. The exhibition was Maryan's first breakout success, establishing him as a singular voice in the bustling Paris art scene. Maryan imagined strange hybrid creatures that at times seem part machine, part human. Mechanical imagery, wheels, robotic cogs, roller skates, and unexplained speckled areas in the compositions suggest restless movement. The accordion-like legs of some figures eerily suggest the phantom of Maryan's own missing limb; likewise, the vehicular chairs with wheels conjure his traumatic convalescence after his imprisonment.

Symbols abound in the *personnage* paintings: there are legible signs such as the Star of David and pointed hoods that echo the Spanish Inquisition and the Ku Klux Klan, as well as more esoteric or personal references. The *personnages* are almost always situated in claustrophobic spatial environments. The box motif in Maryan's breakout body of work in 1960 is repeated and developed in subsequent series and is later revealed, in his 1970s notebooks, to be a direct reference to his experience in the Nazi camps. —AMG

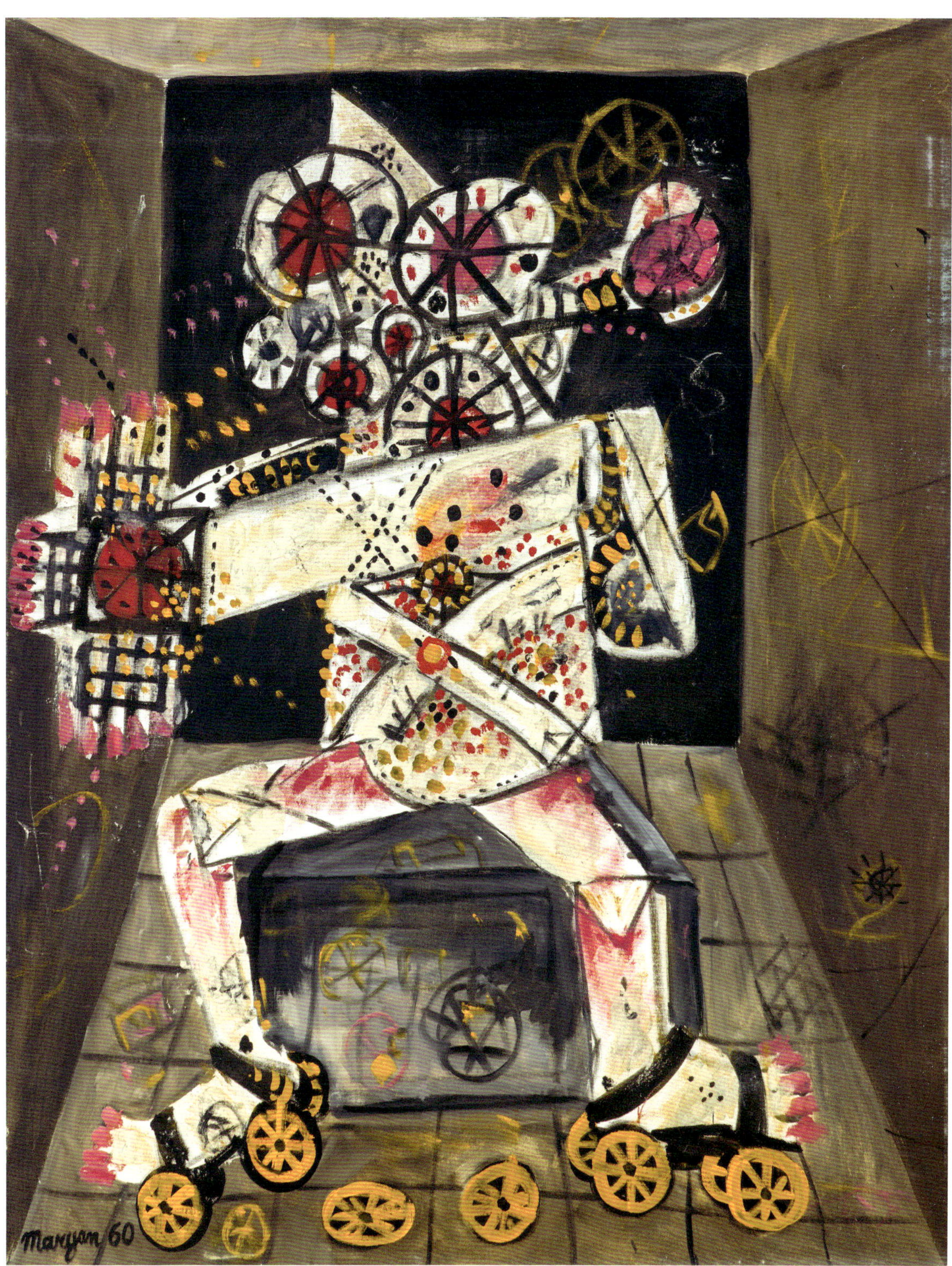

Untitled, 1960. Oil on canvas, 57½ × 45 inches (146 × 114.3 cm). Private Collection

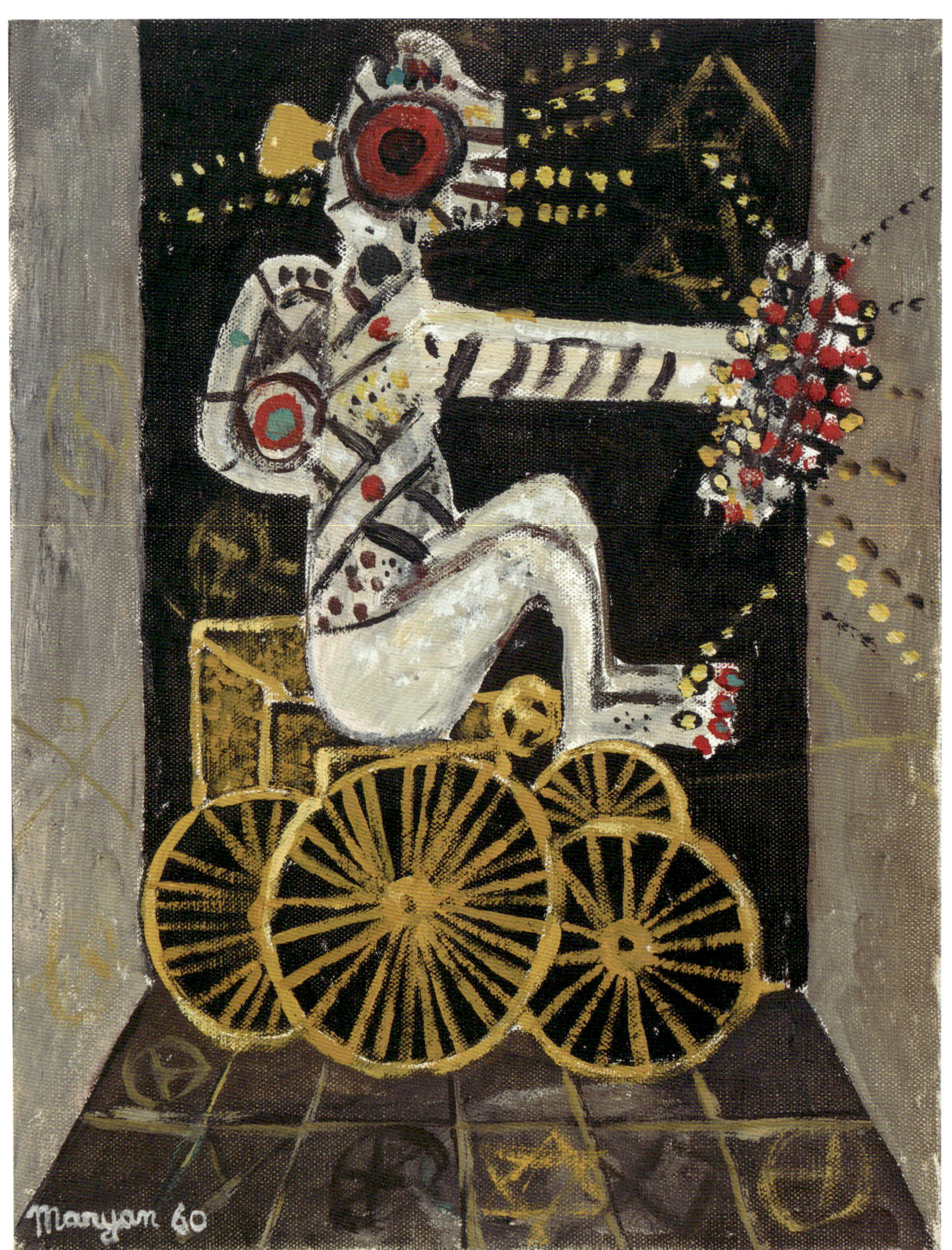

Composition, 1960. Oil on canvas, 13¾ × 10¾ inches (34.8 × 27.3 cm). Collection of Spertus Institute, Chicago

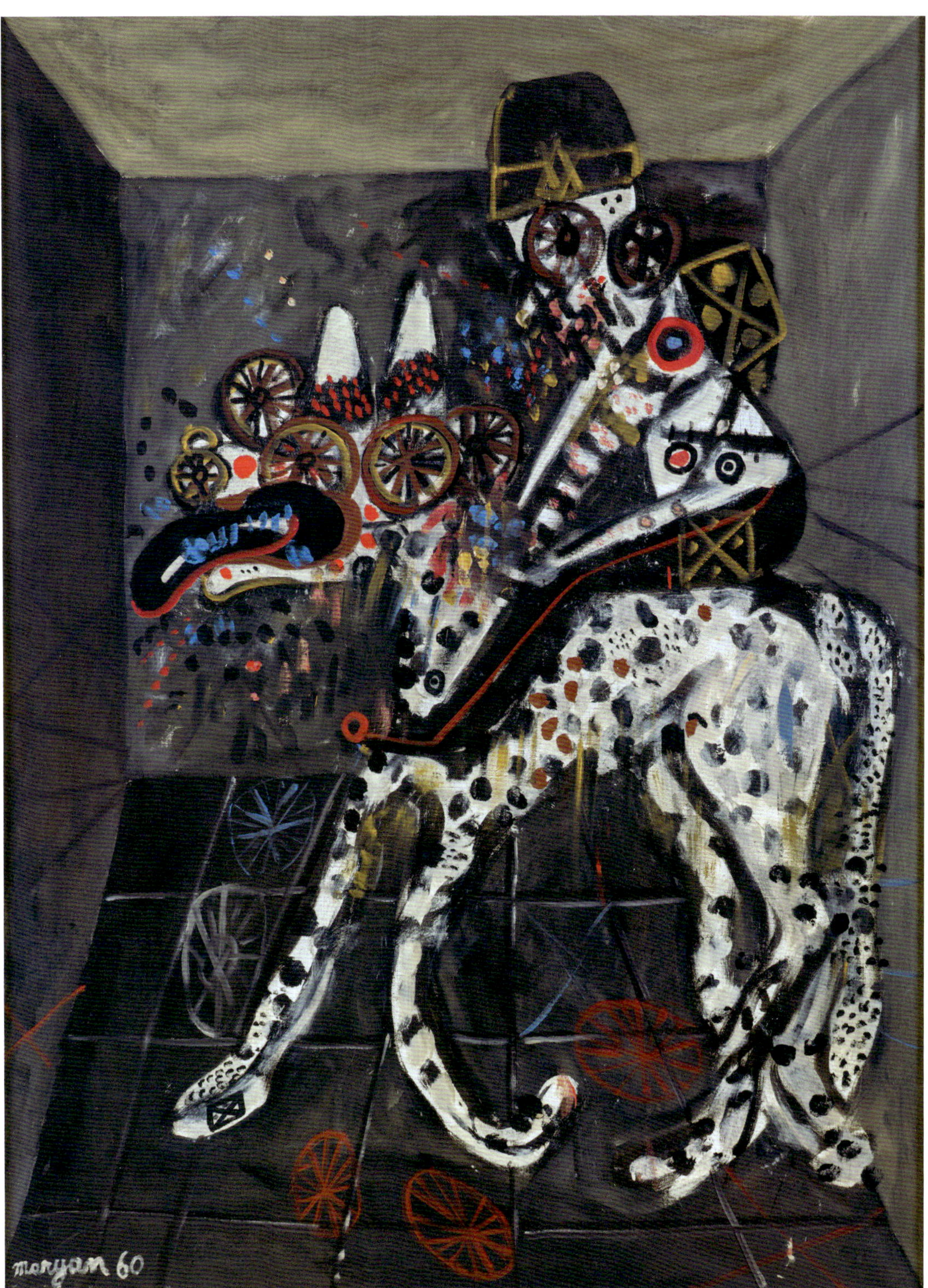

Balak, chien fou, 1960. Oil on canvas, 51 × 37½ inches (129.5 × 95.2 cm). Private Collection

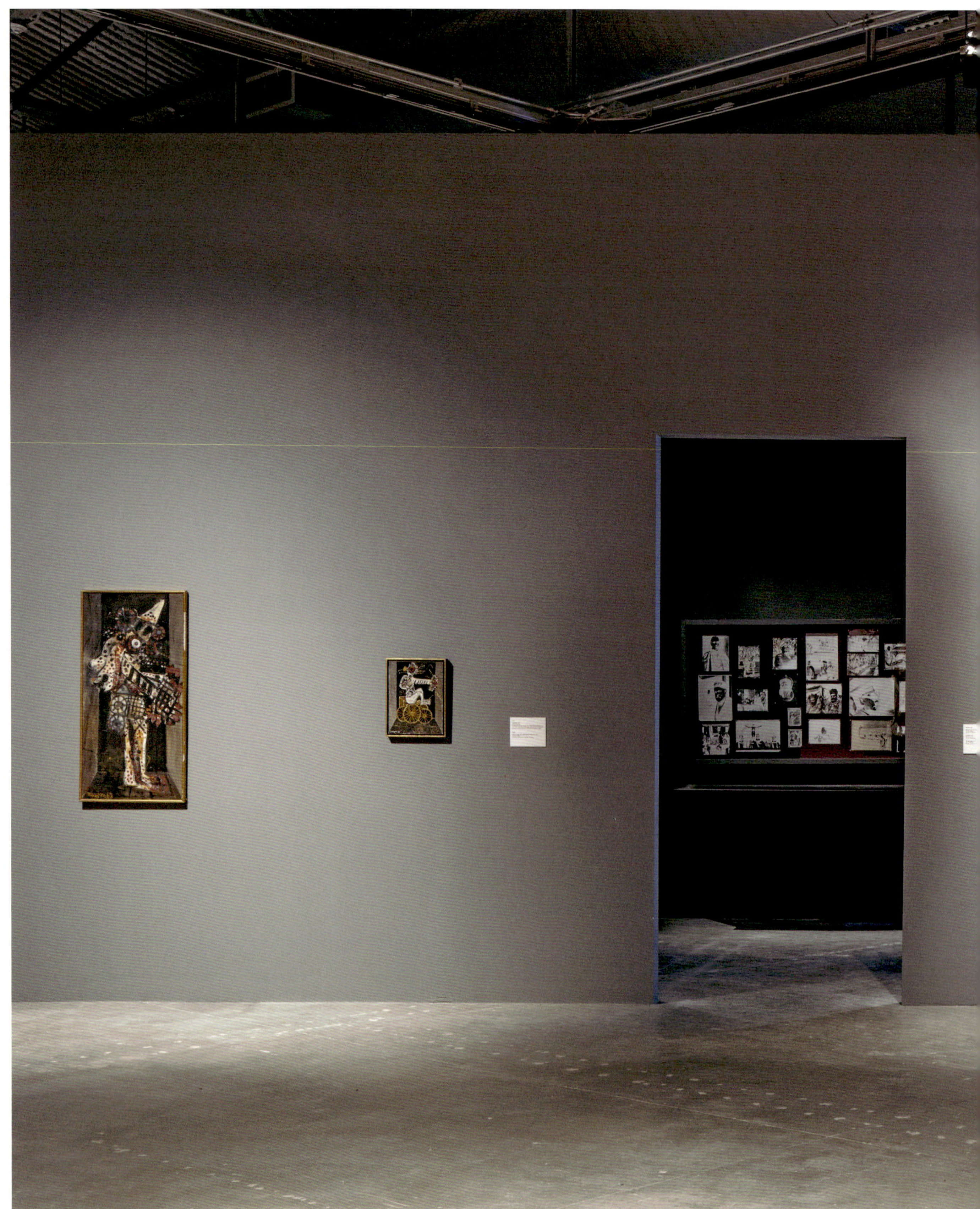

My Name Is Maryan, Museum of Contemporary Art, North Miami, 2022. Installation view

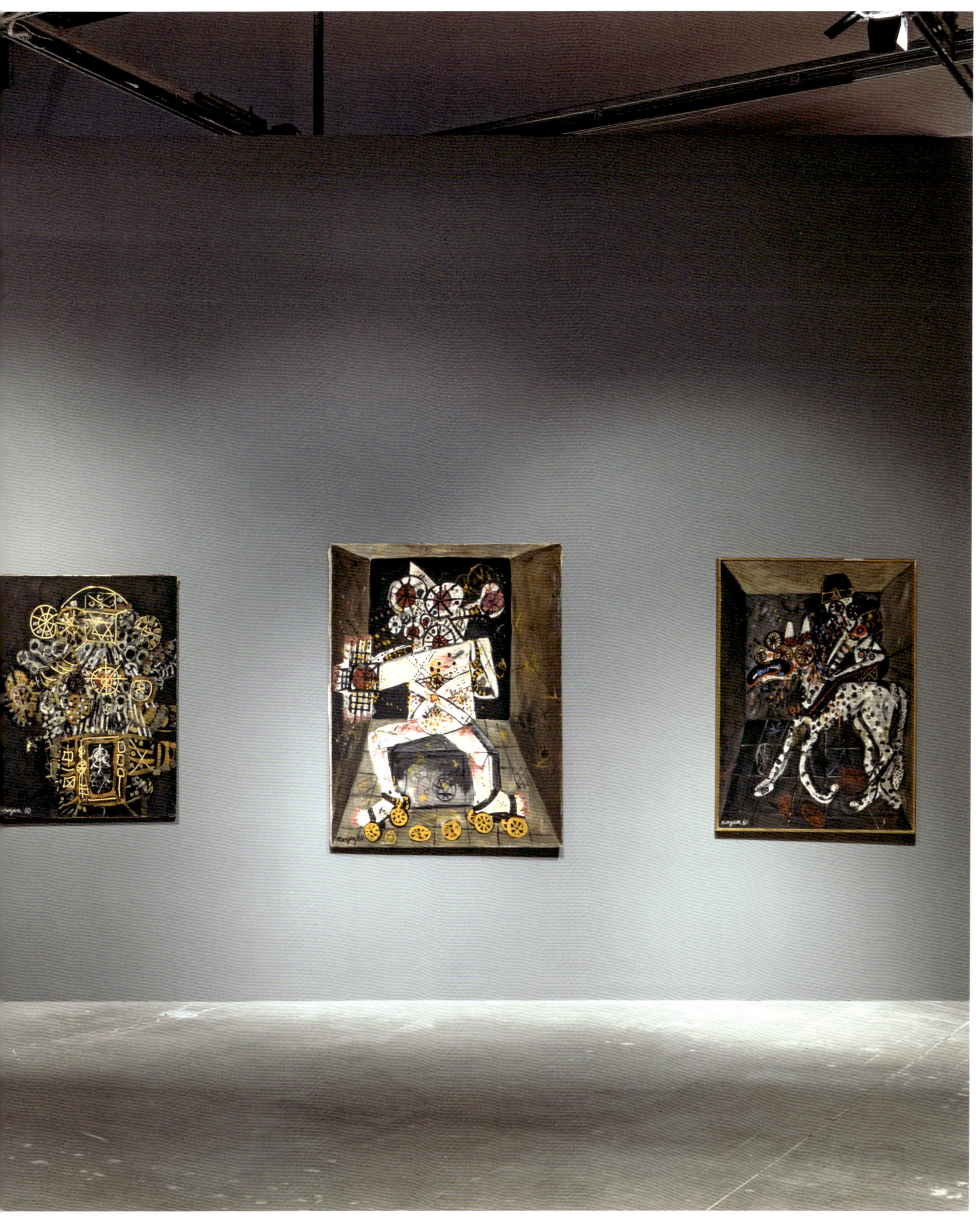

LA MÉNAGERIE HUMAINE

In 1961 a Parisian editor commissioned Maryan to create a book of drawings titled *La ménagerie humaine*. Continuing his exploration of the *personnage* theme, Maryan produced drawings that combine human and animal forms, often in grotesque and disturbing configurations.

This theme of the "human menagerie" was part of the zeitgeist of post-war European art. Maryan developed hybrid iconographies that questioned the foundational understanding of humanism and interrogated the nature of the human condition.

These paintings were made in the early 1960s, when Maryan advanced his unique *personnage* imagery in an intellectual atmosphere of disquiet in Parisian literary and artistic circles. The *personnages* often feature a combination of military regalia, animal heads, grotesque facial distortions, Technicolor bodily fluids, and a preponderance of symbolism. Maryan's imaginary *personnages* fill the canvas and confront the viewer with a theatrical absurdity that resonates with the avant-garde literature of the period. Maryan was inspired by the writings of Alfred Jarry, Franz Kafka, and Samuel Beckett, and incorporated the atmospheres of their tragic-farcical literature into these jarring, monstrous characters.

Maryan also conjures the Jewish holiday Purim—with its elaborate costuming and pageantry and ritual enactments of disorder, excess, and transgression—in his human menagerie paintings and collages. In the autobiographical notebook drawings that Maryan executed a decade later, the psychoanalytical significance of this human menagerie theme reveals itself as animating his entire oeuvre. —AMG

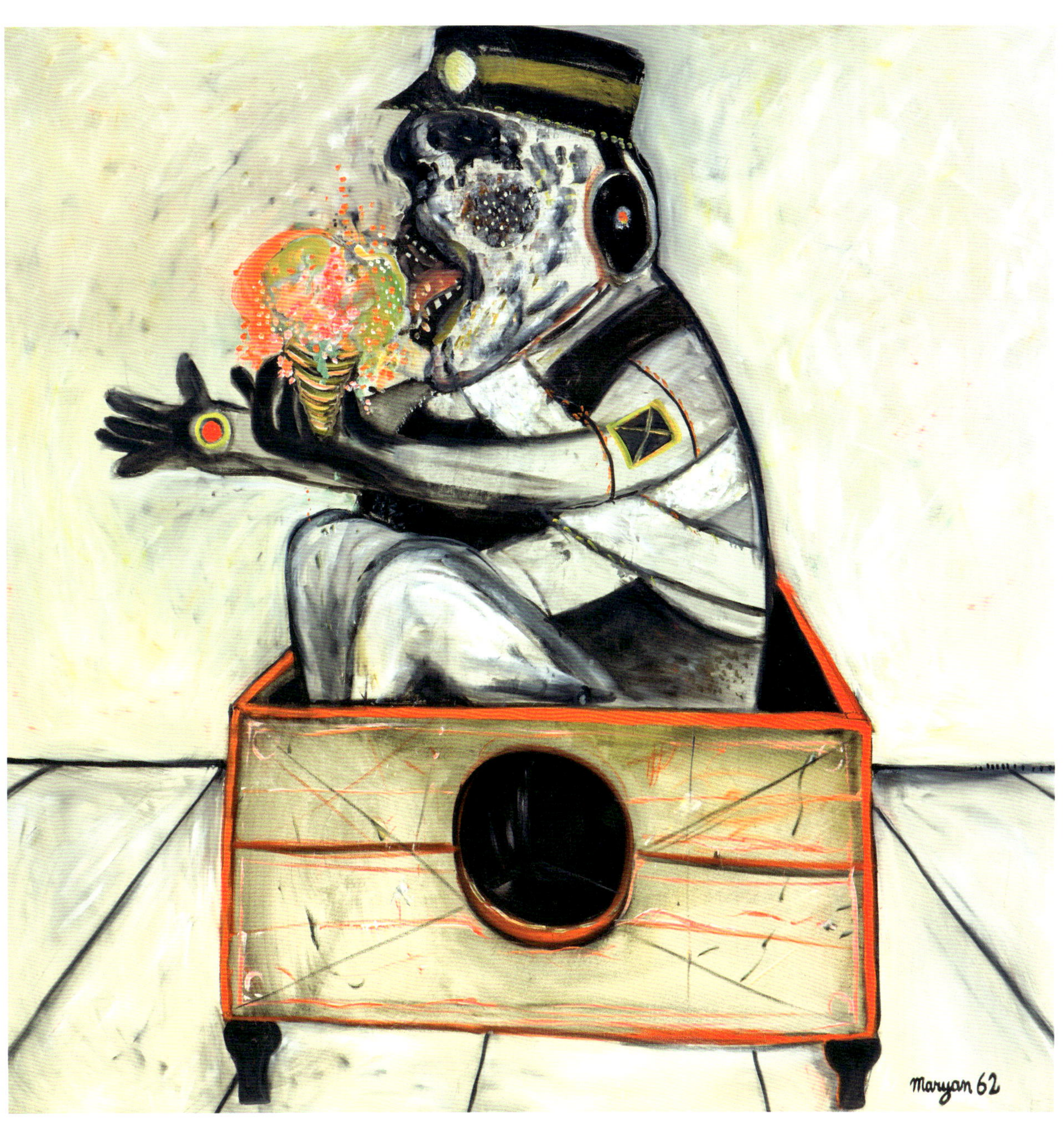

Personnage in a Box, 1962. Oil on canvas, 60¾ × 60¾ inches (154.3 × 154.3 cm).
Courtesy of Venus Over Manhattan, New York

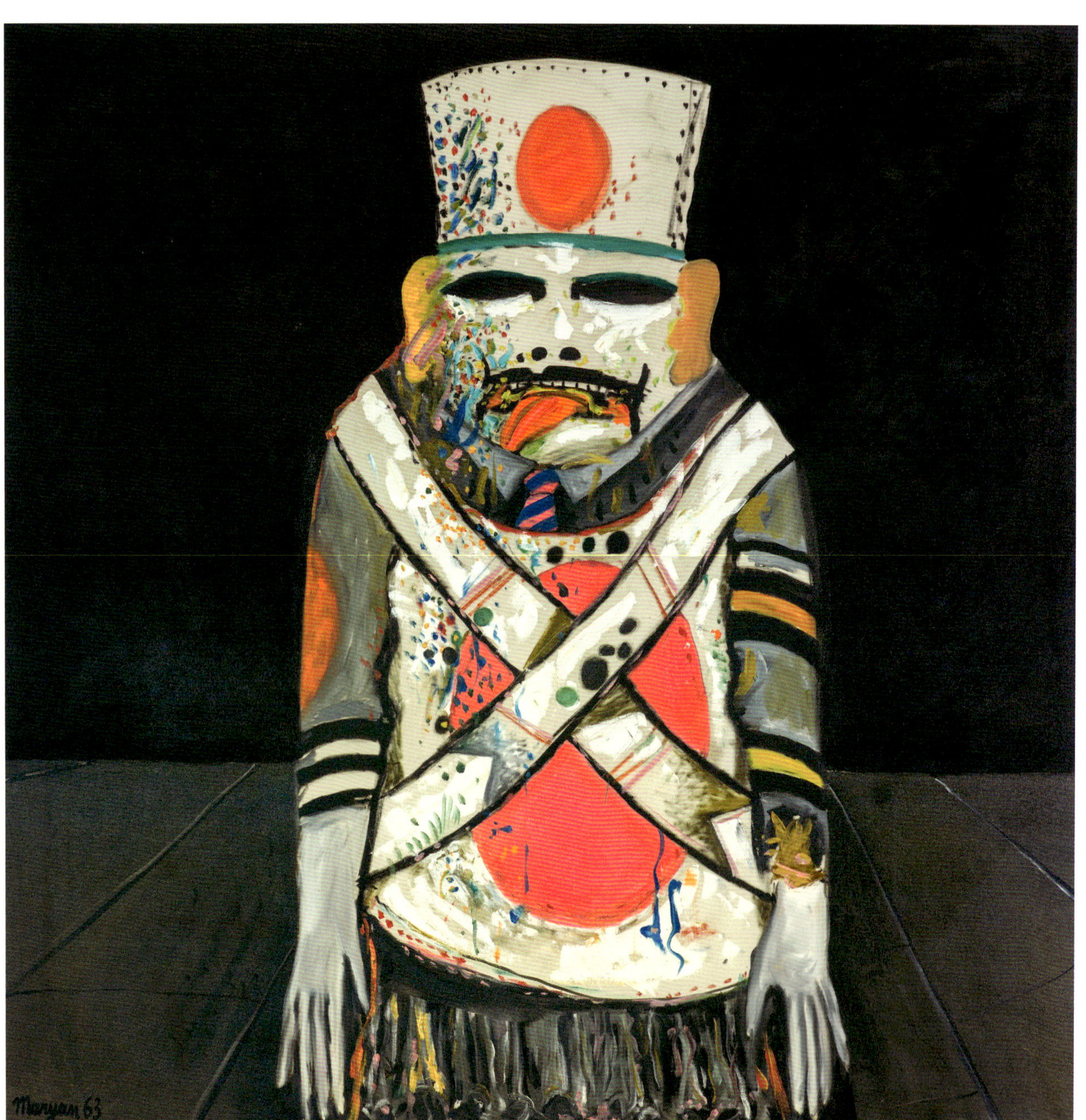

Personnage, 1963. Oil on canvas, 60 × 60 inches (152.4 × 152.4 cm). Collection of Spertus Institute, Chicago

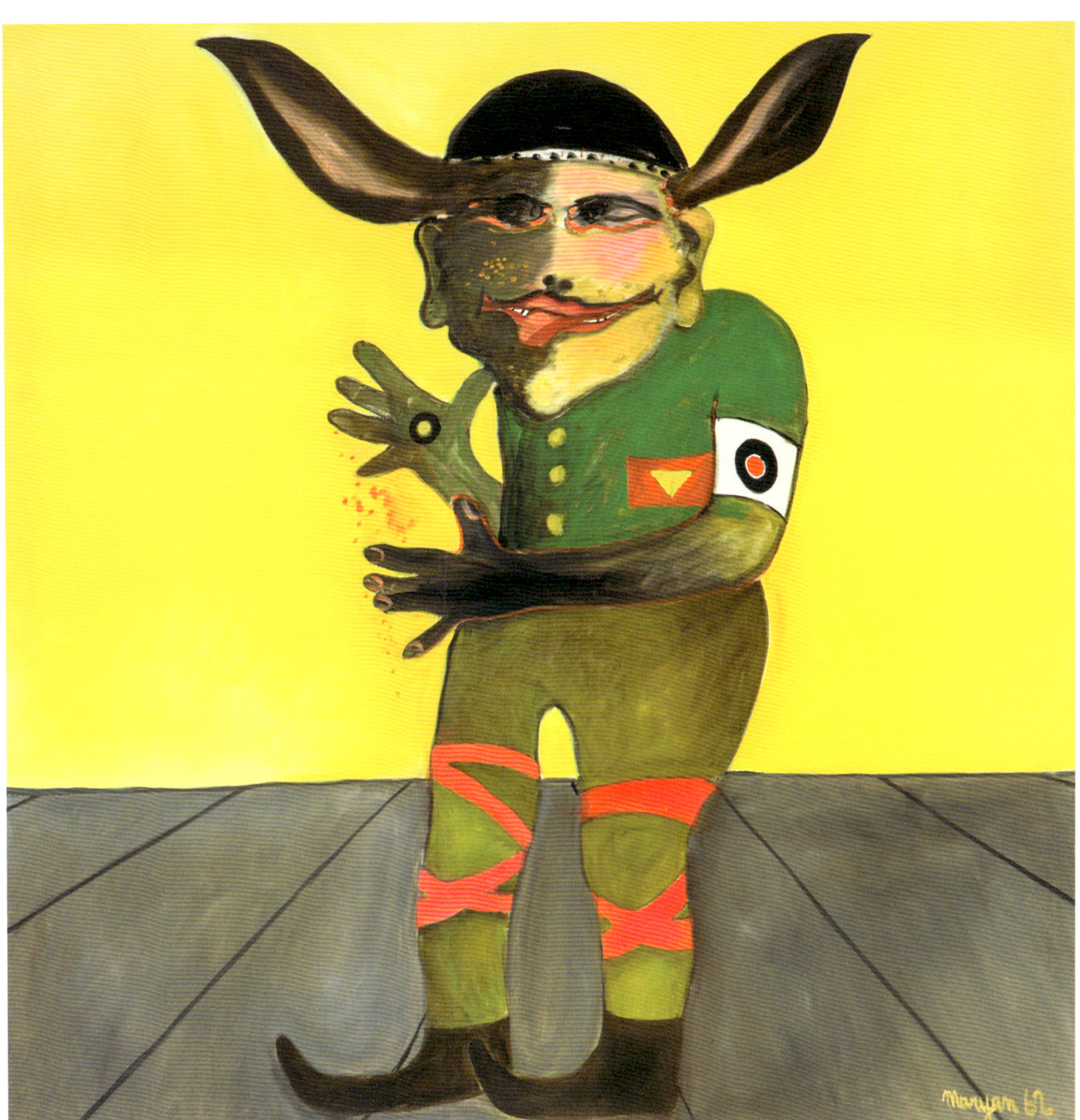

Personnage, 1962. Oil on canvas, 50 × 50 inches (127 × 127 cm). Collection of Anne Wachsmann Guigon

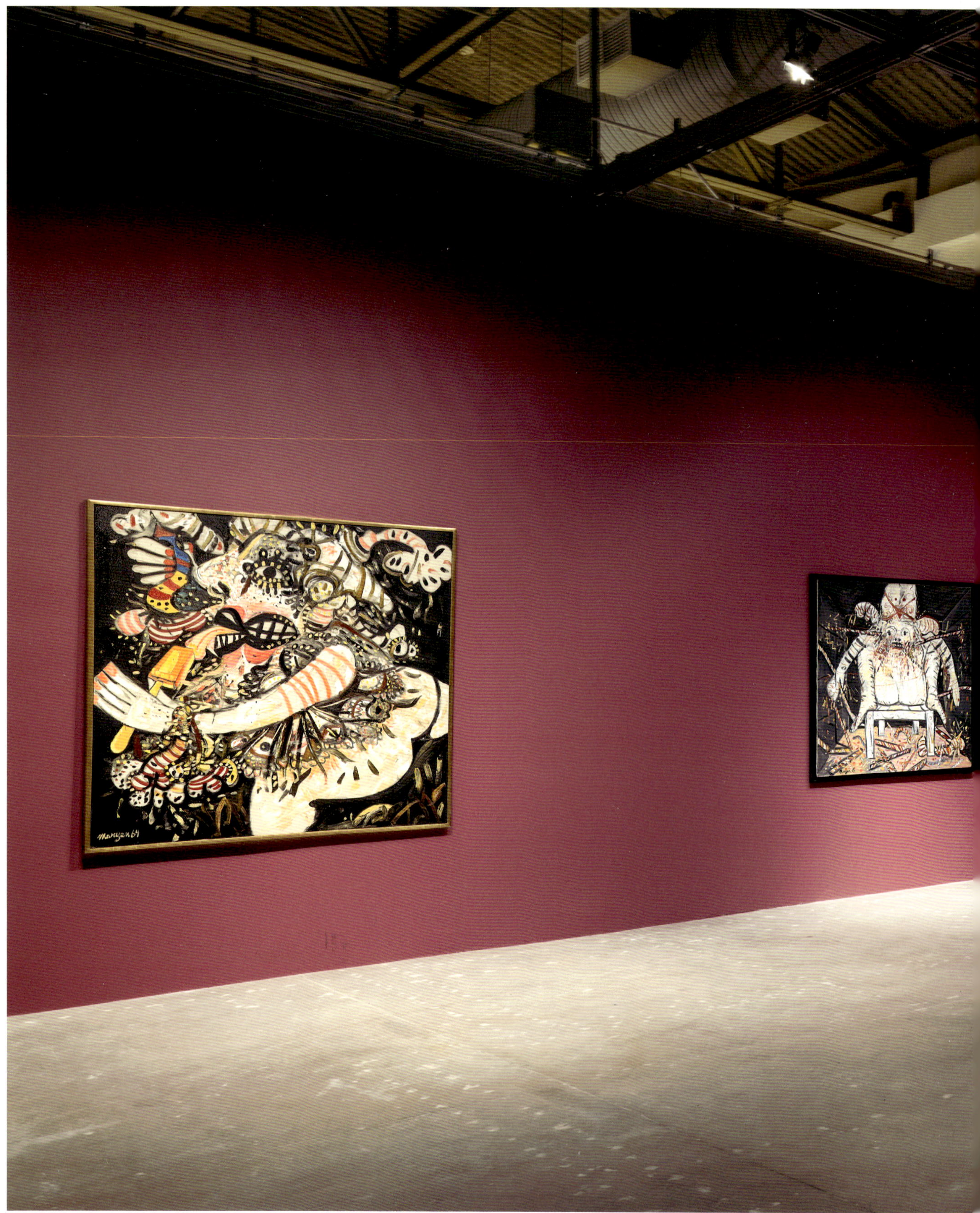

My Name Is Maryan, Museum of Contemporary Art, North Miami, 2022. Installation view

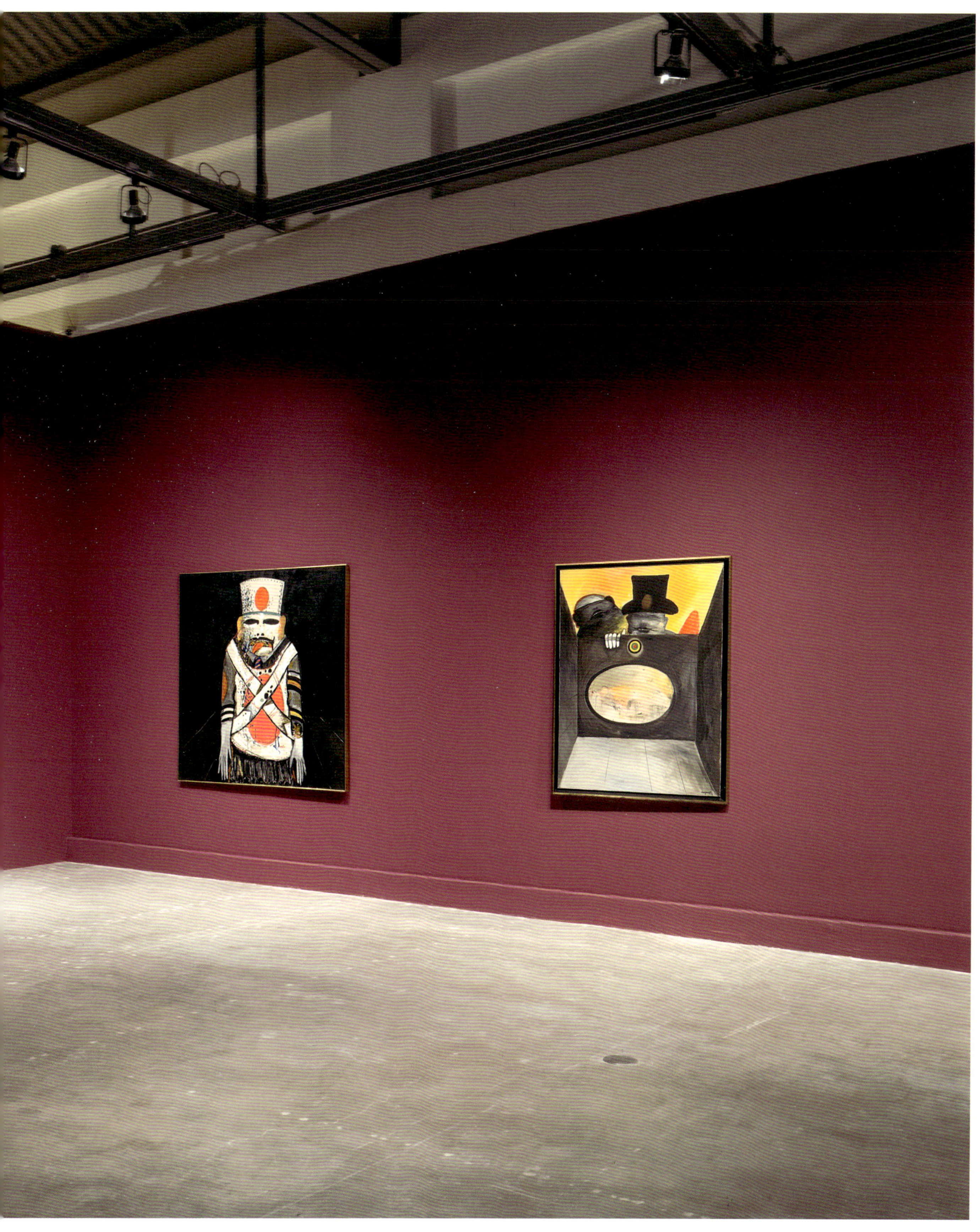

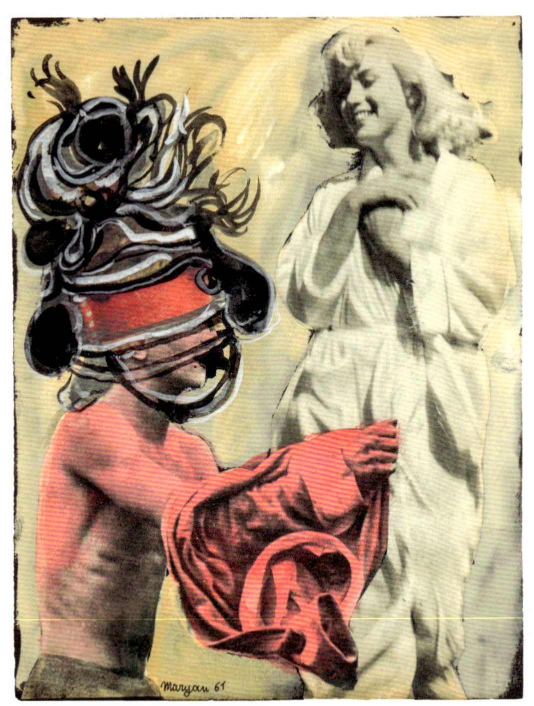
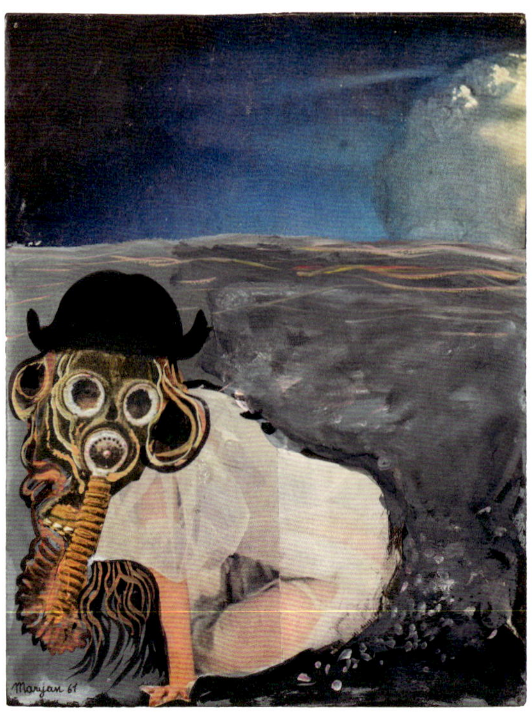
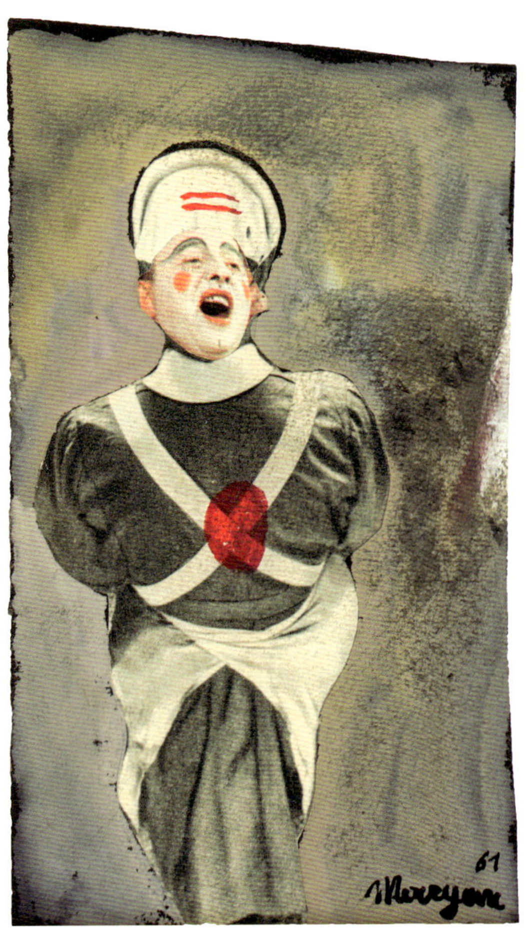
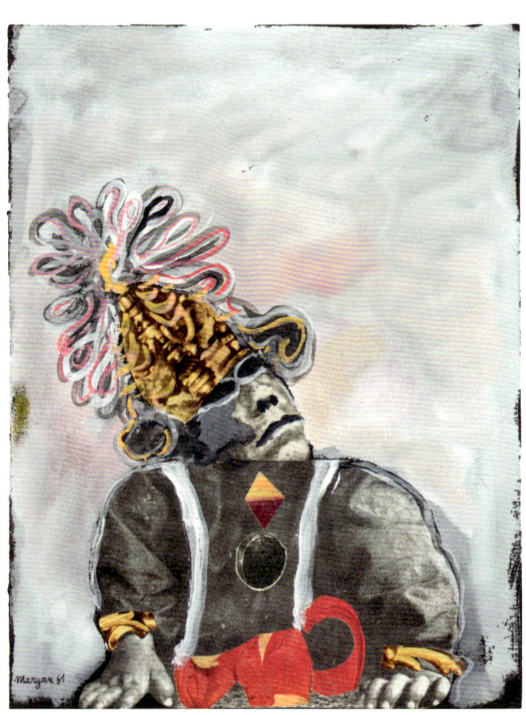

Clockwise from top left
Untitled, 1961. Mixed media on paper, 12¾ × 9⅞ inches (32.5 × 25 cm). Private Collection
Untitled, 1961. Mixed media on paper, 12¾ × 9⅞ inches (32.5 × 25 cm). Private Collection
Untitled, 1961. Mixed media on paper, 12¾ × 9⅞ inches (32.5 × 25 cm). Private Collection
Untitled, 1961. Mixed media on paper, 6½ × 4 inches (16.5 × 10 cm). Private Collection

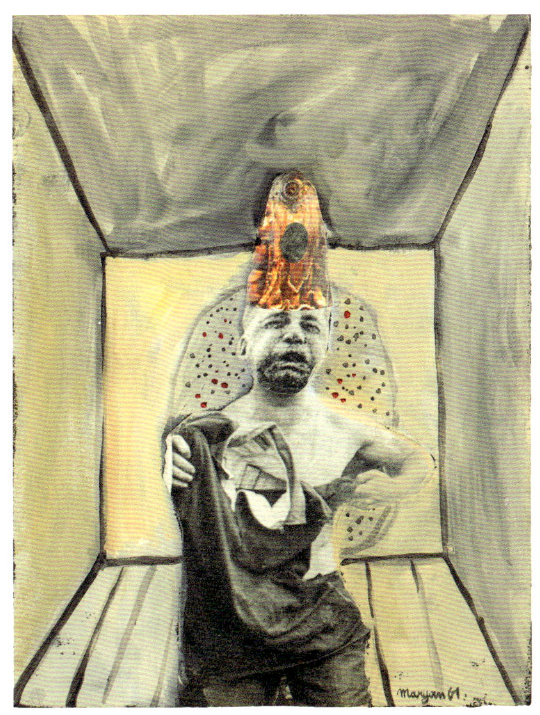
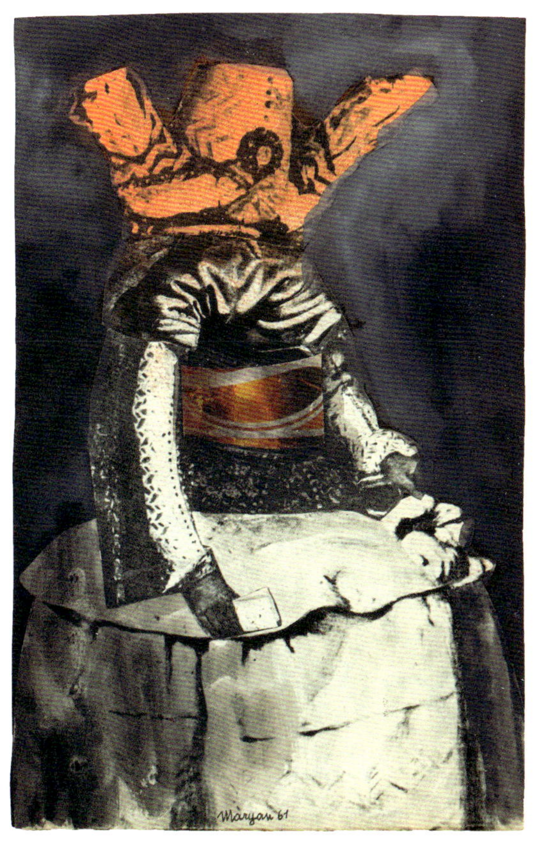
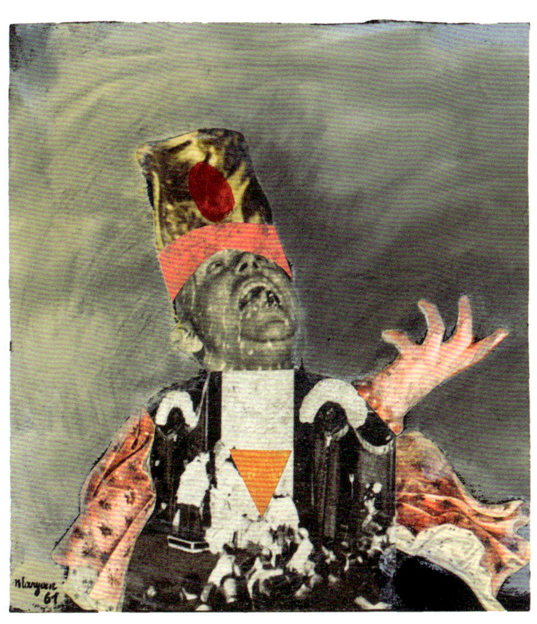
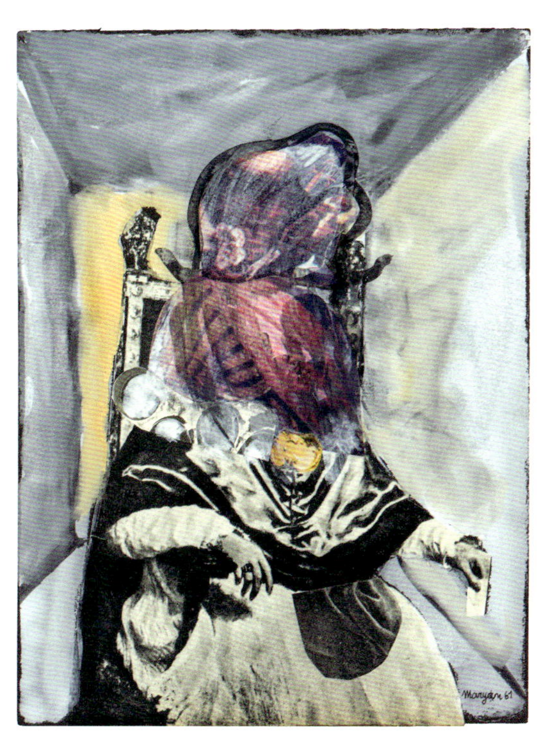

Clockwise from top left
Untitled, 1961. Mixed media on paper, 12¾ × 9⅞ inches (32.5 × 25 cm). Private Collection
Untitled, 1961. Mixed media on paper, 10½ × 6¾ inches (26.7 × 17 cm). Private Collection
Untitled, 1961. Mixed media on paper, 12¾ × 9⅞ inches (32.5 × 25 cm). Private Collection
Untitled, 1961. Mixed media on paper, 8¼ × 7¼ inches (21 × 18.5 cm). Private Collection

MARYAN IN BLACK AND WHITE

While exuberant use of color is one of the hallmarks of Maryan's mature work, his consistent use of black ink was a defining, singular aspect of his practice. From the 1950s in Paris to his later years in New York, Maryan used a pared-down black line on a white ground for some of his most important works. Maryan's black-line works conjure a number of art historical antecedents who influenced his development, from Goya to George Grosz, Max Beckmann, and Fernand Léger.

This pictorial suite is highly representative of Maryan's emblematic black-and-white *personnage* works. Executed in 1963 using ink on white museum board, each of these large-scale drawings depicts a single figure that occupies almost the entire picture plane. The reduced palette showcases Maryan's virtuosic draftsmanship. Many of the characters reappear in his work over the decades: the male figure with donkey ears, a tortured figure with his legs up in the air, figures with strange pointy hats, and an agitated canine modeled after Balak—a dog that was the titular character of a story by the Nobel Prize–winning writer Shmuel Yosef Agnon. In an interview with the Israeli writer Joseph Mundy in 1977, Maryan said of Balak, who wandered the streets of Jerusalem, "I found myself in this story."[1] —AMG

1. Joseph Mundy, "Conversation: Maryan at La Coupole," in *Maryan's Personnages: Works in Chicago Collections, 1958–75*, ed. Michele Vishny (Chicago: Spertus Museum of Judaica, 1983), 53.

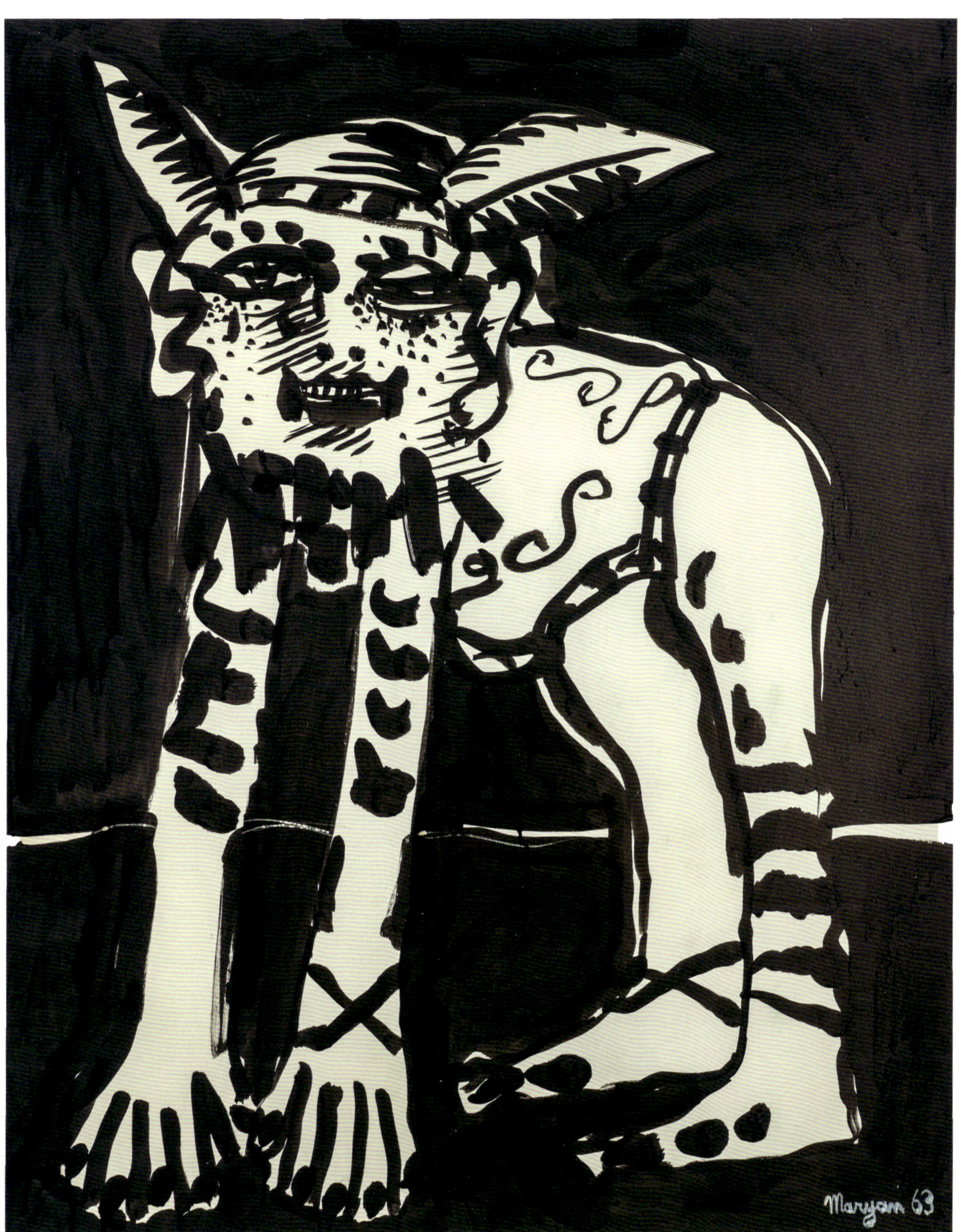

125 *Personnage IV*, 1963. Ink on board, 40 × 32 inches (101.5 × 81.3 cm). Courtesy of Venus Over Manhattan, New York

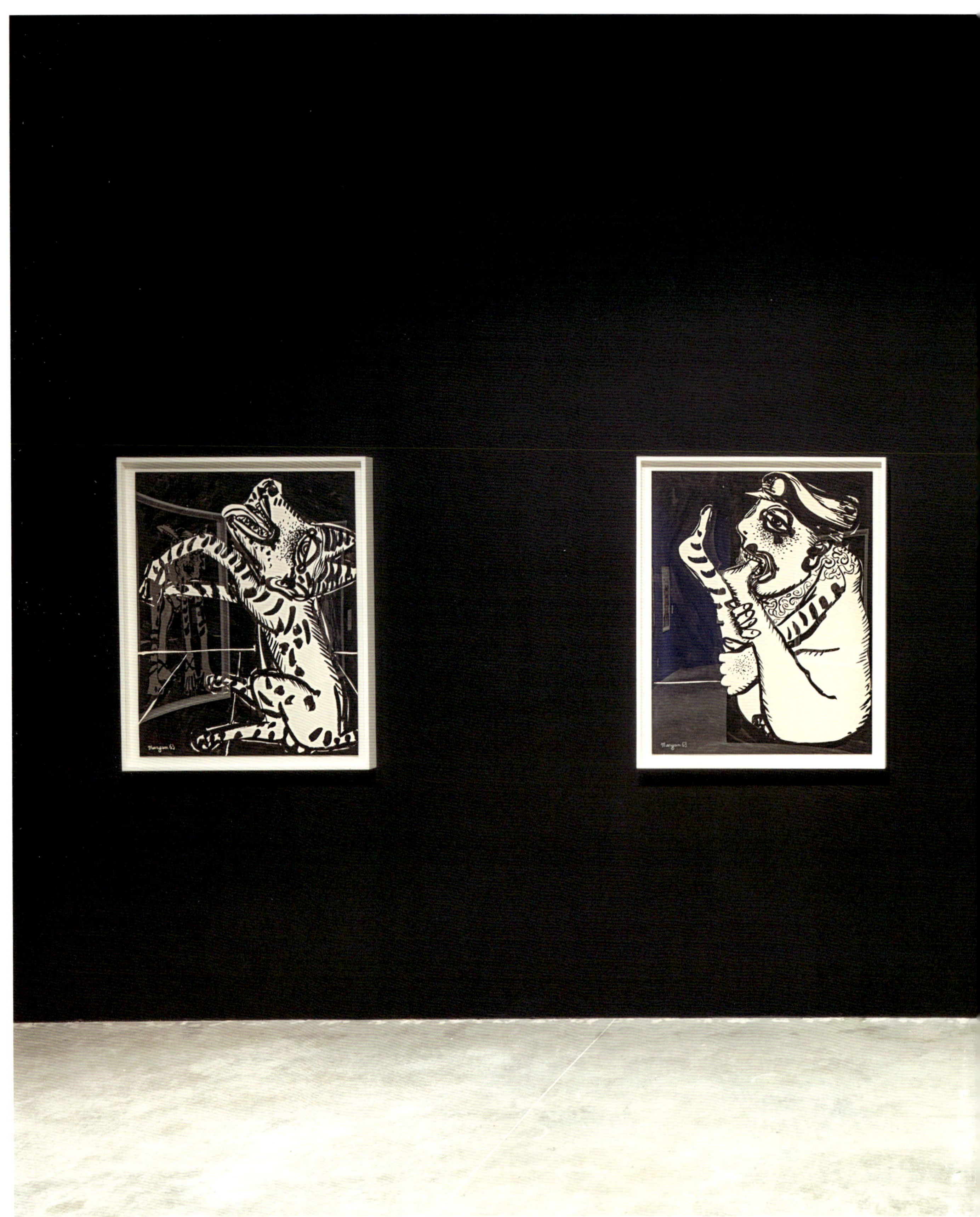

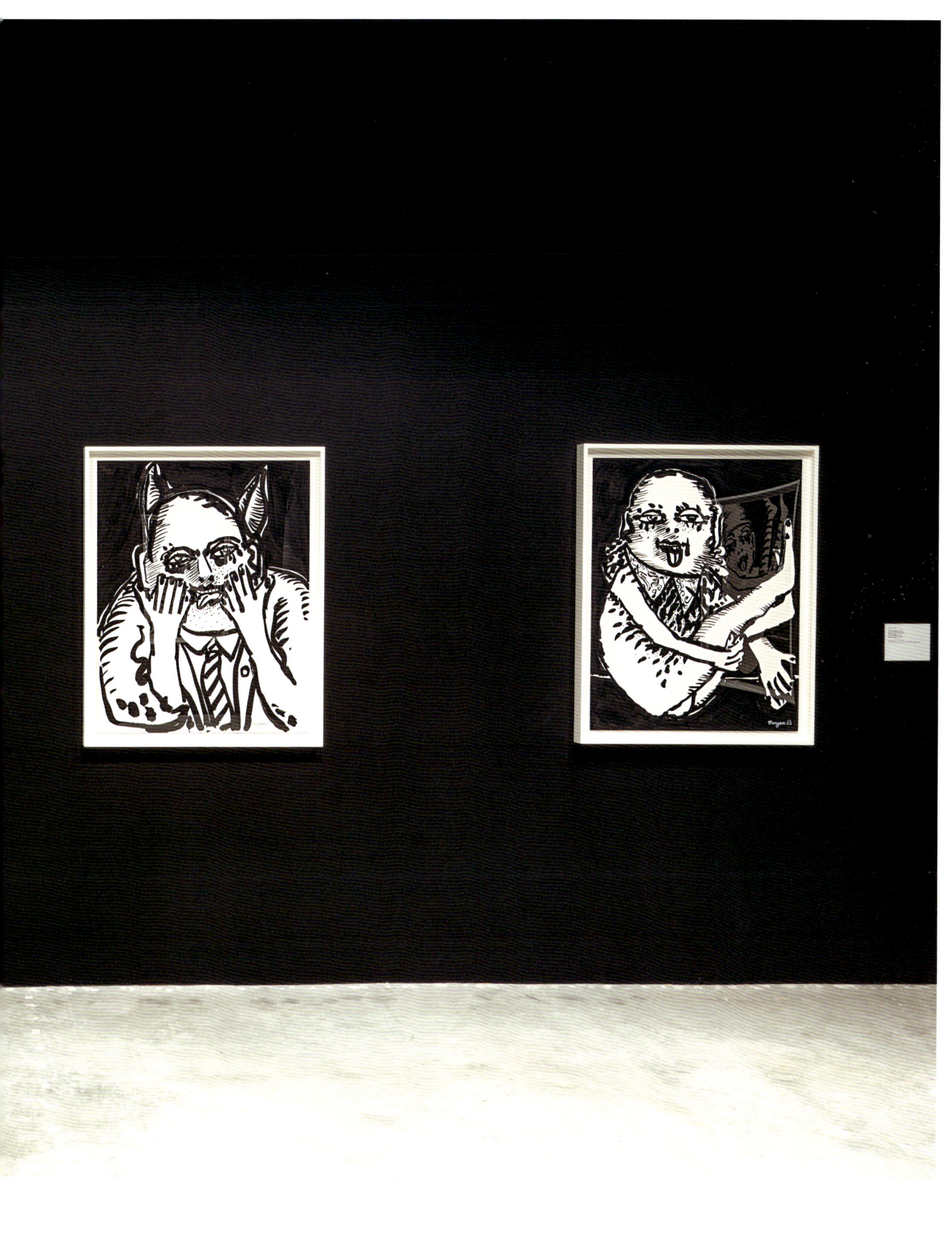

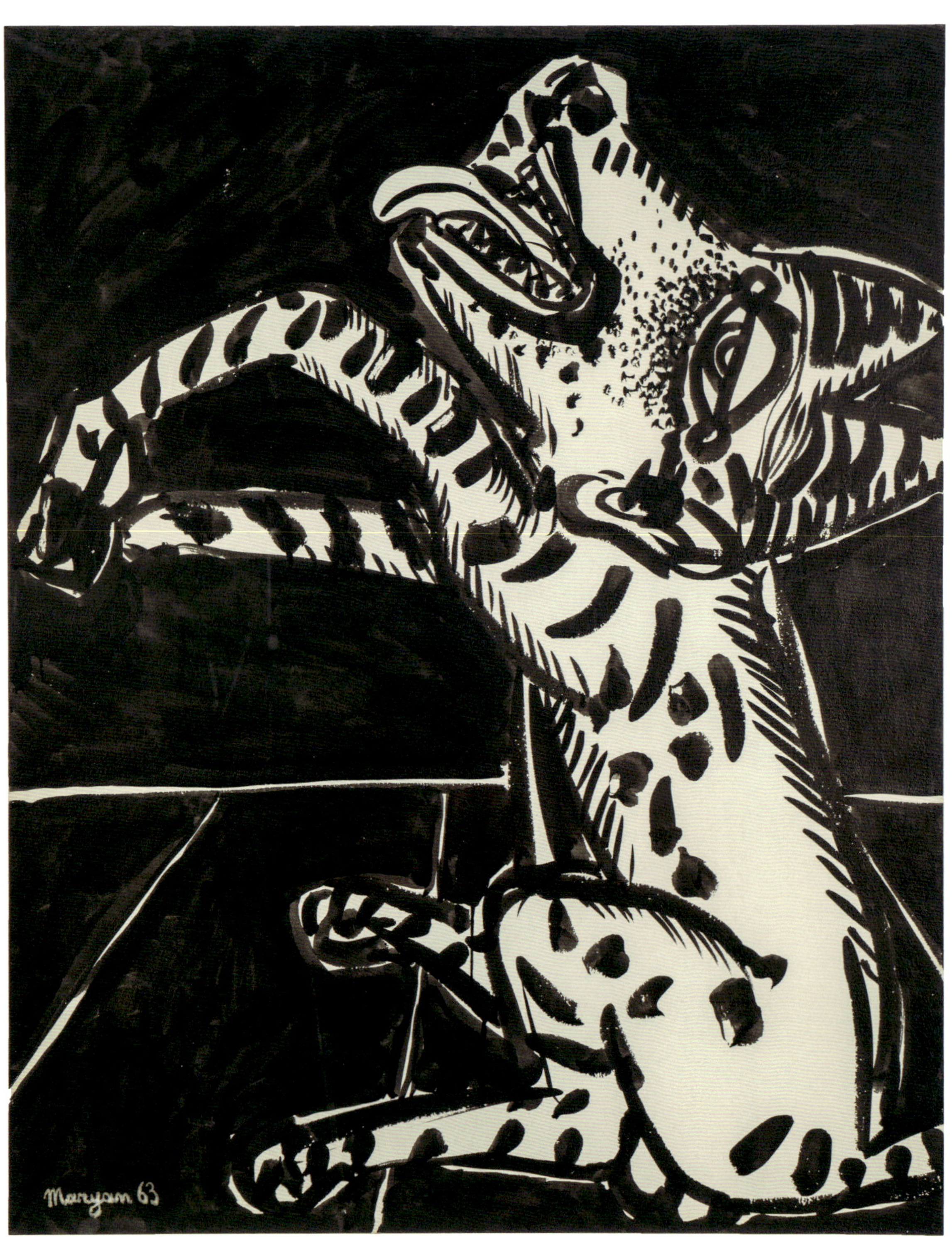

Personnage II, 1963. Ink on board, 40 × 32 inches (101.5 × 81.3 cm). Courtesy of Venus Over Manhattan, New York

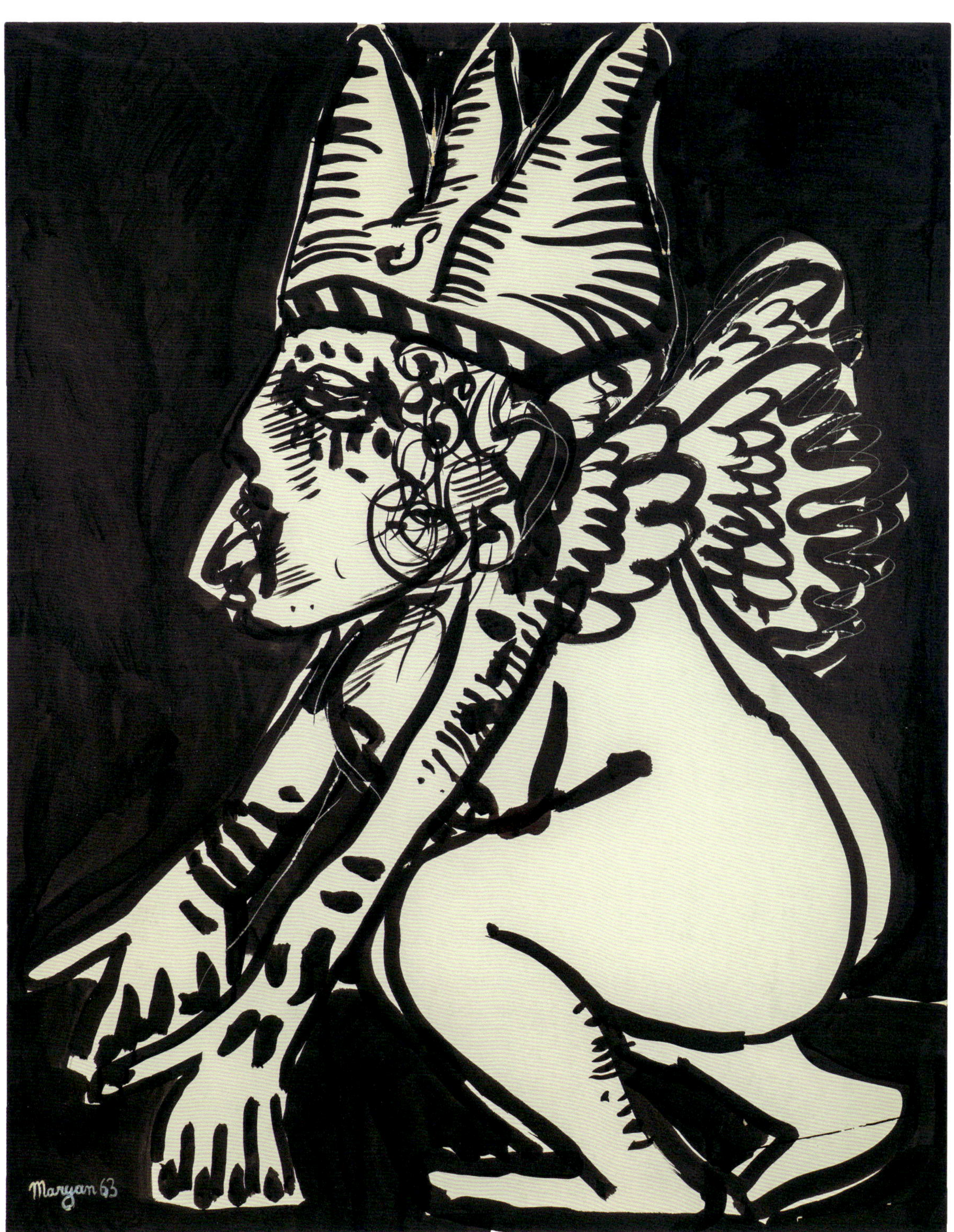

 Personnage VIII, 1963. Ink on board, 40 × 32 inches (101.5 × 81.3 cm). Courtesy of Venus Over Manhattan, New York

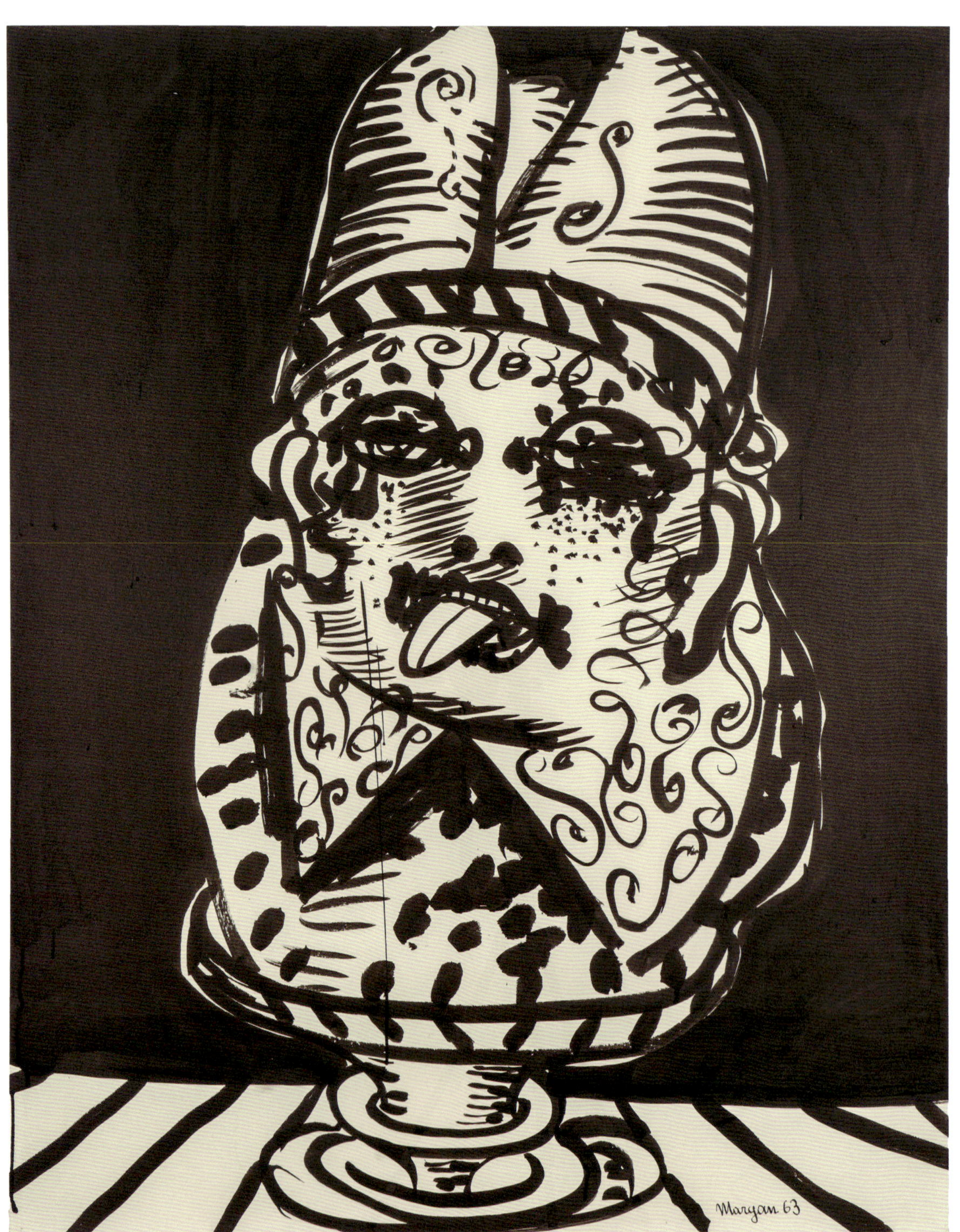

Personnage XII, 1963. Ink on board, 40 × 32 inches (101.5 × 81.3 cm). Private Collection

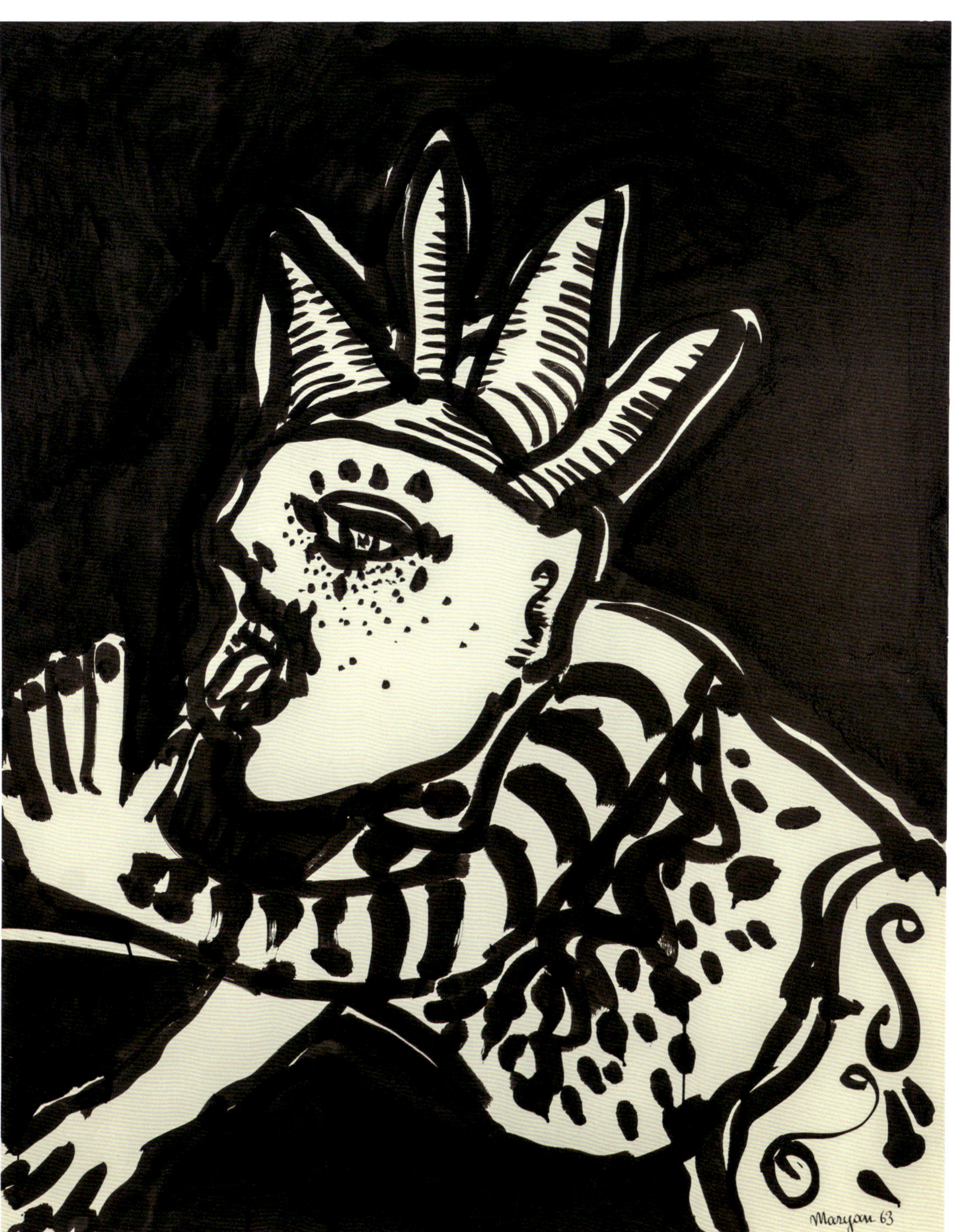

Personnage III, 1963. Ink on board, 40 × 32 inches (101.5 × 81.3 cm). Courtesy of Venus Over Manhattan, New York

1960S: IMMIGRATION TO AMERICA

The 1960s and '70s were the most prolific period of Maryan's life. After his first exhibition in New York in 1960,[1] Maryan and his wife left Paris the following year to immigrate to America. He began to exhibit at the influential Allan Frumkin Gallery, which had branches in New York and Chicago. Through Frumkin, Maryan developed a close friendship with celebrated artists such as H. C. Westermann and June Leaf. He also shared affinities with Leon Golub and the mid-century Chicago artists known as the "Monster Roster."

While never part of their movement, Maryan's exploration of the human figure and intense psychological turmoil mirrors their own. In the Miami exhibition, Maryan's work was hung alongside iconic examples by his American peers, and, in the accompanying vitrines, there were a selection of drawings and friendly correspondence between Maryan and Westermann.

Maryan's American period includes several distinct bodies of work that expand upon his *personnage* paradigm. Psychosexual themes emerged episodically in Maryan's work during these decades, as exemplified by powerful, expressive paintings that fuse snake-like phallus forms with human figures. By the late 1960s, Maryan's *personnages* became more abstract and frenetic. They are often painted on brightly colored solid grounds that contrast the cartoonishly rendered humanoid forms, many of which are reduced to just hands and mouths. —AMG

1.   *Maryan*, André Emmerich Gallery, New York, November 29–December 24, 1960.

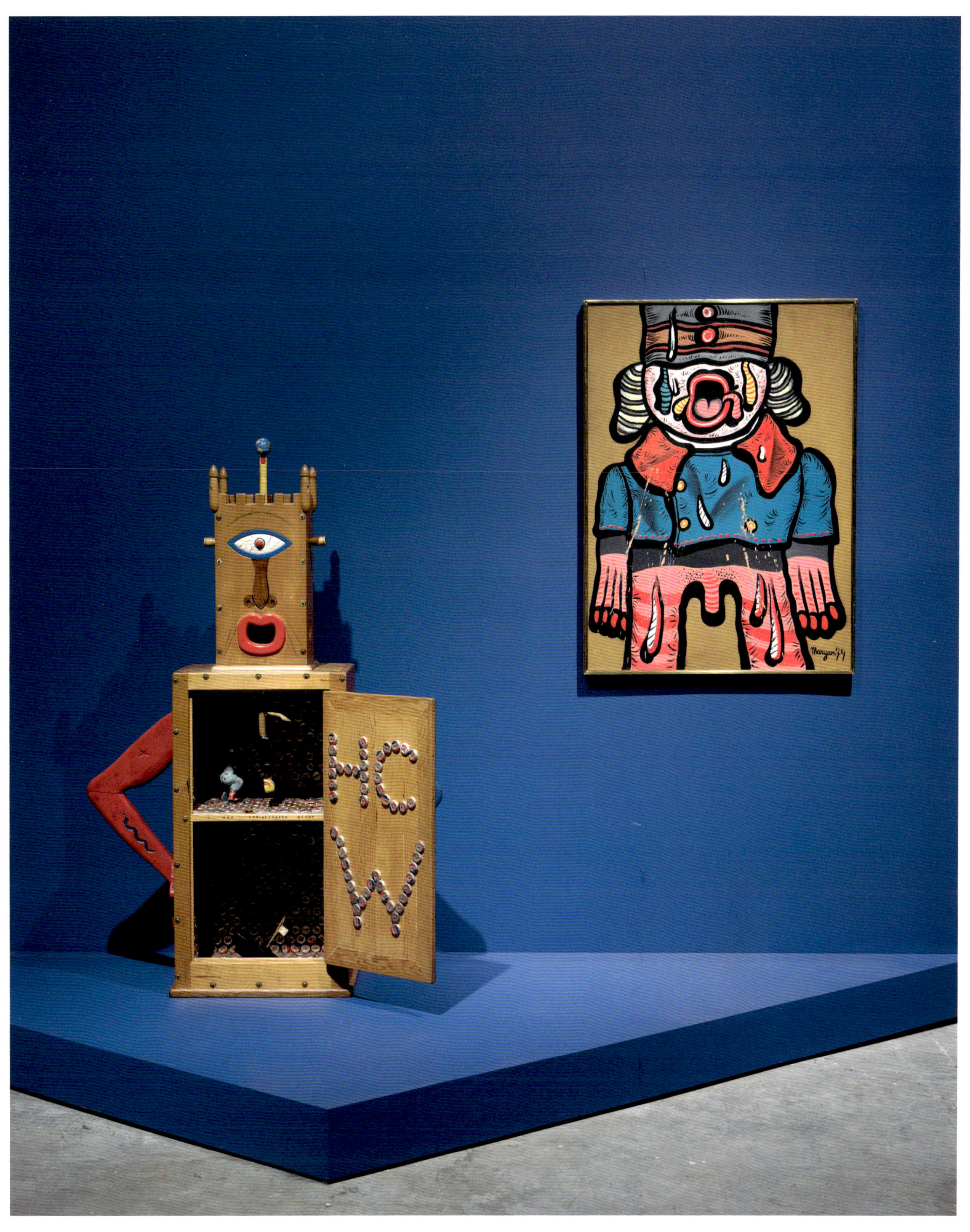

My Name Is Maryan, Museum of Contemporary Art, North Miami, 2022. Installation view.
Left: H. C. (Horace Clifford) Westermann, *Memorial to the Idea of Man If He Was an Idea,* 1958;
right: Maryan, *Personnage (Soldat),* 1974

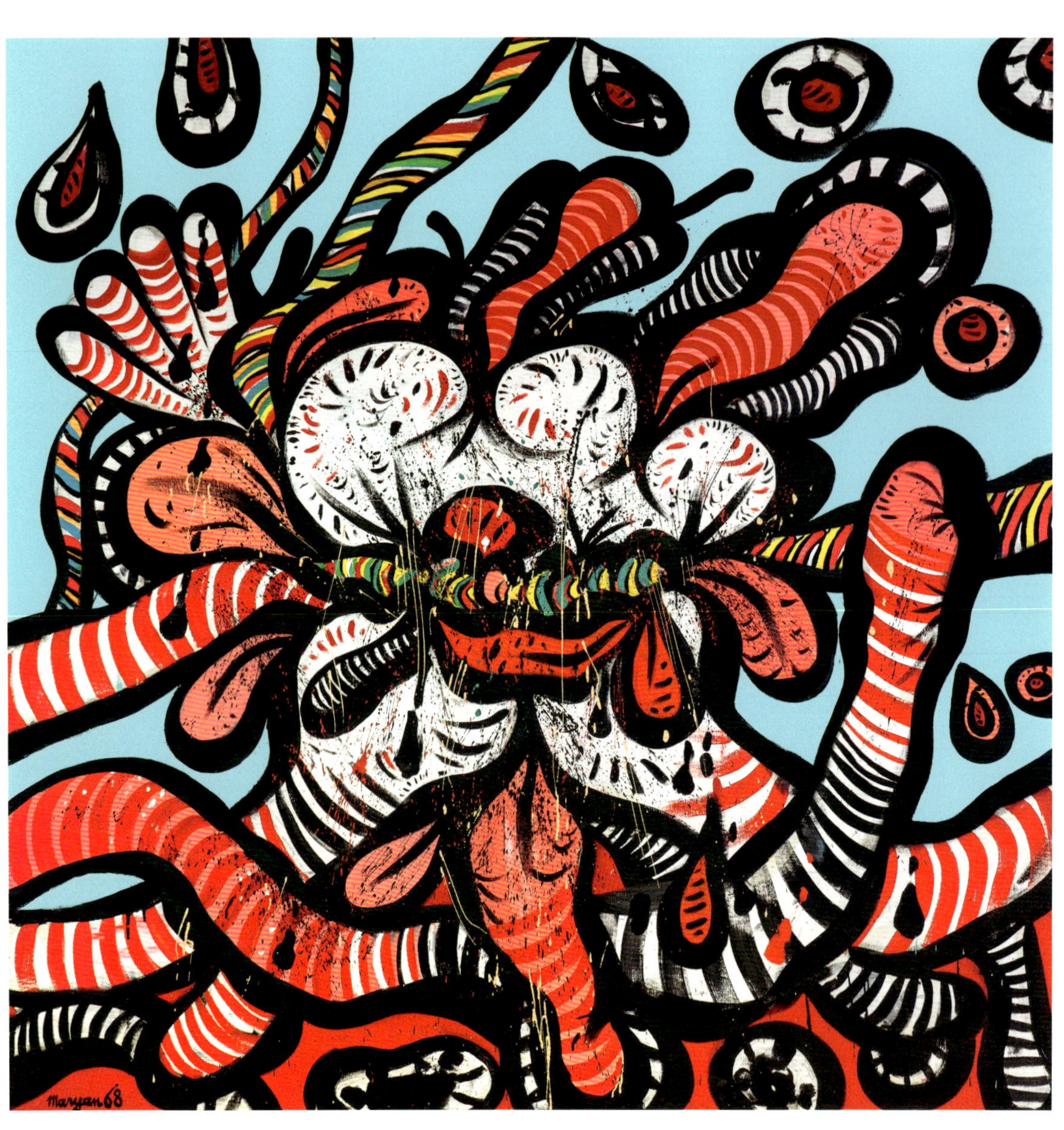

Personnage on a Blue Background, 1968. Oil on canvas, 60 × 60 inches (152.5 × 152.5 cm).
Collection of Ariela and Benito Esquenazi

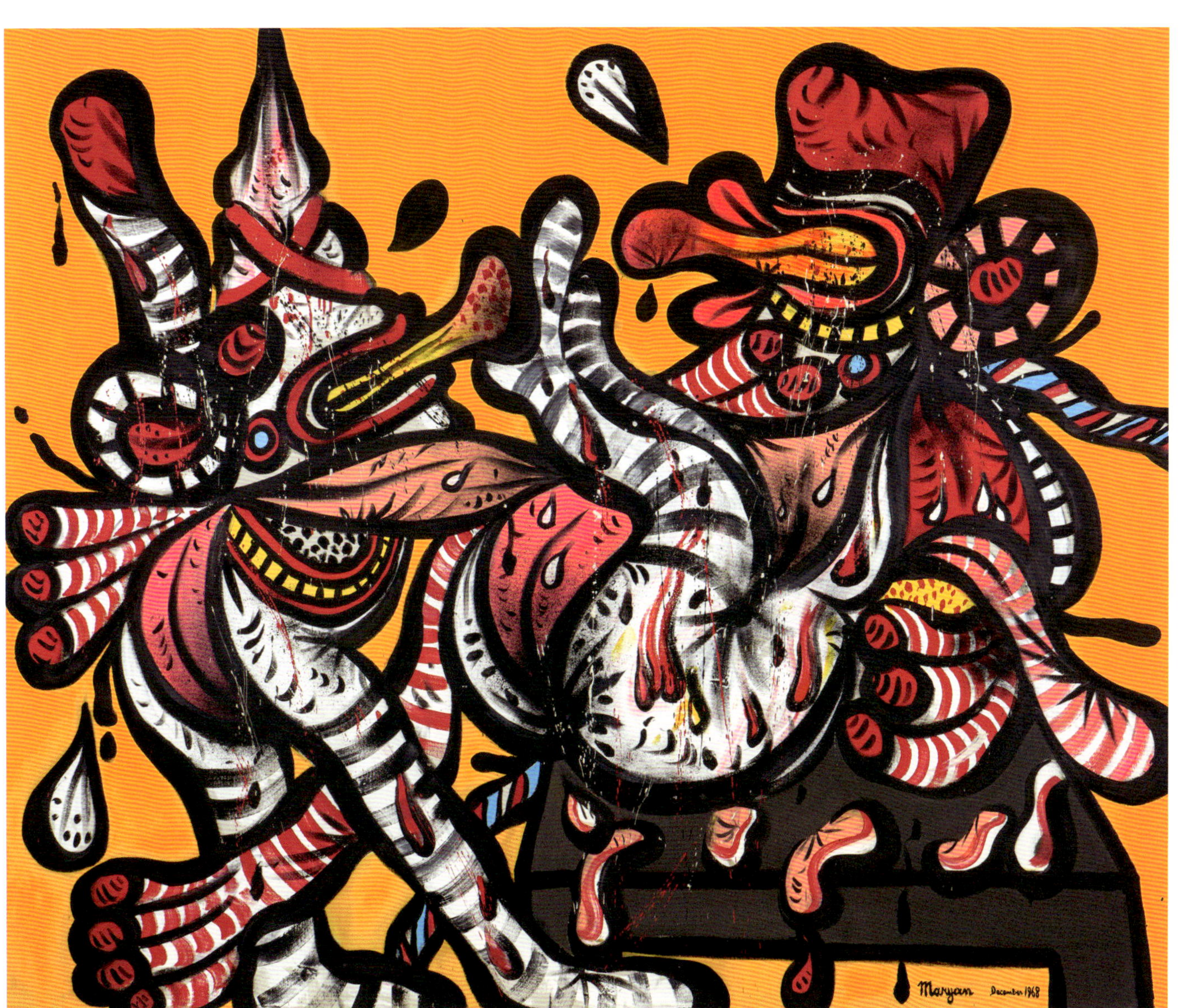

Two Personnages, 1968. Oil on canvas, 52 × 64 inches (132 × 162.5 cm). Private Collection

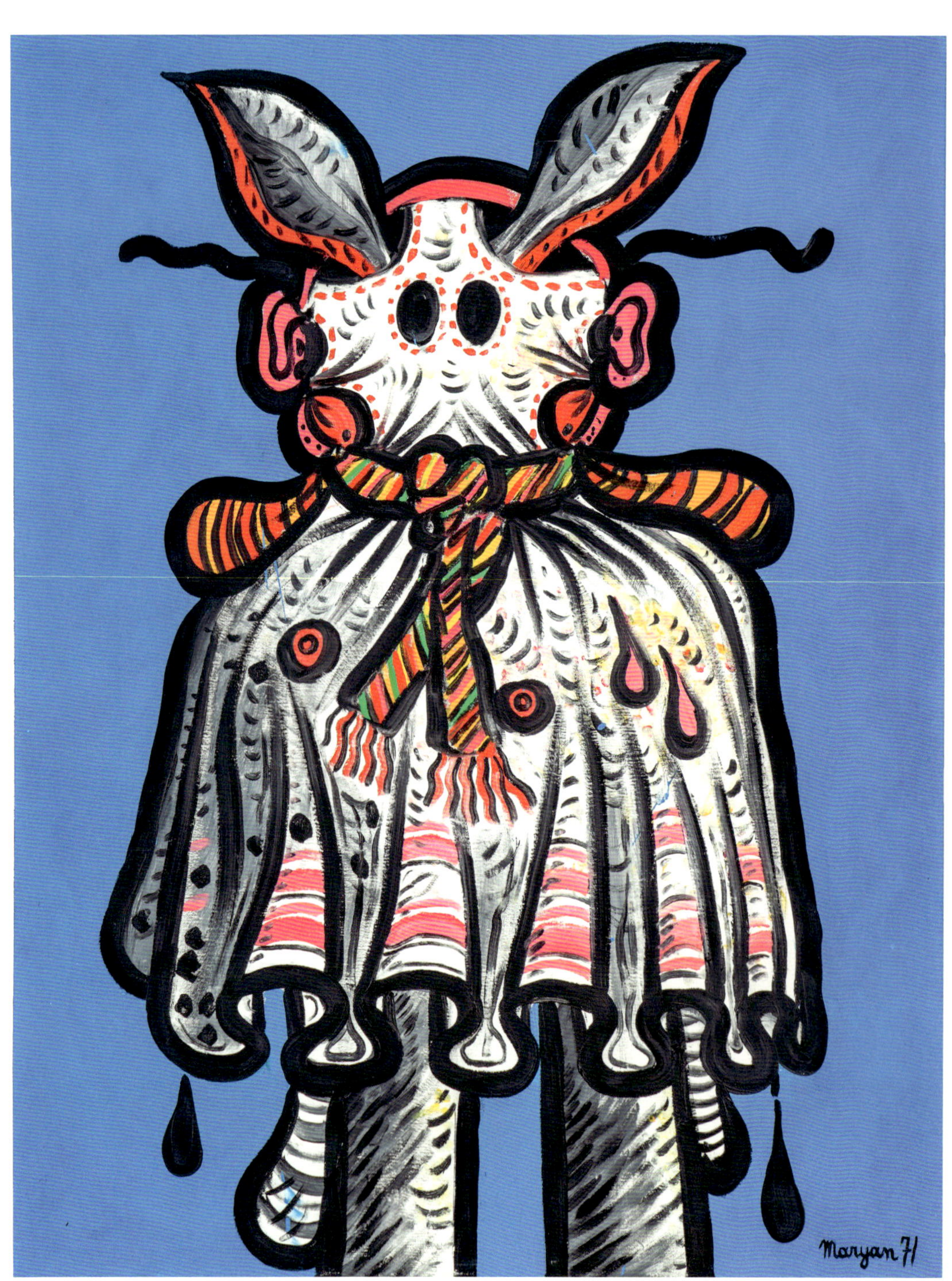

Personnage with Hood and Donkey Ears, 1971. Oil on canvas, 45¼ × 35 inches (115 × 89 cm).
Collection of Spertus Institute, Chicago

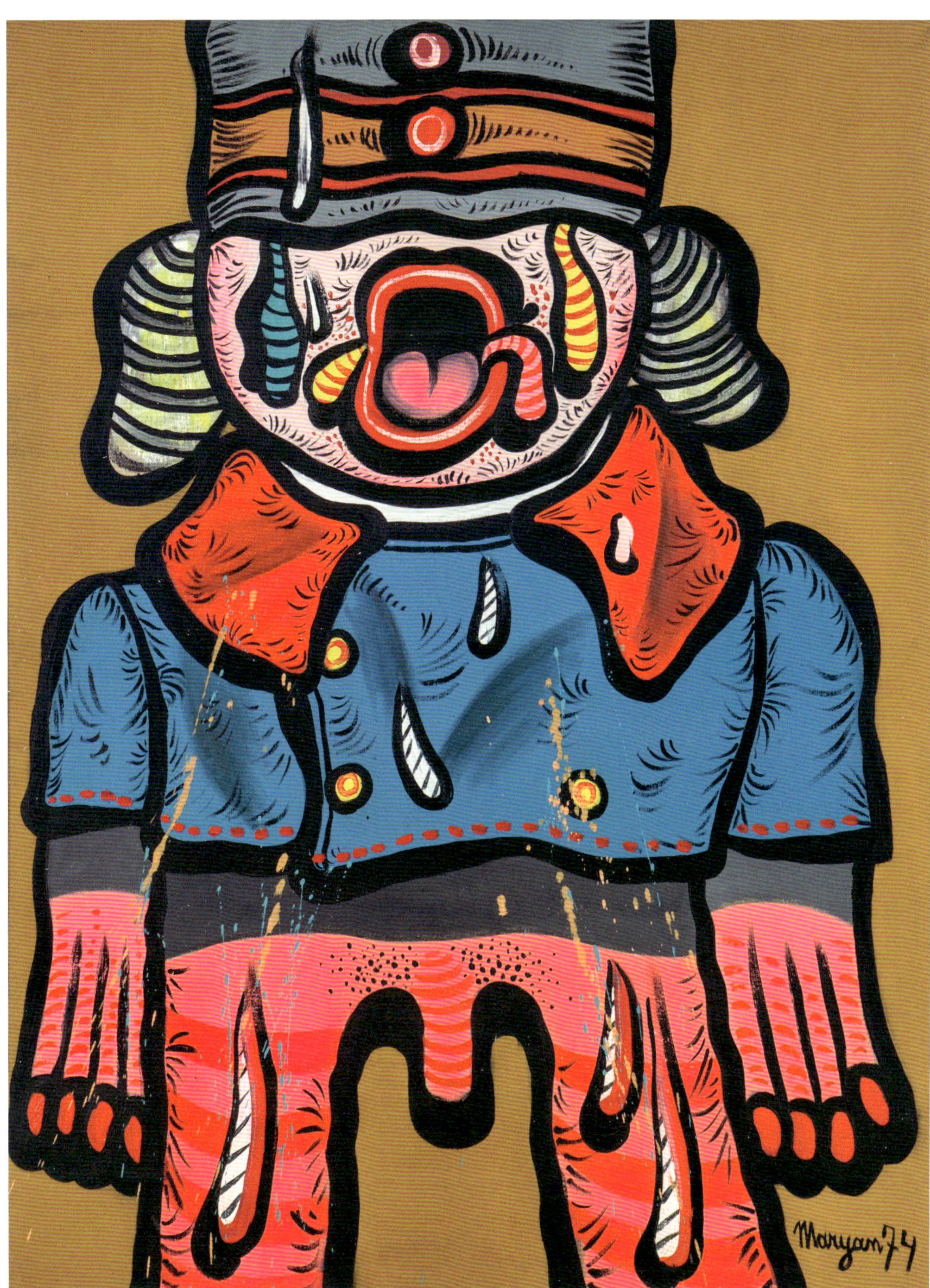

Personnage (Soldat), 1974. Oil on canvas, 40 × 32 inches (101.5 × 81.25 cm). Collection of Beth Rudin DeWoody

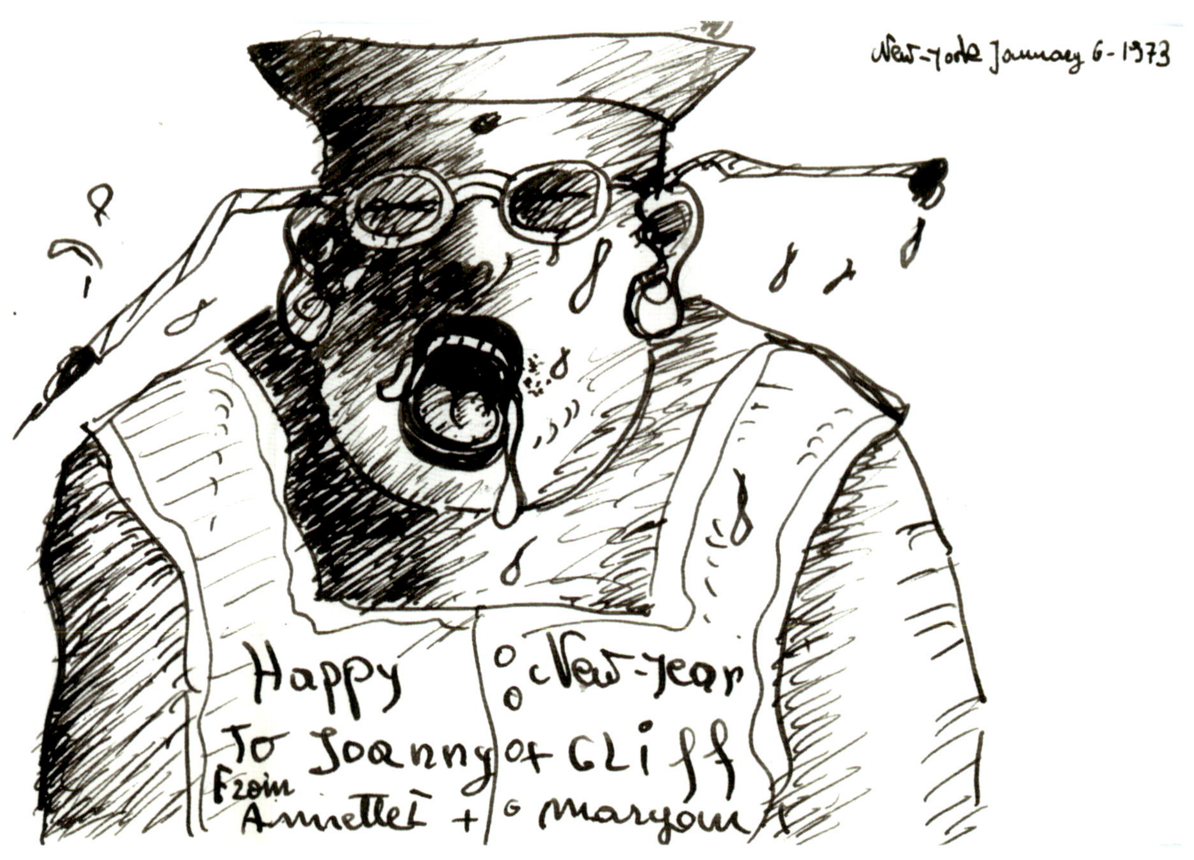

New York, January 6, 73.

Hi!
We are sorry we could not see you when you called us. We tried to call you on the 1st of January around 8 or 8.30 P.M, but there was no answer. We hope to see you both next Saturday. Thanks for the invitation. It is a beautifull dog and beautifull colors. Have a good New Year and good luck for the show. We were thinking a lot about you, and wish we could see each other from time to time.
Be well both of you. Amitiés,
Annette
and Maryan

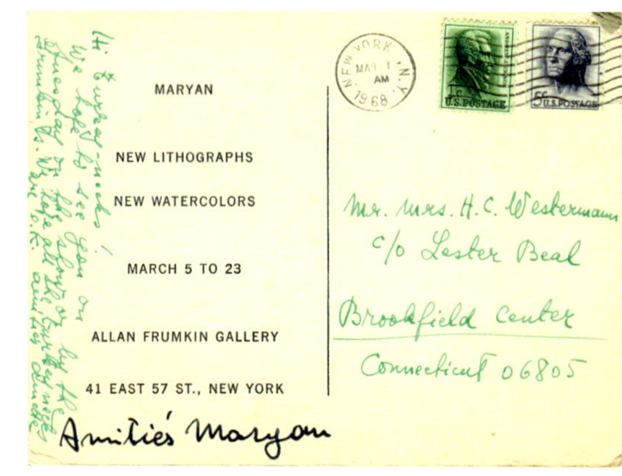

Top and bottom left:
Happy New Year from Annette and Maryan. Enclosed drawing, January 6, 1973. Handwritten letter and ink drawing with envelope. Letter and drawing: 5¾ × 9 inches (14.6 × 22.9 cm); envelope: 3¾ × 6½ inches (9.5 × 16.4 cm). Collection of The David and Alfred Smart Museum of Art, The University of Chicago; The H. C. Westermann Study Collection, Gift of Joanna Beall

Bottom right:
Maryan, H. C. (Horace Clifford) Westermann, Joanna Beall Westermann, *Postcard to [Maryan's] show of lithographs and watercolors at Allan Frumkin Gallery. Hope to see HCW at opening*. Handwritten and typewritten postcard, 6½ × 4⅞ inches (16.5 × 12.4 cm). Collection of The David and Alfred Smart Museum of Art, The University of Chicago; The H. C. Westermann Study Collection, Gift of Joanna Beall

Maryan S. Maryan
301 East 63rd St. Apt. 9F
New York, N.Y. 10021

New-York august I. 1970

Dear Allan,
Thanks a lot for The Three
checks of advanced money, it is
really a big help.
We hope you are all well;
Best regards from us both, for the
whole family..

Maryan

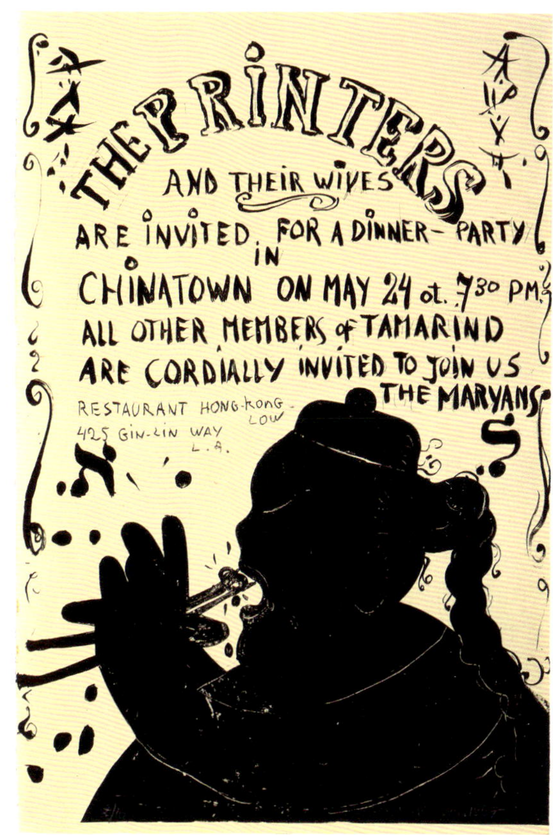

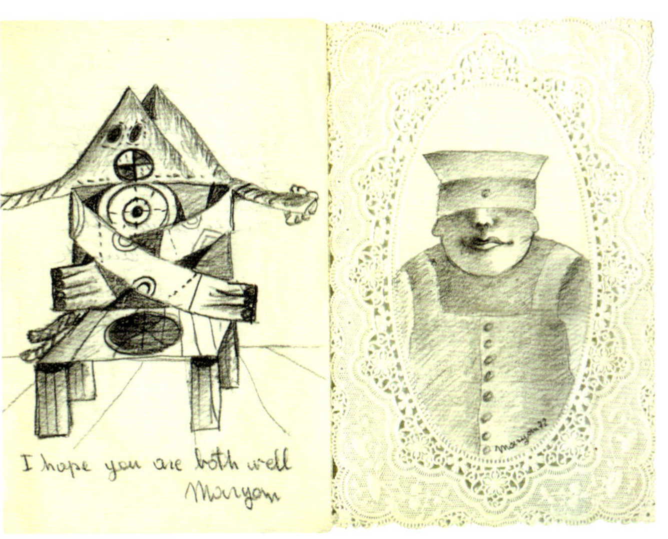

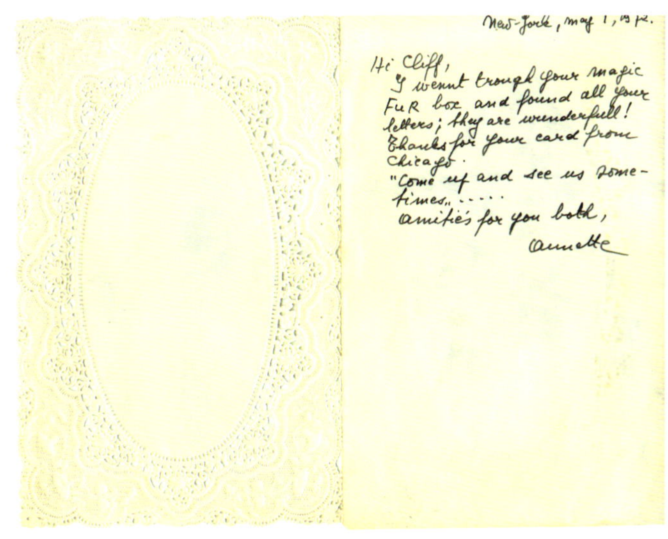

Top left:
Untitled (From Maryan to Allan), 1970. Watercolor and ink on paper, 9½ × 7¼ inches (24.1 × 18.4 cm). Courtesy of Venus Over Manhattan, New York

Top right:
Invitation/poster ("The Printers and Their Wives Are Invited for a Dinner-Party in Chinatown on May 24 at 7:30 PM., All members of Tamarind Are Cordially Invited to Join Us the Maryans, Restaurant Hong-Kong-Low 425 Gin Lin Way L.A."), 1967. Lithograph on red-tan Japanese wove paper, 37¼ × 25 inches (94.6 × 63.5 cm). The David and Alfred Smart Museum of Art, The University of Chicago; Purchase, Anonymous Gift

Bottom, left and right:
Maryan, Annette Maryan, H. C. (Horace Clifford) Westermann, *Annette writes that she found Cliff's letters and they are wonderful. Maryan drawing and "I hope you are well,"* May 1, 1972. Handwritten letter with two pencil drawings, 8⅛ × 10½ inches (20.6 × 26.7 cm). Collection of The David and Alfred Smart Museum of Art, The University of Chicago; The H. C. Westermann Study Collection, Gift of Joanna Beall

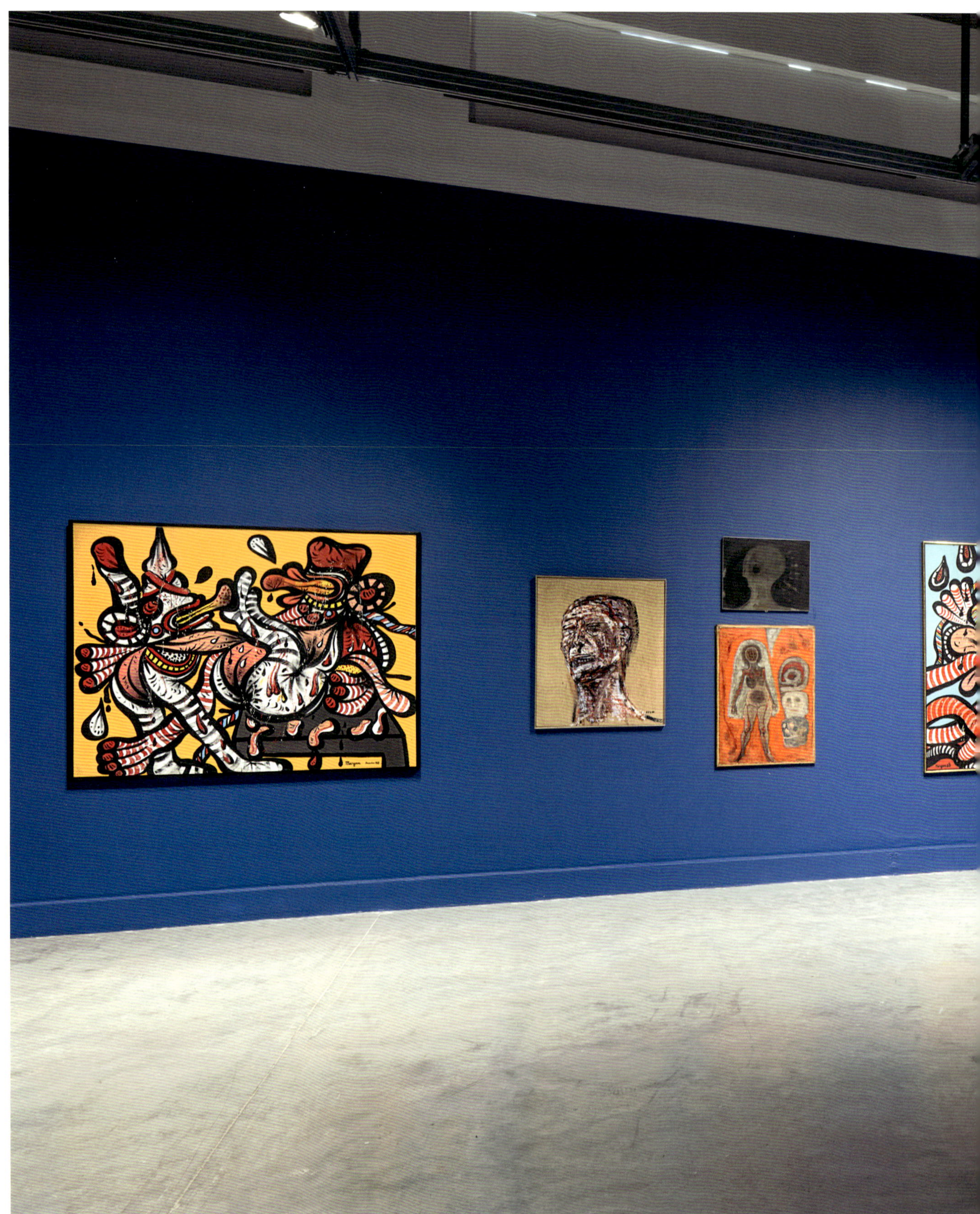

My Name Is Maryan, Museum of Contemporary Art, North Miami, 2022. Installation view

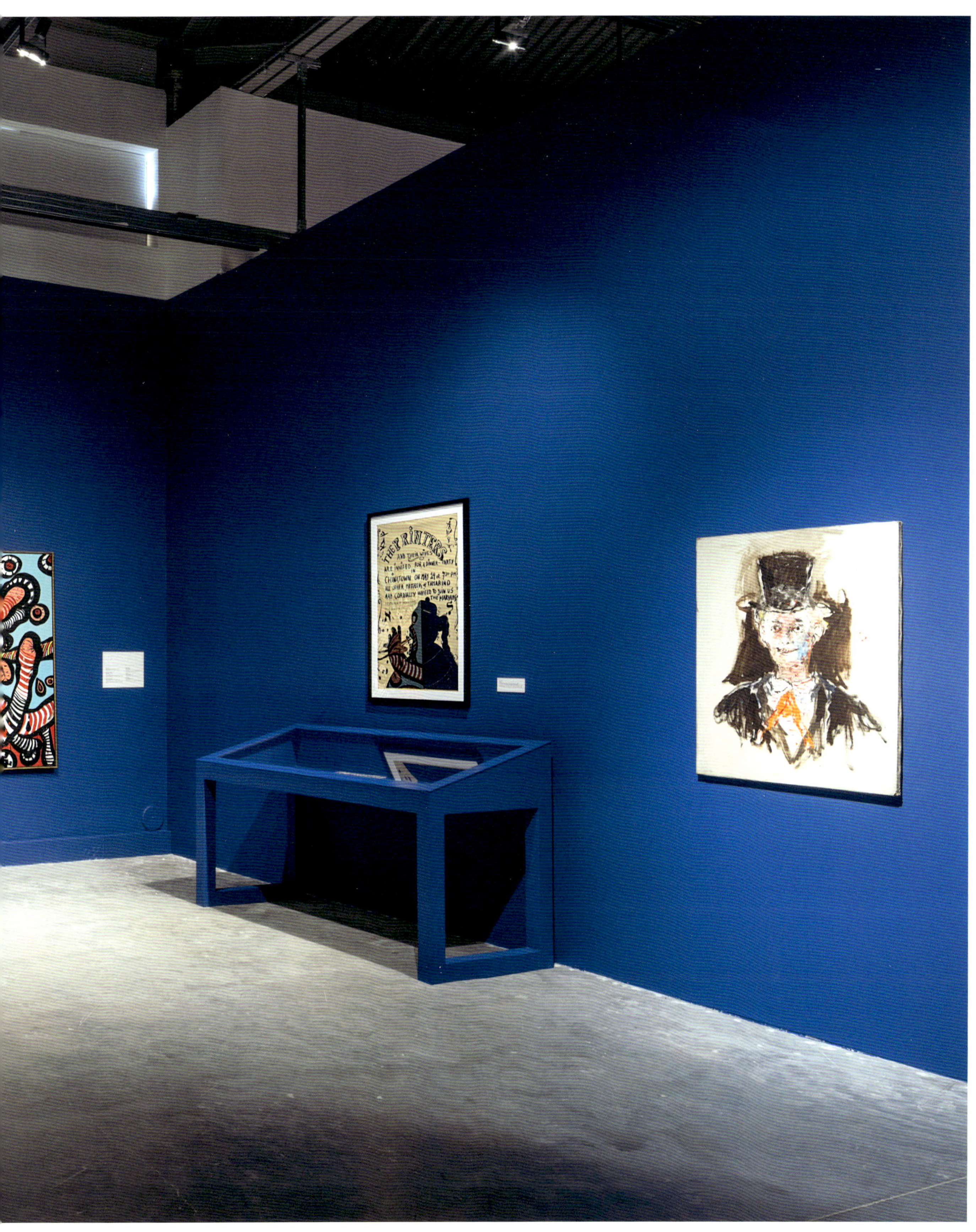

About Maryan (1977)

IN 1958, WHEN I HAD my Fulbright govern-
ment grant to Paris, Allan Frumkin told
me to look at the work of a painter in Paris
named Maryan.

When I saw his work in a group exhibition I
thought—this is the greatest contemporary painter
I have ever seen. It was like a de Kooning painting, full of incredible force but it had humanity!

It was a celebration of life—like an American
Indian Cachina [*sic*] doll. I wrote to Allan and
told him Maryan is the greatest painter in Paris.

I never thought to look him up. What happened
was, Irving Petlin, a young painter who had
just arrived from Chicago, told me that Maryan
wanted to meet me.

There was an exhibition in a Paris gallery that I
had a large painting in which I hated, but probably it is one of my strongest works. It's called
The Operation. Irving Petlin told me that Maryan
liked the painting and wanted to meet me. I was
very depressed and tired at the time but I wanted
to meet Maryan.

I think that meeting with Maryan and Annette,
his wife, was one of the happiest moments of my
life. I remember everything—the warmth of the
small apartment, Annette and Maryan's warmth.
Their house was filled with colors, not decorated
colors but the colors of joy, and there were many
wonderful toys made of wood, so humble, and
they reached out to touch you it seemed.

Maryan stood so proudly and he had the most
beautiful face I've ever seen, because around
him there was a light. He had soft blond hair and
it caught the light like an aureole. They knew
the effect they had on people. He, smiling and
dazzling, and Annette so clean, her house spar-
kling in order to present this gift of Maryan. Yes
it was theater and in it was even a kind of cruelty
because of their awareness of their great power,
their truth.

I believe Annette saw my sadness and depression.
I had been ill from it. We talked, I with my pigeon
[*sic*] French, Annette with her pigeon English.

My strongest memory of that evening was that
Maryan said let's paint. I was bottled up because
for almost two years, if you can imagine such
a thing, I was trying to learn to draw better.
Suppressing my volatile nature copying paint-
ings in the Louvre. Chardin, Goya, even several
Vermeer reproductions. I had stopped doing it.
My fingers were aching to unwind.

Maryan put paper on the floor and we painted.
He was so charming thumping and moving agily
[*sic*] with his crutch on that beautiful well-dressed
leg and shoe. He watched me and he said, "Look,
how she needs to paint." How happy I was even
though I couldn't do it freely.

I left Paris soon because of the death of my broth-
er-in-law and stayed with my sister in Texas for
a month.

Perhaps six months later (I was now married and
living in New York City), Irving Petlin came with
Maryan to my house in Inwood Park. Oh I see I am
aching to tell all of our stories. Joel, my husband's,
story, June's story of her unwinding from the
Vermeer rooms which she had so carefully copied.

So Maryan came again and so cleverly was
speaking English. Irving would help him. He and
Annette would move to America. I wish this story
had a happy ending. But it does not.

We don't have to speak about it as he would say,
"No work on Sunday." Once he laughed to himself
as he walked on the street in NY having heard the
sirens of the fire engines. I knew, as he would know,
that he meant in the concentration camp when the
sirens would sound—no work on Sunday.

So I write about you dear Maryan, the peaked
hats you painted—the exuberant and vulgar
brushstrokes almost like intestines and turds and
ribbons. Our peaked hats! From my painting of
the operation and Goya's inquisition, how you
examined my copies. "Ahh" or "Aghh" you
would say, "If I could only draw like you."

It didn't go to my head, I just watched how later
you made your powerful images no matter what!

People eating ice cream (a memory of your first
trip to Coney Island).

—June Leaf

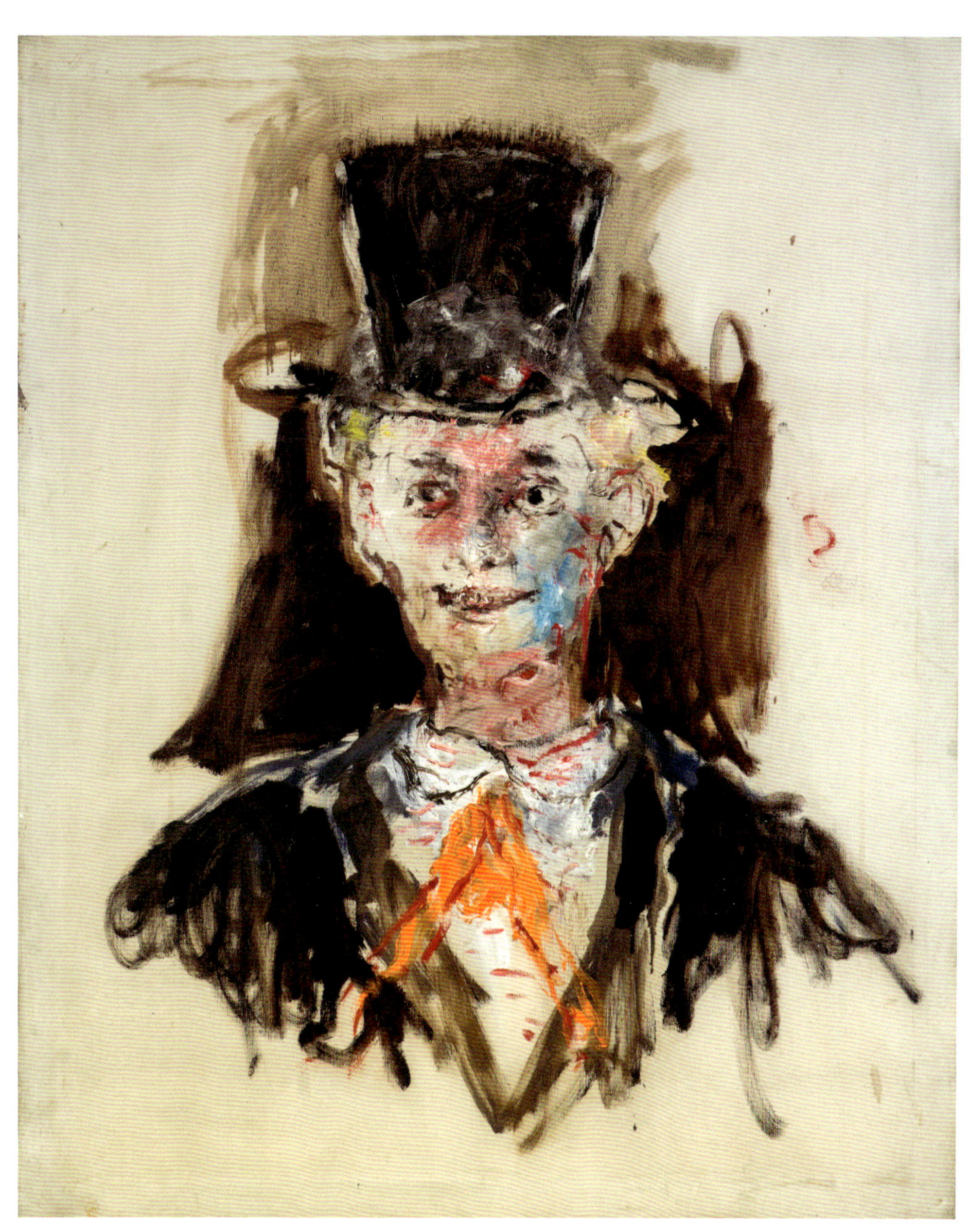

June Leaf, *Portrait of Maryan*, 1968. Acrylic on canvas, 39¼ × 31¾ inches (100 × 81 cm).
Collection of June Leaf; courtesy of Hyphen

ART HISTORY AS MUSE

Artists have always mined the work of their forebears to nourish their practices. Maryan was a voracious, astute student of several centuries' worth of European painters that came before him. This body of work demonstrates the manifold ways in which Maryan treated the old masters as his muses.

Maryan's most explicit acknowledgment of his art historical antecedents is in a series of paintings he titled as "after" artists such as Goya, Velázquez, Hals, Rembrandt, and Vermeer. Goya's influence looms particularly large in Maryan's oeuvre. He frequently returned to the figure of a person wearing a conical hat or "capirote." This character is a direct citation of Goya's iconic work *The Inquisition Tribunal* (1812–19), which depicts the barbarism, public shaming, and torture of Jewish "heretics" by Spanish Catholic clergy.

This section also features never-before-exhibited paintings on panel that render singular figures from various art historical sources. Painted in 1968 with a Pop art palette and cartoony drawing style, this series pays homage to Maryan's own personal literary canon, including Franz Kafka's *Amerika*, Alfred Jarry's *Ubu roi*, Marquis de Sade's eulogy for Jean-Paul Marat, and Jean Genet's *The Balcony*. —AMG

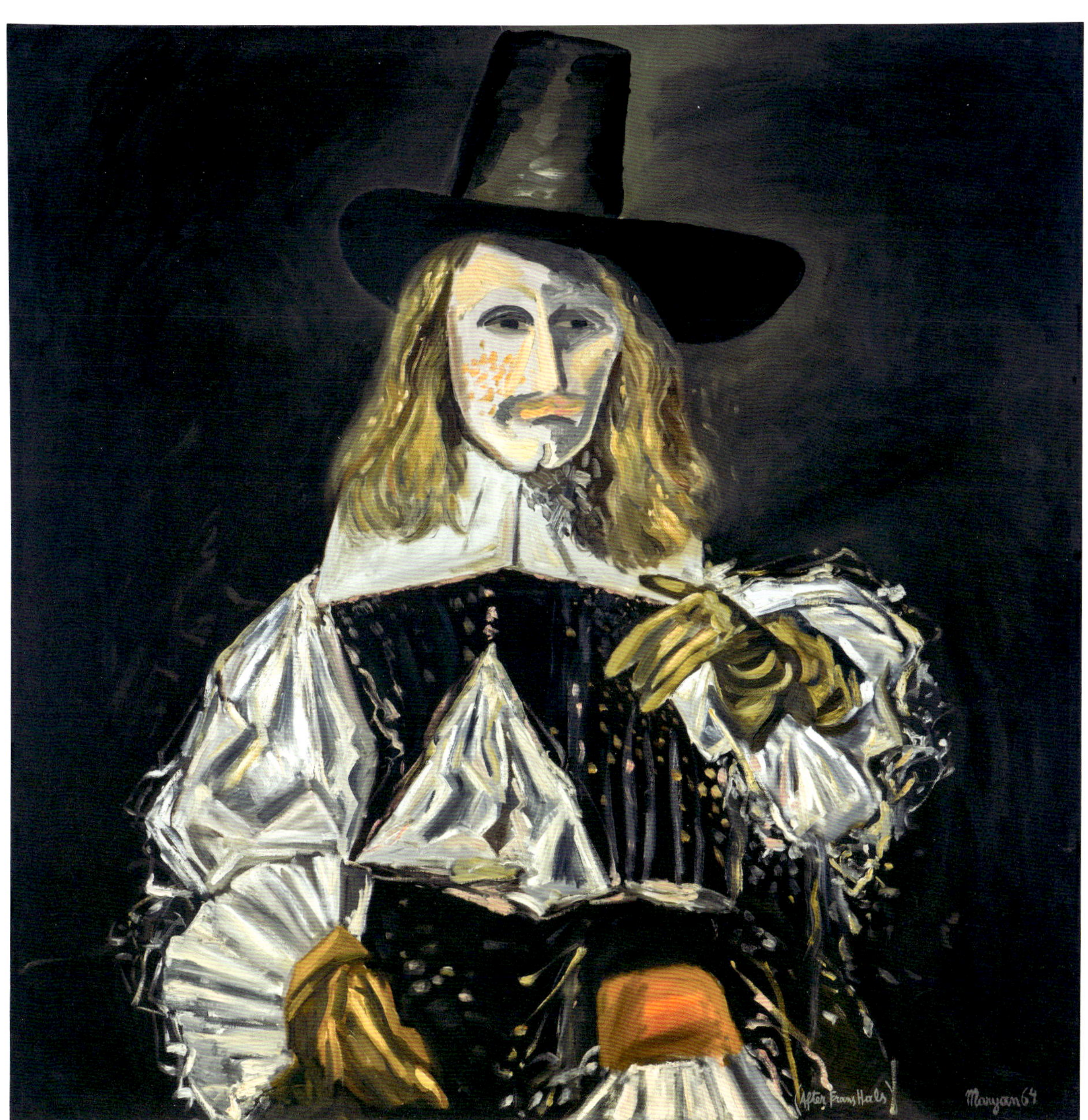

145   *After Frans Hals*, 1964. Oil on canvas, 60 × 60 inches (152 × 152 cm). Private Collection

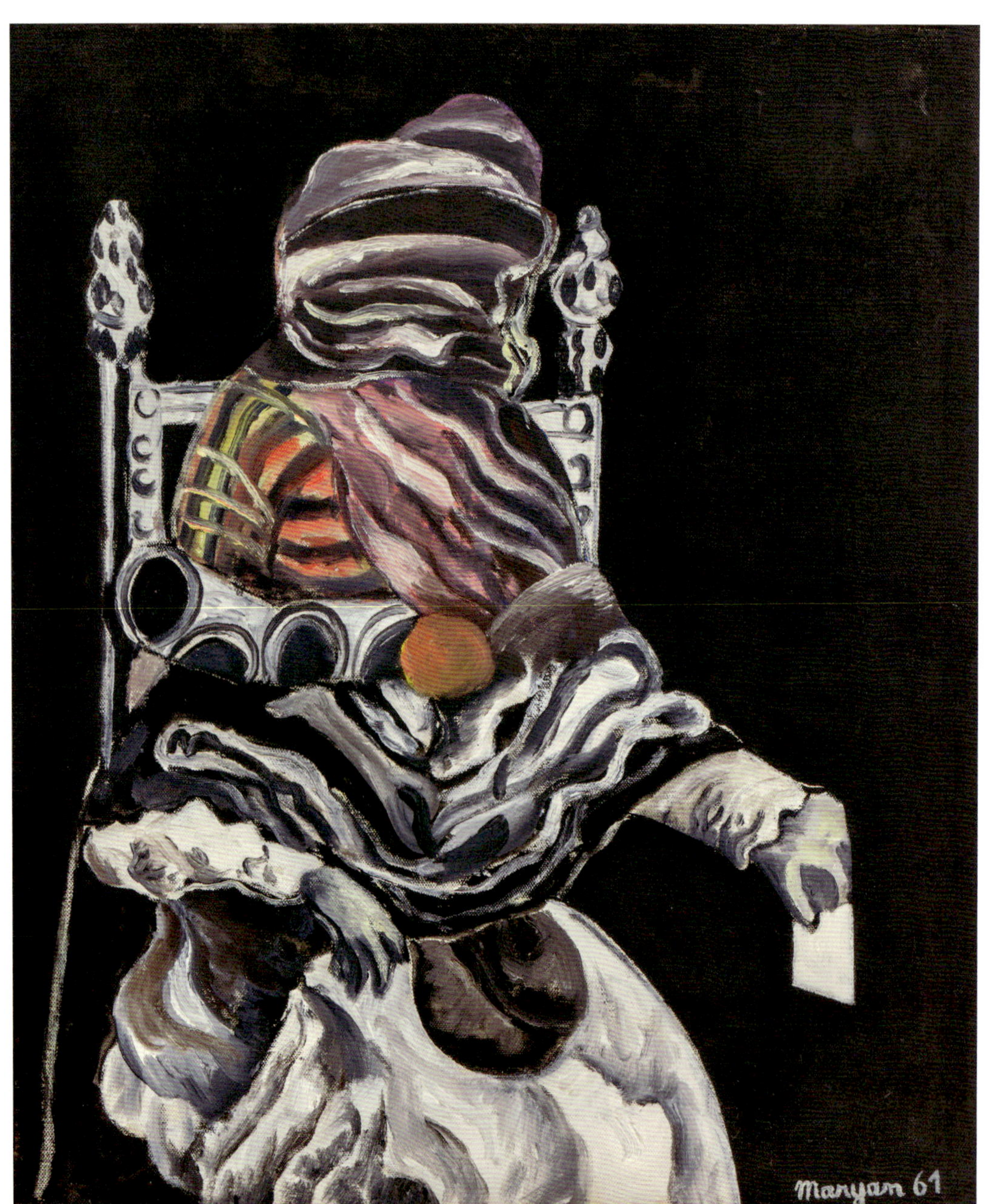

After Velázquez, 1961. Oil on canvas, 21 × 18 inches (55 × 46 cm). Estate of Galerie Jacques Benador, Geneva

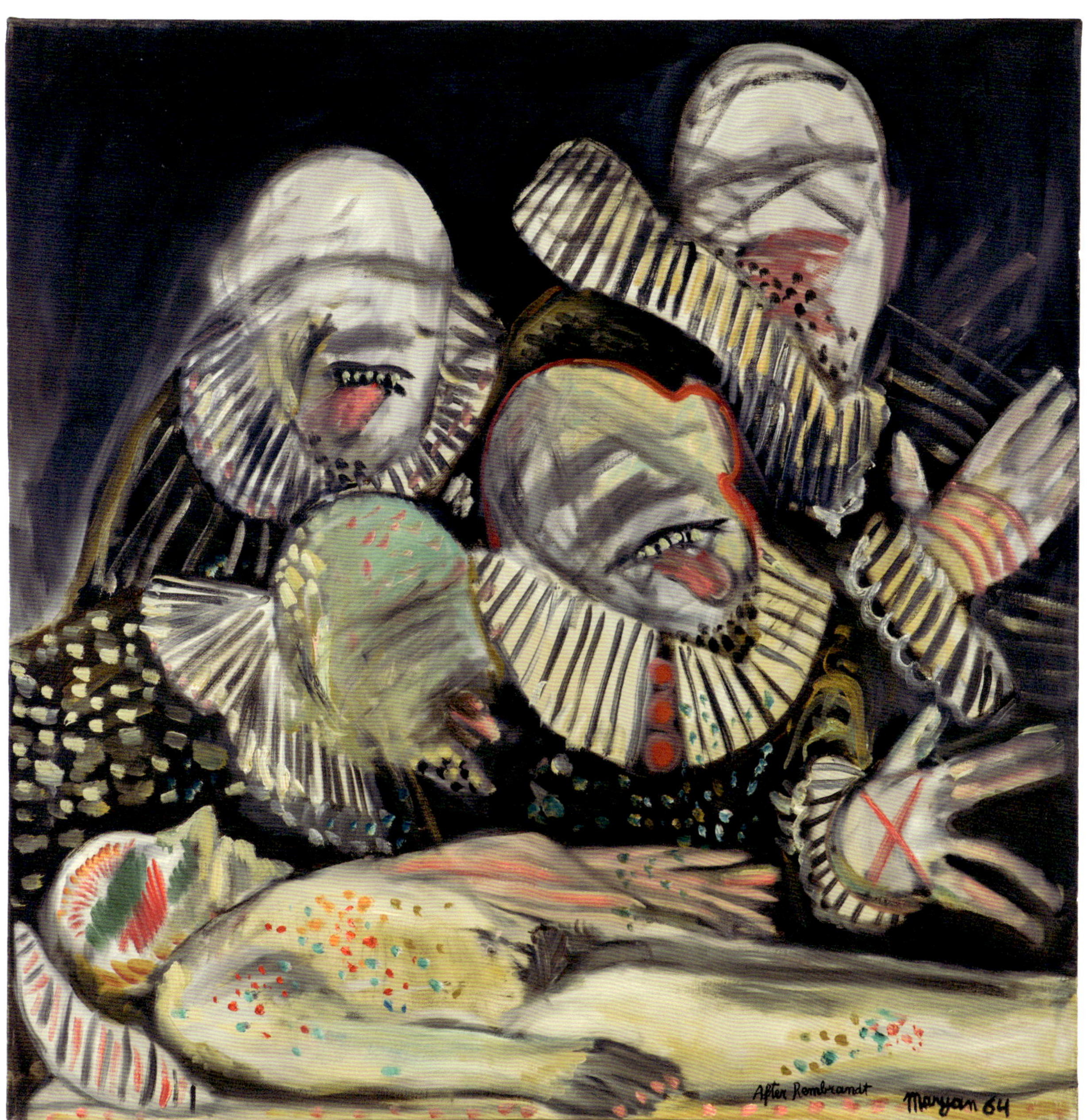

After Rembrandt, 1964. Oil on canvas, 40 × 40 inches (101.5 × 101.5 cm). Private Collection

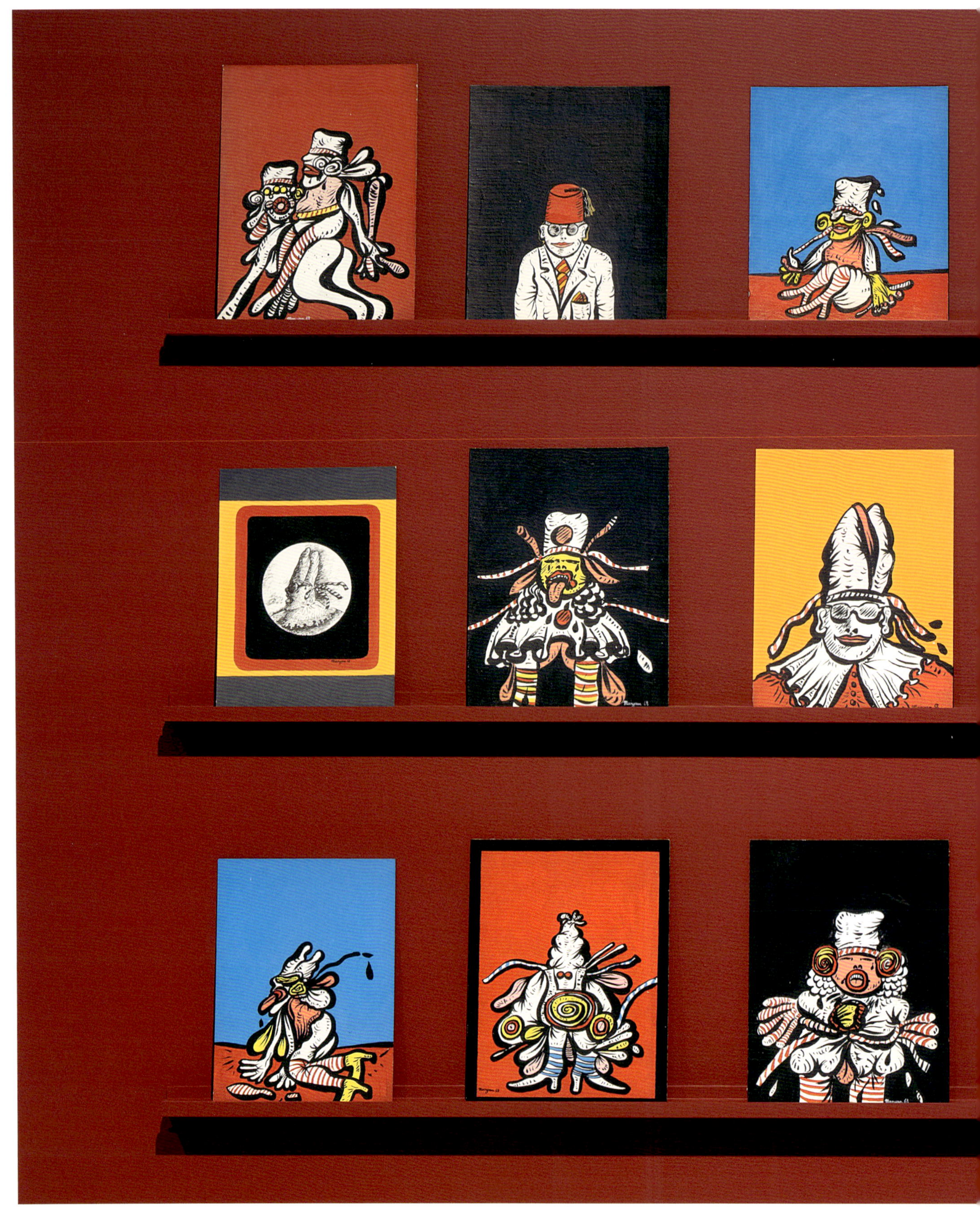

Top row: *Untitled*, 1968; *Untitled*, n.d.; *Untitled*, n.d.; *Franz Kafka: Amerika*, 1968; *Untitled*, 1968; *Untitled*, 1968

Middle row: *Jean Genet: The Balcony*, 1968; *Untitled*, 1968; *Roger Peyrefitte: La Nature du Prince*, 1968; *Untitled*, 1968; *Untitled*, 1968; *Untitled*, n.d.

Bottom row: *Untitled*, n.d.; *Alfred Jarry: Ubu enchaîné*, 1968; *Alfred Jarry: Ubu roi*, 1968; *Untitled*, 1968; *Untitled*, 1968; *Marquis de Sade: Jean-Paul Marat*, 1968

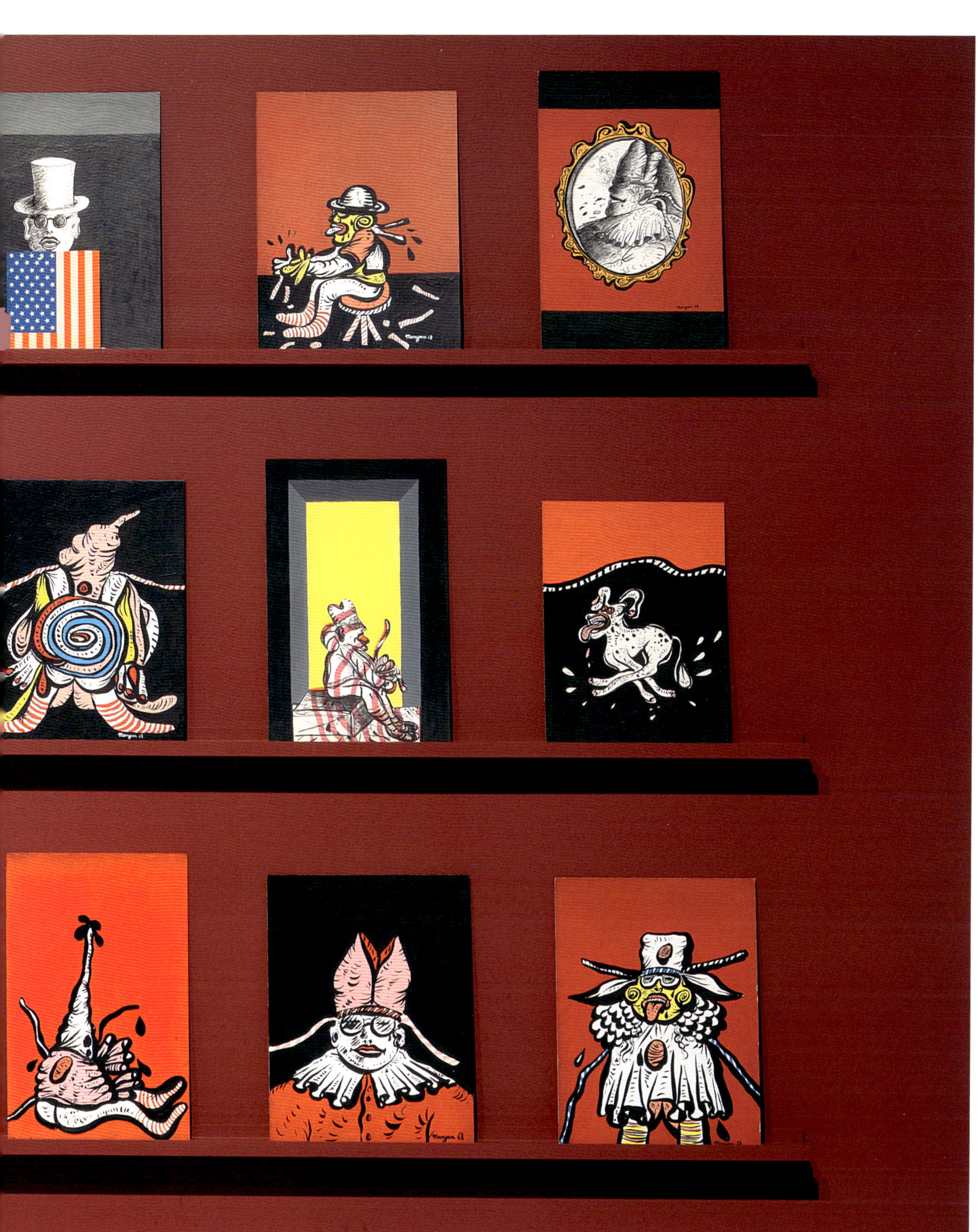

NAPOLEON DRAWINGS

Maryan frequently worked in series, exploring many permutations of a given theme. His wife, Annette, wrote of his studio habits, "painting was his 'liberation.' Once he started to work on a canvas, he usually tried to finish it the same day."[1] Maryan's artist friend Irving Petlin used more visceral terms to describe his working pace: "He made pictures like other people throw up—they were literally spewed out, one after the other with great velocity."[2]

His vigorous, liberatory pace is evident in the series of Napoleon drawings. In 1973–74, Maryan created these iconic, monumental crayon drawings. Maryan transforms the familiar form of the legendary French leader Napoléon Bonaparte (1769–1821) into a grotesque caricature that seems to decompose from one rendering to the next. While most of Maryan's *Napoleon* drawings retain some recognizable features, such as his signature military regalia and distinctive bicorne hat, the figure is shown in various states of distress—sweating, vomiting, splayed open, and with a spliced head. Napoleon becomes another *personnage* in Maryan's theater of human absurdity and cruelty.

The choice of Napoleon as a subject seems bound up with Maryan's complicated relationship to France and the traumatic memories triggered by military regalia. He arrived in Paris to study in 1950. He experienced his first successes as an artist there and felt at home speaking the language, yet after a decade of living in the city, the French state denied his request for citizenship. Maryan left for New York in 1961. It is tempting to speculate that the frenetic energy that went into these Napoleon drawings may have exorcised some of the demons that lurked in his memories of France, or that Napoleon served as a surrogate for his own experiences during the war. —AMG

1.   Annette M. Maryan to Arthur M. Feldman (Director of Spertus Institute), April 4, 1983, Annette M. Maryan papers.
2.   Irving Petlin, quoted in Michele Vishny, "Introduction," in *Maryan's Personnages*.

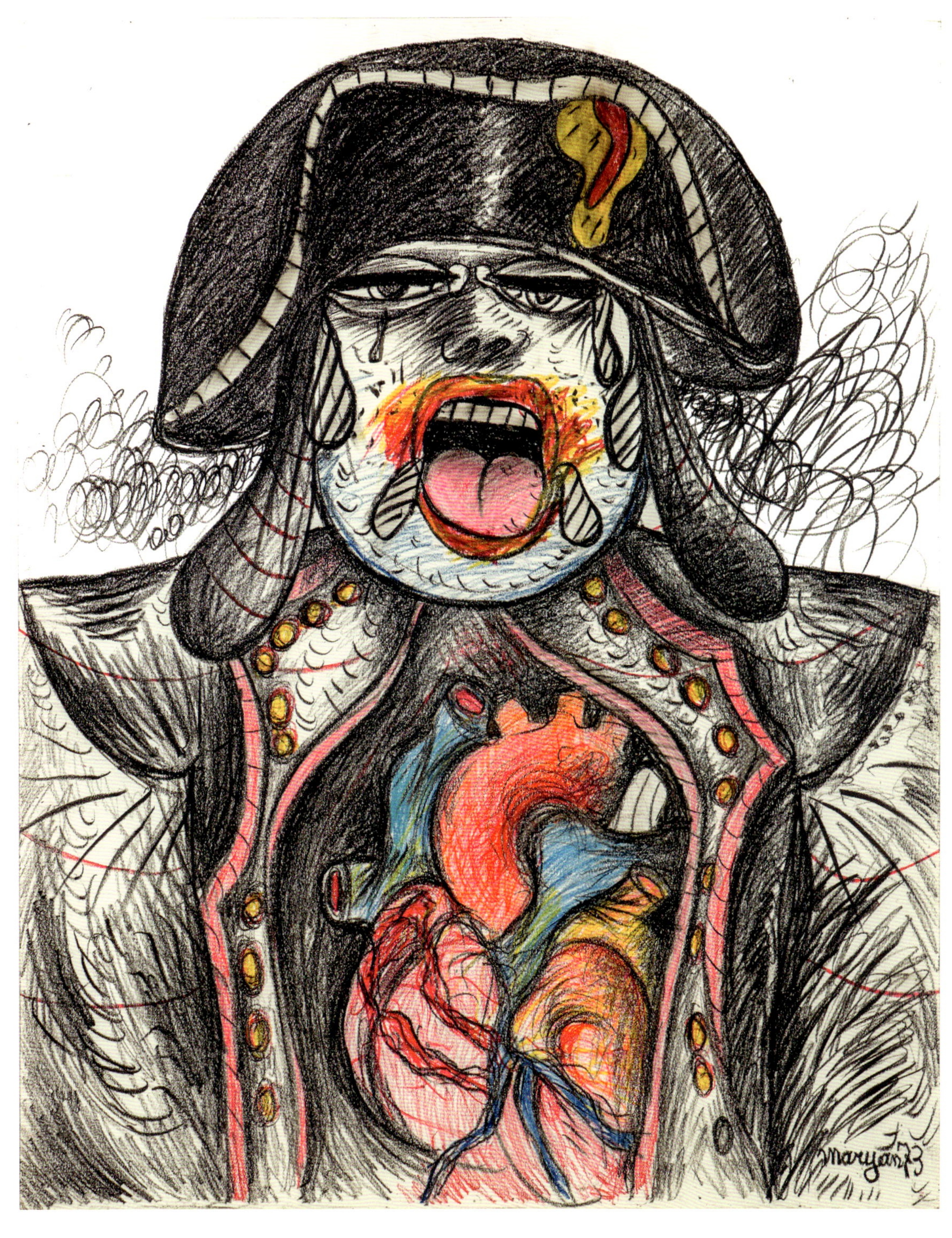

Personnage (Napoléon), 1973. Wax crayon on museum rag board. 40 × 32 inches (101.5 × 81.3 cm).
Collection of The David and Alfred Smart Museum of Art, The University of Chicago; Purchase, Anonymous Gift

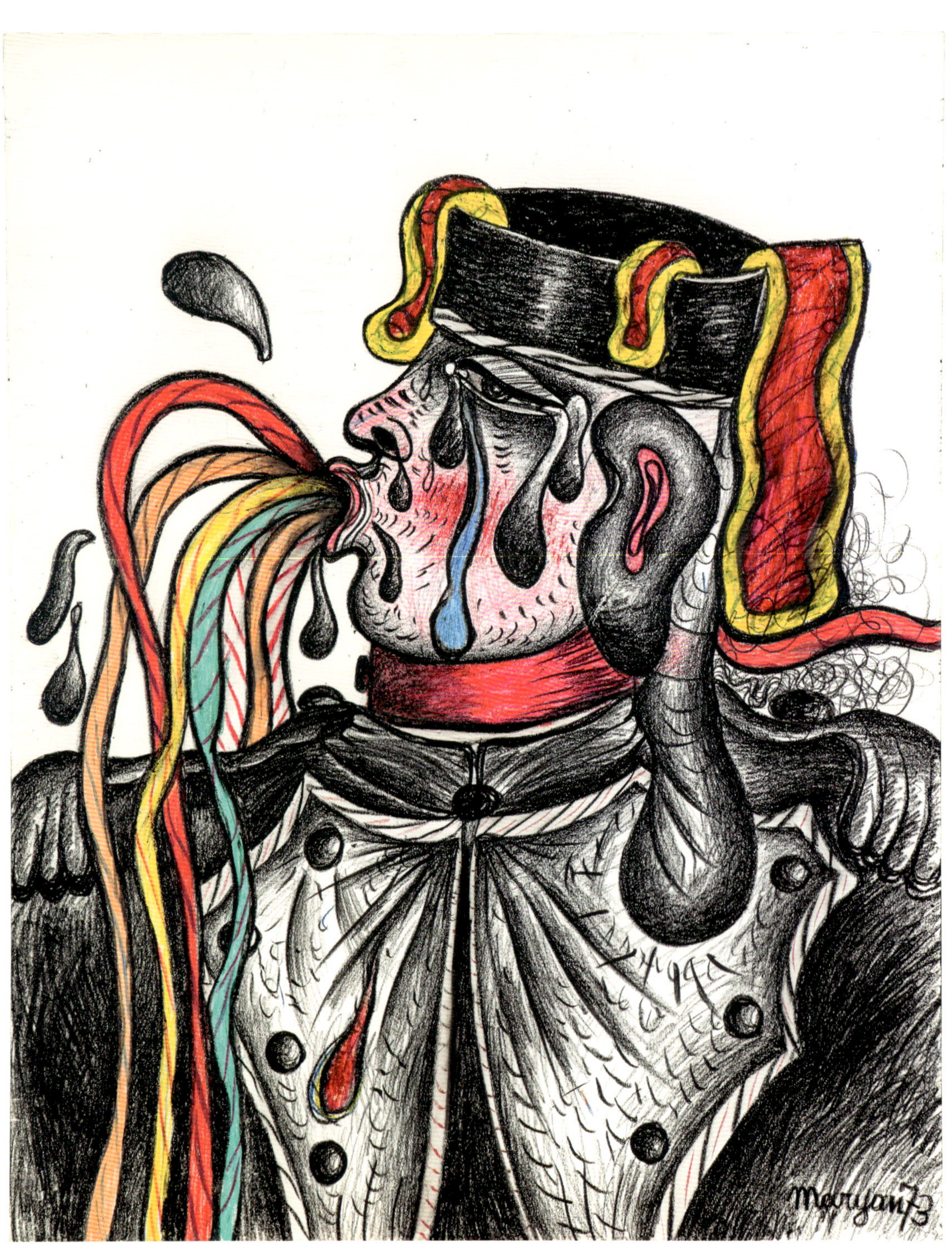

Personnage (Napoléon), 1973. Wax crayon on museum rag board, 40 × 32 inches (101.5 × 81.3 cm). Private Collection

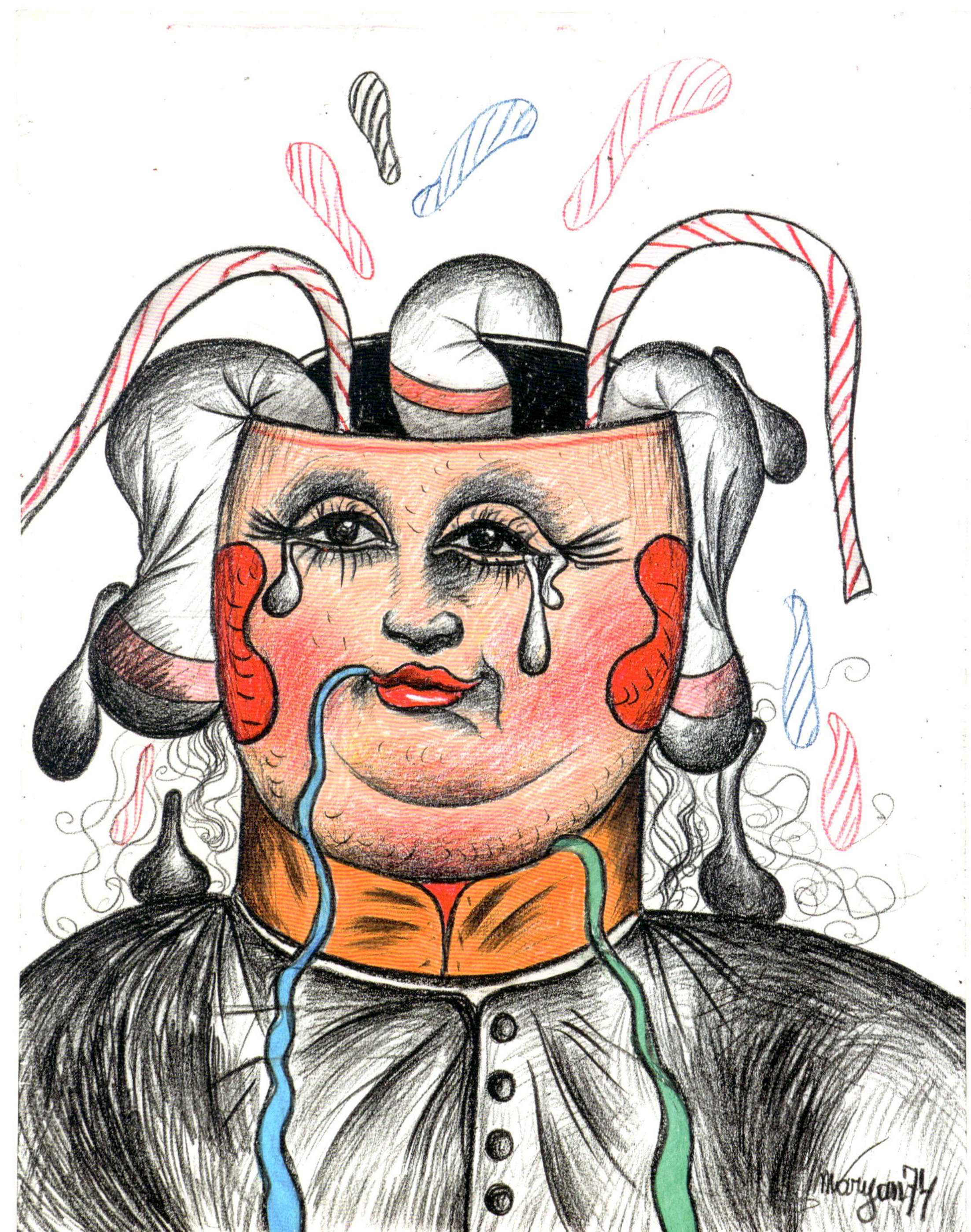

 Personnage (Napoléon), 1974. Wax crayon on museum rag board, 40 × 32 inches (101.5 × 81.3 cm). Private Collection

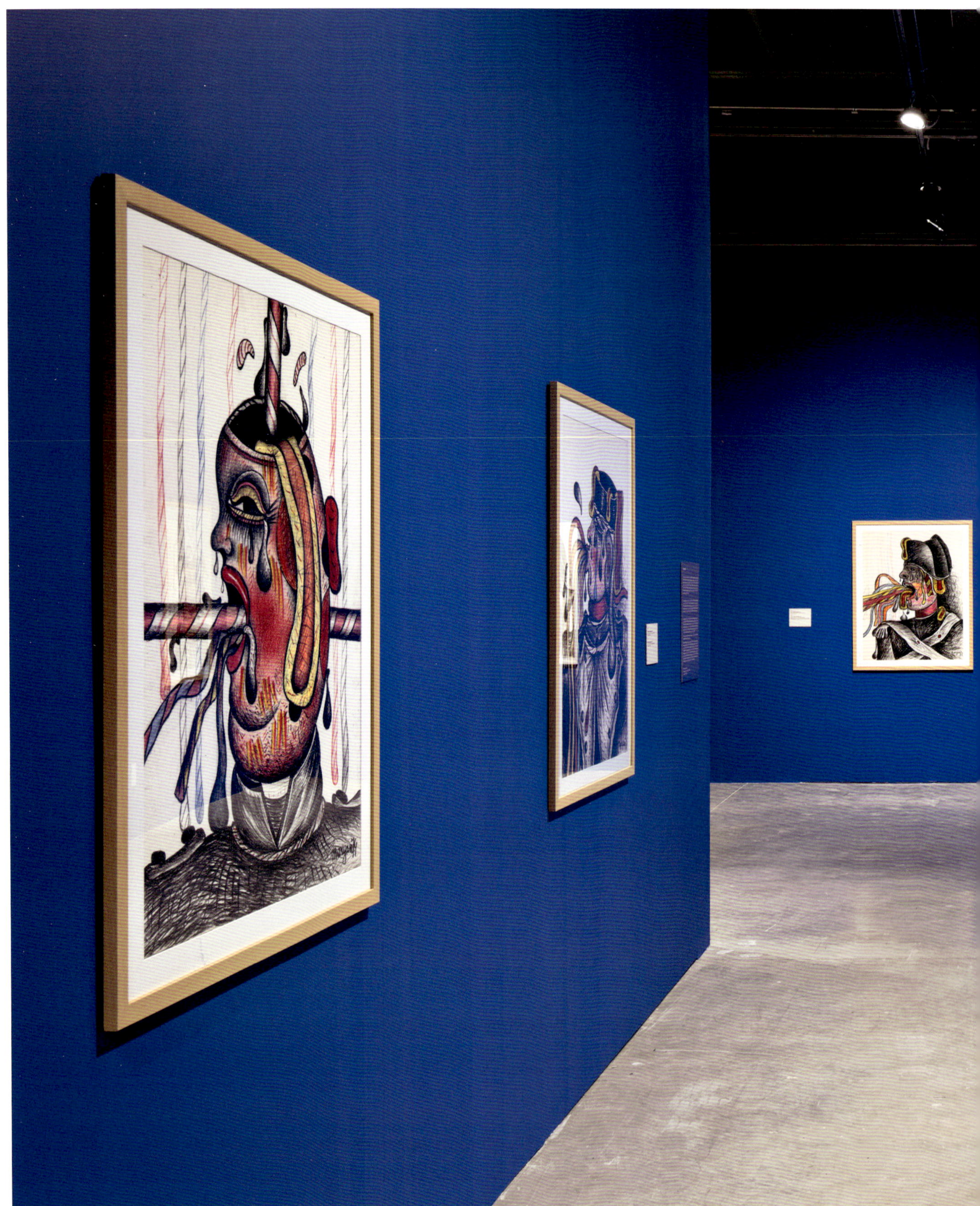

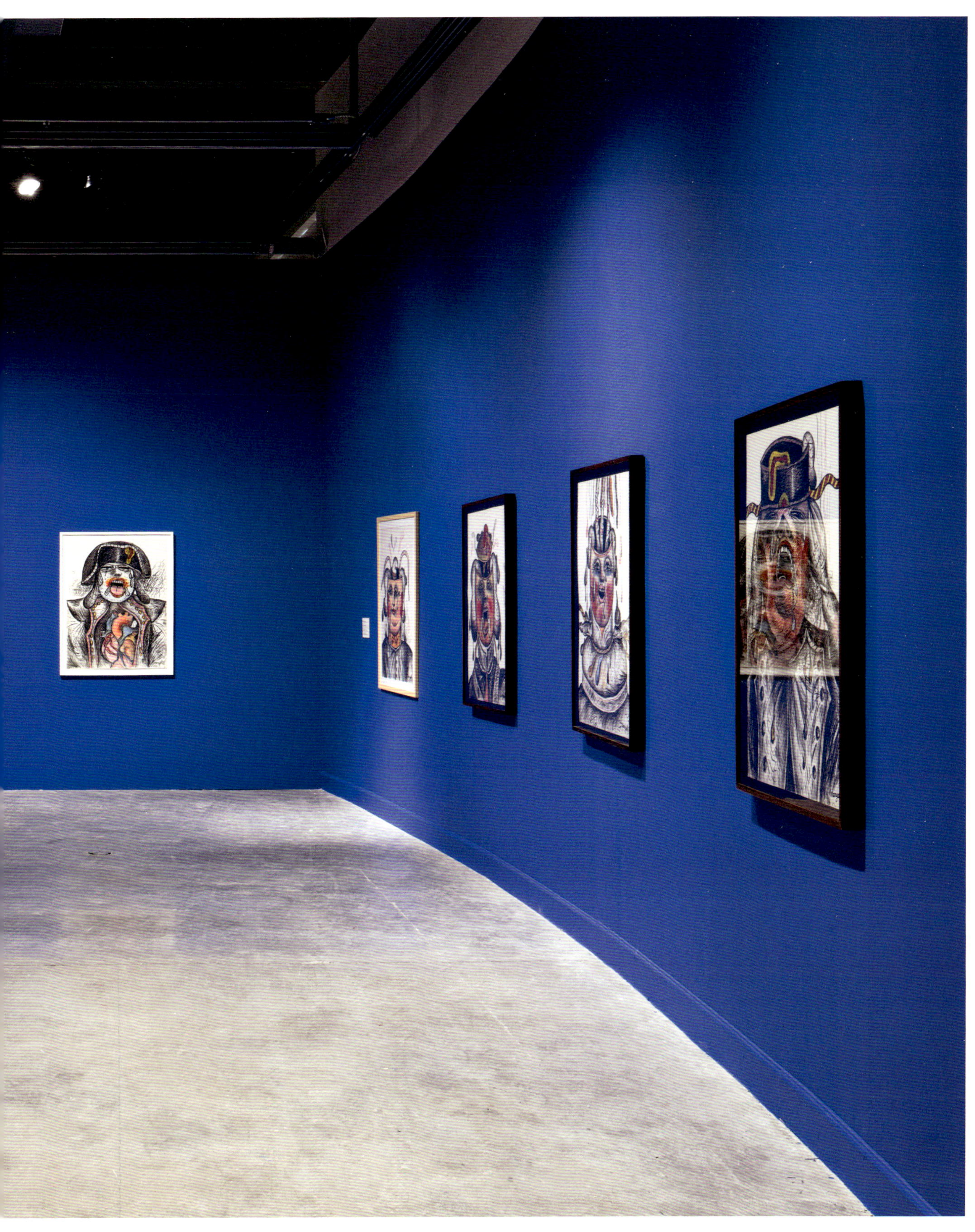

Maryan's Napoleon Drawings:
An Anti-Colonial Perspective

WHO GETS TO BE remembered as a hero? In Maryan's *Napoleon* series, the French emperor appears as a fragmented, disordered, and incongruous soldier, a clownish buffoon who seems to have nothing in his head but tears. What a contrast to the more iconic images of Napoleon the general, riding his horse after victory in the Battle of Austerlitz. Maryan's portrayal begs us to confront rather than cover up Napoleon's many crimes and to discard the lore surrounding the man whose victims span Europe and the Americas.

To reestablish slavery in France's overseas territories, in 1802 Napoleon directed troops to kill all people of color over the age of twelve in French-claimed Saint-Domingue (today, Haiti). French soldiers gassed, drowned, and used dogs to maul the Black inhabitants; French colonists openly bragged that after the "extermination" the island could simply be re-enslaved using more Africans from the continent.

One clearly distraught Polish officer—part of the 5,000 strong Polish expedition sent by Napoléon to assist French troops—wrote in his journal of the French army's infamous usage of imported Cuban dogs deliberately trained to "eat the blacks":

> War is undertaken here differently than it is in Europe—three days ago 200 dogs from the Spanish colonies were brought here . . . tomorrow we are hoping for 400 more. . . . They are unleashed everyday upon living blacks, whom the dogs tear apart without pity as they devour them.

This "auto-da-fé of terror," in one eyewitness's words, led directly to the defection of most of Napoleon's Polish legion, who ended up fighting for the Haitian revolutionaries. After declaring independence in 1804, Haiti became the first modern state to permanently abolish slavery. Formerly enslaved Black people on the Caribbean island of Guadeloupe tried to fight back, too, but they lost their struggle and slavery was officially reinstated in July 1802, where it persisted until 1848.

Maryan seems to ask: How can a man who caused so much suffering be so brazenly honored in France? Only by forgetting.

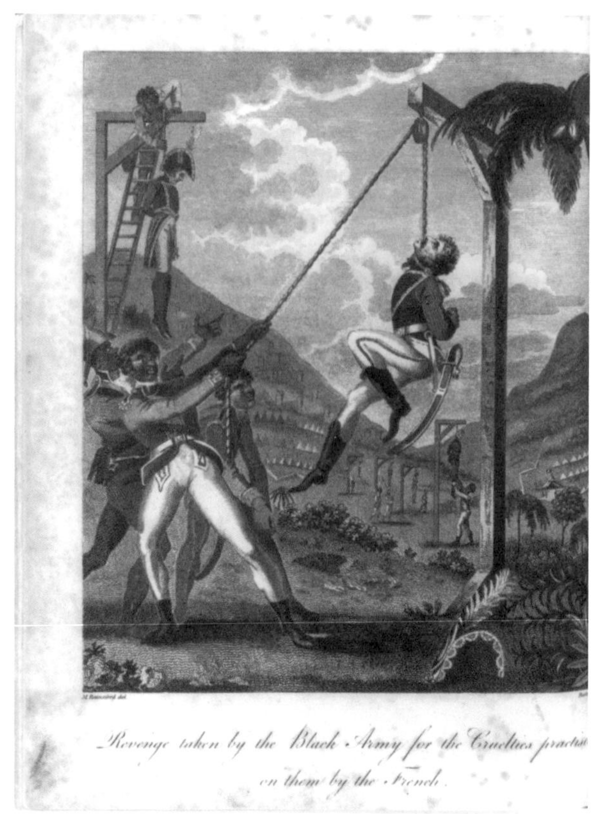

Revenge taken by the Black Army for the cruelties practiced on them by the French, illustrated in Marcus Rainsford's *An Historical Account of the Black Empire of Hayti* (London: James Cundee [Albion Press], 1805). Courtesy of the Library of Congress Prints and Photographs Division, Washington, DC

Maryan's *Napoleon* series well captures the contradictions of portraying as a hero the man who indelibly damaged the French Republic. In 1804 Napoleon declared himself an emperor and proceeded to roll back the gains of the French Revolution. Not only did Napoleon's methods inspire Hitler, but Napoleon's legal code deprived women of individual rights and the restrictions he placed on Jewish marriages and moneylending were aimed, he said, "to weaken, if not to destroy, the Jewish people's inclination to such a great number of practices which are contrary to civilization, and to the good order of society in all the countries of the world."[1] Maryan's paintings encourage painful contemplation of *this* Napoleon—not the conqueror of Europe, but its destroyer; an architect of modern genocide whose legacy of sexism, racism, and religious exclusion unfortunately lives on in today's France.

—Marlene L. Daut

1. Napoleon, in Simon *Schwarzfuchs, Napoleon, the Jews, and the Sanhedrin* (London: Routledge/ Littman Library of Jewish Civilization, 1979), quoted in Alyssa Goldstein Sepinwall, "Napoleon, French Jews, and the Idea of Regeneration," CCAR *Journal 54* (Winter 2007): 65.

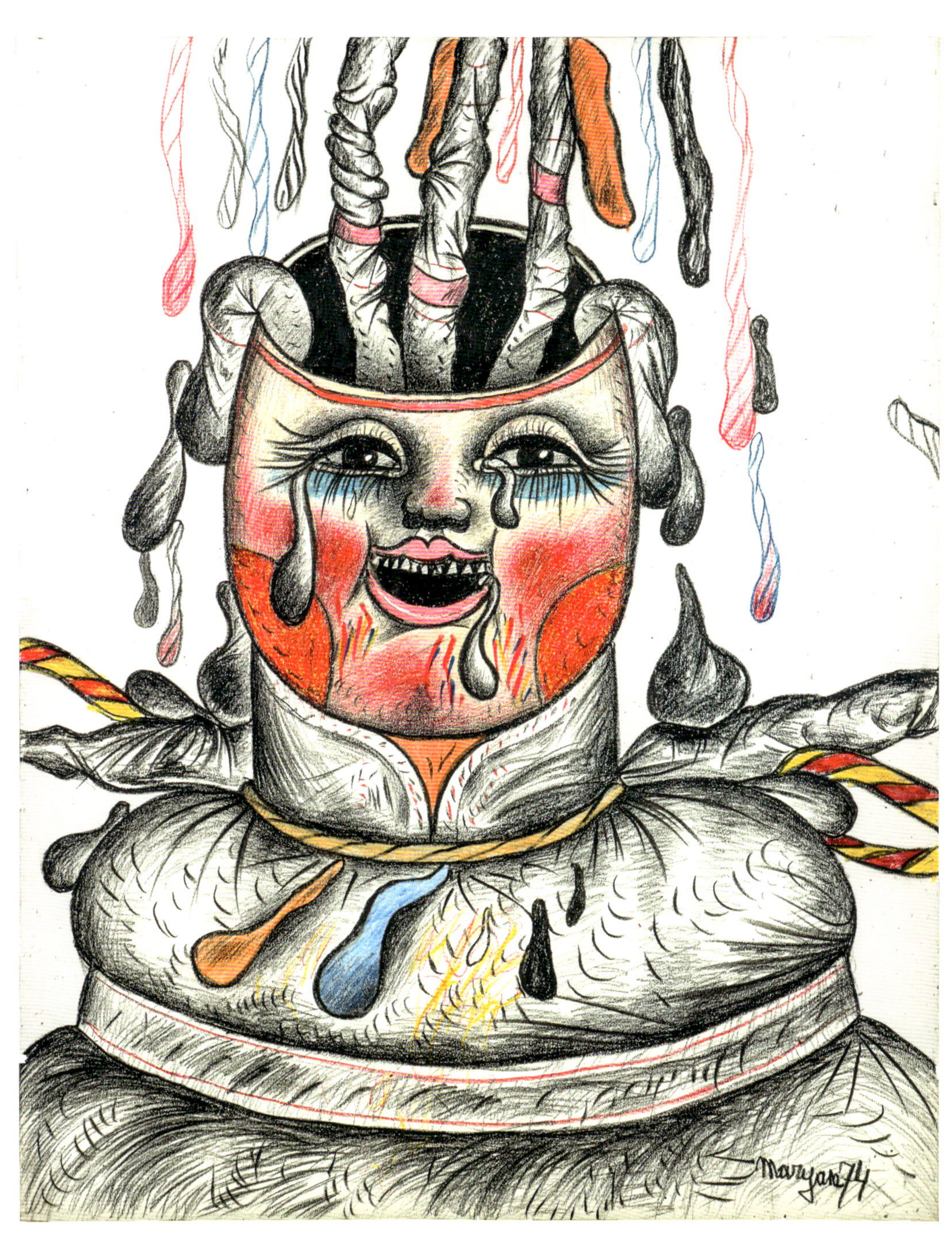

Personnage (Napoléon), 1974. Wax crayon on museum rag board, 40 × 32 inches (101.5 × 81.3 cm).
Courtesy of the William Louis-Dreyfus Foundation

1971–72 NOTEBOOKS

"During the last eight years of his life, [Maryan] became both physically and emotionally exhausted," explained Annette Maryan in a letter she wrote after his death.[1] From 1971 to 1972, on the advice of his doctor, Maryan told the story of his life visually to work through his traumatic memories and residual emotional torment. The resulting nine notebooks are filled with 478 autobiographical drawings captioned in Maryan's handwriting.

These drawings conflate word-and-image recollections of his childhood in Poland, his experiences in the camps, and how those experiences resonated in his later life and in his marriage. During this difficult period, Maryan had trouble communicating verbally with his wife, who was also a Jewish survivor of World War II. Unlike her husband, Annette was not imprisoned; she spent her childhood hiding from the Nazis in the South of France.

Through the captions, these drawings not only tell Maryan's story but partially decode much of the iconography embedded in his paintings made over the two decades preceding the notebooks. The military symbols, prisoners' uniforms, and the tallit that appear in his work are here captioned and contextualized with recalled vignettes from the artist's life. Drawn in a cartoonlike style, he depicts important childhood memories: his father's bakery in Nowy Sącz, his mother arguing with his father, and various Jewish rituals like the kapparah, in which a cock is slaughtered as an act of atonement. The visceral memories of the camps portrayed in the notebooks depict Maryan's nausea, tears, defecation, screaming, and other moments of extreme suffering, rage, and death. Many of these scenes are echoed in more stylized form in his paintings. Because the historical record of Maryan's family life was destroyed by the Nazis, these notebooks are both a therapeutic document and a vital record of lives otherwise extinguished by genocide.

Maryan used the phrase *ecce homo* numerous times in the notebooks to describe scenes of great suffering, which connects these notebooks to the film he created with the same title a few years later. *Ecce Homo* is likewise the title that Annette Maryan gave posthumously to all nine notebooks. It is interesting to note that the Expressionist artist George Grosz, who was an important influence on Maryan, gave his 1923 suite of satirical drawings criticizing German society the same title. Grosz's *Ecce Homo* book was burned by the Nazis. While Maryan was insistent that the understanding of his work should not be reduced to his Holocaust experiences, these notebooks offer valuable insights into what he called his "truth-paintings." —AMG

1. Maryan to Feldman, April 4, 1983.

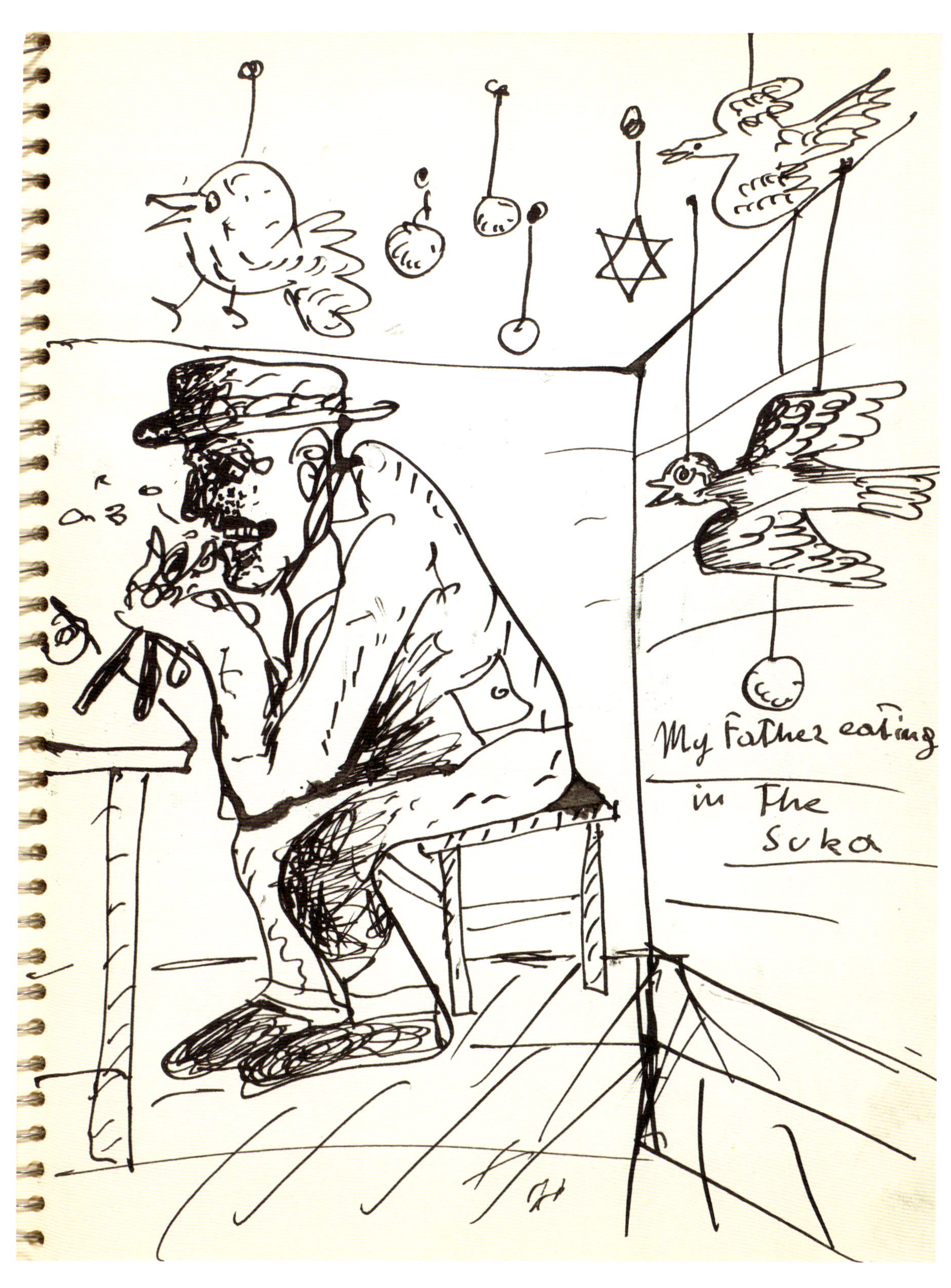

Pages from *Carnet de dessins no. 1 - 9 (Notebook drawings, nos. 1–9)*, 1971
Chinese ink on paper, in 9 spiral-bound notebooks, dimensions variable.
Musée national d'art moderne, Centre Pompidou. Gift of Annette Maryan

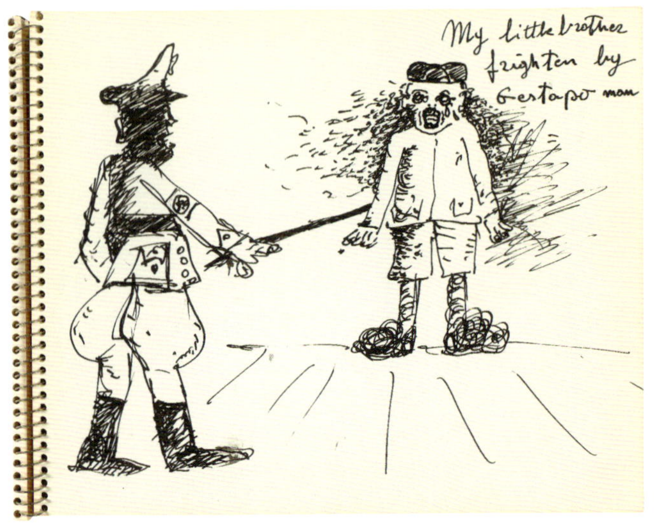

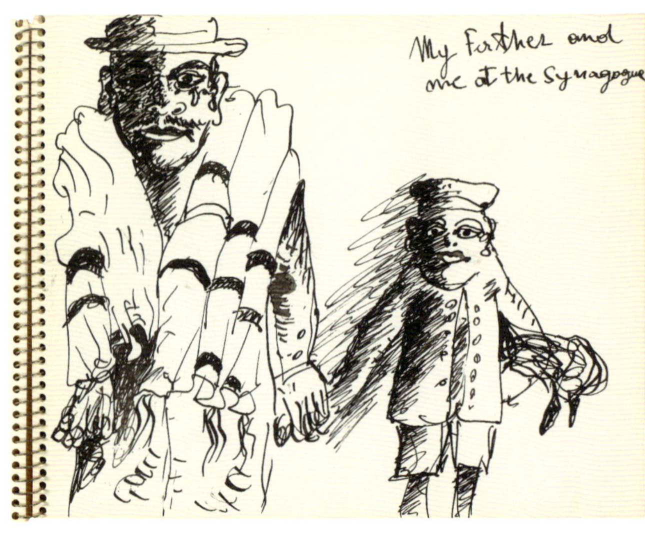

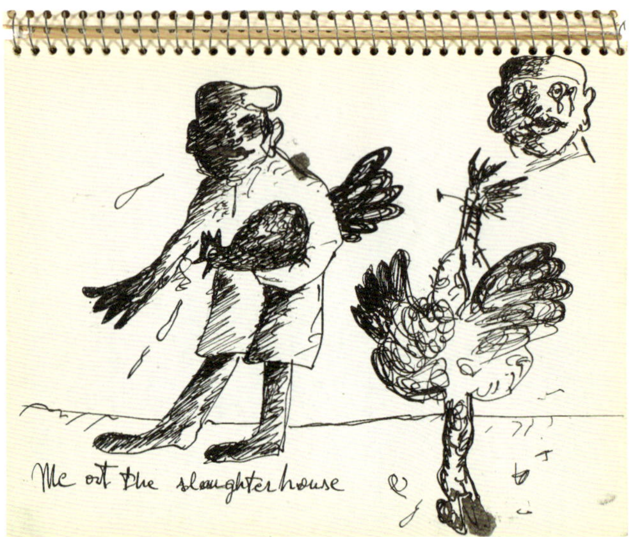

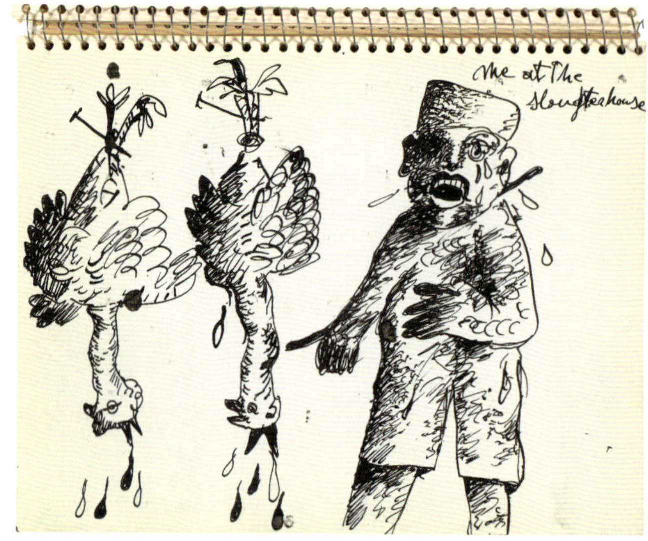

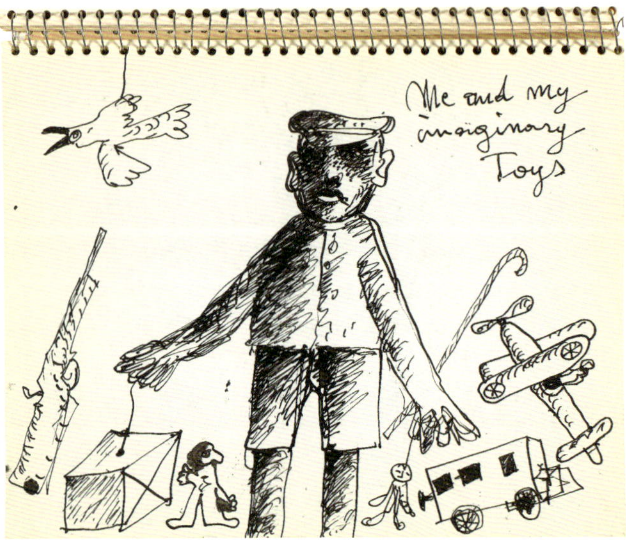

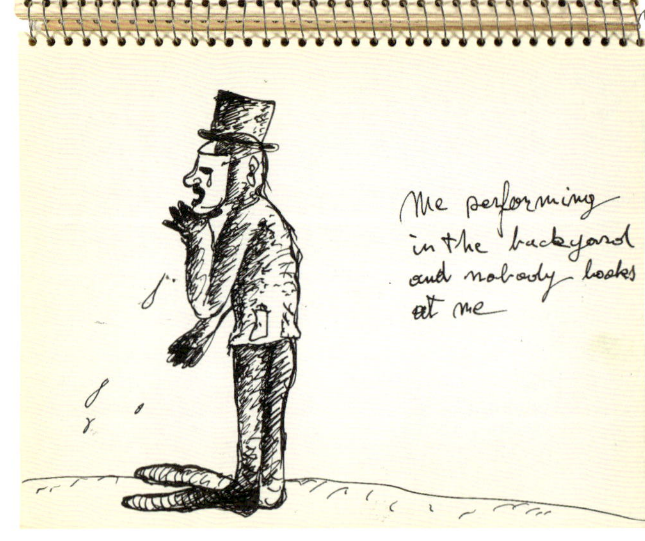

Pages from *Carnet de dessins no. 1 - 9 (Notebook drawings, nos. 1–9)*, 1971
Chinese ink on paper, in 9 spiral-bound notebooks, dimensions variable
Musée national d'art moderne, Centre Pompidou. Gift of Annette Maryan

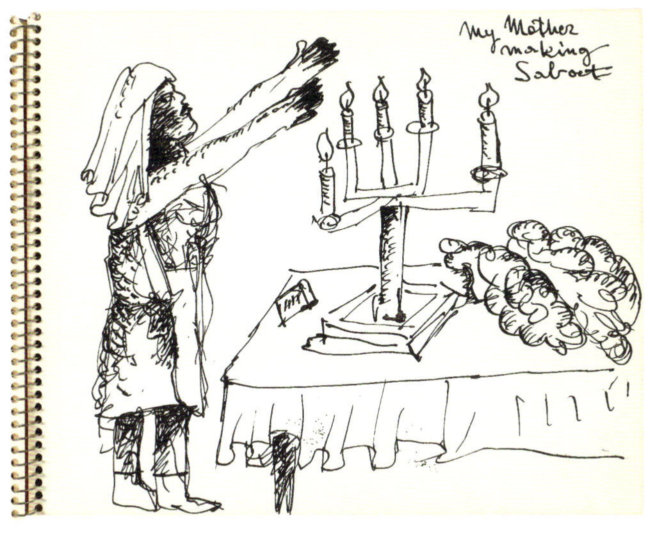

My Mother
making
Sabbat

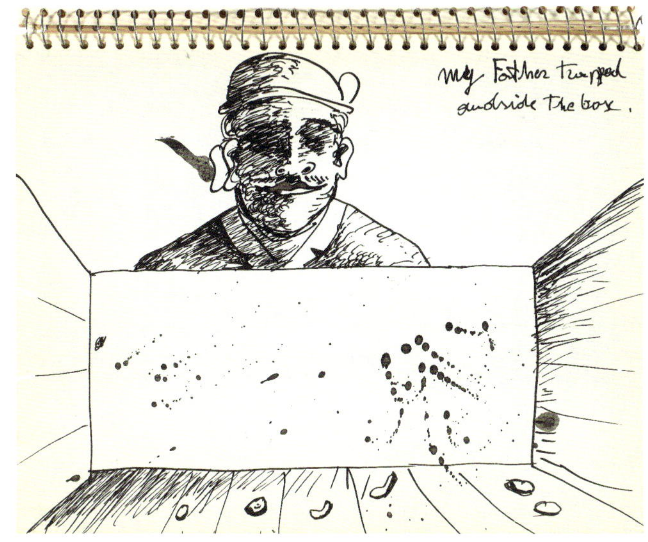

My Father trapped
inside the box.

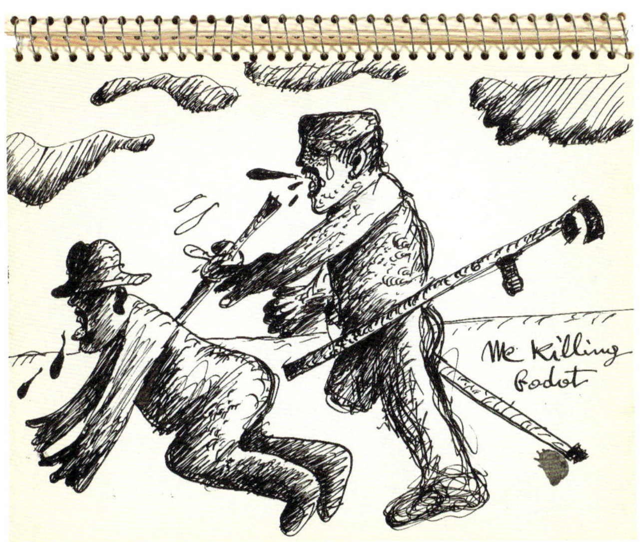

Me Killing
Godot

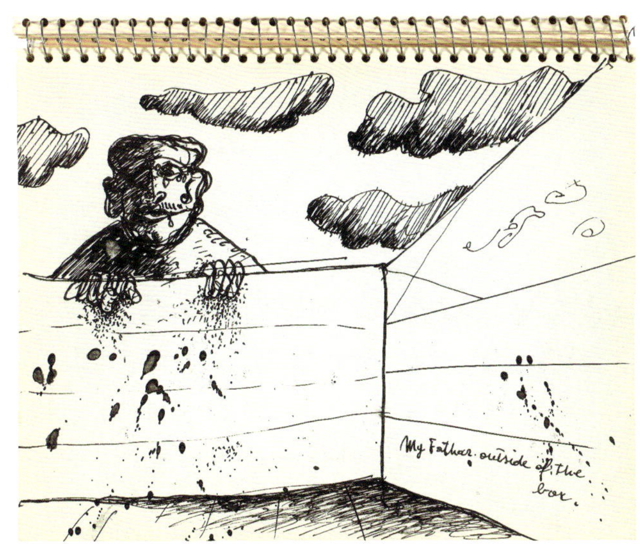

My Father outside of the
box.

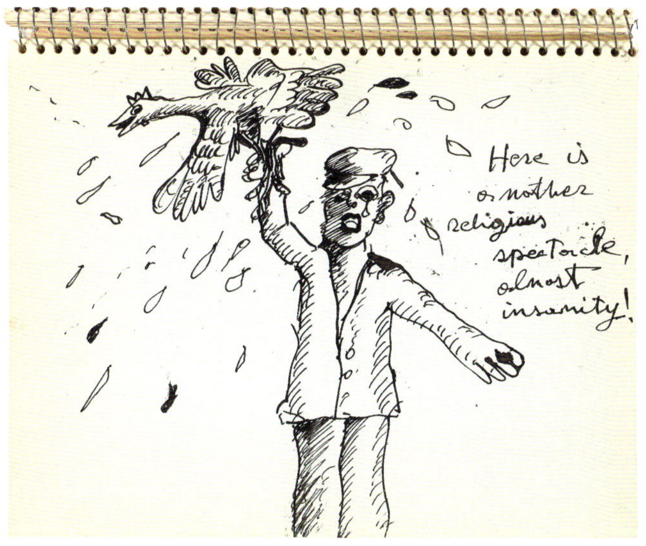

Here is
another
religious
spectacle,
almost
insanity!

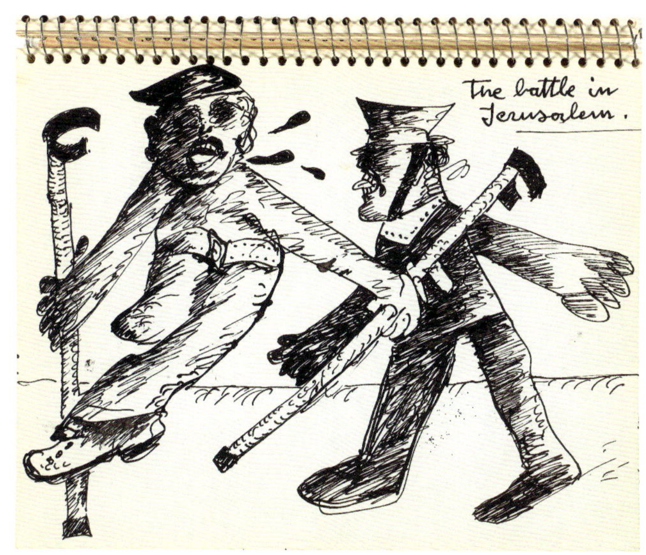

The battle in
Jerusalem.

THE QUIET ONES AND SCREAMING ONES

The series of paintings that came to be known as his *Quiet Ones* and *Screaming Ones* were made in 1971 and '72 after he had been in treatment for his psychological turbulence. These startlingly somber paintings are dominated by a grayscale palette—shades of pink and peach-skin color disturb the otherwise drab compositions.

Each canvas depicts a single *personnage* in a straight-on, head-and-shoulders style. As their titles suggest, they either have a gaping open mouth or a closed mouth—enacting their rage or silence. It is impossible not to connect these paintings with the notebook drawings Maryan made before them, in which various hat shapes correspond to various figures he identified from his biographical experiences. One of the *Quiet Ones* wears the baker's cap that Maryan's father wore before the war. Another *Screaming One* wears the pointed lace hat that Maryan sometimes captioned as a "Pope" or "Vatican Man" in his notebook drawings. With the knowledge that these works were made during a period in which Maryan was confronting his previously repressed memories of his interrupted childhood and the camps, it is impossible not to understand these works as part of the emotional and psychological upheaval that dominated his last decade of work. During this period of his life, Maryan seemed to undergo a transformation from being a "quiet one" who did not openly speak of his wartime traumas during the 1950s and '60s, to becoming a "screaming one" in the 1970s who unleashed his torment in his notebook drawings and later film—a profound conversion that catalyzed some of his most radical works. —AMG

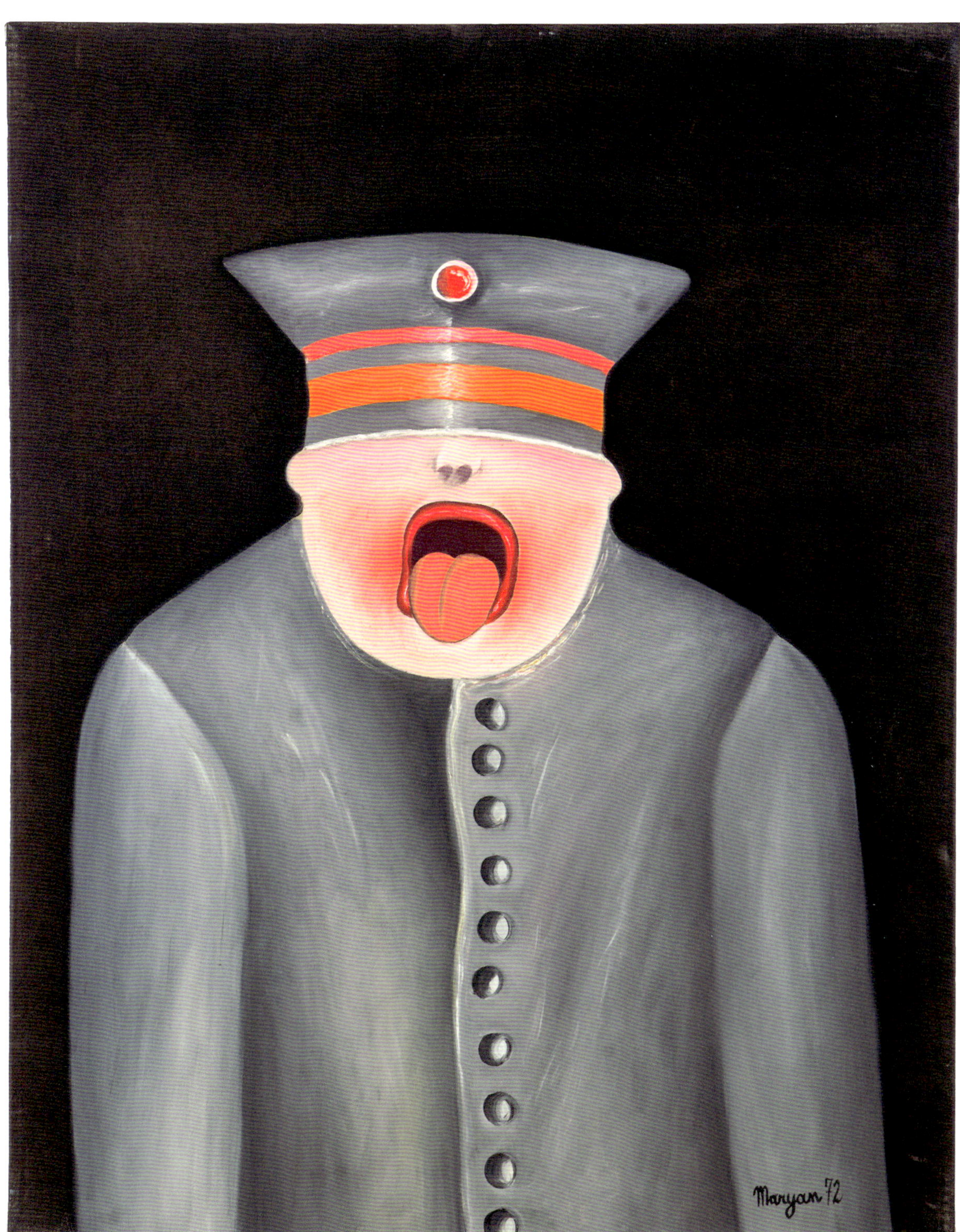

Personnage de la ménagerie humaine, 1972. Oil on canvas, 40 × 32 inches (101.5 × 81.25 cm). Private Collection

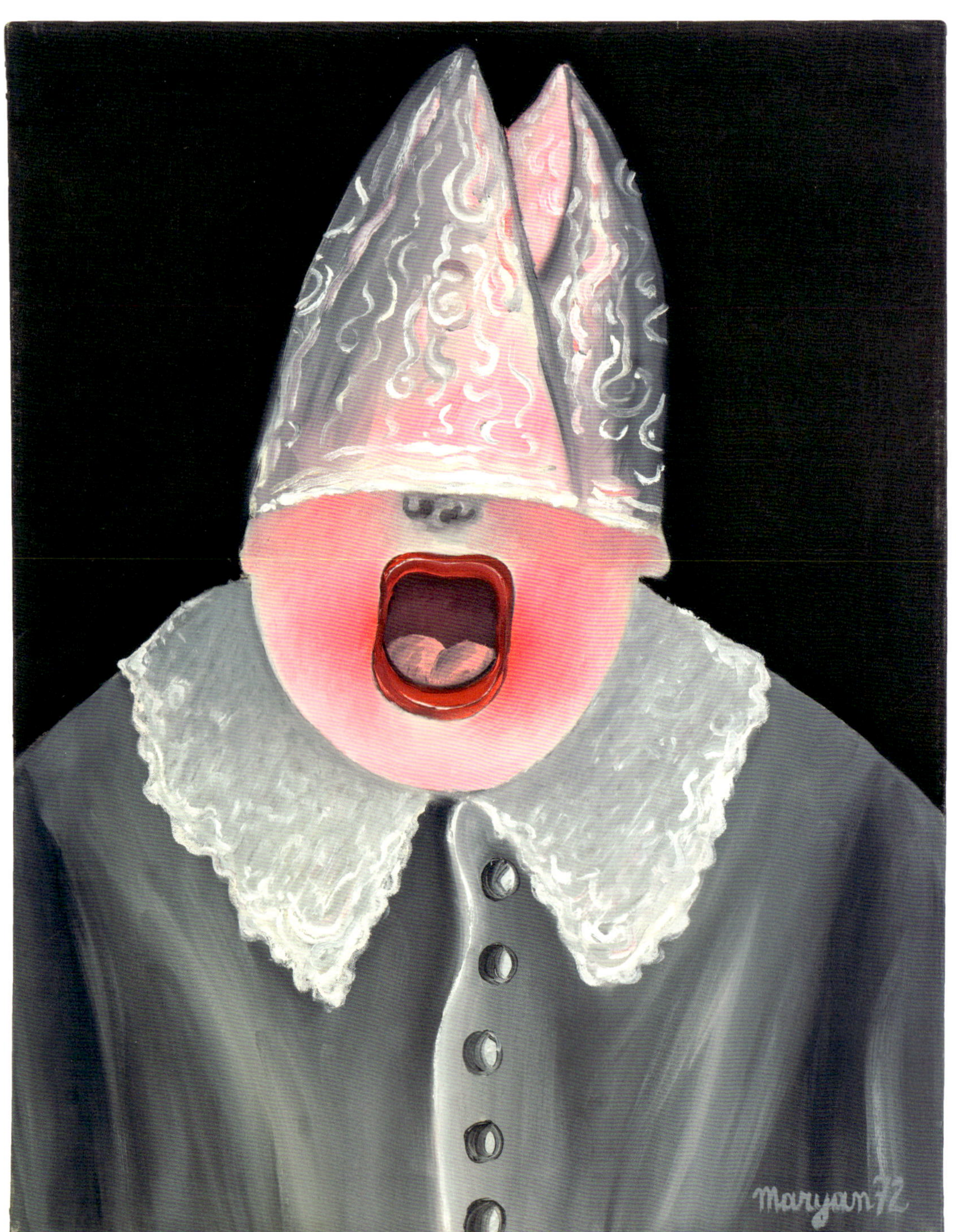

Personnage, 1972. Oil on canvas, 28 × 23¼ inches (71 × 59 cm). Private Collection, Japan

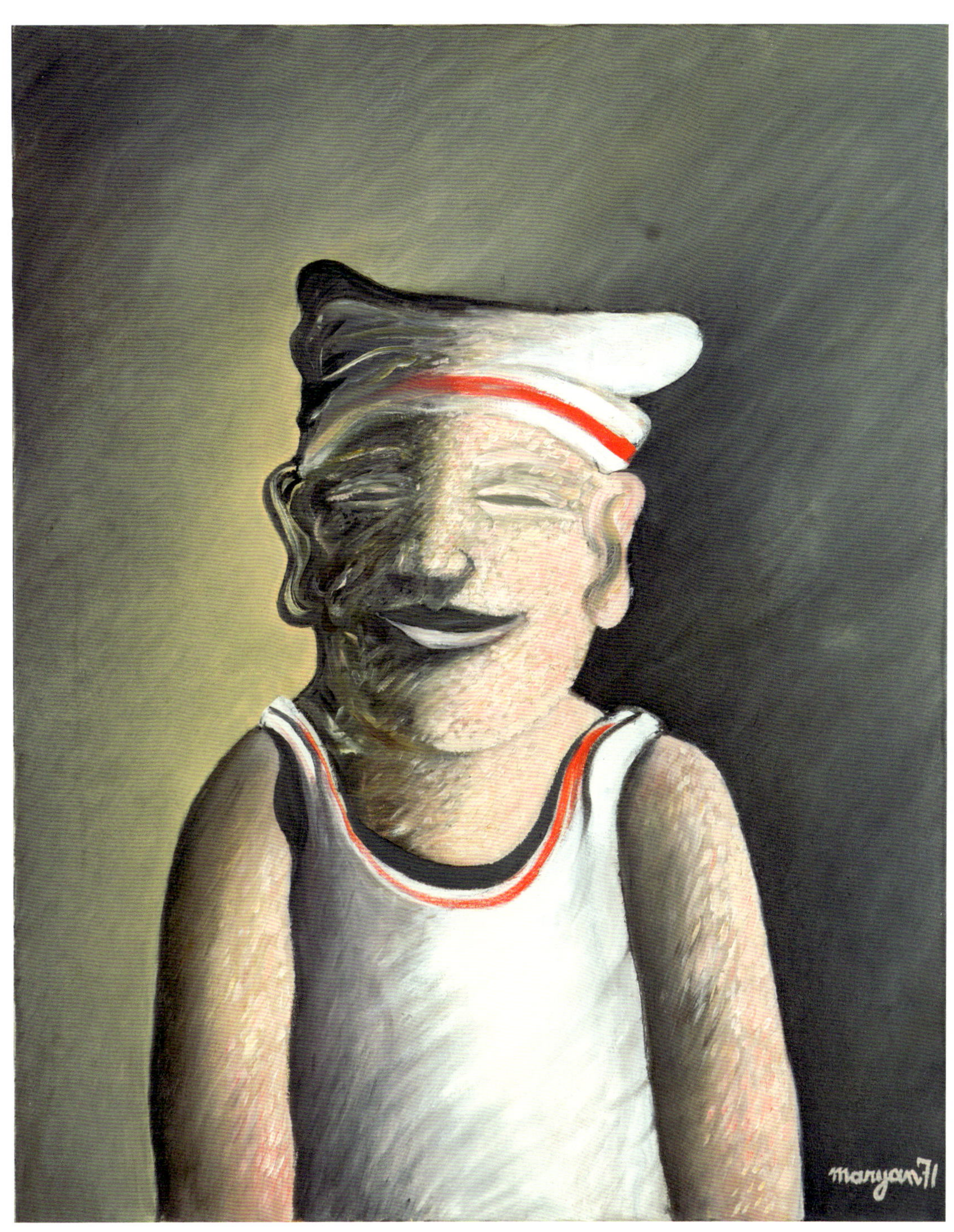

Personnage de la ménagerie humaine, 1971. Oil on canvas, 32 × 25½ inches (81.25 × 64 cm).
Collection of Spertus Institute, Chicago

CHELSEA HOTEL STUDIO

Maryan worked in a room at New York's Chelsea Hotel from the early '70s until his premature death in 1977. Dubbed "the Ellis Island of the avant-garde," this infamous bohemian enclave served as the home of artists and writers like Jackson Pollock, Tennessee Williams, William Burroughs, and Niki de Saint Phalle. Maryan may have been foreign-born, but by working and periodically living at the Chelsea he was at the center of New York's artistic and cultural ferment.

Photographs of Maryan's studio documented his deliberate conflation of his own paintings with African and Oceanic masks, Mexican Day of the Dead papier-mâché skulls, toys, ephemera, and other curiosities that he collected and to which he felt a kindred connection. These late paintings are characterized by their brightly colored palette as well as Maryan's use of shaped canvases. Among his most radical paintings are a series of tondo paintings of distorted and animated heads, a rare polyptych, and his series of crucifixion paintings.

Maryan's Chelsea Hotel *personnages* are portrayed in exaggerated states of distress and suffering; the paintings often show figures with erections, especially in a number from the Crucifixion series. Maryan frequently made reference to Jesus Christ in his work, often using the Latin expression *ecce homo* (behold the man) to conjure Christ's human suffering. Maryan's deliberate Jewish Christian identification was explicitly explored in his 1975 film of that title, in which he recounts his experiences in Nazi concentration camps. These startling cruciform paintings also explore the complex themes of victimhood and sacrifice that preoccupied Maryan deeply at the end of his life.

Another surprising group of works from the Chelsea Hotel began as small charged wooden heads which were souvenirs from Kraków, Poland. They represent a famous decorative feature of Wawel Castle, where generations of Polish kings have been buried. "Wawel Heads" were manufactured in the workshop of Gothic sculptors Sebastian Tauerbach and Hans Snycerz around 1540. Installed on the coffered ceiling inside the castle, these head sculptures originally represented different castes, such as kings, noblemen, and soldiers. The seven heads found in Maryan's Chelsea Hotel studio were modified by the artist, overpainted in his unique style to transform them into his signature *personnage* trope. This surprising and never-before-exhibited aspect of Maryan's work suggests the artist's ongoing preoccupation with his birth country, Poland. —AMG

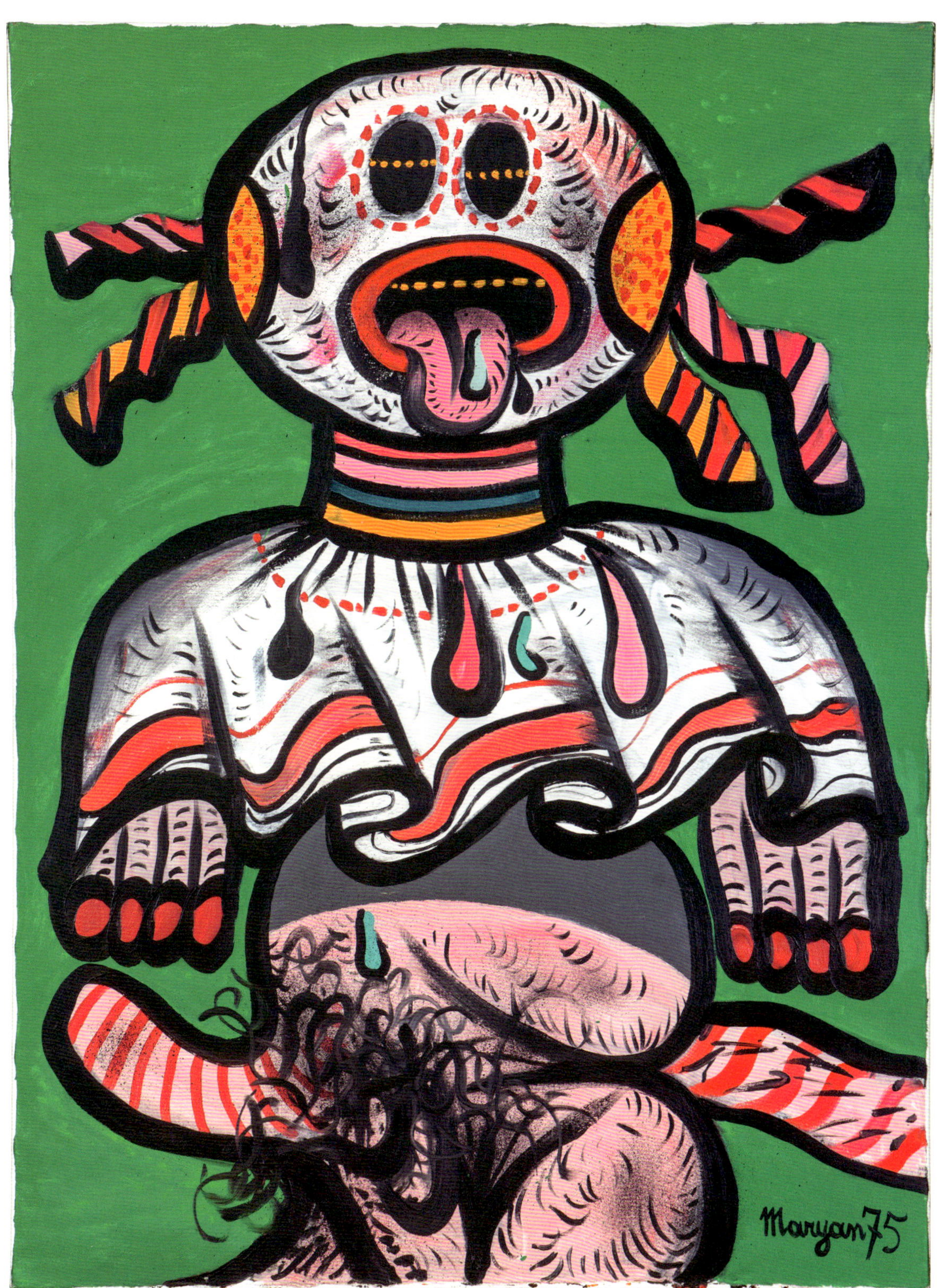

Untitled, 1975. Oil on canvas, 39⅜ × 31¾ inches (100 × 75.5 cm). Private Collection

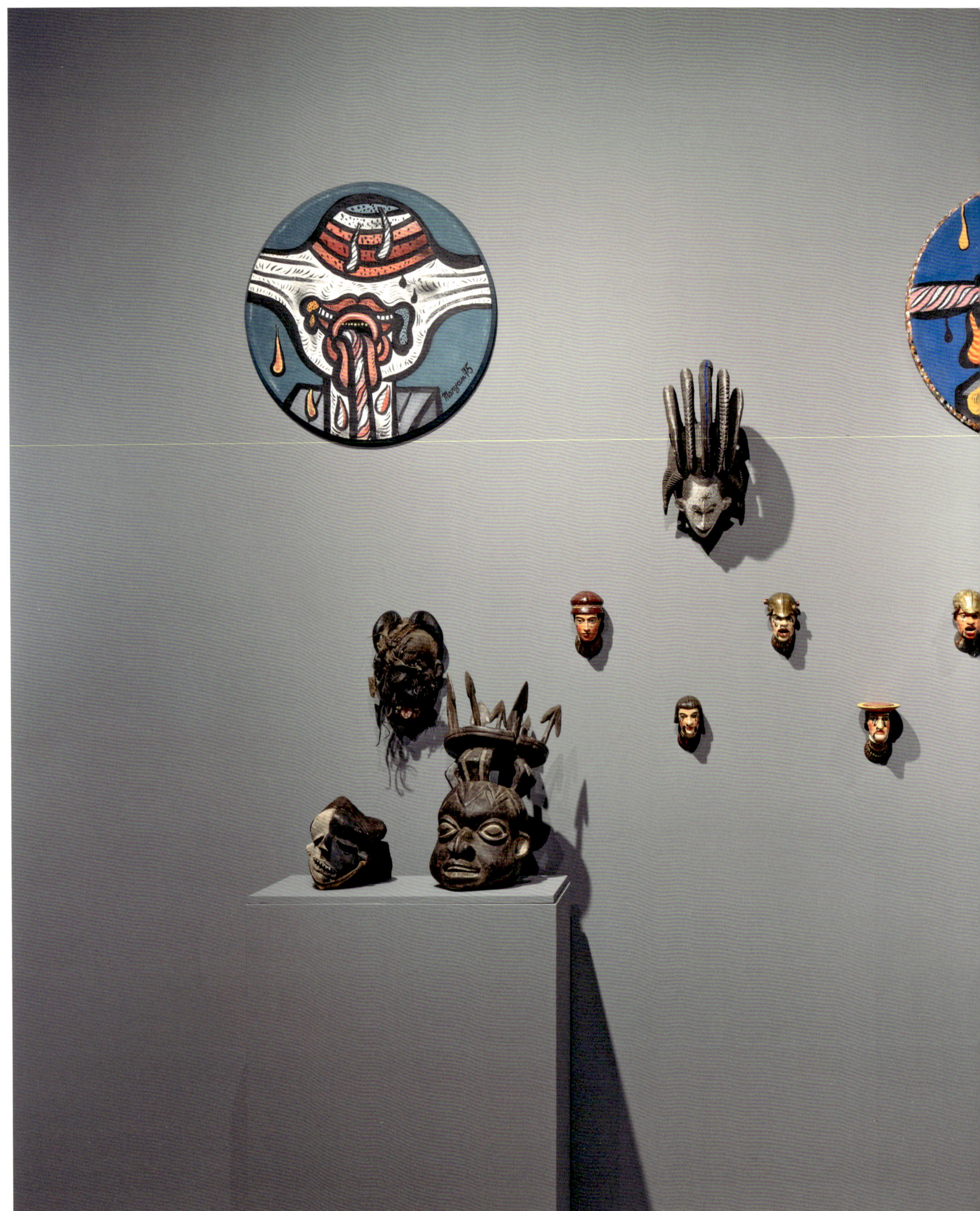

My Name Is Maryan, Museum of Contemporary Art, North Miami, 2022. Installation view

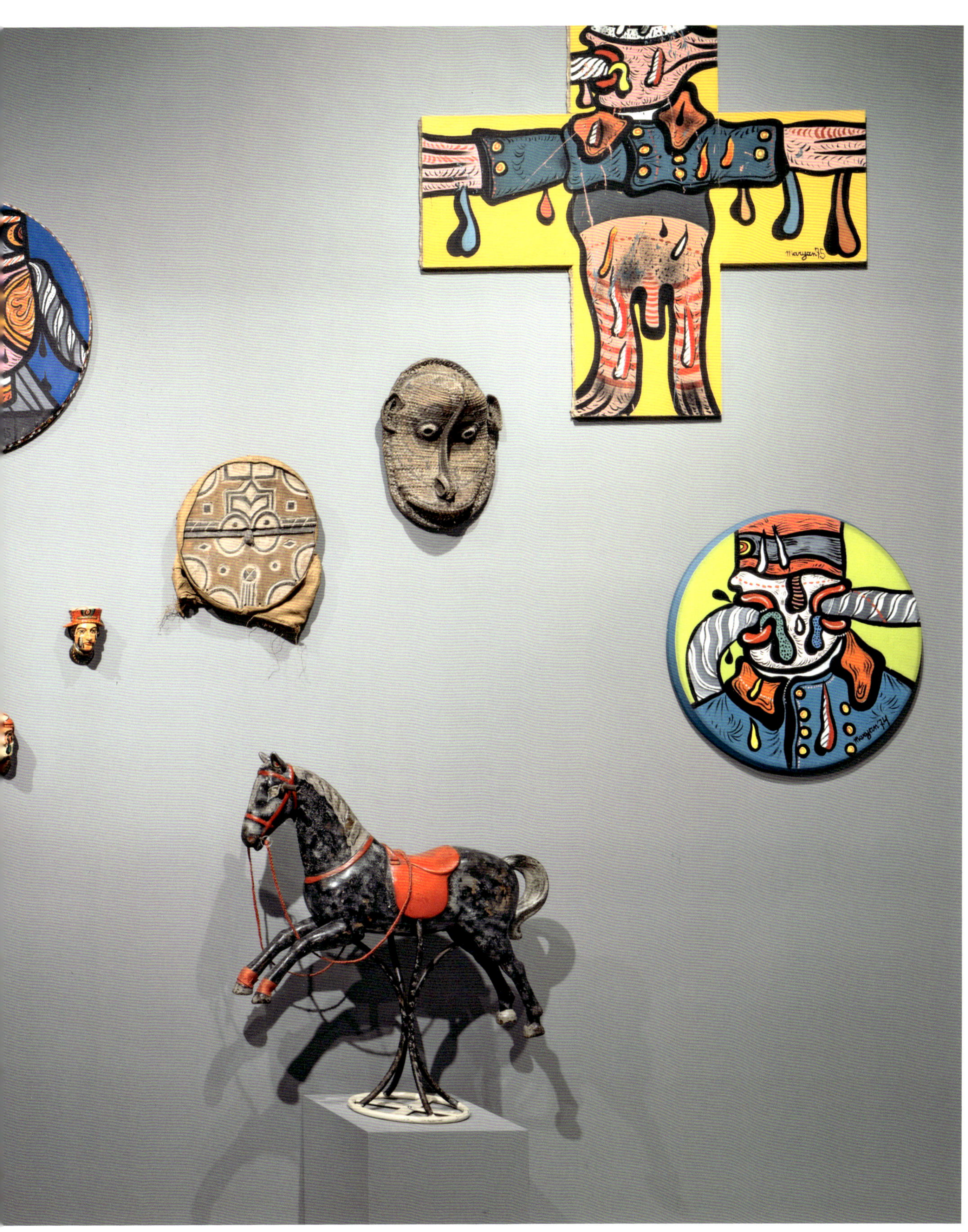

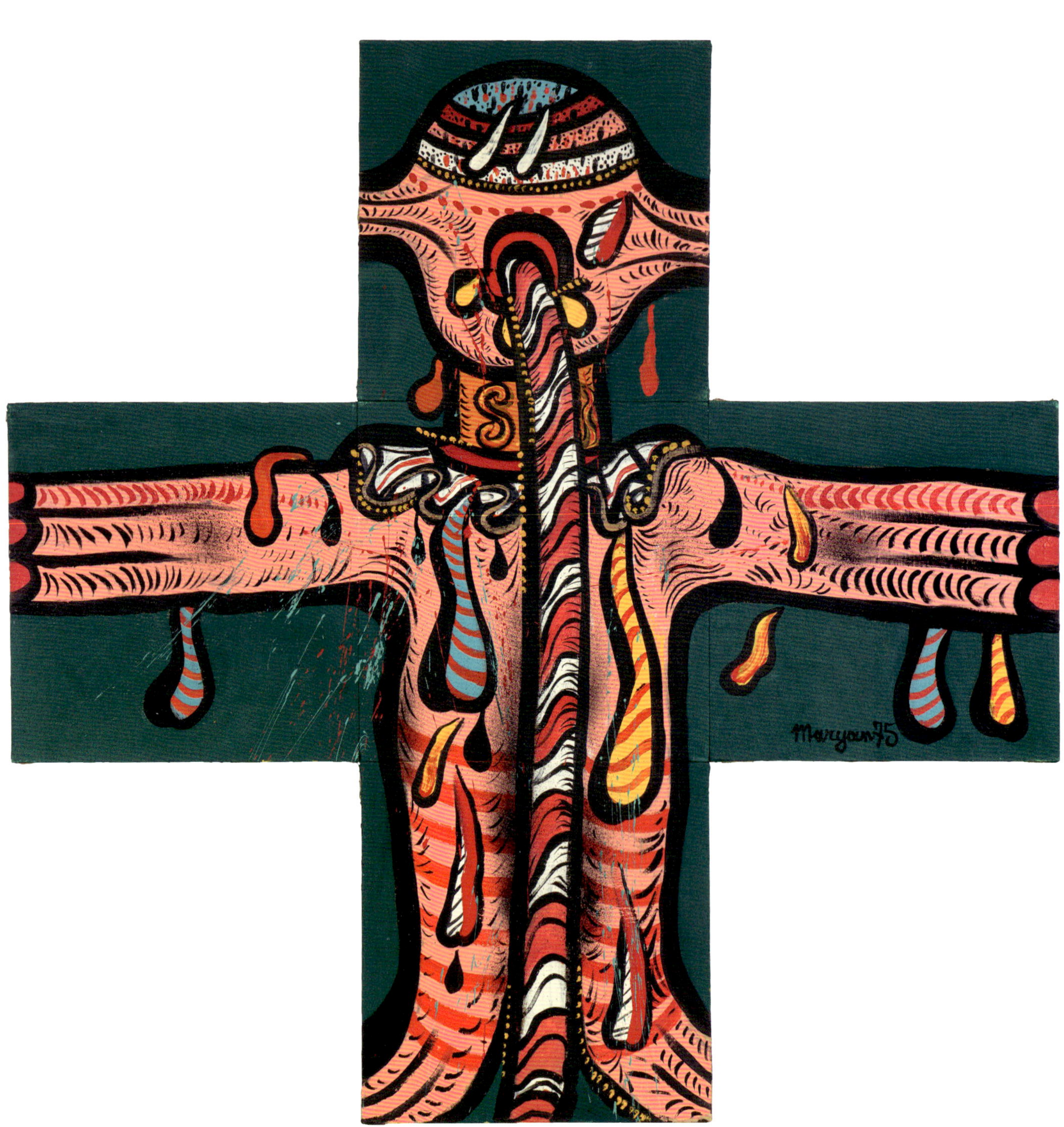

Crucifix, 1975. Acrylic on canvas, 47½ × 47½ inches (120.5 × 120.5 cm). Private Collection

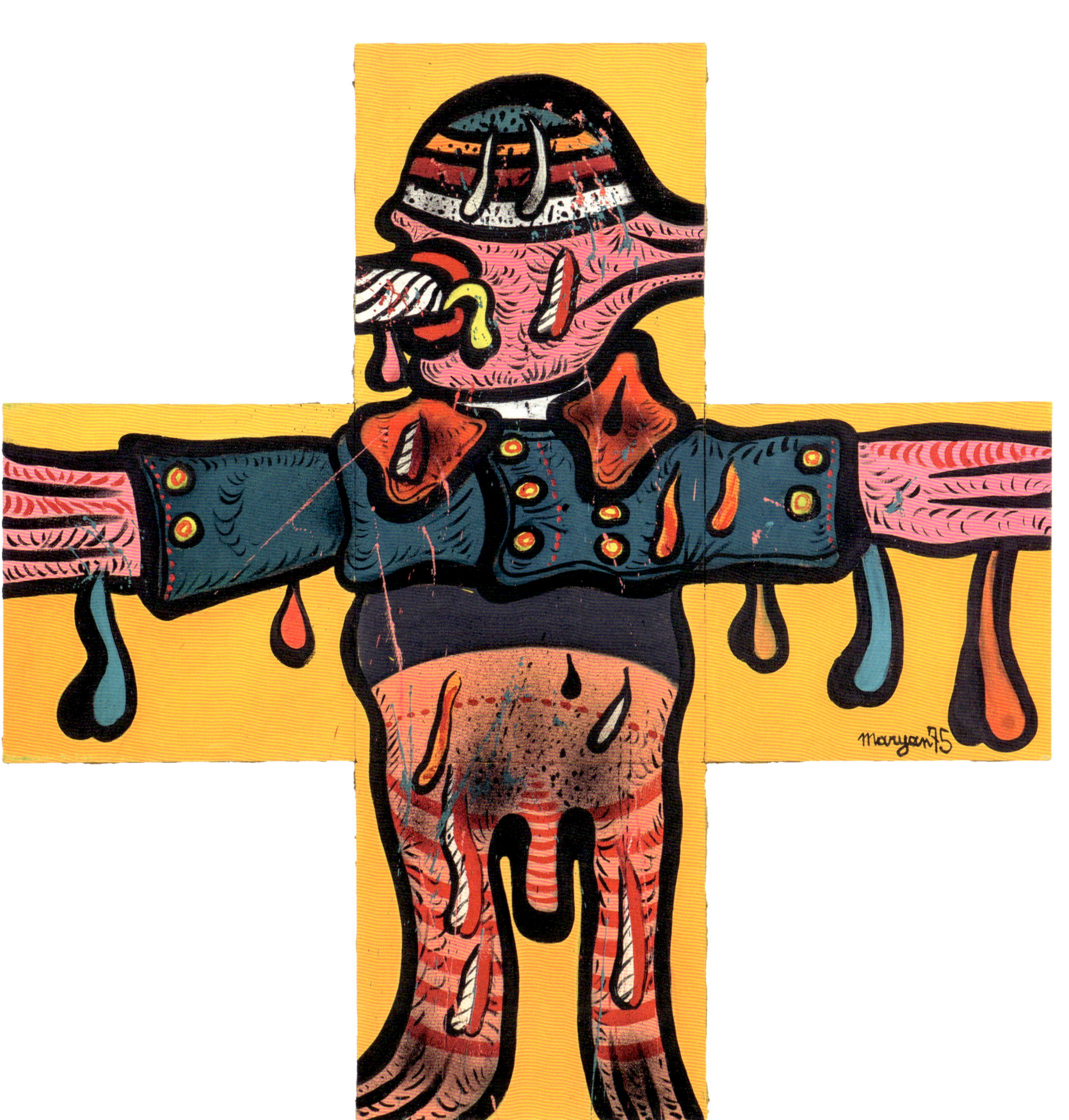

Crucifix, 1975. Acrylic on canvas, 47½ × 47½ inches (120.5 × 120.5 cm). Private Collection

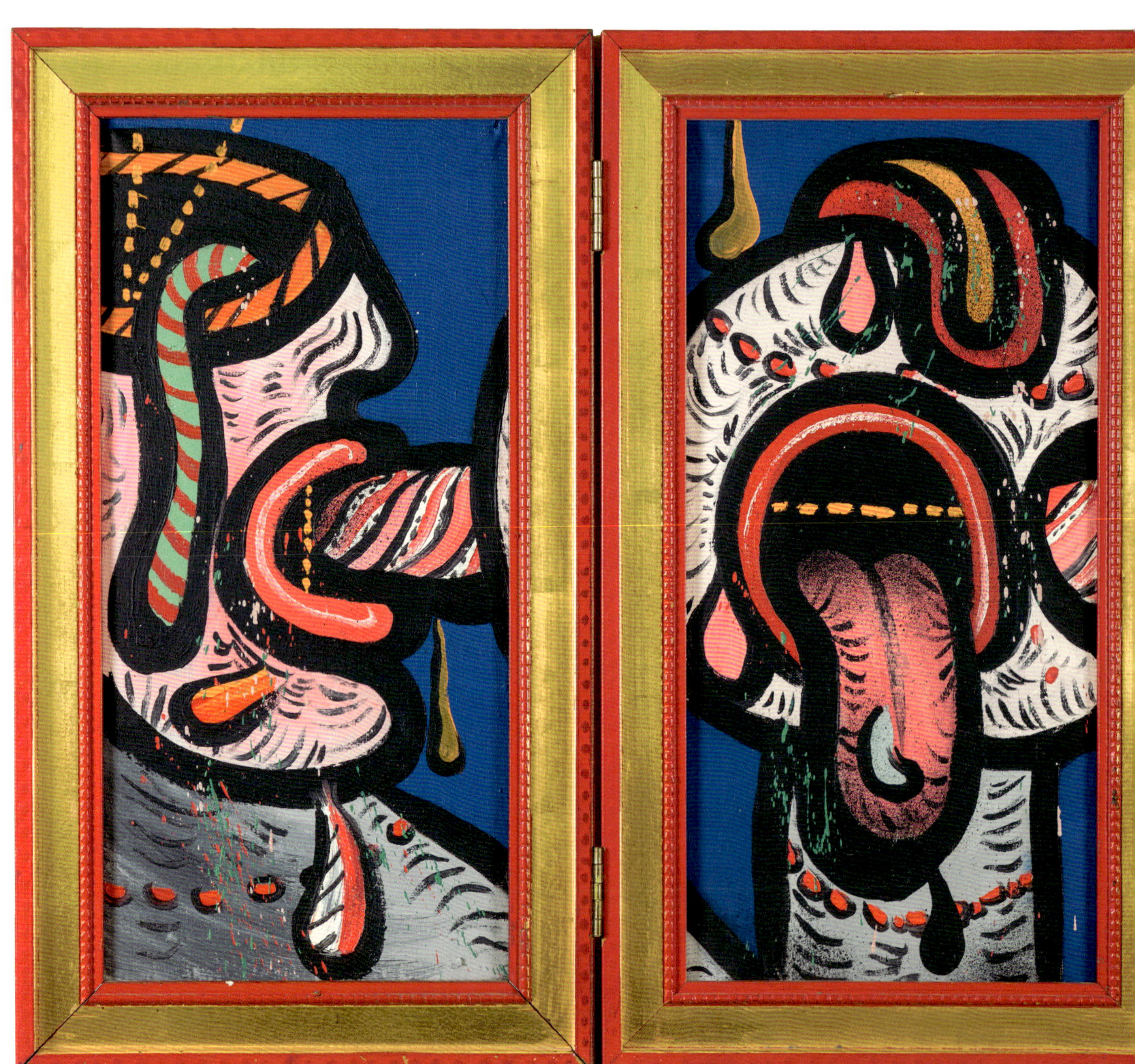

Untitled, ca. 1970. Oil on canvas, 2 panels: 23 × 27 inches (60 cm × 69.5 cm) each, framed. Private Collection

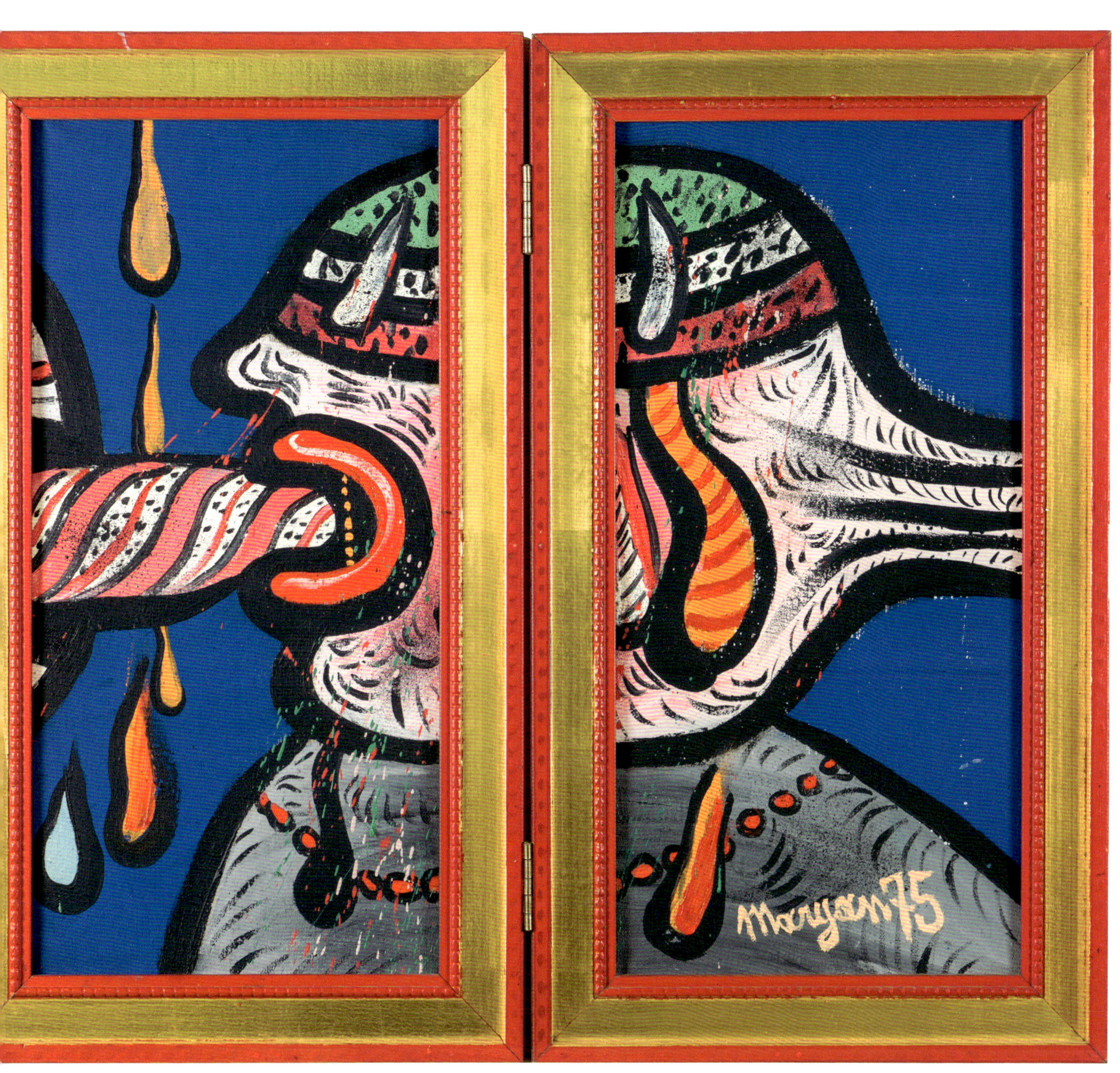
Maryan 75

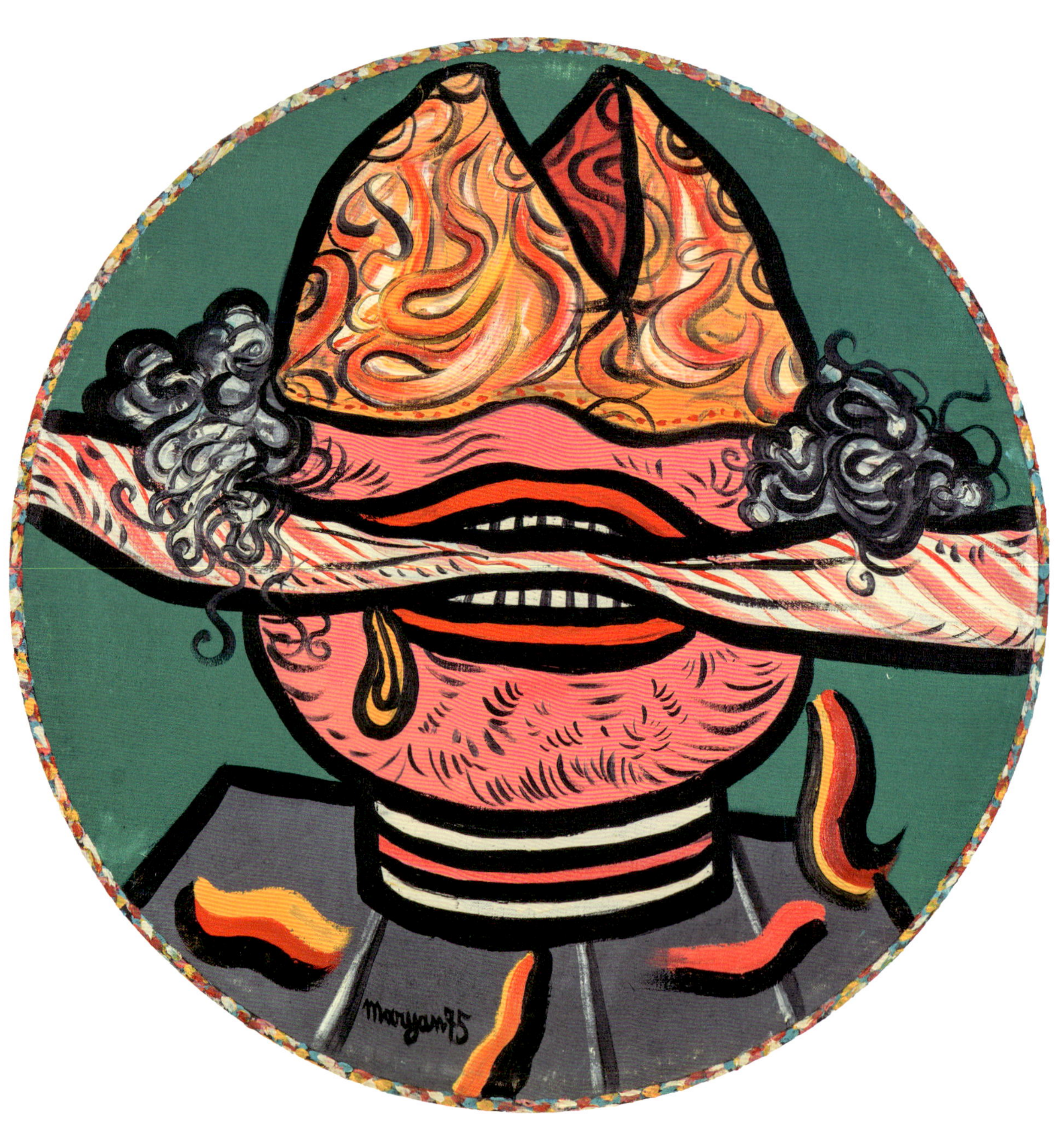

Personnage, 1974–75. Oil on canvas, 27½ inches (70 cm) diameter. Private Collection

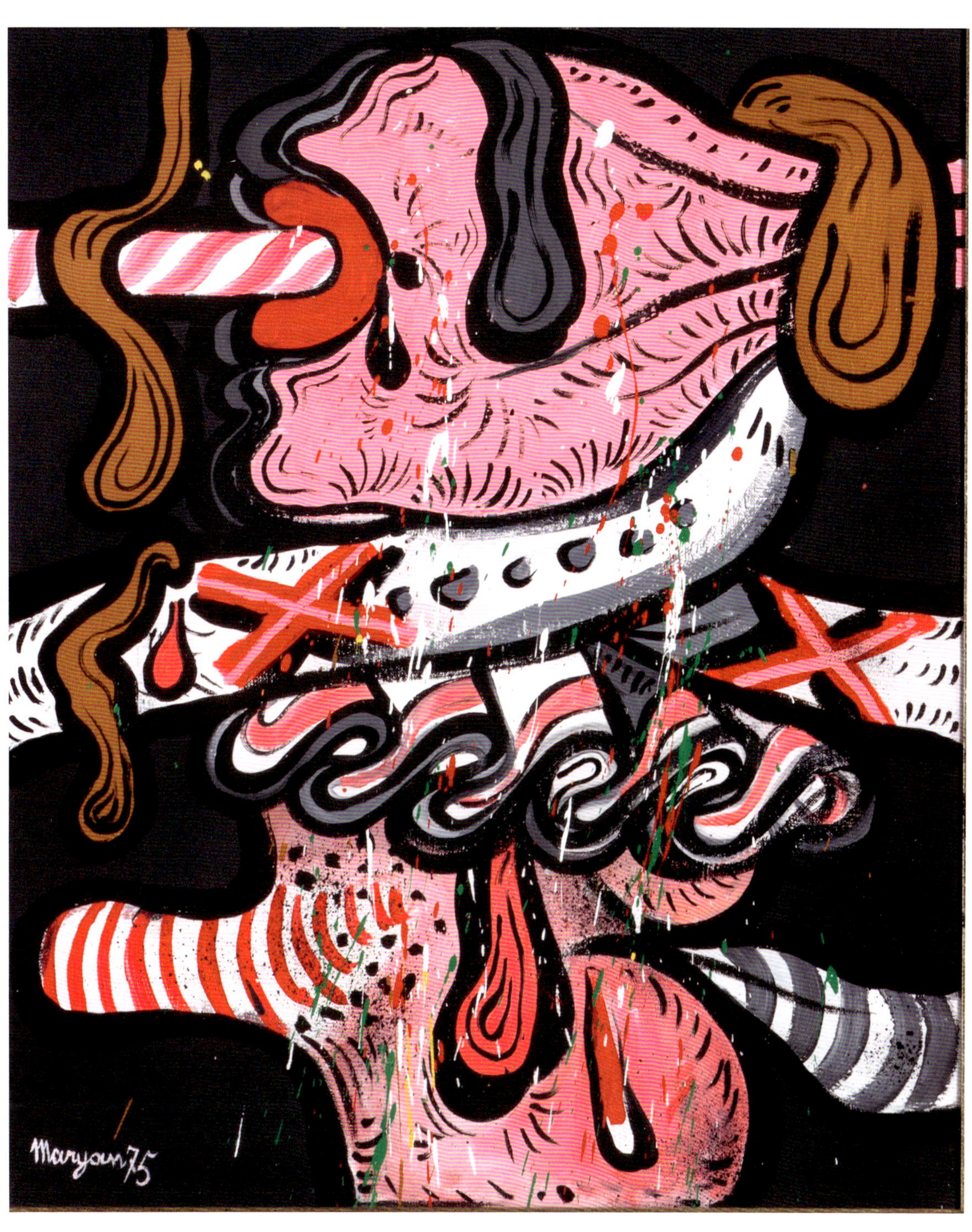

Personnage, 1975. Oil on canvas, 27½ × 23 inches (70 × 58.5 cm). Collection of the Tel Aviv Museum of Art. Gift of Allan Rich, Los Angeles, through the American Friends of the Tel Aviv Museum of Art, 1983

Maryan and African Art in the Chelsea Hotel: Two Perspectives

WHAT DOES IT MEAN to be "traumatically marked"? To lose everything and everyone closest to you? Your family? Your home? Your friends? Your hope? To forever carry the seen and unseen wounds of unfathomable loss in your body? When I look at images of Maryan seated in his room in the Chelsea Hotel, I see an artist surrounded by African sculptures and his unclassifiable paintings; an artist and art objects, all traumatically marked.

Maryan's light-filled room bursts with numerous examples of African art from the Gelede, Bamileke, Ejagham, Igbo, Chokwe, Kifwebe/Luba, Dan (Yakuba), Guere, and Pende peoples, among others. To be present on his walls, this work had to be stripped of cultural meaning and context, disconnected from the animated bodies that danced them. Extracted from the community that gave them form and meaning, they are unable to perform their intended work on Maryan's walls. Do they lose all meaning as a result? Is Maryan's collection even "real"? Do these sculptures have the power to become something else?

The debate over authenticity in African art is unsettled partly because the global art market that sets the value for this work is out of sync with the values of the cultures that produced these objects. Africans have figured out what the market wants and have implemented ways to make an object appear to possess desired qualities. If the art market claims the authenticity of a work is based on it having been used in a ritual that has possibly been eradicated at the hands of colonialism, religion, ideologies, war, famine, displacement, natural cultural change, and the insatiable appetite of the market itself, and an African says the work they produce is authentic because they made it, who is right? Why is the value of African art tied to so much active and passive violence? Why must Africans lose meaningful cultural objects to satisfy the desire of others?

Each of these questions speaks to the extended afterlives of traumatic marking. The value of these African objects to Maryan no doubt lay in part in the very same formal and signifying elements that drew artists like Picasso, Modigliani, and Brâncuși to them. But with Maryan I would like to think that there was something more; that he intuited, even if he couldn't articulate, a familiarity and connection with these works beyond form—a comfort, perhaps, in knowing that they had all been traumatically marked.

—Erica Moiah James

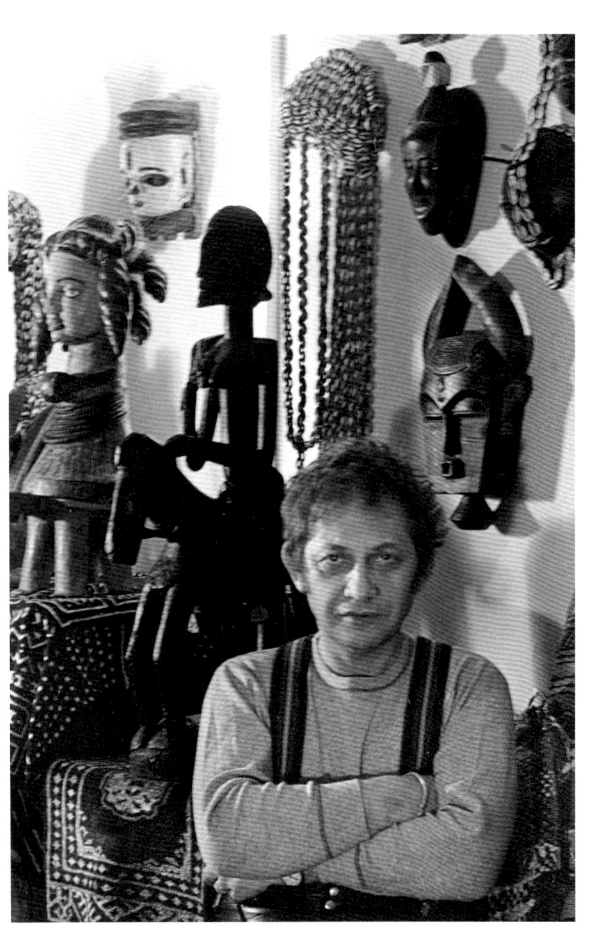

Maryan in his Chelsea Hotel studio with his collection of African sculptures, n.d.

THE THIRTEEN AFRICAN MASKS shown as part of *My Name Is Maryan* represent the types of African sculpture collected by the artist Maryan and displayed in his studio. The masks themselves do not share a cultural background or a common geographic region in Africa. They do, however, in form, refer to their previous function as masquerade headwear. Masquerade is a multi-sensory, community-based performance complete with dance, drumming, audience participation, costume, and, of course, masks. Masks such as these were donned as costume almost exclusively by men at celebratory moments and crucial periods of transition for community members in many societies across west and central Africa. Some performed in conjunction with initiation rites, others at funerals. Africans continue to perform masquerades today, as they address ongoing community anxieties, celebrate milestones that build and reaffirm communities' ties, and, also, generate economic benefit derived from tourists.

But the masks' embodied pasts—to shield a masquerade performer's identity so that he might better embody a spirit or character—are rendered mute after being acquired by Western artists such as Maryan. In these artists' hands, and in the hands of Western collectors more generally, African masks become sculptural objects that provide a stark departure from Western conventions of realism in favor of abstraction. Their confident exaggeration of facial features delights in three dimensions and is made more striking by the addition of paint, white clay, raffia, cloth, and hair. The masks may have served as an inspirational rejoinder to the canon of Western artistic tradition, which, for centuries, prized lifelike portrayal and idealized beauty derived from ancient Greco-Roman standards. These African masks provided another way to reimagine the expressiveness of the human face. Such departures from Western conventions excited many twentieth-century artists in Europe and the United States and led to increased interest in collecting African art.

But while many in the West persisted in the belief that African artists, carvers, and masquerade performers were isolated from Western demand, in fact Africans were aware of and responded to new opportunities for sales. Most African artworks in high demand during the twentieth century were those that Western artists and collectors believed had been made with no influence from the outside world. Perceived as by and for African communities, Western artists and collectors acquired the carved-wood masks with gusto. In turn, African artists responded by carving, and sometimes outright re-creating, well-known mask forms. These masks were likely made for the trade, meaning they approximate earlier and well-known styles of African masks but were likely made for sale rather than carved for use within African communities.

While the African masks displayed here inspired Western artists such as Maryan to experiment with expressive, abstracted representational forms, they are important artworks in their own right. They are evidence of African carving traditions featuring powerful, expressive, and dynamic sculptural forms that preclude any pretensions to Western aesthetic supremacy. They also serve as remnants of dynamic community performances and dances that celebrated African community values. Their presence here tells of a separate life beyond their original contexts, one that pollinated Western artists' fruitful exploration of abstracted and expressive forms.

—MacKenzie Moon Ryan

1977 NOTEBOOK

In the last two years of Maryan's life he made two sketchbooks of autobiographical drawings, several of which are inscribed "B.J.M.G. File." The initials refer to Maryan's girlfriend, "Goldie" Betsy Johnson Gould, with whom he had an affair while living at the Chelsea Hotel.

This series of exquisitely rendered drawings demonstrates the virtuosity of Maryan's hand while also allowing him a forum to vent about the emotional fallout from the end of this relationship. The primary figure in the sketchbook is portrayed as a finely drawn mass of long hair and legs without a body. The psychosexual violence that permeates some of these notebook drawings is echoed in the content of the late paintings he made and displayed at the Chelsea Hotel.

The exposed genitalia of the female figures in these drawings find their male echoes in the numerous phallic depictions in the late paintings made at the Chelsea. The explicit sexuality of these drawings alludes to the liberatory yet violent catharsis that he experienced before his untimely death in 1977. —AMG

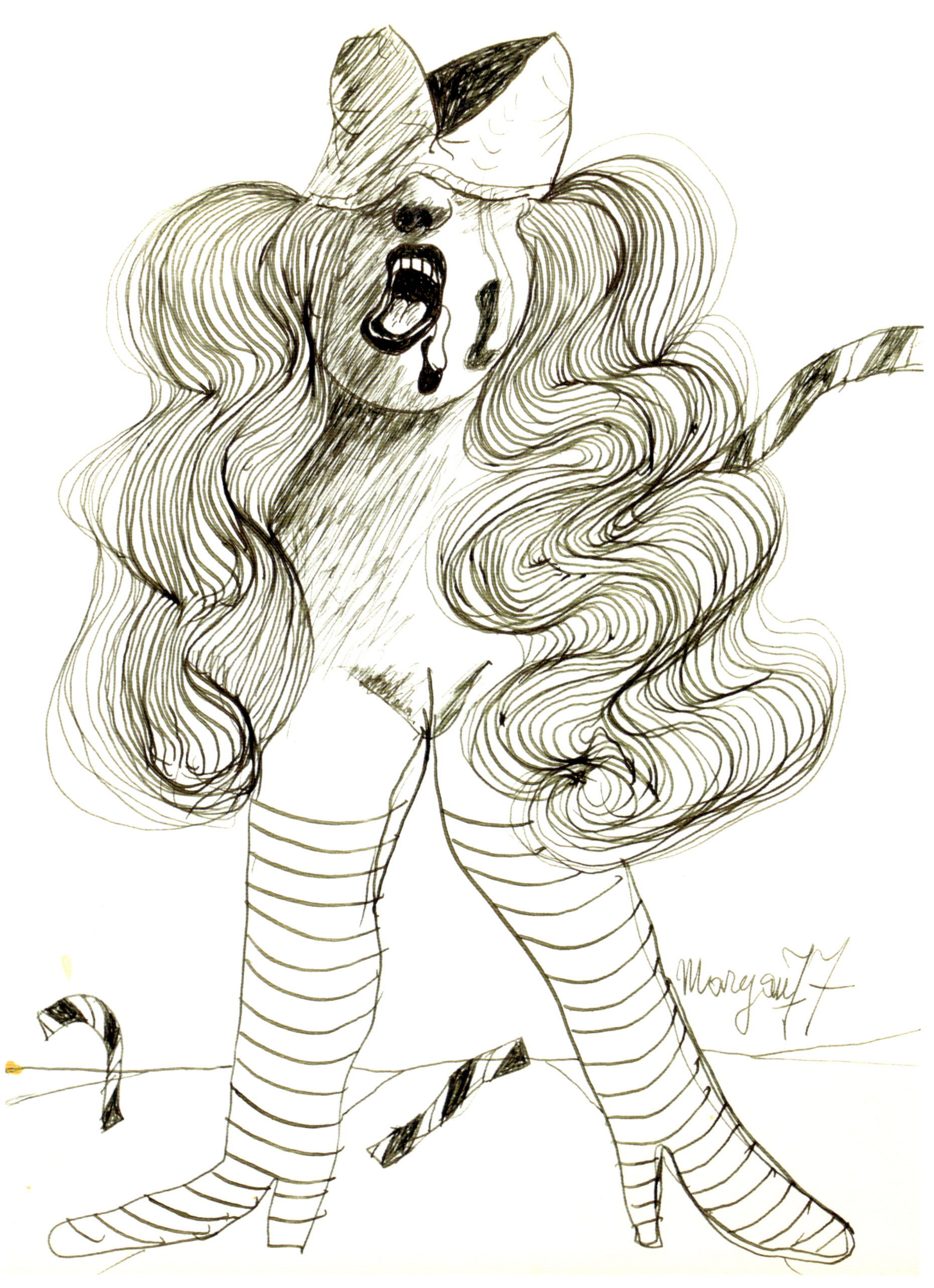

Untitled, 1977. Ink on notebook paper, 14 × 11 inches (35.5 × 28 cm). Private Collection

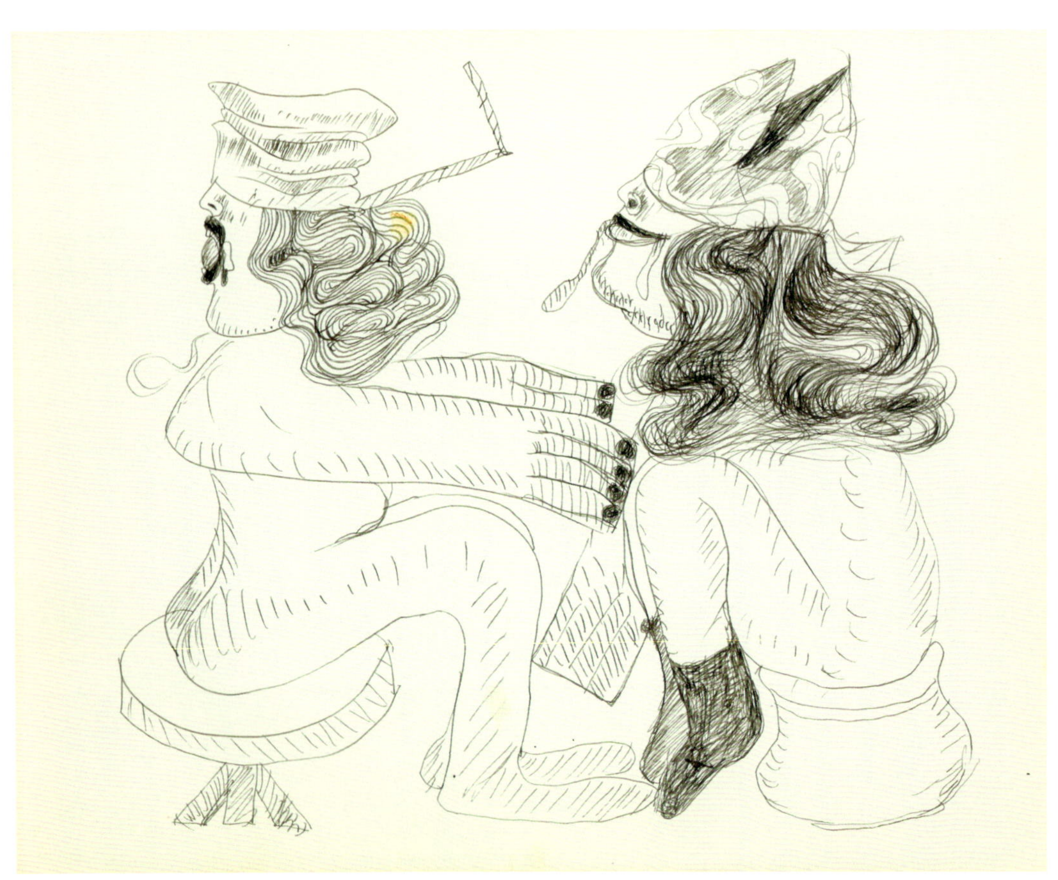

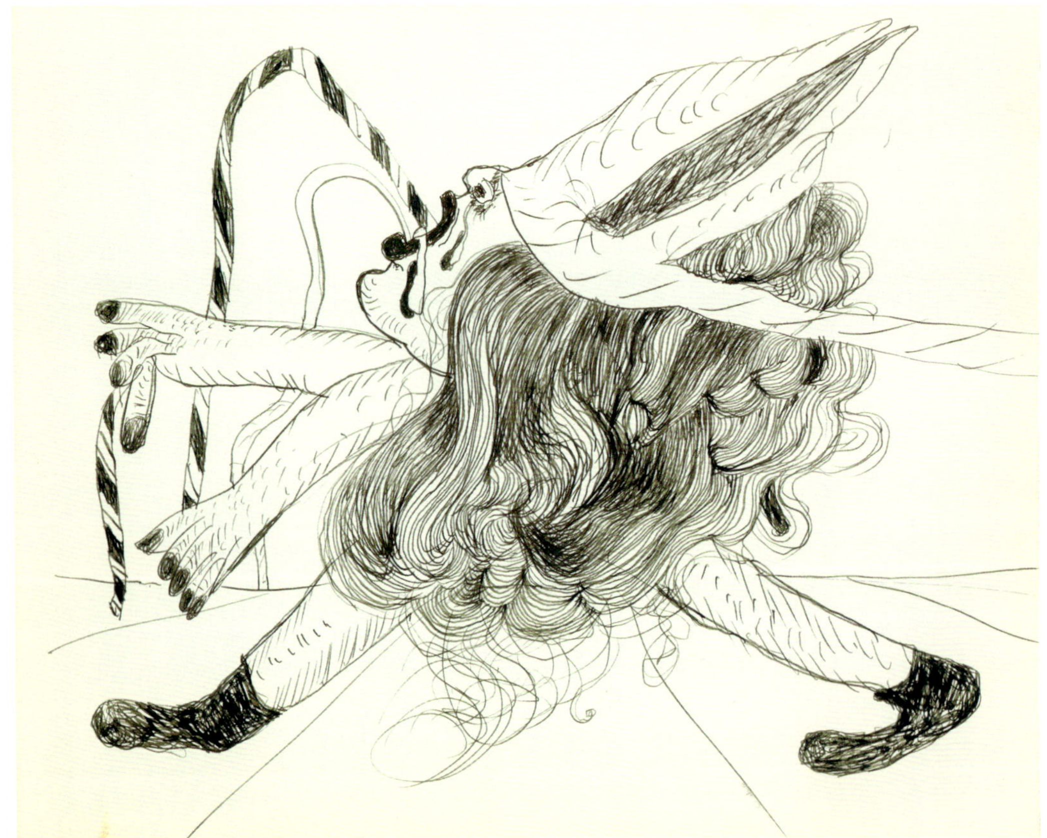

Untitled, 1977. Ink on notebook paper, 12 × 9 inches (30.5 × 22.9 cm). Private Collection

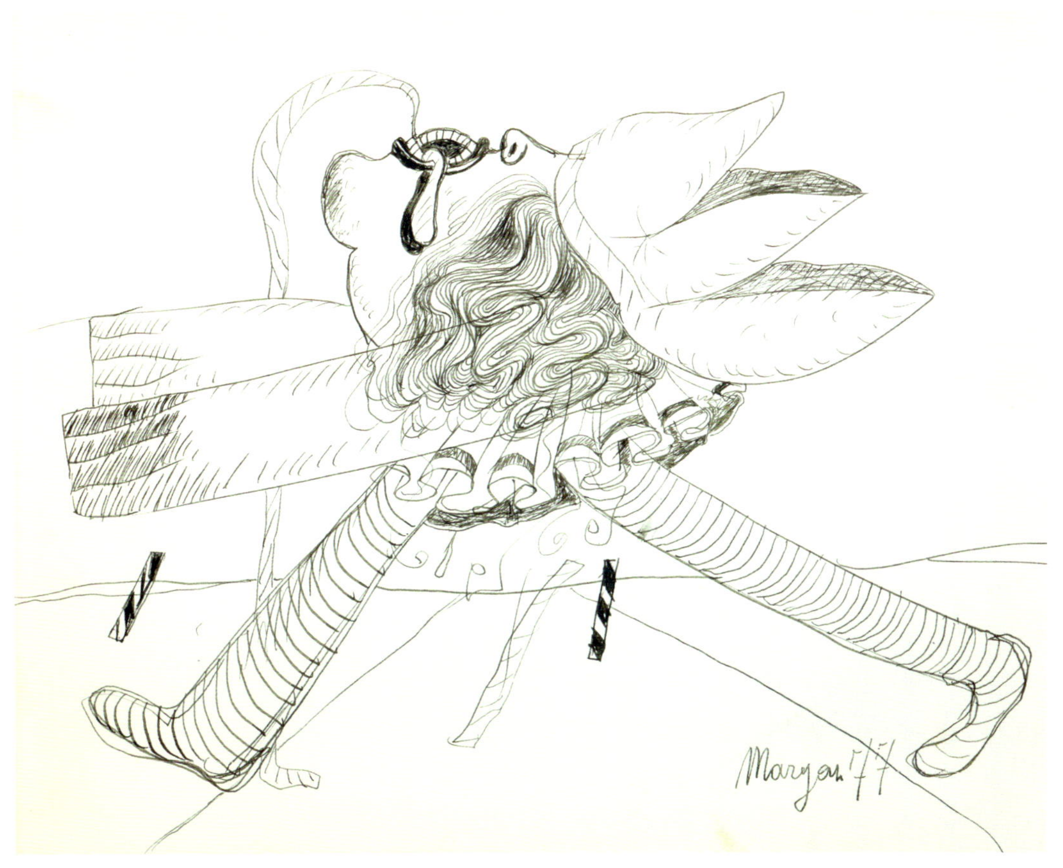

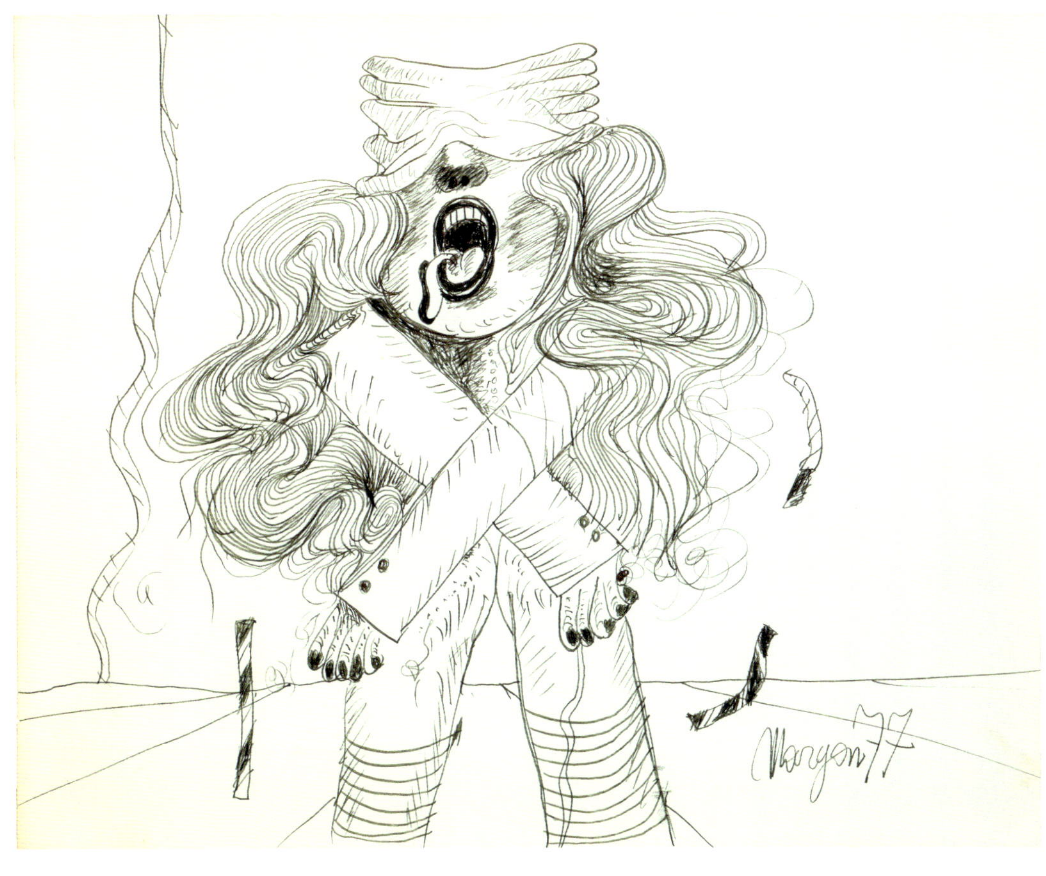

AFTER GOYA

Francisco José de Goya y Lucientes (1746–1828) was one of the few artists Maryan held in the highest esteem. He hung reproductions and postcards of iconic paintings by Goya in his studio.

In 1977, Maryan painted fifteen canvases after Goya's still life entitled *Dead Turkey* (1808–12). This was not a common genre for either Goya or Maryan. In both cases, the artists turned to the subject of a slaughtered animal as a vehicle with which to contemplate human suffering. Goya broke with still life convention by not elevating the dead bird into a trophy or simple vanitas; instead, as art historians William B. Jordan and Peter Cherry explain, Goya was "preoccupied with death and violence [and] seized on the genre [of the still life] as something relevant to his larger concerns . . . If there is an important legacy from Goya's still lifes, it is that he made the still life respectable again, by elevating it to a level of seriousness not to be found in the pretty, bourgeois works of his contemporaries."[1]

Executed just months before his untimely death, Maryan's serial reworkings of Goya's *Dead Turkey* enact a similar radical transformation of the genre. The sacrificial bird motif appears multiple times in Maryan's work, from his early depictions of rabbis performing the kapparah ceremony (in which a cock is slaughtered as a symbolic act of atonement) to his later notebook drawings of a bird nailed to the cross. Maryan's *After Goya* series progressively departs from Goya's original painting, shifting to a brighter palette and with a line that becomes more cartoonish. The last *After Goya* paintings conform to Maryan's own late style. While it is tempting to read these paintings posthumously as a premonition of his own death, the sacrificial theme of the *After Goya* paintings relates closely to Maryan's entire oeuvre. —AMG

1. William B. Jordan and Peter Cherry, Spanish Still Life from Velázquez to Goya (London: National Gallery Publications, 1995), 175.

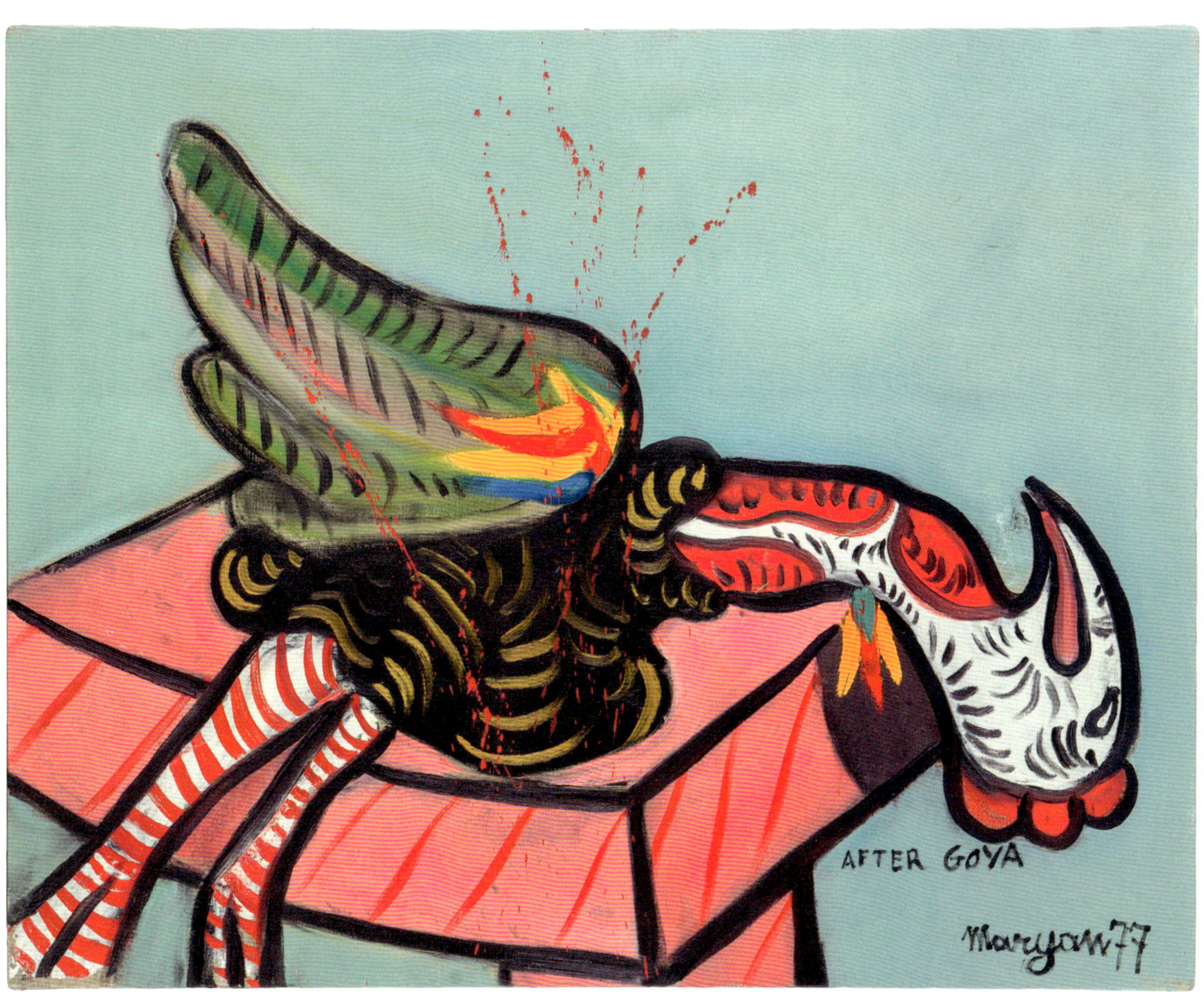

After Goya, 1977. Oil on canvas, 22 × 28 inches (55.9 × 71.1 cm). Private Collection

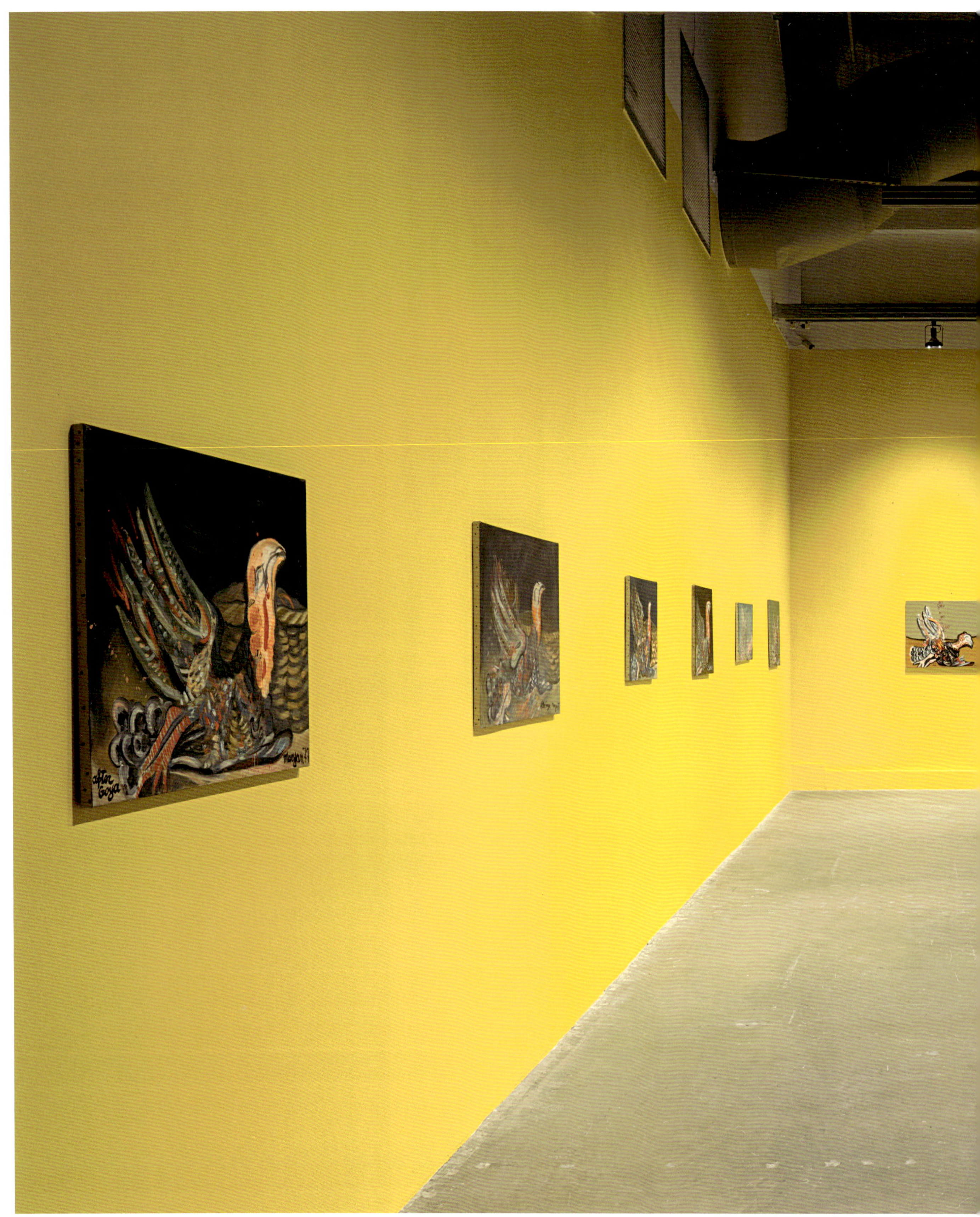

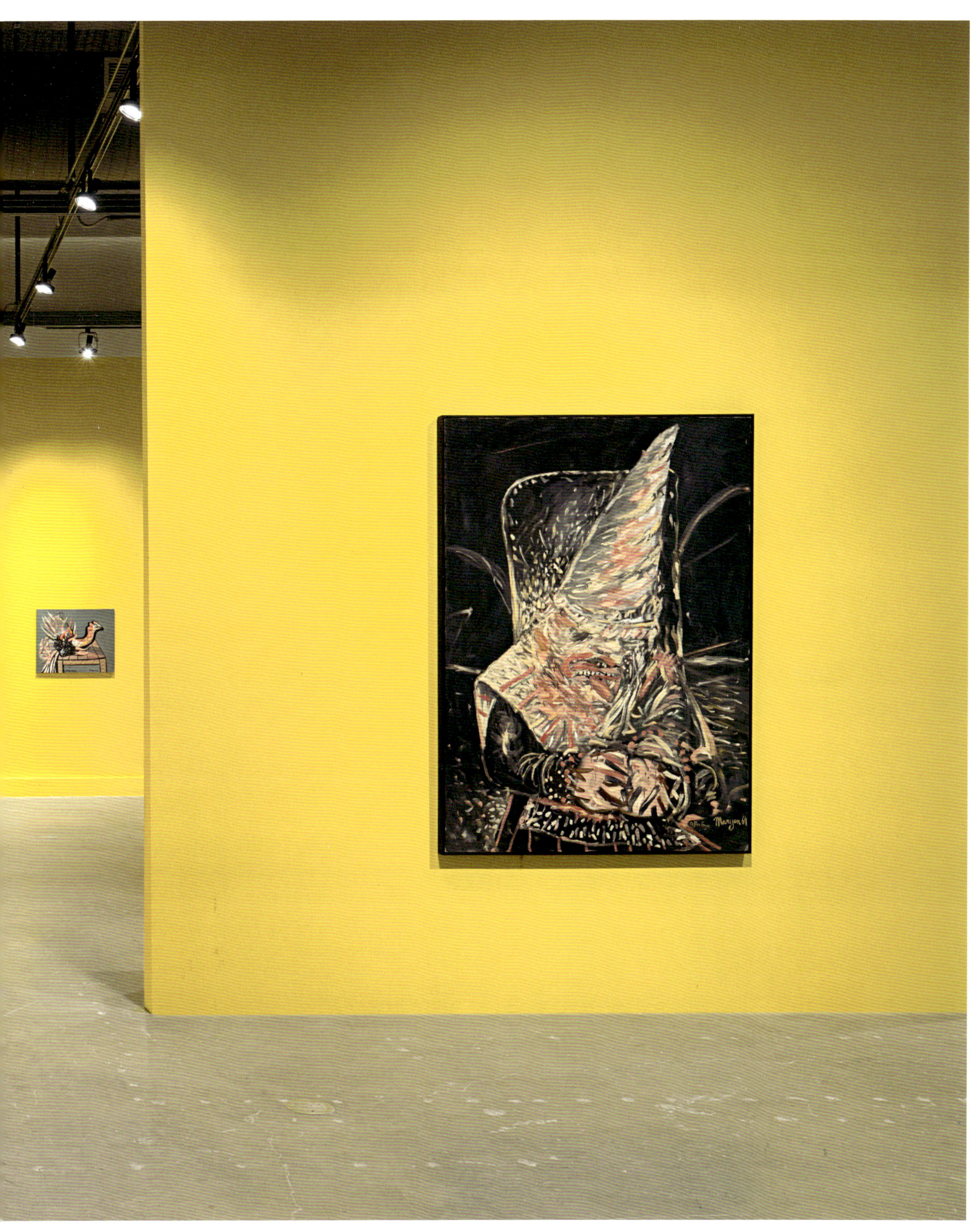

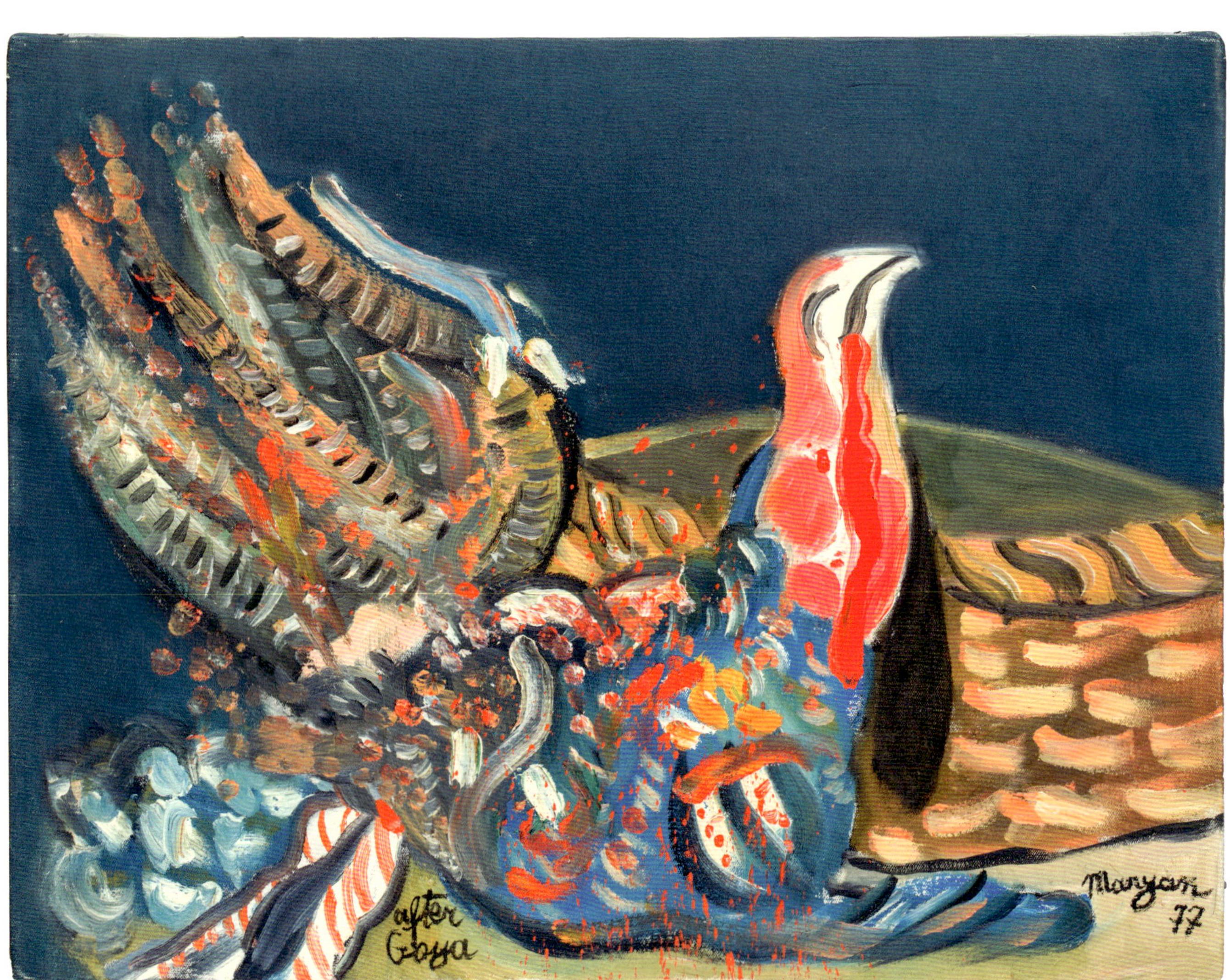

After Goya, 1977. Oil on canvas, 28 × 22 inches (71.1 × 55.8 cm). Private Collection

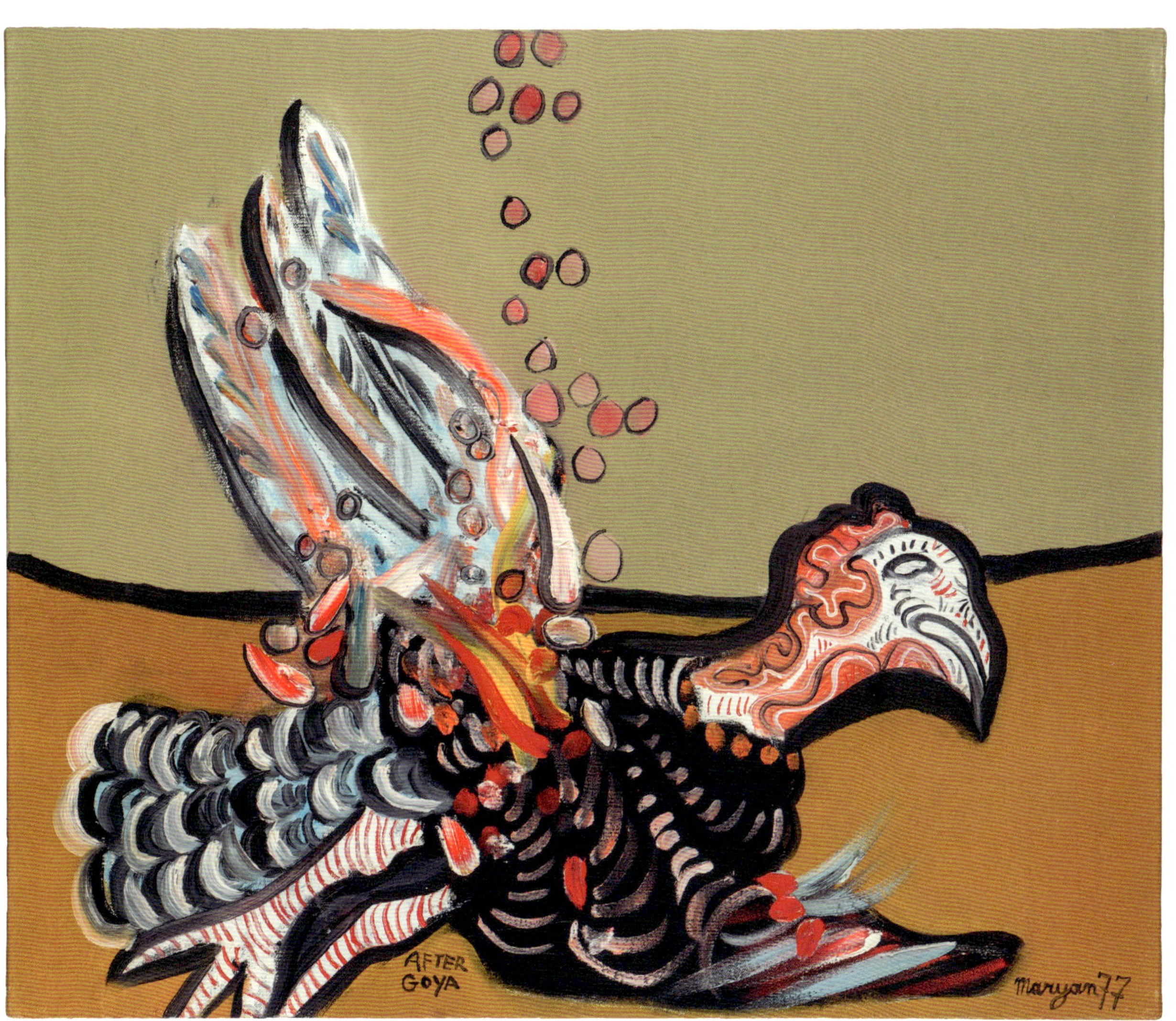

After Goya, 1977. Oil on canvas, 24 × 20 inches (61 × 50.8 cm). Private Collection

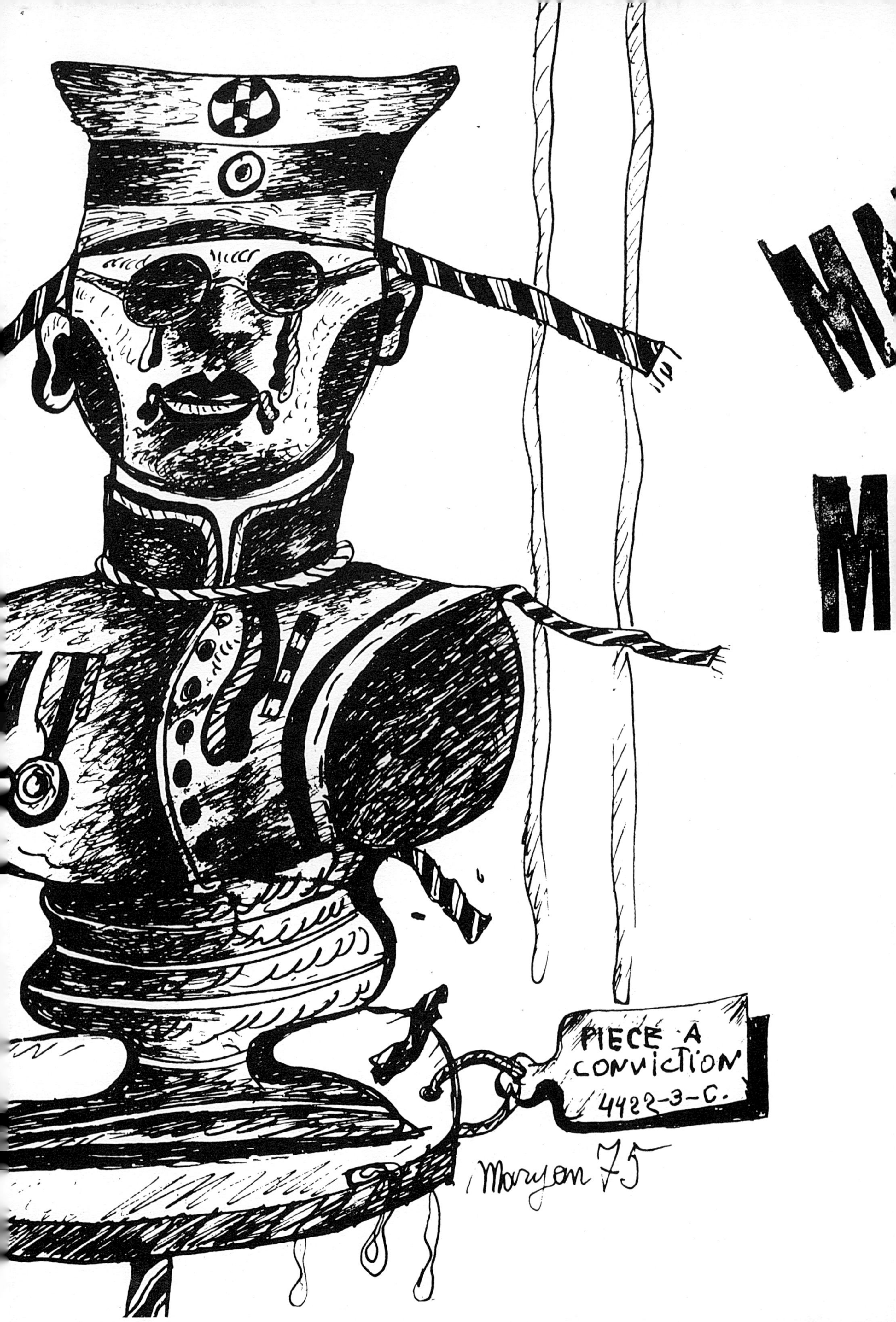
PIECE A
CONVICTION
4422-3-C.
Maryon 75

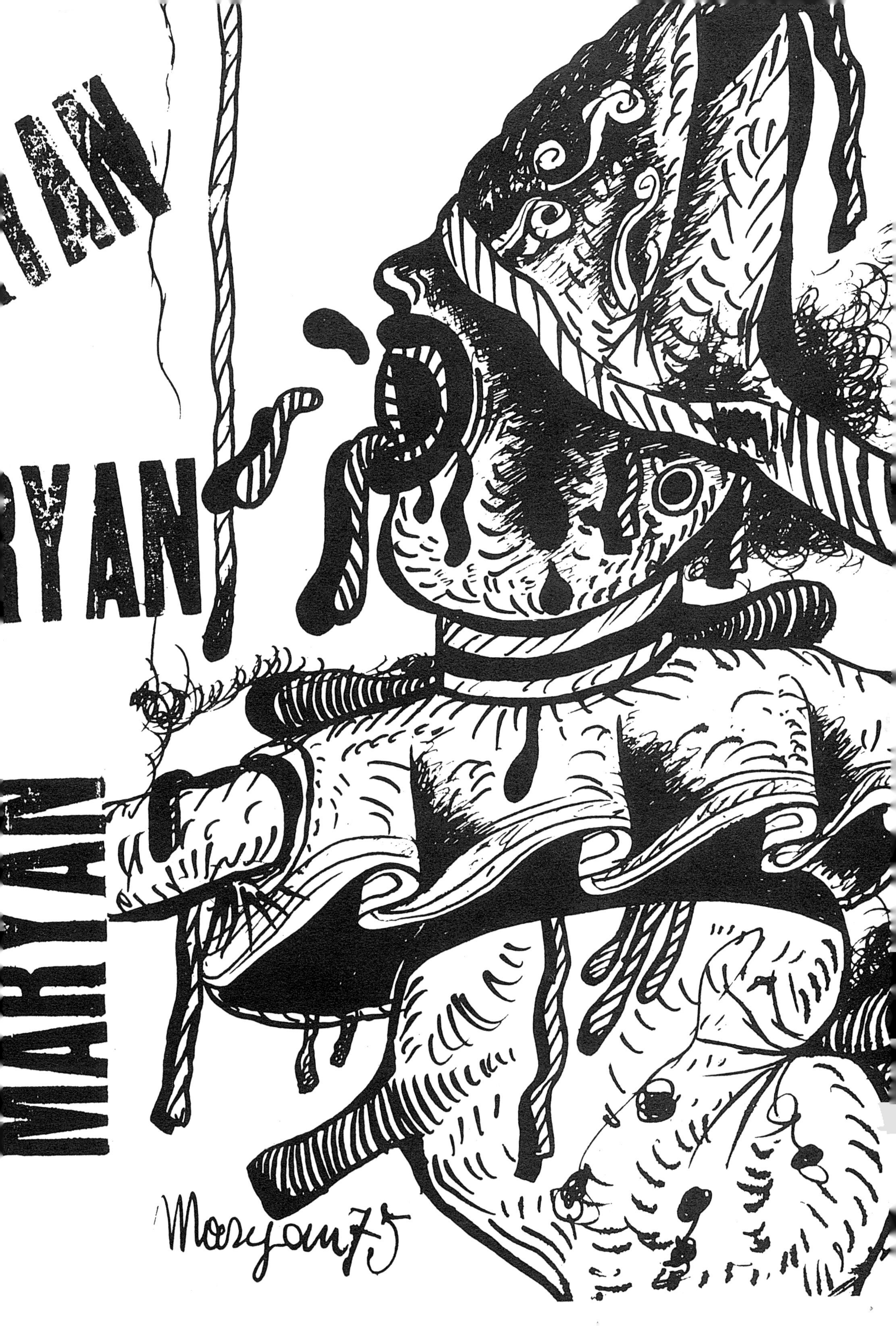
MARYAN
RYAN
MARYAN
Maryan 75

EXHIBITION CHECKLIST

All works are authored by Maryan S. Maryan unless noted otherwise.

Works annotated with a * symbol were only shown the Museum of Contemporary Art, North Miami.

Works annotated with a • symbol were only shown at the Tel Aviv Museum of Art.

ARTWORKS

Pinkas Bursztyn
The Yellow Star, 1947–49
Oil on cardboard
21¾ × 33 inches (55 × 84 cm)
Private Collection
[p. 64]

Pinkas Bursztyn
Two Inmates, 1947–49
Oil on canvas
27½ × 19⅝ inches (70 × 50 cm)
Courtesy of Ghetto Fighters House Archive, Israel
[p. 95]

• Pinkas Bursztyn
Boy Reading Talmud, ca. 1947–50
Oil on cardboard mounted on canvas
27½ × 19⅛ inches (70 × 48.5 cm)
Collection of Tamar and Avner Keshet, Rishon LeZion, Israel
[p. 91]

Pinkas Bursztyn
Crematorium in Auschwitz, 1949
Oil on canvas
63 × 41⅜ inches (160 × 105 cm)
Collection of Mr. Assaph Caspi, Tel Aviv, Israel
[pp. 70, 93]

• Pinkas Bursztyn
Doves (Wounded), 1949
Oil on wooden panel
27½ × 19⅛ inches (70 × 48.5 cm)
Collection of Neomi and David Kolitz, Tel Aviv, Israel
[p. 90, top right]

• Pinkas Bursztyn
The Black Cat, 1949
Oil on cardboard
33 × 22½ inches (84 × 57 cm)
Levin Collection, Jerusalem
[p. 89]

Cover of leaflet for "Exhibition of Paintings and Drawings by Pinhas Burstein [*sic*]", 1950, YMCA, Jerusalem
8¼ × 12¾ inches (21 × 32.5 cm)
Levin Collection, Jerusalem
[pp. 86–87]

Pinkas Bursztyn
An Inmate in the Auschwitz Camp, 1950
India ink drawing
9⅞× 13 inches (25 × 33 cm)
Courtesy of Ghetto Fighters House Archive, Israel
[p. 69, left]

Pinkas Bursztyn
Nude Female Figure, Upper Torso, 1950
India ink drawing
22½ × 16¾ inches (57 × 42.5 cm)
Courtesy of Ghetto Fighters House Archive, Israel
[p. 69, right]

• *Nude Women*, 1950
Pencil on paper
9⅞ × 12¼ inches (25 × 31 cm)
Private Collection, Ramat Gan, Israel
[p. 91, top]

* *Untitled*, n.d.
Acrylic on board
13 × 10 inches (30.5 × 25.4 cm)
Private Collection

* *Untitled*, n.d.
Acrylic on board
13 × 10 inches (30.5 × 25.4 cm)
Private Collection

* *Untitled*, n.d.
Acrylic on board
13 × 10 inches (30.5 × 25.4 cm)
Private Collection

* *Untitled*, n.d.
Acrylic on board
14 × 9 inches (35.5 × 23 cm)
Private Collection

* *Untitled*, n.d.
Acrylic on board
13 × 10 inches (33 × 25.4 cm)
Private Collection

* *Untitled*, n.d.
Ceramic
10¼ × 6¼ × 6¼ inches (26 × 16 × 16 cm)
Private Collection

* *Untitled*, n.d.
Ceramic
13¾ × 10⅝ × 6¼ inches (35 × 27 × 16 cm)
Private Collection

* *Untitled*, n.d.
Ceramic
15 × 5⅞ × 7⅞ inches (38 × 15 × 20 cm)
Private Collection

* *Untitled*, n.d.
Ceramic
16⅛ × 7⅞ × 7⅞ inches (41 × 20 × 20 cm)
Private Collection

• *Shulamite (from Song of Songs)*, ca. 1950
Lithograph
20⅞ × 13⅜ inches (53 × 34 cm)
Collection of the Tel Aviv Museum of Art, purchase
[p. 78]

* *Untitled*, ca. 1950
Ink on paper
3¾ × 6⅝ inches (9.5 × 16.8 cm)
Private Collection
[p. 97, bottom right]

* *Untitled*, ca. 1950
Ink on paper
4⅛ × 5¾ inches (10.5 × 14.5 cm)
Private Collection
[p. 96, bottom right]

* *Untitled*, ca. 1950
Ink on paper
5⅞ × 3⅞ inches (15 × 10 cm)
Private Collection
[p. 96, bottom left]

Untitled, ca. 1950
Ink on paper
12⅜ × 9 inches (31.5 × 23 cm)
Private Collection

Untitled, ca. 1950
Ink on paper
9 × 12⅜ inches (23 × 31.5 cm)
Private Collection

Untitled, ca. 1950
Mixed media on paper
7½ × 10 inches (19.2 × 25.5 cm)
Private Collection
[p. 97, top left]

Untitled, ca. 1950
Ink on paper
8¼ × 10⅝ inches (21 × 27 cm)
Private Collection
[p. 83]

Untitled, ca. 1950
Ink on paper
8¼ × 10⅝ inches (21 × 27 cm)
Private Collection
[p. 96, top left]

Untitled, ca. 1950
Ink on paper
8¼ × 10⅝ inches (21 × 27 cm)
Private Collection

Untitled, ca. 1950
Ink on paper
8¼ × 10⅝ inches (21 × 27 cm)
Private Collection

* *Untitled*, ca. 1950
Ink on paper
8¼ × 10⅝ inches (21 × 27 cm)
Private Collection
[p. 97, bottom left]

* *Untitled*, ca. 1950
Ink on paper
8¼ × 10⅝ inches (21 × 27 cm)
Private Collection

* *Untitled*, ca. 1950
Ink on paper
10⅝ × 8¼ inches (27 × 21 cm)
Private Collection
[p. 97, top right]

* *Untitled*, ca. 1950
Ink on paper
10⅝ × 8¼ inches (27 × 21 cm)
Private Collection

* *Untitled*, ca. 1950
Ink on paper
10⅝ × 8¼ inches (27 × 21 cm)
Private Collection

* *Untitled*, ca. 1950
Ink on paper
9¼ × 8¼ inches (23.5 × 21 cm)
Private Collection

* *Untitled*, ca. 1950
Ink on paper
4¼ × 3 inches (10.7 × 7.4 cm)
Private Collection
[p. 96, top right]

• *The Sacrifice of Isaac*, 1951
Oil on canvas
15 × 21⅝ inches (38 × 55 cm)
Courtesy of Galerie Polysémie,
Marseille
[p. 82]

• *Female Nude*, ca. 1950
Lithograph
20½ × 14⅛ inches (52 × 35.7 cm)
Collection of the Tel Aviv Museum
of Art

Self-Portrait, 1952
Oil on canvas
29½ × 21 inches (75 × 53.4 cm)
Private Collection
[p. 22]

Untitled, 1952
Oil on canvas
45⅝ × 28¾ inches (116 × 73 cm)
Private Collection
[p. 94]

* *L'oiseau*, 1953
Oil on canvas
36 × 28¾ inches (91.4 × 73 cm)
Collection of Mr. David Rosenhaft,
Stamford, CT, courtesy of Taylor
Graham Gallery, New York, NY
[p. 101]

* *Untitled*, 1953
Oil on canvas
28¾ × 21¼ inches (73 × 54 cm)
Courtesy of Galerie Claude Bernard
[p. 104]

* *Chevalier*, 1954
Oil on canvas
39½ × 32 inches (100.3 × 81.3 cm)
Private Collection
[p. 109]

• *Figure with Helmet*, 1955
Gouache on paper
23⅝ × 19⅝ inches (60 × 50 cm)
Collection of the Tel Aviv Museum
of Art
Gift of Claude Bernard, Paris

* *Untitled*, 1955
Oil on canvas
32 × 25⅝ inches (81 × 65 cm)
Courtesy of Galerie Claude Bernard
[p. 105]

• *Personnage*, 1956
Oil on canvas
45⅝ × 35 inches (116 × 89 cm)
Bineth collection, Tel Aviv, Israel

• *Head*, 1958
Oil on canvas
51⅛ × 38⅛ inches (130 × 97 cm)
Collection of Yves and Sandra
Manassé, Tel Aviv, Israel

* *Untitled*, 1959
Oil on canvas
32 × 25½ inches (81.3 × 64.8 cm)
Private Collection, Paris
[p. 108]

Balak, chien fou, 1960
Oil on canvas
51 × 37½ inches (129.5 × 95.2 cm)
Private Collection
[pp. 79, 113]

Composition, 1960
Oil on canvas
13¾ × 10¾ inches (34.8 × 27.3 cm)
Collection of Spertus Institute, Chicago
[p. 112]

* *Untitled*, 1960
Oil on canvas
45½ × 30 inches (115.6 × 76.2 cm)
Private Collection

Untitled, 1960
Oil on canvas
57½ × 45 inches (146 × 114.3 cm)
Private Collection
[p. 111]

* *Untitled*, 1960
Oil on canvas
39½ × 19½ inches (100.3 × 49.5 cm)
Private Collection

After Velázquez, 1961
Oil on canvas
21⅝ × 18⅛ inches (55 × 46 cm)
Estate of Galerie Jacques Benador,
Geneva
[p. 146]

Composition:The Voyeurs, 1961
Oil on canvas
52 × 40 inches (132 × 101.6 cm)
Collection of Spertus Institute, Chicago

Le ménagerie humaine, 1961
Limited-edition artist's book
Courtesy of Venus Over Manhattan

* *Untitled*, 1961
Mixed media on paper
12¾ × 9⅞ inches (32.5 × 25 cm)
Private Collection
[p. 122, top left]

* *Untitled*, 1961
Mixed media on paper
12 ¾ × 9⅞ inches (32.5 × 25 cm)
Private Collection
[p. 122, top right]

* *Untitled*, 1961
Mixed media on paper
12 ¾ × 9⅞ inches (32.5 × 25 cm)
Private Collection
[p. 122, bottom right]

* *Untitled*, 1961
Mixed media on paper
12 ¾ × 9⅞ inches (32.5 × 25 cm)
Private Collection
[p. 123, top left]

* *Untitled*, 1961
Mixed media on paper
12¾ × 9⅞ inches (32.5 × 25 cm)
Private Collection
[p. 123, bottom right]

* *Untitled*, 1961
Mixed media on paper
8½ × 9⅞ inches (21.5 × 25 cm)
Private Collection

* *Untitled*, 1961
Mixed media on paper
10½ × 6¾ inches (26.7 × 17 cm)
Private Collection
[p. 123, top right]

* *Untitled*, 1961
Mixed media on paper
8¼ × 7¼ inches (21 × 18.5 cm)
Private Collection
[p. 123, bottom left]

* *Untitled*, 1961
Mixed media on paper
8¼ × 7¼ inches (21 × 18.5 cm)
Private Collection

* *Untitled*, 1961
Mixed media on paper
6½ × 4 inches (16.5 × 10 cm)
Private Collection
[p. 122, bottom left]

* *Personnage*, 1962
Oil on canvas
50 × 50 inches (127 × 127 cm)
Collection of Anne Wachsmann Guigon
[p. 119]

Personnage in a Box, 1962
Oil on canvas
60¾ × 60¾ inches (154.3 × 154.3 cm)
Courtesy of Venus Over Manhattan,
New York
[p. 117]

* *Man in a Hat with Jacket and Tie*, 1963
Watercolor with oil pastel on Arches
paper
30¼ × 22¼ inches (76.8 × 56.5 cm)
Collection of the Museum of
Contemporary Art, North Miami, Gift of
Adam Lindemann

Personnage, 1963
Oil on canvas
60 × 60 inches (152.4 × 152.4 cm)
Collection of Spertus Institute, Chicago
[p. 118]

* *Personnage*, 1963
Pencil on paper
31 × 20½ inches (78.8 × 52 cm)
Collection of the Museum of
Contemporary Art, North Miami, Gift of
Adam Lindemann

Personnage I, 1963
Ink on board
40 × 32 inches (101.5 × 81.3 cm)
Courtesy of Venus Over Manhattan,
New York

Personnage II, 1963
Ink on board
40 × 32 inches (101.5 × 81.3 cm)
Courtesy of Venus Over Manhattan,
New York
[p. 128]

Personnage III, 1963
Ink on board
40 × 32 inches (101.5 × 81.3 cm)
Courtesy of Venus Over Manhattan,
New York

Personnage IV, 1963
Ink on board
40 × 32 inches (101.5 × 81.3 cm)
Courtesy of Venus Over Manhattan,
New York
[p. 125]

Personnage VI, 1963
Ink on board
40 × 32 inches (101.5 × 81.3 cm)
Courtesy of Venus Over Manhattan,
New York

Personnage VIII, 1963
Ink on board
40 × 32 inches (101.5 × 81.3 cm)
Courtesy of Venus Over Manhattan,
New York
[p. 129]

Personnage IX, 1963
Ink on board
40 × 32 inches (101.5 × 81.3 cm)
Courtesy of Venus Over Manhattan,
New York

Personnage XI, 1963
Ink on board
40 × 32 inches (101.5 × 81.3 cm)
Courtesy of Venus Over Manhattan,
New York

Personnage XII, 1963
Ink on board
40 × 32 inches (101.5 × 81.3 cm)
Private Collection
[p. 130]

Personnage XIII, 1963
Ink on board
40 × 32 inches (101.5 × 81.3 cm)
Courtesy of Venus Over Manhattan,
New York
[p. 131]

* *After Frans Hals*, 1964
Oil on canvas
60 × 60 inches (152 × 152 cm)
Private Collection
[p. 145]

After Goya, 1964
Oil on canvas
40 × 30 inches (101.5 × 76.2 cm)
Collection of Spertus Institute, Chicago

After Rembrandt, 1964
Oil on canvas
40 × 40 inches (101.5 × 101.5 cm)
Private Collection
[p. 147]

* *Image of Seated Cardinal*, 1964
Charcoal on paper
20¼ × 14 inches (51.4 × 35.6 cm)
Courtesy of Venus Over Manhattan,
New York

Personnage, 1964
Oil on canvas
40 × 40 inches (101.5 × 101.5 cm)
Courtesy of Venus Over Manhattan,
New York

Personnage, 1964
Oil on canvas
60 × 60 inches (152.5 × 152.5 cm)
Collection of Spertus Institute, Chicago

* *Figure on Orange and Blue
Background*, 1965
Watercolor on wove paper
22¼ × 15½ inches (56.5 × 39.4 cm)
Private Collection, courtesy of Venus
Over Manhattan, New York

*Figure on Purple and Blue
Background*, 1965
Watercolor and gouache on
wove paper
22½ × 15½ inches (57.2 × 39.4 cm)
Collection of the Museum of
Contemporary Art, North Miami, Gift of
Adam Lindemann

* *Image of Man in a Hat with Glasses*,
1965
Pastel on felted paper
26 × 20 inches (66 × 50.8 cm)
Collection of the Museum of
Contemporary Art, North Miami, Gift of
Adam Lindemann

* *Personnage*, 1965
Ink on paper
20 × 14 inches (50.8 × 35.6 cm)
Collection of the Museum of
Contemporary Art, North Miami, Gift of
Adam Lindeman

* *Personnage with Hat Holding Wand*,
1965
Watercolor on paper
22½ × 15½ inches (57.2 × 39.4 cm)
Courtesy of Venus Over Manhattan,
New York

* *Untitled*, 1965
Charcoal on paper
22 × 26 inches (55.9 × 66 cm)
Collection of the Museum of
Contemporary Art, North Miami, Gift of
Adam Lindemann

* *Untitled*, 1965
Pastel on paper
30¾ × 23¾ inches (78.1 × 60.3 cm)
Courtesy of Venus Over Manhattan,
New York

Untitled, 1965
Acrylic on canvas
50 × 50 inches (127 × 127 cm)
Courtesy of Galerie Claude Bernard

• *Personnage*, 1966
Oil on canvas
45⅝ × 35 inches (116 × 89 cm)
Bineth collection, Tel Aviv, Israel

* *Alfred Jarry: Ubu enchainé*, 1968
Acrylic on board
13 × 10 inches (33 × 25.4 cm)
Private Collection

* *Alfred Jarry: Ubu roi*, 1968
Acrylic on board
13 × 10 inches (33 × 25.4 cm)
Private Collection

* *Franz Kafka: Amerika*, 1968
Acrylic on board
13 × 10 inches (33 × 25.4 cm)
Private Collection

* *Jean Genet: The Balcony*, 1968
Acrylic on board
11¾ × 9 inches (30 × 23 cm)
Private Collection

* *Marquis de Sade: Jean-Paul Marat*,
1968
Acrylic on board
13 × 10 inches (33 × 25.4 cm)
Private Collection

Personnage on a Blue Background,
1968
Oil on canvas
60 × 60 inches (152.5 × 152.5 cm)
Collection of Ariela and Benito
Esquenazi
[p. 134]

* *Roger Peyrefitte: La Nature du Prince*,
1968
Acrylic on board
13 × 10 inches (33 × 25.4 cm)
Private Collection

Two Personnages, 1968
Oil on canvas
52 × 64 inches (132 × 162.5 cm)
Private Collection
[p. 135]

* *Untitled*, 1968
Acrylic on board
13 × 10 inches (33 × 25.4 cm)
Private Collection

* *Untitled*, 1968
Acrylic on board
13 × 10 inches (33 × 25.4 cm)
Private Collection

* *Untitled*, 1968
Acrylic on board
13 × 10 inches (33 × 25.4 cm)
Private Collection

* *Untitled*, 1968
Acrylic on board
13 × 10 inches (33 × 25.4 cm)
Private Collection

* *Untitled*, 1968
Acrylic on board
13 × 10 inches (33 × 25.4 cm)
Private Collection

* *Untitled*, 1968
Acrylic on board
13 × 10 inches (33 × 25.4 cm)
Private Collection

* *Untitled*, 1968
Acrylic on board
13 × 10 inches (33 × 25.4 cm)
Private Collection

• *Personnage*, 1970
Watercolor and ink on paper
24 × 18 inches (60.8 × 45.9 cm)
Collection of the Tel Aviv Museum of Art
Gift of Alex Maguy, Paris

• *Personnage*, 1970
Watercolor and ink on paper
24 × 18 inches (60.8 × 45.9 cm)
Collection of the Tel Aviv Museum of Art
Gift of Alex Maguy, Paris

• *Personnage*, 1970
Watercolor and ink on paper
24 × 18 inches (60.8 × 45.9 cm)
Collection of the Tel Aviv Museum of Art
Gift of Alex Maguy, Paris

Untitled, ca. 1970
Oil on canvas
2 panels: 23⅝ × 27⅜ inches (60 cm ×
69.5 cm) each, framed
Private Collection
[pp. 172–73]

Smoking Figure on Pink Background,
1970
Watercolor and ink on paper
24 × 18 inches (61 × 45.7 cm)
Courtesy of Venus Over Manhattan,
New York

Untitled (From Maryan to Allan), 1970
Watercolor and ink on paper
9½ × 7¼ inches (24.1 × 18.4 cm)
Courtesy of Venus Over Manhattan,
New York
[p. 139]

*Carnet de dessins no. 1 - 9 (Notebook
drawings, nos. 1–9)*, 1971
Chinese ink on paper, in 9 spiral-bound
notebooks, dimensions variable
Musée national d'art moderne, Centre
Pompidou. Gift of Annette Maryan
[pp. 35, 159–61. Note: A selection of
these drawings were presented as
projections in *My Name Is Maryan*]

Personnage de la ménagerie humaine,
1971
Oil on canvas
32 × 25½ inches (81.25 × 64 cm)
Collection of Spertus Institute, Chicago
[p. 165]

*Personnage with Hood and Donkey
Ears*, 1971
Oil on canvas
45¼ × 35 inches (115 × 89 cm)
Collection of Spertus Institute, Chicago
[p. 136]

Untitled, 1971
Oil on canvas
25 × 30 inches (63.5 × 76.3 cm)
Private Collection

* *Untitled*, 1971
Oil on canvas
32 × 23⅝ inches (81.3 × 60 cm)
Collection of The David and Alfred
Smart Museum of Art, The University
of Chicago; Gift of Dennis Adrian in
memory of the artist and memory of
Cynthia E. Basil

Personnage, 1972
Oil on canvas
28 × 23¼ inches (71 × 59 cm)
Private Collection, Japan
[p. 164]

Personnage de la ménagerie humaine,
1972
Oil on canvas
40 × 32 inches (101.5 × 81.25 cm)
Private Collection
[p. 163]

• *Personnage*, 1972
Acrylic and gouache on paper
12 × 16 inches (30.5 × 40.5 cm)
Collection of the Tel Aviv Museum of
Art
Gift of Allan Rich, Los Angeles, through
the American Friends of the Tel Aviv
Museum of Art, 1983
[p. 81]

• *Personnage*, 1972
Acrylic and gouache on paper
12 × 16 inches (30.5 × 40.5 cm)
Collection of the Tel Aviv Museum of
Art
Gift of Allan Rich, Los Angeles, through
the American Friends of the Tel Aviv
Museum of Art, 1983

• *Personnage*, 1972
Acrylic and gouache on paper
12 × 16 inches (30.5 × 40.5 cm)
Collection of the Tel Aviv Museum of
Art
Gift of Allan Rich, Los Angeles, through
the American Friends of the Tel Aviv
Museum of Art, 1983

• *Personnage*, 1972
Acrylic and gouache on paper
12 × 16 inches (30.5 × 40.5 cm)
Collection of the Tel Aviv Museum of
Art
Gift of Allan Rich, Los Angeles, through
the American Friends of the Tel Aviv
Museum of Art, 1983

• *Personnage*, 1972
Acrylic and gouache on paper
12 × 16 inches (30.5 × 40.5 cm)
Collection of the Tel Aviv Museum of
Art
Gift of Allan Rich, Los Angeles, through
the American Friends of the Tel Aviv
Museum of Art, 1983

• *Personnage*, 1973
Oil on canvas
39⅜ × 31⅞ inches (100 × 81 cm)
Bineth collection, Tel Aviv, Israel

* *Personnage (Napoléon)*, 1973
Wax crayon on museum rag board
40 × 32 inches (101.5 × 81.3 cm)
Collection of The David and Alfred
Smart Museum of Art, The University
of Chicago; Purchase, Anonymous Gift
[p. 151]

Personnage (Napoléon), 1973
Wax crayon on museum rag board
40 × 32 inches (101.5 × 81.3 cm)
Private Collection
[p. 152]

Personnage (Napoléon), 1973
Wax crayon on museum rag board
40 × 32 inches (101.5 × 81.3 cm)
Private Collection

Personnage (Napoléon), 1974
Wax crayon on museum rag board
40 × 32 inches (101.5 × 81.3 cm)
Private Collection
[p. 153]

Personnage (Napoléon), 1974
Wax crayon on museum rag board
40 × 32 inches (101.5 × 81.3 cm)
Courtesy of the William Louis-Dreyfus
Foundation
[p. 157]

Personnage (Napoléon), 1974
Wax crayon on museum rag board
40 × 32 inches (101.5 × 81.3 cm)
Courtesy of the William Louis-Dreyfus
Foundation

Personnage (Napoléon), 1974
Wax crayon on museum rag board
40 × 32 inches (101.5 × 81.3 cm)
Private Collection

Personnage (Napoléon), 1974
Wax crayon on museum rag board
40 × 32 inches (101.5 × 81.3 cm)
Courtesy of the William Louis-Dreyfus
Foundation

Personnage (Soldat), 1974
Oil on canvas
40 × 32 inches (101.5 × 81.25 cm)
Collection of Beth Rudin DeWoody
[p. 137]

Personnage, 1974–75
Oil on canvas
27½ inches (70 cm) diameter
Private Collection
[p. 174]

Personnage, 1974–75
Oil on canvas
27½ inches (70 cm) diameter
Private Collection

Personnage, 1974–75
Oil on canvas
27½ inches (70 cm) diameter
Private Collection

Personnage, 1974–75
Oil on canvas
27½ inches (70 cm) diameter
Private Collection

Personnage, 1974–75
Oil on canvas
27½ inches (70 cm) diameter
Private Collection

Personnage, 1974–75
Oil on canvas
27½ inches (70 cm) diameter
Private Collection

Personnage, 1974–75
Oil on canvas
27½ inches (70 cm) diameter
Private Collection

Personnage, 1974–75
Oil on canvas
27½ inches (70 cm) diameter
Private Collection

Crucifix, 1975
Acrylic on canvas
47½ × 47½ inches (120.5 × 120.5 cm)
Private Collection
[p. 170]

Crucifix, 1975
Acrylic on canvas
47½ × 47½ inches (120.5 × 120.5 cm)
Private Collection
[p. 171]

Ecce Homo, ca. 1975
Unique artist's book, acrylic paint
Private Collection

Ecce Homo, 1975
VHS to digital video transfer, black and
white, sound
Produced by M. S. Maryan with Kenny
Schneider
1 hour 31 minutes
Courtesy of Kenny Schneider
[pp. 40–61]

Untitled, 1975
Oil on canvas
39⅜ × 29¾ inches (100 × 75.5 cm)
Private Collection
[p. 167]

Untitled, 1975
Oil on canvas
39⅜ × 31⅞ inches (100 × 81 cm)
Private Collection

* *Personnage*, 1975
Oil on canvas
27½ × 23 inches (70 × 58.5 cm)
Collection of the Tel Aviv Museum of
Art
Gift of Allan Rich, Los Angeles, through
the American Friends of the Tel Aviv
Museum of Art, 1983
[p. 175]

Untitled, 1977
Ink on notebook paper
19 drawings: 14 × 11 inches (35.5 × 28
cm); 17 drawings: 12 × 9 inches (30.5
× 22.9 cm)
Private Collection
[pp. 179–81]

After Goya, 1977
Oil on canvas
30 × 16 inches (76.2 × 40.6 cm)
Private Collection

After Goya, 1977
Oil on canvas
28 × 22 inches (71.1 × 55.8 cm)
Private Collection
[p. 186]

After Goya, 1977
Oil on canvas
22 × 28 inches (55.9 × 71.1 cm)
Private Collection
[p. 183]

After Goya, 1977
Oil on canvas
30 × 24 inches (76.2 × 61 cm)
Private Collection

After Goya, 1977
Oil on canvas
24 × 18 inches (61 × 45.7 cm)
Private Collection

After Goya, 1977
Oil on canvas
24 × 20 inches (61 × 50.8 cm)
Private Collection
[p. 187]

After Goya, 1977
Oil on canvas
30 × 16 inches (76.2 × 40.6 cm)
Private Collection

After Goya, 1977
Oil on canvas
30 × 24 inches (76.2 × 61 cm)
Private Collection

After Goya, 1977
Oil on canvas
24 × 18 inches (61 × 45.7 cm)
Private Collection

After Goya, 1977
Oil on canvas
28 × 22 inches (71.1 × 55.8 cm)
Private Collection

After Goya, 1977
Oil on canvas
24 × 20 inches (61 × 50.8 cm)
Private Collection

After Goya, 1977
Oil on canvas
18 × 24 inches (45.7 × 61 cm)
Private Collection

Maryan with anonymous artisans
Wawel Head, n.d.
Acrylic on wood
6⅝ × 3½ × 3¾ inches (17 × 9 × 9.5 cm)
Private Collection

Maryan with anonymous artisans
Wawel Head, n.d.
Acrylic on wood
5¾ × 3⅜ × 3½ inches (14.5 × 8.5 × 9 cm)
Private Collection

Maryan with anonymous artisans
Wawel Head, n.d.
Acrylic on wood
6¾ × 2¾ × 3⅛ inches (17 × 7 × 10 cm)
Private Collection

Maryan with anonymous artisans
Wawel Head, n.d.
Acrylic on wood
5⅞ × 4¾ × 3¾ inches (15 × 12 × 9.5 cm)
Private Collection

Maryan with anonymous artisans
Wawel Head, n.d.
Acrylic on wood
6½ × 3⅛ × 3⅛ inches (16.5 × 10 × 10 cm)
Private Collection

Maryan with anonymous artisans
Wawel Head, n.d.
Acrylic on wood
6½ × 3½ × 3¾ inches (16.5 × 9 × 9.5 cm)
Private Collection

Maryan with anonymous artisans
Wawel Head, n.d.
Acrylic on wood
6⅛ × 4¾ × 4½ inches (15.5 × 12 × 11.5 cm)
Private Collection

* Anne Abrons
Annette at Home Transcribing Her Memoirs, 1996
Oil on linen
25 × 25 inches (56 × 56 cm)
Collection of Anne Abrons and David Sharpe

* Mogens Balle
Langsom Opvågnen (Expanded Wake), 1962
Oil on canvas
25⅝ × 21¼ inches (65 × 54 cm)
Collection of NSU Art Museum Fort Lauderdale; Cobra Collection, Gift of Golda and Meyer Marks

* Constant
Vogel met wielen (Bird with Wheels), 1949
Tempera and gouache on paper
17¾ × 20⅛ inches (45 × 51.1 cm)
Collection of NSU Art Museum Fort Lauderdale; Cobra Collection, Gift of Golda and Meyer Marks

* Dominick Di Meo
Algonquin, ca. 1950
Oil on canvas
18 × 22 inches (45.7 × 55.9 cm)
Collection of The David and Alfred Smart Museum of Art, The University of Chicago; Gift of the artist and Corbett vs. Dempsey

* Jacques Doucet
Untitled, 1947
Oil on canvas
19¼ × 15⅛ inches (49 × 38.5 cm)
Private Collection

* Stephen Gilbert
Untitled, 1948
Oil and pencil on canvas
19½ × 15⅞ inches (49.5 × 40.3 cm)
Collection of NSU Art Museum Fort Lauderdale; Cobra Collection, Gift of Golda and Meyer Marks

* Stephen Gilbert
Untitled #28, 1949
Ink on paper
12¼ × 9 inches (31.1 × 23.9 cm)
Collection of NSU Art Museum Fort Lauderdale; Cobra Collection, Gift of Golda and Meyer Marks

* Leon Golub
Portrait, 1965
Oil on burlap
36 × 29¼ inches (91.5 × 74.3 cm)
Collection of the Museum of Contemporary Art, North Miami, Gift of Joan and Roger Sonnabend

* Egill Jacobsen
Two Yellow Figures, 1949
Oil on canvas
21¾ × 25½ inches (55.2 × 64.8 cm)
Collection of NSU Art Museum Fort Lauderdale; Cobra Collection, gift of Golda and Meyer Marks

* Asger Jorn
Tête (Head), 1940
Oil on canvas
17⅝ × 15½ inches (44.8 × 39.4 cm)
Collection of NSU Art Museum Fort Lauderdale; Cobra Collection, Gift of Golda and Meyer Marks

* Asger Jorn
Pauvre poète (Poor Poet), 1962
Oil on canvas
32 × 25½ inches (81.3 × 64.8 cm)
Collection of NSU Art Museum Fort Lauderdale; Cobra Collection, Gift of Golda and Meyer Marks

* June Leaf
The Vermeer Box, 1966
Mixed media
25¼ × 24 × 25¼ inches (64 × 61 × 64 cm)
Collection of The David and Alfred Smart Museum of Art, The University of Chicago; Gift of Joel Press

* June Leaf
Portrait of Maryan, 1968
Acrylic on canvas
39¼ × 31¾ inches (100 × 81 cm)
Collection of June Leaf; courtesy of Hyphen
[p. 143]

* Carl-Henning Pedersen
Untitled, 1941
Watercolor and crayon on paper
15⅞ × 17½ inches (40.3 × 44.5 cm)
Collection of NSU Art Museum Fort Lauderdale; Cobra Collection, Gift of Golda and Meyer Marks

* Seymour Rosofsky
Female Personage and Three Heads, 1951
Oil on canvas
34 × 24 inches (86.4 × 61 cm)
Collection of The David and Alfred Smart Museum of Art, The University of Chicago; Gift of the Rosofsky Estate

* H. C. (Horace Clifford) Westermann
Memorial to the Idea of Man If He Was an Idea, 1958
Pine, bottle caps, cast-tin toys, glass, metal, brass, ebony, and enamel
56½ × 38 × 14¼ inches (143.5 × 96.5 × 36.2 cm)
Collection of the Museum of Contemporary Art Chicago, Susan and Lewis Manilow Collection of Chicago Artists, 1993.34

MASKS

* Bangwa People
Bangwa Helmet Mask, n.d.
Wood, kaolin clay
15 × 9 × 7½ inches (38.1 × 22.9 × 19.1 cm)
Collection of the Patricia and Phillip Frost Art Museum, Gift of Jack Baruch, M.D.

* Bangwa People
Bangwa Helmet Mask, 20th century
Wood, kaolin clay
15 × 11 × 8 inches (38.1 × 27.9 × 20.3 cm)
Collection of the Patricia and Phillip Frost Art Museum, Gift of Jack Baruch, M.D.

* Bapende People
Katundu Inititiation Mask, 20th century
Wood, pigment, raffia, and fabric
8 × 10¾ × 7½ inches (20.3 × 27.3 × 19.1 cm)
Collection of the Patricia and Phillip Frost Art Museum, Gift of Dr. and Mrs. Edward D. Saltzman

* Bini People
Bini Mask, 1900–25
Wood, paint
10 × 5⅜ × 4¼ inches (25.4 × 13.7 × 10.8 cm)
Collection of the Patricia and Phillip Frost Art Museum, Gift of Dr. and Mrs. Arthur I. Segaul

* Bini People
Bini Mask with Coral Earrings, 20th century
Wood, paint, and coral
10½ × 5¼ × 4 inches (26.7 × 13.3 × 10.2 cm)
Collection of the Patricia and Phillip Frost Art Museum, Gift of Dr. and Mrs. Edward D. Saltzman

* Bobo People
Bobo Antelope Mask, ca. 20th century
Wood, paint
61 × 10 inches (155 × 25.4 cm)
Collection of the Patricia and Phillip Frost Art Museum, Gift of Linda and Martin Gallant

* Cameroon Grasslands
Helmet Mask, n.d.
Wood, kaolin clay
22 × 10 × 20 inches (55.9 × 25.4 × 50.8 cm)
Collection of the Patricia and Phillip Frost Art Museum, Gift of Jack Baruch, M.D.

* Dan (Kran) Culture
Chimpanzee Mask, 20th century
Wood
11 × 6 × 5 inches (28 × 15 × 12.7 cm)
Collection of the Patricia and Phillip Frost Art Museum, Gift of Jack Baruch, M.D.

* Ibibo People
Mask, face deformed by Gangosa, n.d.
Wood, pigmentation, hair, fur, and
nails
11¾ × 7¾ × 5½ inches (29.8 × 19.7 ×
14 cm)
Collection of the Patricia and Phillip
Frost Art Museum, Gift of Jack Baruch,
M.D.

* Ibo (Igbo) Culture
Mask with Mmwo Society Spirit Motif,
20th century
Wood, paint, and kaolin
18½ × 8½ × 10 inches (47 × 21.6 × 25.4
cm)
Collection of the Patricia and Phillip
Frost Art Museum, Gift of Dr. and Mrs.
Edward D. Saltzman

* Teke People
Mask, n.d.
Wood, burlap, and paint
16¼ × 15 × 5 inches (41.3 × 38.1 ×
12.7 cm)
Collection of the Patricia and Phillip
Frost Art Museum, Gift of Susan Yecies

* *Basketry Mask*, ca. 1910
Basketry with traces of polychrome
17 × 12 × 7 inches (43.2 × 30.5 × 20.3 cm)
Collection of the Patricia and Phillip
Frost Art Museum, Gift of Ann and
Robert Walzer

Day of the Dead Masks

Unknown artist
Day of the Dead Mask, n.d.
Painted papier-mâché
7½ × 5⅛ × 3 inches (19 × 15 × 7.5 cm)
Collection of Maryan Association,
Nowy Sącz, Poland

Unknown artist
Day of the Dead Mask, n.d.
Painted papier-mâché
8¼ × 6¼ × 4⅜ inches (21 × 16 × 11 cm)
Collection of Maryan Association,
Nowy Sącz, Poland

Unknown artist
Day of the Dead Mask, n.d.
Painted papier-mâché
7⅛ × 5⅜ × 3⅞ inches (18.5 × 13.5 × 10 cm)
Collection of Maryan Association,
Nowy Sącz, Poland

Unknown artist
Day of the Dead Mask, n.d.
Painted papier-mâché
7⅛ × 7⅛ × 4⅜ inches (20 × 20 × 11 cm)
Collection of Maryan Association,
Nowy Sącz, Poland

Unknown artist
Day of the Dead Mask, n.d.
Painted papier-mâché
10⅜ × 7⅛ × 6¾ inches (26.5 × 18 × 12 cm)
Collection of Maryan Association,
Nowy Sącz, Poland

Unknown artist
Day of the Dead Mask, n.d.
Painted papier-mâché
7⅞ × 7⅛ × 3½ inches (20 × 18.5 × 9 cm)
Collection of Maryan Association,
Nowy Sącz, Poland

Unknown artist
Day of the Dead Mask, n.d.
Painted papier-mâché
7⅛ × 9 × 3¾ inches (18 × 23 × 9.5 cm)
Collection of Maryan Association,
Nowy Sącz, Poland

EPHEMERA

* Packing list from one of Annette and
Maryan's joint trips, n.d.
Collection of Maryan Association,
Nowy Sącz, Poland

Photograph of Maryan's Chelsea Hotel
studio, n.d.
Photo by John Lefebre
Courtesy of the Lefebre Gallery Archives
[p. 200]

* Photographs of Maryan's Chelsea
Hotel studio, n.d.
Photos by Susan Weiley
Courtesy of Venus Over Manhattan

A group of Jewish Holocaust survivors
in Częstochowa, Poland, in 1945. They
lived in a "House for the Crippled" at
11 Garibaldi Street after their
discharge from various hospitals
beginning in May 1945.
Photographic print
8 × 11 inches (23.3 × 28 cm)
Courtesy of Ghetto Fighters House
Archive, Israel
[p. 72]

* Annette and Maryan (far right)
with their friends at the Dôme,
Montparnasse, Paris, ca. 1950s
Photographer unknown

* Maryan at work, 1951
Photographer unknown

* Maryan and gallerist Claude Bernard
Photo by C. Damann, Paris, 1954
Private Collection

* Annette and Maryan
Studio on rue des Suisses, Paris, 1955
Photo by Izis Bidermanas
[p. 19]

* Annette and Maryan
Studio on rue des Suisses, Paris, 1955
Photo by Izis Bidermanas

* Maryan in his studio on the rue des
Suisses, Paris, ca. 1955–56
Photographer unknown
Private Collection

* Annette and Maryan
Hotel Michele's, Paris, ca. 1957
Photo by Izis Bidermanas

* Maryan in his studio on the rue des
Suisses, Paris, ca. 1959
Photographer unknown
Private Collection

* A selection of photographs of young
Maryan, ca. 1959–63
Private Collection
[p. 201]

* Maryan exhibition catalogue and
lithograph, Galerie de France, 1960
Collection of Maryan Association,
Nowy Sącz, Poland

* Annette and Maryan, in front of a
hanging of Maryan's paintings, late
1960s
Photographer unknown

* Allan Frumkin Gallery "H. C.
Westermann" poster, 1961
Paper, ink
21⅞ × 16 inches (55.6 × 40.6 cm)
Collection of The David and Alfred
Smart Museum of Art, The University
of Chicago; The H. C. Westermann
Study Collection, Gift of Martha
Westermann Renner

* Annette and Maryan
301 E. 63rd Street, New York, 1962
Photo by Nathan Rabin
[p. 33]

* Annette and Maryan
301 E. 63rd Street, New York, in front of
the Queensboro Bridge, 1963
Photographer unknown
[p. 202]

* Maryan, Annette Maryan, H. C.
(Horace Clifford) Westermann
*Think the new sculpture at the gallery
is terrific. Illustration of two of HCW's
sculptures, including Antimobile.
Postcard: Buffalo Bill's Wild West,
1885*, March 7, 1966
Handwritten and illustrated postcard
5⅝ × 4 inches (14.3 × 10.2 cm)
Collection of The David and Alfred
Smart Museum of Art, The University
of Chicago; The H. C. Westermann
Study Collection, Gift of Joanna Beall
[p. 34]

* Maryan, H. C. (Horace Clifford)
Westermann, Joanna Beall
Westermann
*Has seen HCW's sculptures in the
Museum. Doesn't like L.A. Illustration
with car and figure. Postcard: The
Watts Towers, Los Angeles*, May 6,
1967
Handwritten and illustrated postcard
5½ × 3½ inches (14 × 8.9 cm)
Collection of The David and Alfred
Smart Museum of Art, The University
of Chicago; The H. C. Westermann
Study Collection, Gift of Joanna Beall

* Invitation/poster ("The Printers and
Their Wives Are Invited for a Dinner
Party in Chinatown on May 24 at
7:30 PM., All members of Tamarind Are
Cordially Invited to Join Us the
Maryans, Restaurant Hong-Kong-Low
425 Gin-Lin Way L.A."), 1967
Lithograph on red-tan Japanese
wove paper
37¼ × 25 inches (94.6 × 63.5 cm)
Collection of The David and Alfred
Smart Museum of Art, The University
of Chicago; Purchase, Anonymous Gift
[p. 139, top right]

CONTRIBUTOR BIOGRAPHIES

Alison M. Gingeras is a curator and writer based in New York and Warsaw. Gingeras has served as curator at the Solomon R. Guggenheim Museum, the Musée National d'Art Moderne, Centre Pompidou, Paris, and Palazzo Grassi, Venice. Currently she serves as an adjunct curator at Dallas Contemporary and a guest curator at MOCA North Miami, in addition to working independently. Known for her scholarly yet anarchic approach to art history, Gingeras has organized several groundbreaking exhibitions, including *Dear Painter, Paint Me: Painting the Figure Since Late Picabia* at the Centre Pompidou (2002), and co-curated *Pop Life* at Tate Modern (2009). Most recently, she curated *John Currin: My Life as a Man* at Dallas Contemporary (2019) and *New Images of Man* at Blum & Poe, Los Angeles (2020). Her writing regularly appears in such periodicals as *Artforum*, *Playboy*, *Spike*, and *Tate Etc.*, as well as in scores of books and exhibition catalogues. The cult imprint Heinzfeller Nileisist recently published *Totally My Ass and Other Essays* (2019)—a collection of Gingeras's writing.

Noa Rosenberg is Curator and Head of the Modern Art Department at the Tel Aviv Museum of Art (TAMA). She is a researcher and lecturer at the Ben-Gurion University of the Negev, whose work centers on the Holocaust as the central instance of modernity; "multiple modernities"—national models in visual culture and print media in the Ottoman Empire/Turkey Republic and Palestine/Israel in the early twentieth century; and the history of the Tel Aviv Museum, 1929–36. Rosenberg has curated exhibitions dealing with nationality and contemporary Israeli identity, including *Tamir Zadok: A Guide to the Arab World* (2017), and exhibitions of modern Israeli artists who worked outside of the local canon, including *Hagit Lalo: A Painter who Begins at the End* (2015). She is currently working on an anthology to be published in conjunction with TAMA's ninetieth anniversary.

Piotr Słodkowski is an art historian, assistant professor at the Academy of Fine Arts in Warsaw, and a guest curator at the Museum of Modern Art, Warsaw. His research focuses on Polish and Central European twentieth-century art in relation to contemporary thought in the humanities. Słodkowski recently curated *Henryk Streng/Marek Włodarski and Jewish-Polish Modernism* (2021). He is the editor of *Przestrzeń społeczna. Historie mówione Złotego Grona i Biennale Sztuki Nowej* (Social space: oral histories of the Golden Grapes avant-garde plein-airs and the New Art Biennale) (2014) and, with Agata Pietrasik, coeditor of *Czas debat. Antologia krytyki artystycznej z lat 1945–1954* (Time of debate: an anthology of Polish art criticism, 1945–1954) (2016).

ACKNOWLEDGMENTS

A project of this magnitude and complexity relies upon the generosity of many of the people who personally knew Maryan S. Maryan and his wife, Annette Maryan. In Israel, we are deeply indebted to those Holocaust survivors who shared their stories and memories of Pinkas Bursztyn in Mandatory Palestine–Eretz Israel and the young State of Israel (1947–50), especially Yehuda Bacon, an Israeli artist and close friend of Maryan at Bezalel in those years. Heartfelt thanks to Betty Karchi, the niece of Annette Maryan, who told us much about her aunt's life in prewar Belgium and about Annette and Maryan's life in Paris in the early 1950s. In the US, Belgium, and France, we would like to thank a number of individuals who shared their personal and family memories of Maryan with us as well as opening their archives as this project took shape: Anne Abrons, Michel Auder, Claude Bernard, Miriam Haim, June Leaf (with additional support from Andrea Glimsher and Leaf's studio), Jan Nieuwenhuizen Segaar, Joel and Maya Press, Nicolas Saada, David Sharpe, Ruth Shomron (and Michael Rips, who introduced us to the community of Chelsea Hotel residents who knew Maryan), Michel Soskin, Catherine Thieck, Jeanne Marie Wasilik, and Samuel Cohen Solal. Marion Lefebre was very generous with her father's Lefebre Gallery archive, providing us with crucial documentation and portraits that John Lefebre took of Maryan in Paris and New York. Founding member of the CoBrA group, artist Pierre Alechinsky, shared his recollections of Maryan, with whom he shared a gallery in France and whose milieu overlapped with Maryan's in Paris and New York in the 1960s and '70s.

The research that enriched our exhibition traversed multiple countries and institutions. We are grateful to Eliad Moreh-Rosenberg, curator of art at the Yad Vashem Museum in Jerusalem, for her generous help, and to the archives who welcomed us and assisted our research, especially the Jerusalem City Archive and the Bezalel Archive. Curator Nathalie Brunet and her colleagues at the Musée d'art et d'histoire du Judaïsme in Paris were extremely supportive in sharing their research at the earliest stages of this project. Our colleague Jennifer Carty, curator at the Smart Museum of Art at the University of Chicago, and Dr. Dean Bell, president of the Spertus Institute for Jewish Learning and Leadership in Chicago, were very generous in sharing their collections and archives with us. In Maryan's hometown of Nowy Sącz in Poland, Krzysztof Bojarczuk , Ewa Andrzejewska and the Society of the Friends of Maryan very graciously opened their archives of Maryan's personal and studio objects, and provided excellent information about the Jewish communities of Galicia before and during the war. Curator Anda Rottenberg was also very supportive of the Polish research related to this project. Dr. Piotr Rypson, Noam Silberberg, and Anna Przbyszewska Drozd at the Jewish Genealogy & Family Heritage Center of the Emanuel Ringelblum Jewish Historical Institute in Warsaw provided vital research support in uncovering previously unknown aspects of Maryan's family history and helped us to connect to his living descendants, including members of the Eisen family in the United States.

Antonina Gułaga provided us with much-needed curatorial assistance at the outset of our journey, as did the team at Venus Over Manhattan, especially the gallery's founder, Adam Lindemann, along with Zach Fischman and Anna Furney. Dr. Olivier Philippe, Andrea Schwan, Simone Taylor, and Piotr Uklański supported our efforts from the beginning. Nathalie Andrijasevic, assistant curator of the Tel Aviv exhibition, contributed invaluable research and help in all matters, as did Daphna Raz, Sivan Raveh, Orna Yehudiaoff, and Tamar Fox, who were excellent editors and translators of the Hebrew and Arabic versions of the catalogue essays and documents.

Alison M. Gingeras
Noa Rosenberg

MOCA ACKNOWLEDGEMENTS

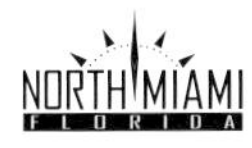

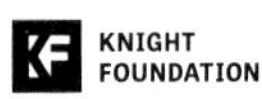

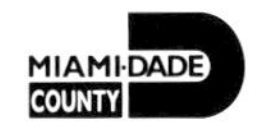

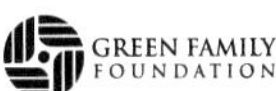

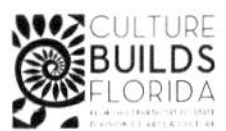

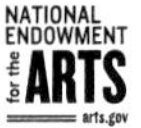

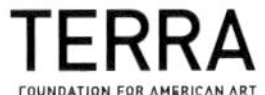

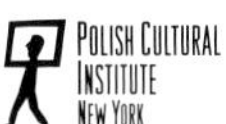

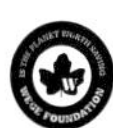

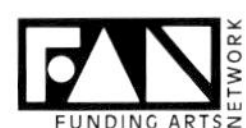

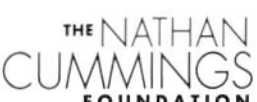

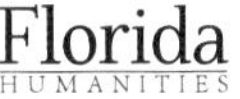

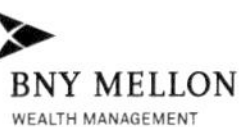

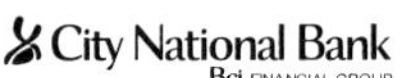

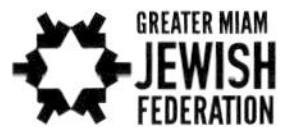

My Name is Maryan is made possible with lead support from the Terra Foundation for American Art and Shirley and William M. Lehman, Jr. Major support was provided by the Miami-Dade County Tourist Development Council, The Polish Cultural Institute New York, The Wege Foundation, the Schottenstein Family, and the Simkins Family. We thank the Funding Arts Network, the Galbut Family, and Adele and Joel Sandberg for their generosity, and our partners BNY Mellon Wealth Management, Florida Humanities, William Louis-Dreyfus Foundation, Ariela and Benito Esquenazi, Arlene Kahn, and Richard Yulman. We are also grateful to Bal Harbour Village, City National Bank, Greater Miami Jewish Federation, Robert Russell Memorial Foundation, Brian Bilzin, Dr. Helen Sachs Chaset and Mr. Alan Chaset, Isaac Fisher, Daniel Lewis, David and Sydney Schaecter, and Judi Witkin. Special thanks to Venus Over Manhattan, New York.

The catalogue is made possible with partial support from kamel mennour.

MOCA North Miami is generously funded by the North Miami Mayor and Council and the City of North Miami; the John S. and James L. Knight Foundation; the Miami-Dade County Department of Cultural Affairs and the Cultural Affairs Council, the Miami-Dade County Mayor and Board of County Commissioners; and the State of Florida, Department of State, Division of Arts and Culture and the Florida Council on Arts and Culture (Section 286.25, Florida Statutes). MOCA is supported in part by an American Rescue Plan Act grant from the National Endowment for the Arts to support general operating expenses in response to the COVID-19 pandemic. Additional support is provided by the Fine & Greenwald Foundation; The Nathan Cummings Foundation; and the Sol Taplin Charitable Foundation. Founding support for the MOCA Sustainability Fund provided by the Green Family Foundation Trust. Major support provided by Shirley and William M. Lehman, Jr. We also thank our Board of Trustees, Curator's Circle, and MOCA Members for their meaningful support.

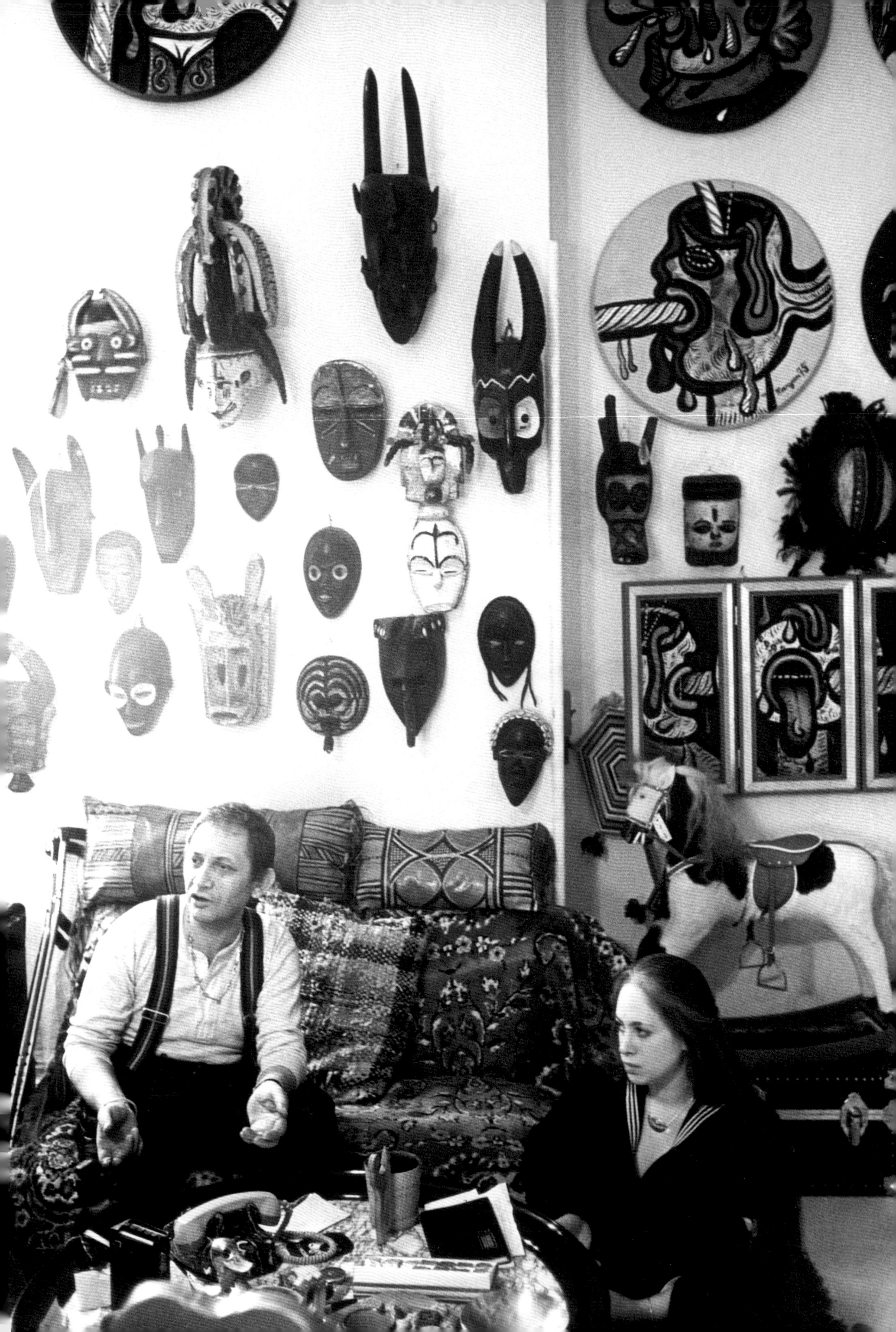

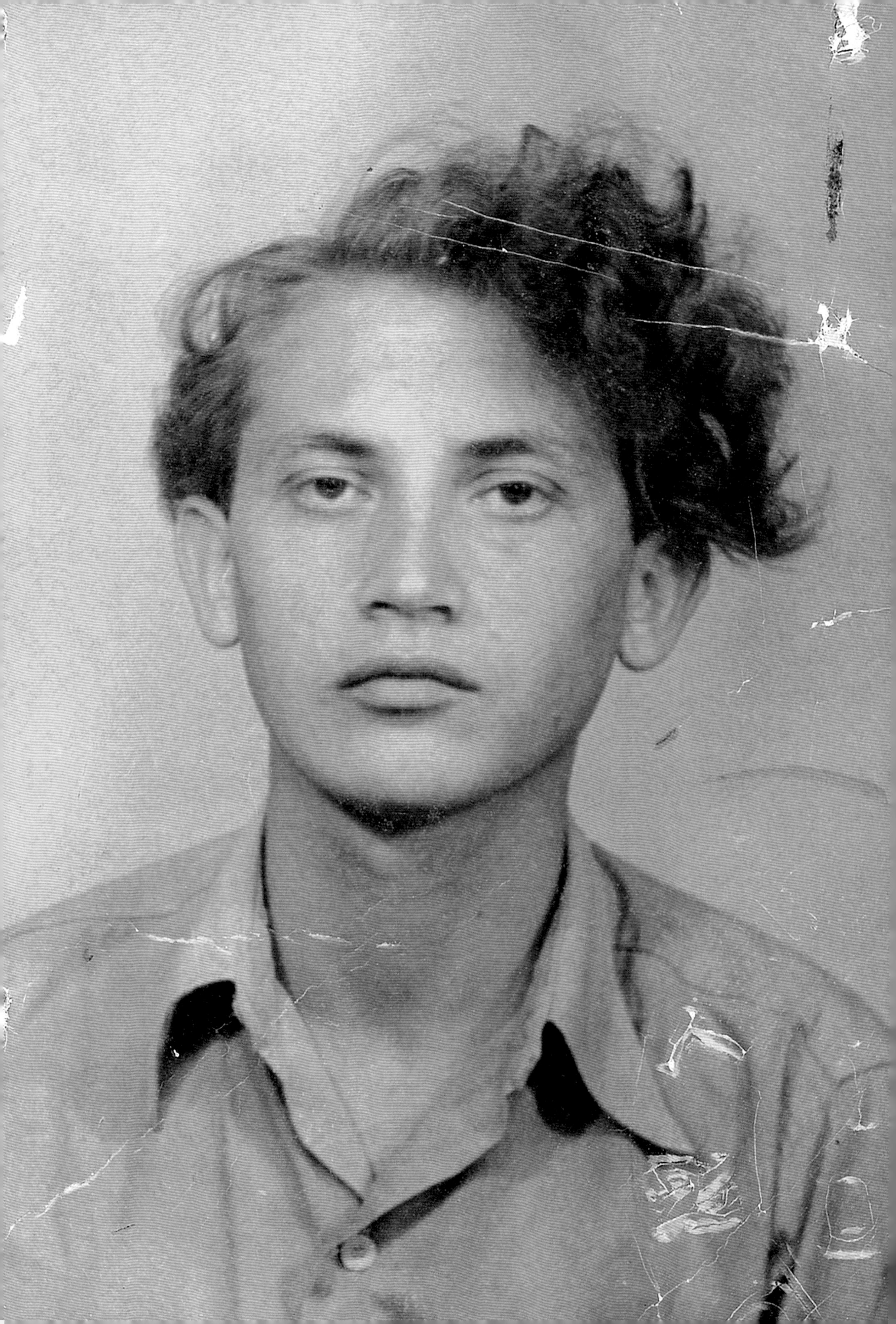

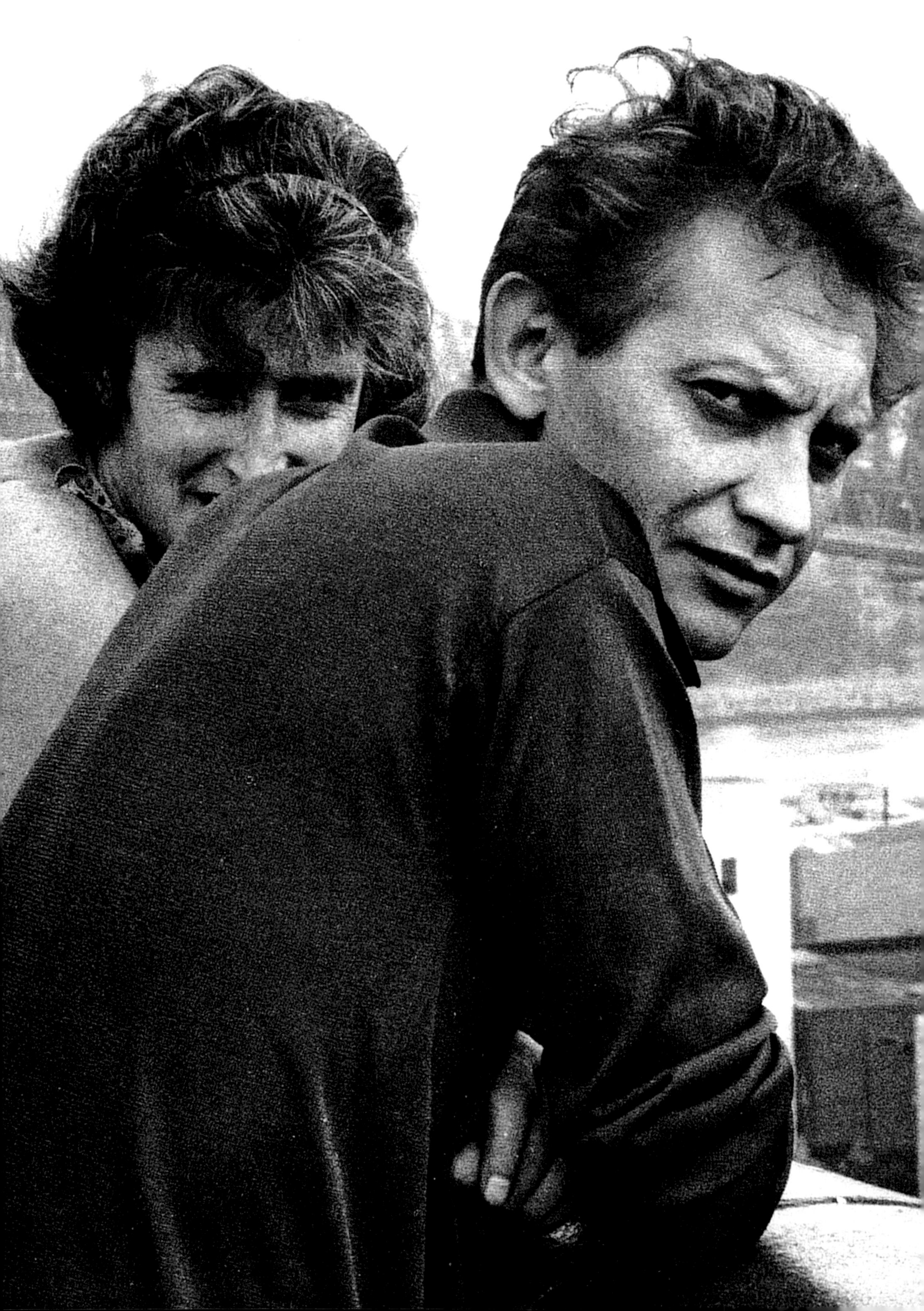

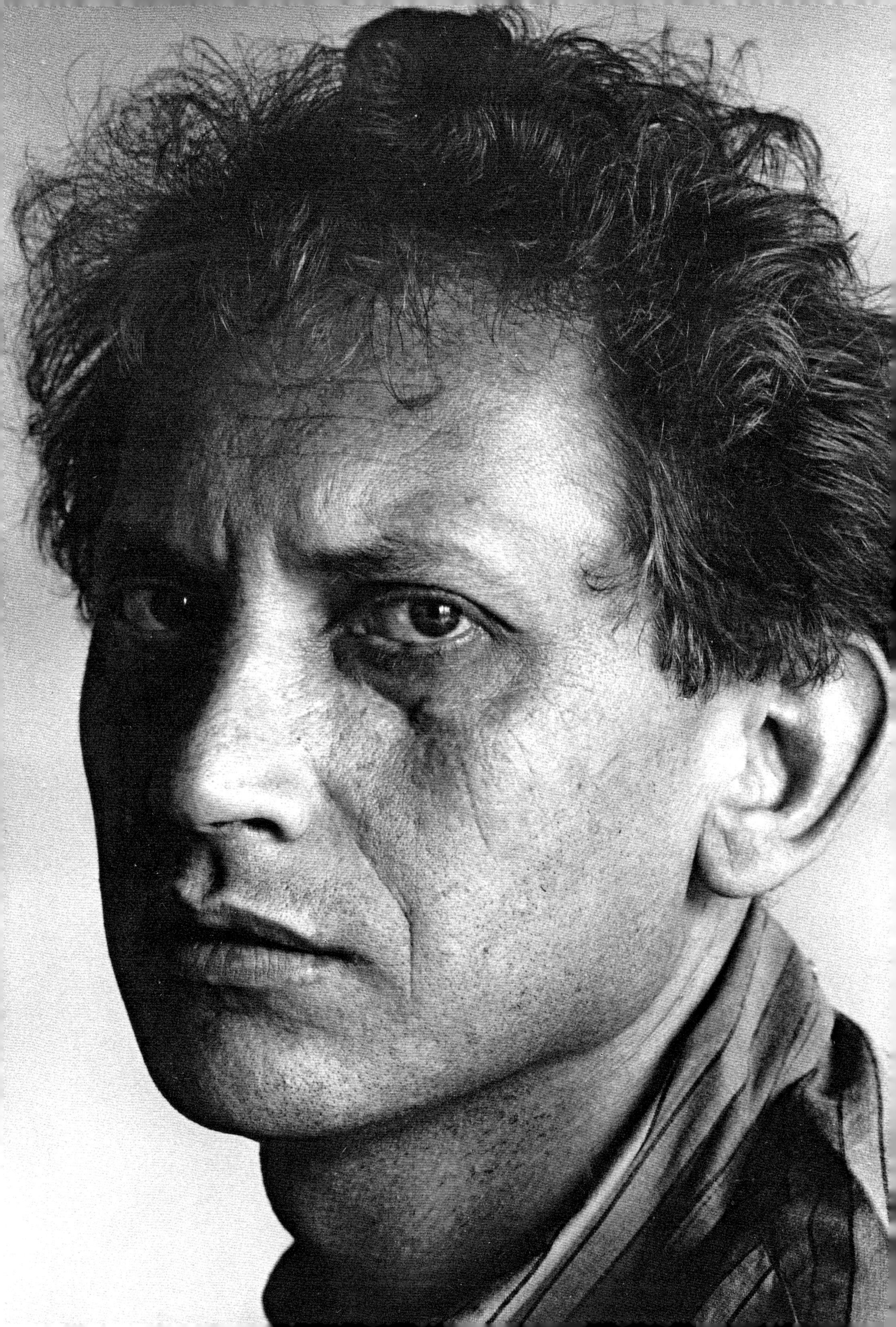

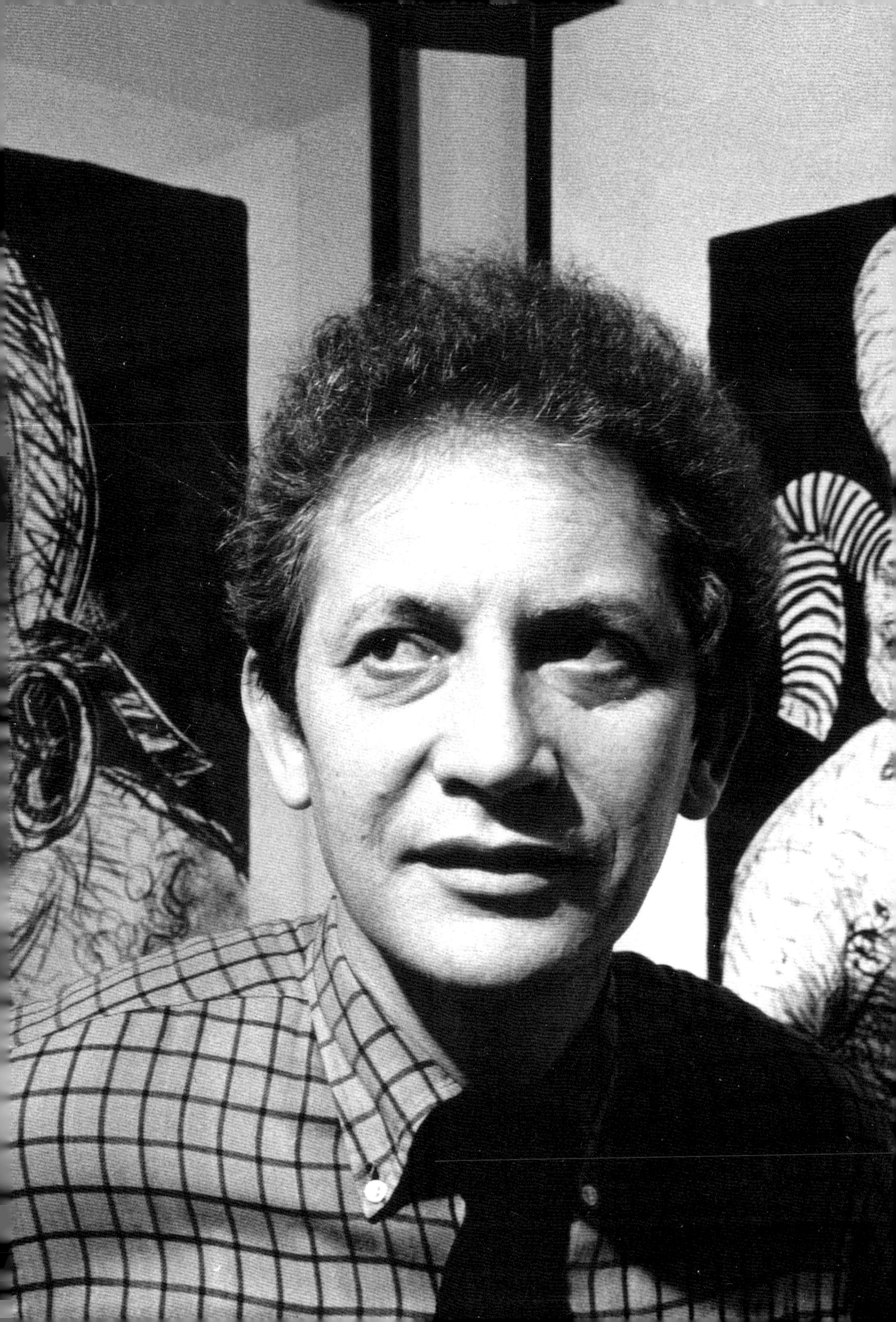

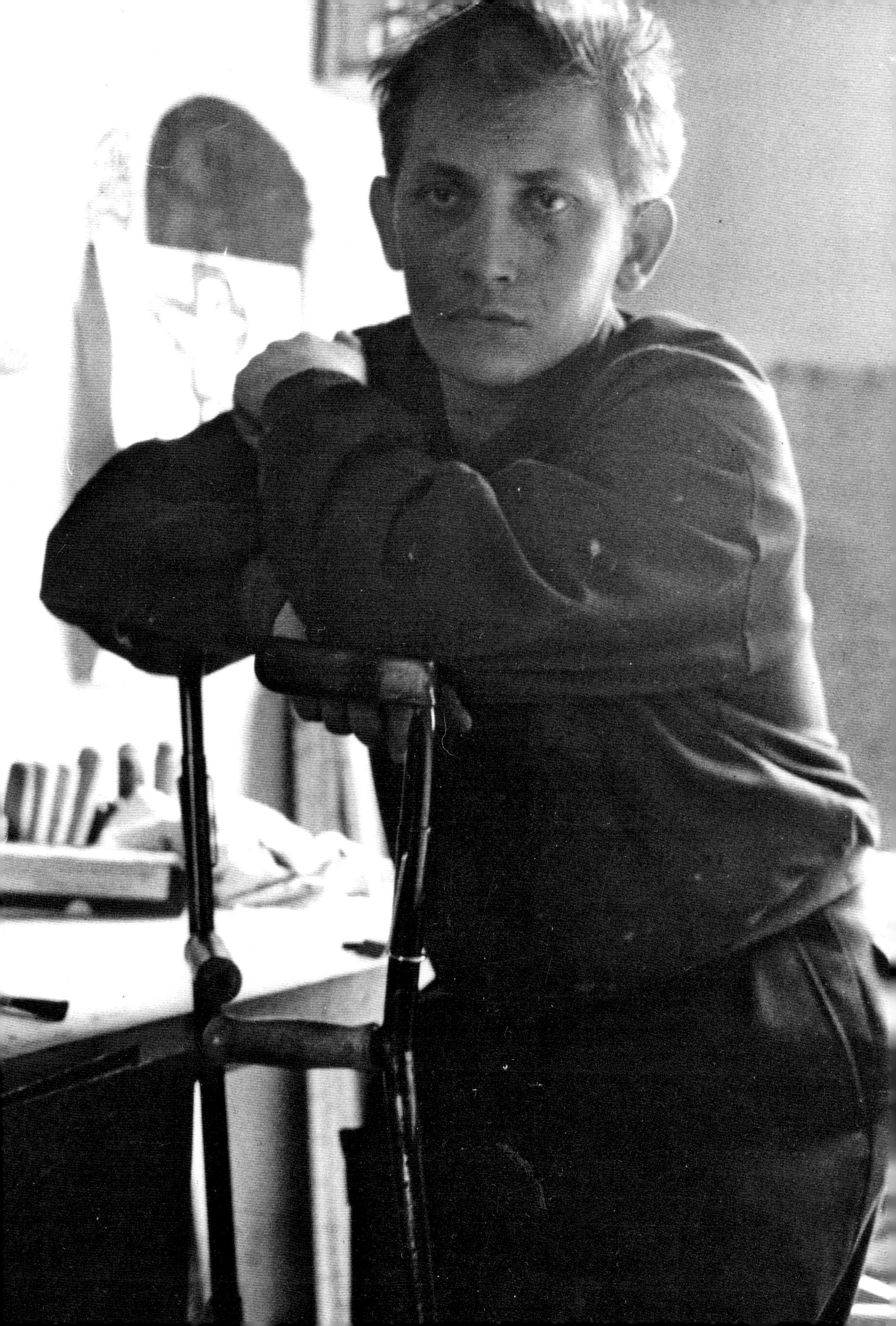

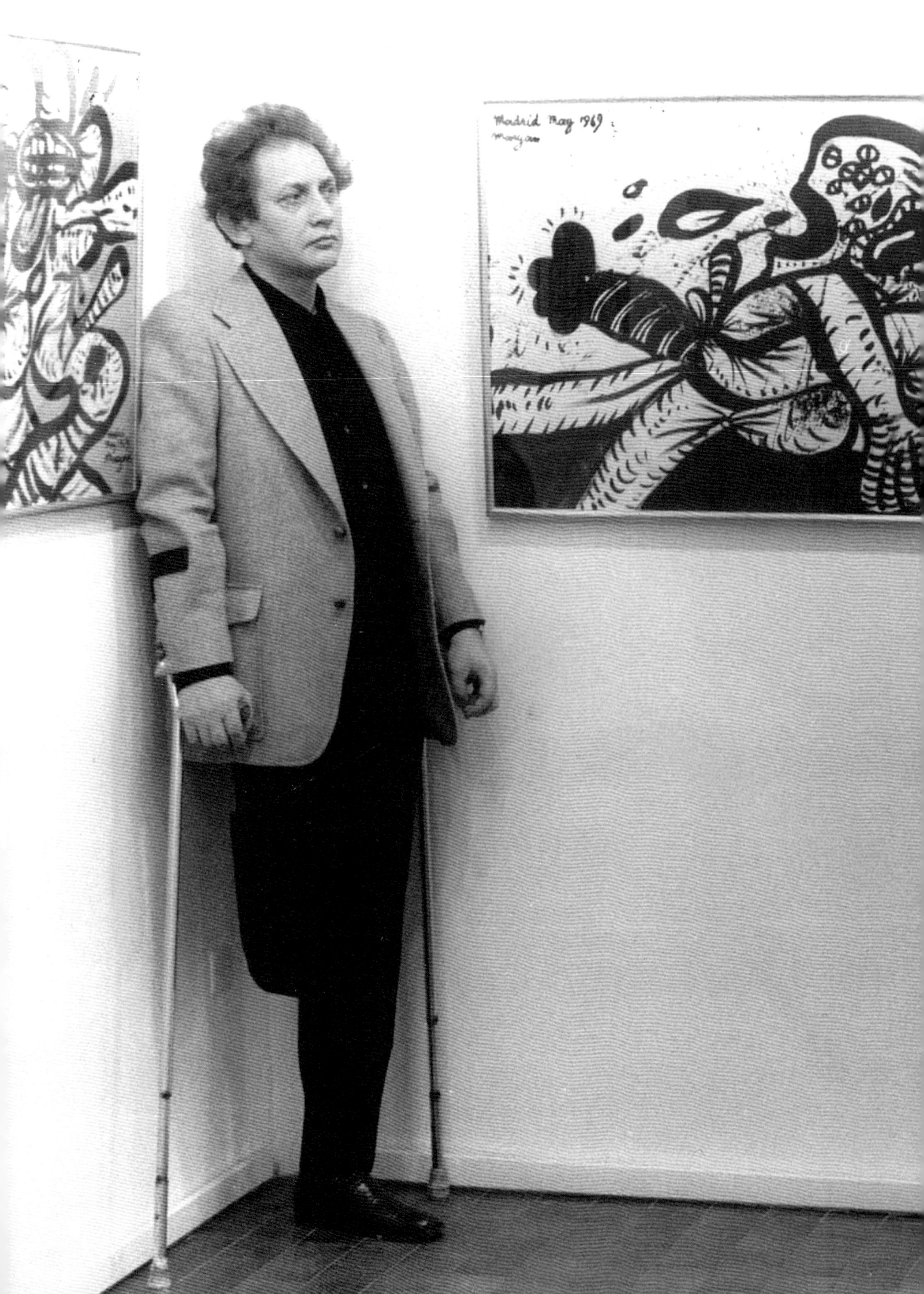
Madrid May 1969

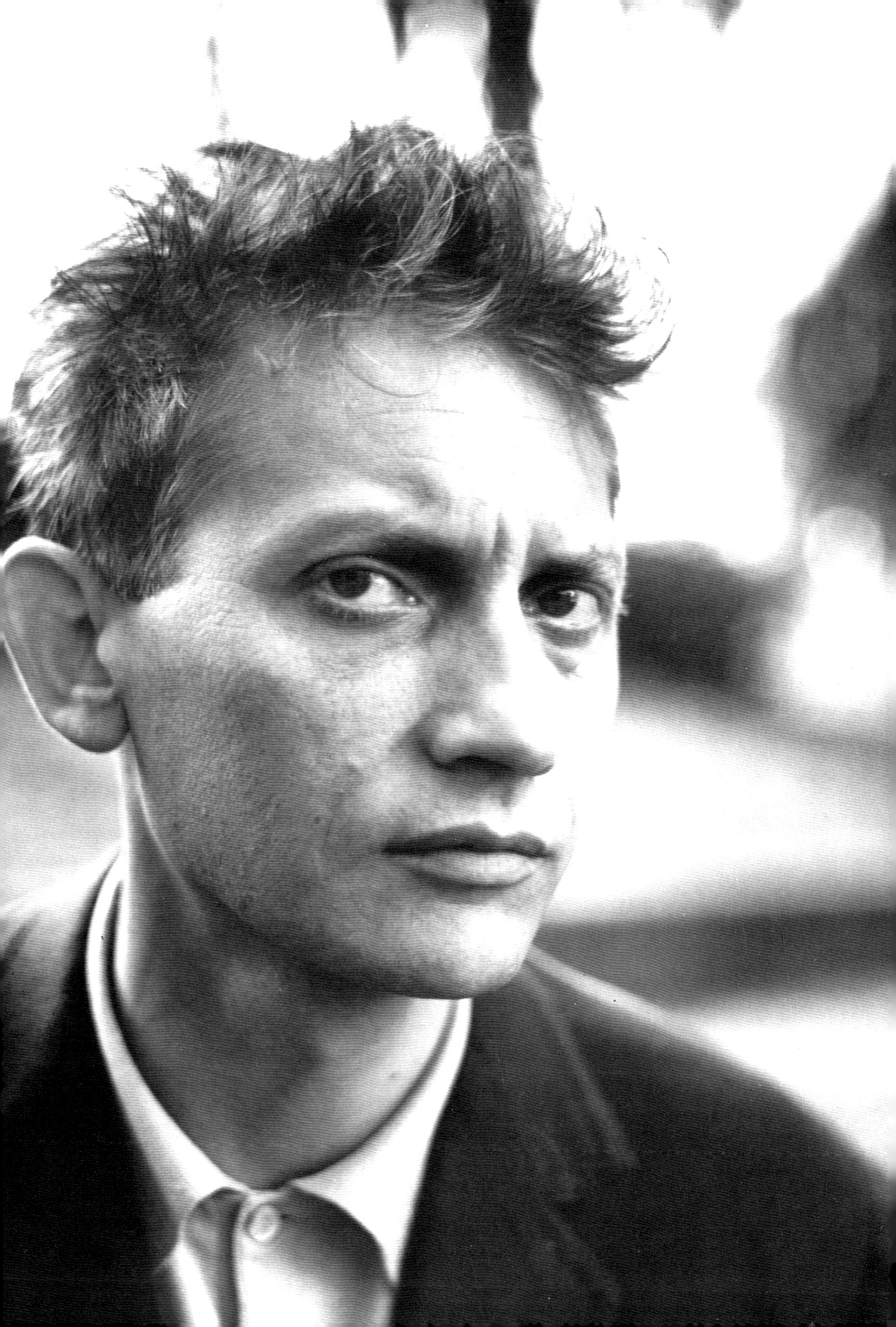

My Name Is Maryan is published in conjunction with the exhibition curated by Alison M. Gingeras and presented at the Museum of Contemporary Art, North Miami, November 17, 2021–October 2, 2022, and co-curated with Noa Rosenberg at the Tel Aviv Museum of Art, December 19, 2022–May 27, 2023.

Published by
Museum of Contemporary Art,
   North Miami
770 NE 125th Street
North Miami, FL 33161
mocanomi.org

Tel Aviv Museum of Art
27 Shaul HaMelech Blvd.
The Golda Meir Cultural and Art Center
Tel Aviv Jaffa
tamuseum.org.il/en/

Verlag der Buchhandlung Walther
   und Franz König
Ehrenstraße 4, D-50672
Köln

Distribution:

Europe
Buchhandlung Walther König
Ehrenstraße 4
D - 50672 Köln
Tel: +49 (0) 221 / 20 59 6 53
verlag@buchhandlung-walther-koenig.de

UK & Ireland
Cornerhouse Publications Ltd. - HOME
2 Tony Wilson Place
UK - Manchester M15 4FN
Tel: +44 (0) 161 212 3466
publications@cornerhouse.org

Outside Europe
D.A.P. / Distributed Art Publishers, Inc.
75 Broad Street, Suite 630
USA - New York, NY 10004
Tel: +1 (0) 212 627 1999
orders@dapinc.com

ISBN 978-3-7533-0142-6

Editor: Alison M. Gingeras
Design: Joseph Logan, assisted by
   Katy Nelson and Anamaria Morris
Project Manager: Todd Bradway
Copy Editor: Miles Champion
Hebrew Text Editor: Orna Yehudiaoff
Translator: Sivan Raveh, Paul Vickers
Printing: Lösch GmbH & Co. KG,
   Germany

Front cover: Maryan, *Personnage (Soldat)*, 1974. Detail

My Name Is Maryan logo design by Jonelle Demby

Back cover: Maryan in his Paris atelier, ca. 1955–56. Photo: J.P. Dutour

Pp. 6–15, 98–99, 102–103, 114–15, 120–21, 133, 140–41, 148–49, 154–55, 168–69, 184–85: *My Name Is Maryan,* Museum of Contemporary Art, North Miami, November 17, 2021–October 2, 2022. Installation views